Anecdota Oxoniensia

THEOLOGICAL TEXTS FROM COPTIC PAPYRI

EDITED WITH AN APPENDIX UPON THE ARABIC AND COPTIC VERSIONS OF THE LIFE OF PACHOMIUS

BY

W. E. CRUM, M.A.

HON. PH.D. BERLIN

WIPF & STOCK · Eugene, Oregon

Wipf and Stock Publishers
199 W 8th Ave, Suite 3
Eugene, OR 97401

Theological Texts from Coptic Papyri
Edited with an Appendix Upon the Arabic and Coptic
Versions of the Life of Pachomius
By Crum, Walter E.
ISBN 13: 978-1-4982-8142-3
Publication date 2/22/2016
Previously published by Clarendon Press, 1913

RESPECTFULLY DEDICATED

TO THE

PHILOSOPHICAL FACULTY OF

THE UNIVERSITY OF BERLIN

PREFACE

THE papyrus fragments here published were acquired in the winter of 1905–6 by the late Lord Amherst of Hackney, who kindly entrusted me with their publication. During the course of printing they became the property of Mr. J. Pierpont Morgan. Professor Sayce, who had already seen them at the dealer's in Luxor,[1] was told that they had been brought from Hou, some 30 miles below Denderah. There is no internal evidence as to their *provenance*. Probably they had been part of the library of one of the monasteries once numerous in that district.[2] It is melancholy to reflect that these poor remnants of some thirty volumes—assuming each script to indicate a distinct volume—are all that have survived.

The language in which the texts are written is a pure Saʿidic, such as one might expect in the district whence they came. Peculiar however is, in several cases,[3] the superlineation, which I have tried to reproduce in print as nearly as may be.[4] This matter of superlineation is one to which various scholars have given attention—notably M. Amélineau[5]—but as yet no systematic, statistical investigation has shown how it may be used as a means towards determining the dates of manuscripts.

Neither, in the present case, can any very definite indication of age be had from palaeographical features, the script of most of our papyri, including both the finest (No. 13) and the roughest (Nos. 8, 16) types, being of the class which it is still necessary vaguely to assign to about the 7th century.[6] For No. 7 a *terminus ante quem* is indeed given, since its author was

[1] That Prof. Sayce saw these identical fragments is proved by his having then and there copied part of one, that printed here as No. 25, fol. 14.

[2] The presence here of two Lives of Pachomius might suggest one of the Pachomian foundations, seven at least of which lay close around Hou. It may be observed that the position of Tabennêse, as being 10 m. from Shenesêt (Bo. 25), is confirmed by Av. 12 b تقدير عشرة اميال (*cf.* Amélineau *Gêogr.* 469 n.). There is still obscurity as to some of these names (*cf.* Ladeuze 173 ff.). For شدسنا (Am. 569) = ⲧⲥⲏ, I would suggest شدستا ϫⲉⲧⲥⲏⲧⲉ.

[3] Particularly Nos. 1, 4 (fol. 3), 7, 9, 11, 12, 15, 16, 18, 23. Examples of similar abnormal usage can be seen in Br. Mus. Cat., Pl. 10, nos. 278, 967.

[4] The frequent comma in the text of No. 25 is, as elsewhere, merely a word-divider; the + above ⲏ the breathing.

[5] In the Introduction to his *Œuvres de Schenoudi*, Paris 1907.

[6] Most of the Turin papyri should belong to this period. *V.* also Brit. Mus. Cat., Pll. 8–10.

patriarch from 578 to 605; and this, considering the paucity of datable uncial hands, is not without importance. It may perhaps be assumed that the rest of the collection also is of about that age.

Though so fragmentary, these papyri include remnants of more than one interesting work: foremost probably, as also most extensive, the new Lives of Pachomius (Nos. 24, 25); then the Sermon attributed to Gregory Nazianzen (No. 9) and that above referred to, bearing the name of Damianus (No. 7). A certain historical value attaches to the evidence, in No. 13, for a Coptic version of the anecdotes embodied by John of Maiuma in his *Testimonies*; nor is a fresh addition to Enoch literature (No. 3), even when manifestly of late origin, without its interest. Indeed there are few of the remaining pieces but contribute something, either in the persons whom they mention or the relations which they show to other works, to enlarge our knowledge of Coptic literature.

Little need be said regarding the manner of publication. Though all revised once, several (*e.g.* No. 25) more often, my copies cannot claim finality. The dark colour of the papyrus in some cases, in others faded ink or a damaged surface, made certainty well nigh unattainable. I have preferred to abstain from many a seemingly obvious completion of *lacunae*, where reflection showed that such was not the sole restitution possible and the several alternatives would have overloaded the page unduly. The translations aim at literalness, so long as that remained intelligible.

In an Appendix I have taken the opportunity to attempt a preliminary estimate of two hitherto unstudied Arabic versions of the history of Pachomius and to give summary accounts of the various Saʿidic recensions, a critical edition whereof is promised by Professor Théodore Lefort.

A list of the principal abbreviations used will be found at the head of the Appendix.

My grateful thanks are due to Lady Amherst for her kindness in leaving the papyri at my disposal and to the Delegates of the Press for generously undertaking their publication; to Prof. Nau for lending me his copy of the Metaphrastic text of the Pachomian biography (*Paris* 881), to Prof. Pietschmann for facilitating my use of an important Arabic MS. (*v.* p. 176), and to Marcus bey Simaika for a valuable communication (*v.* p. 175); also to Sir Herbert Thompson and Mr. H. I. Bell for help in verifying occasional references otherwise beyond my reach.

CONTENTS

No. 1.

Ruth iv. 5–10, with *lacunae*. This is clearly by the scribe of no. 9, and lay together with those fragments. But I have assumed that it has merely a fortuitous connexion with them, for it is improbable that the long biblical passage would be cited by the preacher of a sermon. Nor can I recall a Coptic MS. which contained both a biblical and a non-biblical text.[1] Sir H. Thompson's text (*A Coptic Palimpsest*) is unfortunately deficient here.

→ *Recto.*	
ⲙⲟⲩ [ⲉϫⲛ-]	
ⲧⲉϥⲕⲗⲏⲣⲟ-	
ⲛⲟⲙⲓⲁ ·	ⲧ[
+ⲁⲩⲱ ⲡⲉⲧ-	ⲛ[
(*lacuna*)	+ (*lacuna*)
	ⲛ̄ⲧⲉⲧϩⲏ̣[ⲛ]
[ⲛ]ⲟⲙⲓⲁ’ · ⲛ̄-	ⲉⲣⲟϥ’ · ⲁⲩ[ⲱ]
ⲧⲟⲕ’ ⲇⲉ’ ϫ̄ⲓ̄	ⲡⲁϊⲡⲉ ⲡⲙ[ⲁⲣ-]
ⲙ̄ⲙⲟⲥ’ ⲛⲁⲕ’	ⲧⲩⲣⲓⲟⲛ’ ⲉ̣[ⲧ-]
ⲉⲡⲁⲙⲁ’	ϩ̄ⲙ̄ⲡⲉⲥⲣⲁ[ⲏⲗ’] (*sic*)
ϫⲉⲁⲛⲟⲕ’	+ⲡⲉⲧϫ̄ⲓ̄ ⲇⲉ
ⲛ̄ϯⲛⲁϣϫⲓⲧⲥ’	ⲉϩⲟⲩⲛ̄’ ⲉⲡ̣ⲡ̣[[a]
margin	

↑ *Verso.*	[ⲙ̄ⲡⲉⲛ]ⲧⲁϥ-
[ⲡⲉϫⲁ]ϥ ⲛ-	[ⲙ]ⲟⲩ ⲉϫⲛ-
[ⲛⲉⲡⲣⲉ]ⲥ̣ⲃⲩ̣-	ⲧⲉϥⲕⲗⲏⲣⲟ-
[ⲧⲉⲣⲟⲥ ⲙ]ⲛ-	ⲛⲟⲙⲓⲁ ⲛϥ-
(*lacuna*)	ⲧⲙϥⲱⲧⲉ [b]
ⲉⲗⲓ-]	(*lacuna*)
ⲙⲉⲗ[ⲉⲭ ⲧⲏ-]	
ⲣⲟⲩ’ · ⲁⲩⲱ	
ⲡⲉⲧϣⲟⲟⲡ’	ⲫⲩⲗⲏ̣ [ⲙ̄-]
ⲧⲏⲣⲟⲩ’ ⲛ̄ϫⲉ-	ⲡⲉϥⲗⲁ[ⲟⲥ .]
ⲗⲁ̄ⲓ̄ⲱⲛ ⲙ̄ⲛ̄	+ⲛ̄ⲧⲱⲧⲛ̄’
ⲙⲁⲗⲗⲱⲛ’	ⲧⲉⲧⲛ̄ⲟ̄
ⲛ̄ⲧⲟⲟ̄ⲧⲥ’ ⲛ̄-	ⲙ̄ⲙⲛ̄ⲧⲣⲉ
ⲡ̣ⲱⲉⲛⲓⲙ’ (*sic*) · ⲁⲩⲱ	ⲙ̄ⲡⲟⲟⲩ’ ·
margin	

[a] Should be ⲉⲃⲟ[ⲉⲥ. [b] Here Thompson's text (p. 267), which fills the gap thus: ⲉⲃⲟⲗ ⲛϭⲓ ⲡⲣⲁⲛ ⲙⲡⲉⲛⲧⲁϥⲙⲟⲩ ⲉⲃⲟⲗ ϩⲛⲛⲉϥⲥⲛⲏⲩ ⲁⲩⲱ ⲉⲃⲟⲗ ϩⲛⲧⲉ- (*i.e.* probably six lines of our MS.).

[1] Unless it be a volume with 'Exodus and the Canons of Apa Athanasius', in the catalogue, *Rec.* xi. 132.

No. 2.

Fragments of a Lectionary. Text in one column. The sequence of foll. 1 and 2 is obvious; that of fol. 3 uncertain.

I have to thank Dr. Anton Baumstark for the following valuable observations:—'The Bohairic directories indicate Ps. xcvii. 1 ff. and Eph. iv. 20–v. 14 as lections for Low Sunday (*Dom. in Albis*); *v.* Lagarde's *Orientalia* 8; likewise Ps. xxviii. 3 ff. and Titus ii. 11–iii. 7 for Epiphany; *l.c.* 10. With the Blessing of the Water at Epiphany Ps. l. 7 might well be connected; note that it was read in Egypt at a similar rite (Foot Washing) on Holy Thursday. The divergences in detail of the lections, here and in the far younger Bohairic uses, are of small moment compared with the remarkable agreement, maintained over so long a period, to which these important fragments testify.'

The only other Lectionary on papyrus known to me is a small fragment (no. 12) in the Strassburg University Library, which shows a lection ending 1 John iii. 11 (or 2 John v.?) followed by Acts ix. 36 ff. and, on its other side, an unidentified passage from St. John's Gospel.

Fol. 1. ↑ *Recto* (?).

]ⲟ̅ⲩ̅ⲥ̅ (*red*)[a]
]ⲧ̣ϩⲧⲛ̣̄ . (*black*)
]ϩ̓ ⲁⲡ̣ .
ϣ]ⲡ̣ⲛ̄ϣⲱⲡ
]ⲁ̣ⲩ ⲉ̣ⲧ̣

→ *Verso.* Ps. xcvii. 1, 2.

(*red*) ⲡⲉⲡⲣⲟ[ⲕⲉⲓⲙⲉⲛⲟⲛ]
∽ ∽[
(*red*) Ⲭⲱ̣ [ⲉⲡϫⲟⲉⲓⲥ ⲛⲟⲩϫⲱ ⲛⲃ̄ⲣⲣⲉ]
(*black*) ϫⲉⲁⲡ[ϫⲟⲉⲓⲥ ⲉⲓⲣⲉ ⲛϩⲉⲛϣⲡⲏⲣⲉ]
ⲁ̣ⲥ̣ⲧ[ⲟⲩϫⲟ ⲛⲁϥ ⲛϭⲓ ⲧⲉϥⲟⲩⲛⲁⲙ]
ⲁⲩⲱ [ⲡⲉϥϭⲃⲟⲓ ⲉⲧⲟⲩⲁⲁⲃ·]
ⲁⲡϫ[ⲟⲉⲓⲥ ⲟⲩⲱⲛϩ ⲉⲃⲟⲗ ⲙⲡⲉϥⲟⲩϫⲁⲓ]

[a] From a Pauline Epistle.

Fol. 2. → *Recto.* Ps. xcvii. 2–5.

ⲥⲩⲛⲏ ⲙⲡⲉ[ⲙⲧ]ⲟ ⲉⲃⲟⲗ ⲛ[ⲛϩⲉ-]
ⲑⲛⲟⲥ ⲧⲏ[ⲣ]ⲟⲩ·[a]
ⲁϥⲣ̄ⲡⲙⲉⲉⲩⲉ ⲙⲡⲉϥⲛⲁ ⲛ[ⲓⲁⲕⲱⲃ]

↑ *Verso.* Eph. v. 17–20.

[ⲗ]ⲁ̣ ⲉ̣ⲓ̣ⲙⲉ̣ ϫ̣ⲉⲟ[ⲩⲡⲉ] ⲡⲟⲩⲱϣ ⲛ̄-
[ⲡϫ]ⲟⲉⲓⲥ· ⲁⲩⲱ [ⲙ̄]ⲡⲣϯϩⲉ ϩ̄ⲛⲟⲩⲏ-
[ⲣⲡ] ⲡⲁⲓ ⲉⲧⲉ̣ⲟⲩⲛ ⲟⲩⲙⲛ̄ⲧϣⲛⲁ’

[a] ⲧⲏⲣⲟⲩ not elsewhere. *Cf.*? Ps. lxvi. 2.

ⲁⲩⲱ ⲧⲉϥⲙⲉ ⲙⲡⲏⲓ ⲙⲡ[ⲓⲏ̅ⲗ]
ⲁⲛⲉⲕⲣⲱⲟⲩ ⲧⲏⲣⲟⲩ ⲙⲡ[ⲕⲁϩ ⲛⲁⲩ]
ⲉⲡⲟⲩϫⲁⲓ ⲙⲡⲉⲛⲛⲟⲩ[ⲧⲉ]
ⲡⲕⲁϩ ⲧⲏⲣϥ ⳾ ⲗⲟⲩⲗⲁⲓ ⲙ̣[ⲡ-]
ⲛⲟⲩⲧⲉ
ϫⲱ ⲛⲧⲉⲧⲛⲧⲉⲗⲏⲗ ⲛⲧⲉⲧ̣ⲛ̣-
ⲯⲁⲗⲗⲉⲓ ⲉⲣⲟϥ
[ⲯⲁⲗⲗⲉⲓ ⲉⲣⲟϥ ϩⲛⲟⲩ]ⲕ̣ⲓ̣ⲑ̣ⲁ̣ⲣ̣ⲁ̣

[ϣⲟ]ⲟⲡ ⲛ̣ϩⲏⲧϥ ⲁⲗⲗⲁ ⲛ̅ⲧⲉⲧⲛ-
[ϫⲱ]ⲕ̣ ⲉⲃⲟⲗ ϩⲙ̅ⲡⲉⲡⲛ̅ⲁ · ⲉⲧⲉⲧⲛ̅-
[ϣⲁ]ϫ̣ⲉ ⲙ̅ⲙⲛⲉⲧⲛⲉⲣⲏⲩ ϩⲛ̅ϩⲉⲛ-
[ⲯⲁⲗ]ⲙⲟⲥ ⲙ̅ⲛ̅ϩⲉⲛⲥⲙⲟⲩ ⲙ̅ⲛ̅ϩⲉⲛ-
ⲱ̣ⲇⲏ ⲙ̅ⲡⲛ̅ⲁⲕⲟⲛ ⲉⲧⲉⲧⲛ̅ϫⲱ’
ⲁⲩⲱ ⲉⲧⲉⲧⲛⲯⲁⲗⲗⲉⲓ ϩⲙ̅ⲡⲉ-
ⲧⲛϩⲏⲧ’ ⲉⲡϫⲟⲉⲓⲥ · ⲉⲧⲉⲧⲛ̅ϣⲡ̅

Fol. 3. ↑ *Recto* (?). Ps. l. 7–9.

margin

ed) ☰ ⁝⁝ ⲯ̅ⲁ̅ⲗ̅ⲧ̅ⲏ̅ⲣ̅ⲓ̣[ⲟⲛ
lack) ⲕⲛⲁϭⲉϣϭⲱⲱϣ̅ⲧ [ⲛⲟⲩϩⲩⲥⲥⲱⲡⲟⲥ]
ⲉⲃⲟⲗ’ ϩⲙ̅ⲡⲉⲥⲛⲟϥ’ ⲙ̅[ⲡϣⲉ ⲧⲁⲧⲃⲃⲟ]
ⲕⲛⲁϫⲟⲕⲙⲉⲧ ⲉⲃ[ⲟⲗ ⲛϩⲏⲧϥ ⲁⲩⲱ]
sic ⲧⲁⲟⲩⲃⲁϣ’[a] ⲛ̅ϩ[ⲟⲩⲉⲟⲩⲭⲓⲱⲛ]
[ⲉ]ⲕⲛⲁⲧⲣⲁⲥⲱⲧ[ⲙ ⲉⲩⲧⲉⲗⲏⲗ ⲙⲛⲟⲩ-
[ⲟⲩⲛⲟϥ[b]
[ⲥ]ⲉⲛⲁⲧⲉⲗⲏⲗ’ ⲛ̅[ϭⲓ ⲛⲕⲉⲉⲥ ⲉⲧⲑⲃⲃⲓⲏⲩ]
[ⲕⲧⲉ] ⲡⲉⲕϩⲟ ⲛ̅ⲥ[ⲁⲃⲟⲗ ⲛⲛⲁⲛⲟⲃⲉ]
[ⲁⲩⲱ] ⲛⲁⲁⲛⲟ[ⲙⲓⲁ ⲧⲏⲣⲟⲩ ϥⲟⲧⲟⲩ ⲉⲃⲟⲗ]

→ *Verso* (?). Ps. xxviii. 8 and Titus ii. 11 (?).

margin

[ⲧⲉⲥⲙⲏ ⲙⲡϫⲟ]ⲉ̣ⲓ̣ⲥ · ϥⲕⲓⲙ’ ⲉⲧⲉⲣⲏⲙⲟⲥ
[ⲡϫⲟⲉⲓⲥ ⲛⲁⲕⲓⲙ] ⲉⲧⲉⲣⲏⲙⲟⲥ’ ⲛ̅ⲕⲁⲇⲏⲥ ·
]— — . . . ——
ⲡⲣ]ⲟ̣ⲥ ⲧⲓⲧⲟⲥ — (*red*)
]— — . . . ——
[ⲁⲡⲉϩⲙⲟⲧ ⲅⲁⲣ ⲙⲡ]ⲛⲟⲩⲧⲉ ⲡⲉⲛ̣- (*black*)
[ⲥⲱⲧⲏⲣ ⲟⲩⲱⲛϩ ⲉⲃ]ⲟⲗ’ ⲛ̅ⲣⲱⲙⲉ’ ⲛ[ⲓⲙ]
]ⲁⲥ̣’ ⲉ̣ . . ⲕ[
]ⲧⲉ̣ . . . [

[a] Elsewhere ⳾ⲛⲁⲟⲩⲃⲁϣ.
[b] The end of this must have been inserted above or below the line.

No. 3.

These remnants of a new text connected with the once extensive Enoch literature are, owing to my failure to discover elsewhere any guiding version of the story[1], printed in a merely tentative sequence. An alternative order might, for instance, begin with foll. 2, 6, 8. All is so ill preserved that scarcely a phrase can be translated without hesitation. Pronouns, of decisive importance for the intelligence of the narrative, are too often missing or, owing to imperfect context, ambiguous. Needless to say, the order of *recto* and *verso* is usually an open question.

[1] The recently published Ethiopic 'Clement' (Grébaut, *ROC*. xvi. 230) is of no help.

Both Enoch's mother and sister—assuming 'my son' and 'my brother' to have their literal meaning—have parts in this legend.[1] That the latter is the speaker in foll. 7, 9, is an assumption based simply upon the traditional relationship of the Sibyl to Enoch[2] and the probability that prophetic information would be ascribed to her wisdom. A gnostic element in the work might perhaps be recognized in fol. 2, but the references to the persons of the Trinity would suffice to separate this text from the more venerable literature relating to Enoch.

Fol. 1. ↑ *Recto.* margin | → *Verso.*

Recto margin	Recto	Verso	
	]ⲕ[	[.]ⲉ[	ϩⲣ[
	[ϥ · ⲉ	[. .]ⲡⲉ[	ⲉϥ[
	ⲧ[ⲉⲡⲁⲓ]ⲡⲉ ⲡⲣ[ⲁⲛ]	[.]ⲉ ⲥⲧⲱ[ⲧ ⲉ]ϥ-	[.]ⲟⲩⲕ ⲉϥ[
	ⲙ̄ⲡϣⲏⲣⲉ [ⲙ̄-]	ϣⲁⲛⲛⲁⲩ ⲉⲣⲟ-	ⲛⲟⲩ . ⲁⲛ[
]ⲉ ⲙⲡⲁⲣ-	ⲡⲛⲟⲩⲧⲉ ⲉϥ-	ⲟⲩ ϩⲛⲛⲉⲩⲙⲛⲧ-	ⲧⲉ · ϥⲛⲁ[
[ⲭⲁⲅ]ⲅⲉⲗⲟⲥ ⲁϥ-	ϩⲙⲟⲟⲥ ⲛ̄ⲥⲁ-	ϣⲁϥⲧⲉ ⲧⲏ-	ϫⲉⲛⲟ[
[ⲕ]ⲁⲁϥ[a] ⲉϫⲛ̄ⲙ̄ⲙⲁ-	ⲟⲩⲛⲁⲙ ⲙ̄ⲡⲉϥ-	ⲣⲟⲩ ⲉϣⲁⲩⲁⲁⲩ	ⲛ̄ϭⲟⲛⲥ . [
[ⲁϣ]ⲉ ⲛ̄ⲧⲇⲓ̈ⲕⲁⲓ-	ⲉⲓ̈ⲱⲧ · ⲁϥ-	ϥⲛⲁⲥⲉ̄ϩⲁⲓ̈ⲥⲟⲩ	ⲧⲉϥϭⲟⲙ · [
[ⲟⲥ]ⲩⲛⲏ ⲁϥⲉⲓ̈-	ⲡⲁϩⲧϥ ⲉϫⲛ̄-	ⲛ̄ⲧⲉⲩⲛⲟⲩ ⲛ̄-	ⲙ[. .]ϣⲉϩ[
[ⲛⲉ] ⲛ̄ⲕⲉⲁⲅⲅⲉ-	ⲙ̄ⲡ[ⲁⲧ][b] ⲙ̄ⲡⲉϥ-	ⲧⲉⲧⲉⲕ[ϩ]ⲓⲕⲱ̄	ϩ̄ⲙⲡⲕⲟ[
[ⲗⲟ]ⲥ ⲛϫⲱⲱⲣⲉ	ⲉⲓ̈[ⲱⲧ] ⲉϥϫⲱ	ⲧⲏⲣⲥ̄ ⲃ[ⲱ]ⲕ ⲉⲡ-	ⲉ[.]ⲙⲙⲁ[
[. . . . .] ⲟ [ⲛ]ϣⲁϩ	ⲙⲙ[ⲟⲥ] ϫⲉⲱ̄-	ⲧⲁⲕⲟ · [ⲁⲗ]ⲗⲁ	[. .]ⲩⲉⲡ[
	ⲡⲁ[ⲉⲓⲱ]ⲧ ⲙ̄-	ϣⲓ̈ⲛ[ⲉ .]ⲧⲡ .	
	ⲡⲣ[. . . .]ⲙⲡϥ	ⲛ̄ⲥⲁ[. . . .]ⲙ[c]	

[a] Or ⲧⲁⲁϥ. [b] Altered. [c] ⲡ]ⲧⲟϥ ⲛⲥⲁ[ⲟⲩⲣⲱ]ⲙ[ⲉ ?

Fol. 1. *Recto.* . . . the archangel (ἀρχ.) and he placed him (it ?) at (upon ?) the ba[lan]ces of righteousness (δικαιοσύνη), and broug[ht] other mighty angels (ἄγγ.), . . . being flame (?) . . . . .

[1] In an Ethiopic legend his mother's name is Bareka (*Livre des Mystères*, p. 138, ed. Grébaut, *Patr. Or.* vi).

[2] *V.* my note *ZNTW.* 1911, 352. I may here add that the sibylline quotation in the Turin papyrus is to be referred to the Tiburtian Sibyl; *cf.* Sackur, *Sib. Texte u. Forsch.* 181; further, as to the invocations of Enoch on grave stones, *v.* H. Thompson in Quibell's *Saqqara*, 1912, p. 48. Prof. Pietschmann has referred me to certain versions of the History of Alexander, wherein the Sibyl appears as Solomon's sister (A. N. Vesslovsky's work on the *History of the Novel*, vol. i, 1886, and his article in *Vizant. Vrem.* 1897). On Tabitha associated with Enoch and Elias, *v.* also Steindorff's *Apok. des Elias* 92.

. . . which is (?) the name (?) of the son of God, sitting on His father's right. He cast himself at His father's feet, saying, 'O (?) my father, do not . . . . .

Verso. . . . 'tremble (?) if he behold them in all their wickedness which they do, he shall straightway write them down and all thy image[1] (*εἰκών*) shall go to destruction. But (*ἀλλά*) rather (?) seek for' . . . . .[2]

. . . *nothing intelligible in col. 2.*

Fol. 2.	→ *Recto.*	↑ *Verso.*	
	[.]ⲛ̣ⲟⲩ[. .]ⲟ̣ⲛ̣ .	[. . ⲁⲛⲁ]ⲗ̣ⲁ[ⲙ-]	
	ⲣⲱⲙⲉ ⲛ̣[ⲇⲓ-]	[ⲃ]ⲁⲛⲉ̣ ⲙⲙⲟϥ ⲉ̣-	
	ⲕⲁⲓⲟⲥ ⲉⲧ̣[ⲉⲡⲁⲓ-]	[ⲧ]ⲡⲉ· ⲁϥⲛⲟⲓ ⲛⲙ̄-	
	ⲡⲉ ⲓ̈ⲁⲣ[ⲉⲇ ⲁϥⲣ̄-]	[ⲙⲩⲥⲧⲏ]ⲣⲓⲟⲛ	
]ⲛ	ϩⲟⲧⲉ ϩⲏⲧϥ [ⲙ-]	[ⲉ]ⲑⲏ[ⲡ] ϩⲛⲛⲁ̣ⲓ-	ⲉ[
]ⲉ̣	ⲡⲛⲟⲩⲧ[ⲉ ⲁⲩⲱ]	ⲱ̣ⲛ ⲙⲡϫⲓⲥⲉ	ⲛ[
]ⲗ̣ⲡ̣ⲟϥ[a]	ⲡⲛⲟⲩⲧⲉ ⲟ[ⲛ]	[ⲁⲩ]ⲱ̣ ⲛⲛⲟⲩⲥ	ϫ[
]ϩⲁ-	ⲉⲣⲉⲛⲉϥ[ⲁⲅⲅⲉ-]	ⲧ̣ⲏ̣ⲣⲟⲩ ⲉⲑⲏⲡ	ⲉⲛ[
]ⲡⲉ	ⲗⲟⲥ ⲙⲉ ⲙⲙ[ⲟϥ]	[ϩ]ⲛ̣ⲛⲁⲓⲱⲛ ⲙ-	ⲣⲉ[
]ϫⲓ	[ⲉ]ⲧⲃⲉⲡ̣ . . [	[ⲡ]ⲟ̣ⲩⲟⲉⲓⲛ· ⲁⲩⲱ̣	ⲁⲥ̣[
]ⲡⲉ		[. . .]ⲓⲁ ⲛⲛ[	ⲡ̣[
]ⲏ̣			

[a] Or ϫⲡⲟϥ.

Fol. 2. *Recto.* . . . [3]righteous (*δίκαιος*) man, namely Iar[ed, and he] feared God. [And] the [an]gels (*ἄγγ.*) of God al[so] loved him[4] by reason of . . . . .

Verso. . . . took him up (? *ἀναλαμβάνειν*) to heaven and he knew (*νοεῖν*) the [mys]teries (*μυστ.*) that are hidden in the *aeons* (*αἰών*) of the height, and all the minds (*νοῦς*) that are hidden in the *aeons* (*αἰ.*) of light, and . . . of the (*pl.*) . . . . .

[1] The human race.

[2] Perhaps: seek out a man to mitigate the severity of the recording angel.

[3] Presumably 'son of a], or something similar.

[4] *Lit.* (if my suggestion be accepted) 'And God also, His angels loved him'. But this construction is unlikely.

Fol. 3. ↑ *Recto.* ? margin		→ *Verso.*	margin
	ⲙⲡ[. . .]ⲉ[	]ⲛⲁ	
	ϩⲟ[.]ⲩ [ⲉ]ϥⲁϩⲉⲣ[ⲁ-]	ⲥⲁ. ⲉⲛⲱⲭ ⲡ-	
	ⲧ̅ϥ̅ ϩⲓϫⲙ̅ⲡⲧⲟ-	ϣⲏⲣⲉ [ⲛⲓ]ⲁⲣⲉⲇ	
	ⲟⲩ · ⲉⲓ̈ (*sic*) ⲟⲩⲁ[ⲅ]ⲅⲉ-	[ϫⲓ ⲙⲡⲉ]ϊϫⲱ-	ⲃ[
	ⲗⲟⲥ ⲛ̅[ⲧⲉ ⲡⲛⲟⲩ-]	ⲱⲙⲉ ϩⲛⲧⲁϭⲓ̈ϫ	ⲟⲉ[ⲓ
]ⲧ	ⲧⲉ ⲁϥⲟⲩⲱⲛ[ϩ]	[ⲛⲅ]ⲱϣ ⲛ̅ϩⲏ-	Ⲡⲁⲙ[
]ⲩⲙⲛ-	ⲛⲁϥ ⲉⲃⲟ[ⲗ ⲉϥ-]	[ⲧ]ϥ ⲛⲅⲟⲩⲱⲛϩ	ⲛⲁ[
]ϣⲁϫⲉ	ⲙⲏⲣ ⲉϫⲛⲧ[ⲉϥ-]	[ⲉ]ⲃⲟⲗ ⲙ̅ⲡⲣⲁⲛ (*sic*)	ⲙ̅ⲡⲉ[
] · ⲁ-	ϯⲡⲉ ⲛⲟⲩⲙ[ⲟ-]	[Ⲡⲉ]ϫⲉ ⲉⲛⲱⲭ	ⲙⲉϩ[
]ϥⲧⲙ-	ϫ̅ϩ̅ ⲛ̅ⲛⲟⲩⲃ [ⲉ-]	[ⲛ]ⲁϥ [a] ϫⲉⲛⲓ̈ⲙ	ⲛ̅ⲅ̅[
]ϫⲓ	ⲣⲉⲟⲩⲕⲗⲟⲙ [ⲛⲁ-]	?	ⲧϥ[
]ⲟⲥ	ⲧⲁⲙⲁⲛⲧ[ⲓⲛⲟⲛ		
	?		

[a] Not ⲛⲁⲥ.

Fol. 3. *Recto.* . . . while he stood upon the mount, lo, an angel (ἀγγ.) of God appeared unto him, girt about his loins with a golden girdle, a crown of adamant (ἀδαμάντινος) being [upon his head . . . . .

Verso. . . . 'Enoch, son of Iared, [take] this book of my hand and read therein and reveal the(?)[1] name.' Enoch said unto him, 'Who [art thou?' . . . . .

Fol. 4. → *Recto.*		↑ *Verso.*	
]ⲉⲧ[	ⲡⲁ[	]ⲧⲉ.	ⲱⲙ[
]ⲛⲧ[	ⲱⲙ[. . . ⲡⲛⲟⲩ-]	]ⲛ[	ϩⲓ̈ϫ[
]ⲧ[	ⲧⲉ ⲛ[ⲁⲭⲁⲣⲓⲍⲉ]	]ⲣⲡ.	[.]ⲧ̅ⲛ̅[
]ⲁⲛⲟⲩϣ	ⲛⲁⲕ [ⲛ]ⲟⲩⲣ[ⲁⲛ]	[. . .]ⲕⲟⲥ ⲛ̅ϥ̅-	ⲫⲁⲅ[ⲓⲟⲥ ⲙ̅ⲡϫⲟ-]
]ⲁϣⲱⲡⲉ	ⲛⲥⲟⲉⲓ̈ⲧ ⲉ[ϩⲟⲩ-]	ϫⲓ ⲛⲧⲁⲡⲁⲅ-	ⲉⲓⲥ ⲧ̅ⲩ̅. [
]ⲟϥ ⲉⲓⲧⲉ	ⲉⲣⲱⲙⲉ ⲛⲓ̈ⲙ	[ⲅⲉ]ⲗⲟⲥ ⲧⲁⲙⲟϥ	ⲡⲁⲣⲑ[ⲉⲛⲟⲥ
]ⲉⲥⲟⲗ-	⟋ Ⲥⲉⲛⲁϫⲓ̈ⲧⲕ ⲉⲧ-	ⲉⲣⲟⲟⲩ ϩⲓ̈ϫⲙ-	ϫⲉⲥ. [
]ⲥϩⲁⲓ̈ⲥⲟⲩ	ⲡⲉ ϩ̅ⲙ̅ⲡⲉⲕ-	ⲡⲧⲟⲟⲩ · ⲁϥ-	ⲛⲁⲉⲓ̈ⲣ[ⲉ

[1] Perhaps 'my', ⲡⲁ-.

]ϫⲓⲛⲧⲉϥ-	ⲥ[ⲱ]ⲙⲁ ⲛ̄ⲥⲉⲕⲁ-	ϭⲛ ϣⲟⲙ[ⲧ]ⲉ	ϣⲟ ⲛ̄[ⲣⲱⲙⲉ][a]
]ⲉ̣ ⲙⲡⲁ-	ⲁⲕ ϩ̄ⲛ̄ⲧⲙⲏⲧⲉ	ⲛ̄ⲥⲫⲣⲁⲅⲓ̈[ⲥ]	ϩⲓ̈ϫⲙ[ⲡⲕⲁϩ
]ⲁⲁϥ ⲉⲧ-	[ⲛⲑ]ⲩⲡⲟⲑⲩⲕⲏ	ⲁ̣ⲩⲱ ⲡⲉ[. .	ϣⲁⲧⲛ̄[
]ⲛ̣ⲛ̄ⲧϥ-	[. .]ⲧ̣ⲉ ⲟⲩⲥ̣ⲓ̈ⲉ	[.]ⲩ . ⲛⲥϩⲁⲓ̈ .	ⲛⲟⲩ . . [
?	]ⲡ[	]ⲧ	
	traces of two lines.	]ⲙ̣ⲥ	

[a] Stroke over ⲛ̄ not certain.

Fol. 4. *Recto.* . . . 'God [shall grant (χαρίζεσθαι)] thee a name (?) famous [above] all men. Thou shalt be taken to heaven in thy body (σῶμα) and shalt be set in the midst of the store-house (? ἀποθήκη [1]) ' . . . . .

Verso. . . . whereof the angel (ἄγγ.) had told him upon the mount. He found three seals (σφραγίς) and the . . . writings . . . . .
. . . the ho[ly one (ἅγιος) of the Lo]rd . . . .[2] vir[gin (παρθ.)], that . . . should spend . . . hundred [years] upon [the earth,] all but . . . . .

Fol. 5. ↑ *Recto* (?).

]ⲛ̄[	ⲙⲏ̣[
]ⲟⲩ-	?
ϣⲟϫ[ⲛⲉ] ⲛⲟⲩ-	ⲣ . [
ⲱⲧ ⲡ[ⲉ]ⲧ̣ⲛ̄ϩⲏ-	ⲉϫ[
[ⲧ]ⲟ̣ⲩ ⲛ[ⲧ]ⲟⲟⲩ ⲥⲉ-	ⲧⲏ̣[
ⲉ̣ⲣϩⲙⲙⲉ ⲛ̄ⲧ-	ⲙⲉ[
[ⲡ]ⲉ ⲙ̄ⲡ̄ⲕⲁϩ	ⲱ[
Ⲡⲣⲁⲛ ⲙⲡⲉⲓ̈ⲱⲧ	ⲥⲏ[
[.]ⲱ̣ϩ ⲛⲡⲙⲉϩ-	ⲛ[
ϣⲟⲙⲛ̄ⲧ ⲛ̄ .	ⲧ[
[.]ⲛ̣ ⲉⲧϩⲓ̈ϫⲛ̄-	ⲡ̣[

→ *Verso* (?).

	ⲙ̣ⲉ[
] . ⲛ .	ⲁϥϭⲛ̣[ⲧϥ ϫⲉⲡ-]
]ⲉ ϩⲛ-	ⲣⲁⲛ [ⲙ]ⲡⲉⲡ̣-
?	ⲛⲁ ⲉⲧ̣[ⲟⲩⲁⲁⲃ]
]ⲉ	Ⲡⲉϫⲉ ⲉⲛⲱⲭ
]ⲟⲛ	ⲛⲁϥ ϫⲉⲡⲁ-
]ⲕ	ϫⲟⲉⲓ̈ⲥ ⲉⲓ̈[ⲥ ϣⲟ-]
] ⲉⲃⲟⲗ	ⲙⲛ̄ⲧ ⲛⲣⲁⲛ̣
]ⲉⲧ-	ⲛⲁϩⲟⲣⲁⲧⲟⲛ̣
]ⲛ̣	ⲁⲓ̈ϭⲛⲧⲟⲩ ⲉ[ⲩ-]
?	[ⲥ]ⲏϩ ϩ̄ⲙ̄ⲡ̄ϫ̣ⲱ-
?	ⲱ̣ⲙ̣ⲉ[

[1] In the Book of Enoch 'store-houses' are mentioned, but the Greek words are ταμεῖον or θησαυρός (ch. xi, xviii).

[2] ⲧⲛ[ⲛⲟⲟⲩ ⲧ-] 'send the', might be read hardly space for ⲟⲩ- 'send a'.

Fol. 5: *Recto* (?). . . . 'a single purpose is in them.[1] They it is do guide heaven and earth. The name of the Father is written (?) [2] on the third . . . that is upon ' . . . . .

Verso (?). . . . and he found [it to be the] name [of] the [Holy] Ghost (? *πνεῦμα*). Enoch said unto him, 'My lord, lo, three invisible (*ἀόρατος*) names have I found written in the book (?) . . . . .

Fol. 6. → *Recto.*		↑ *Verso.*	
]ϣ̣[	]ⲁⲥ̣	[. . . .]ⲛⲥ̣	
]ⲡ	ⲓ̣ⲉϩ[. . . . .]ⲡ̣	ϫ̅ⲡ̣̅[. . .]ⲁ̣ⲛⲉ̣	ⲟⲛ[
ϣ̣ ⲛ̅-	ⲃⲟⲗ . . . . ⲟ̣	ⲕ . . . ⲛ̣ⲧⲉⲩ-	ϯⲁⲡ̣ . . ⲙ̣ⲡ̣[
ⲛϣⲁϫⲉ ⲛ-	ⲙ̅ⲡ̣ⲕ̣ⲟ̣ⲓⲧⲱ̣̅	ⲛ[ⲟⲩ ⲛⲧ]ⲁ̣ⲥⲥⲱ-	ϯϫ[ⲓ] ⲉⲕⲓ̈ⲃ[ⲉ ⲛ̅-]
[ⲛϩⲉ]ⲗ̣ⲗⲏⲛ ⲙ̅-	ⲛⲧⲡⲁⲣⲑⲉ-	ⲧ̅ⲙ̅ ⲉ[ⲧ]ⲉⲫⲱ-	ⲧ̅ⲛ̅ⲧⲁⲙⲁ[ⲁⲩ]
]ⲥ̣ⲱ̣ⲧ̅ⲙ̅	ⲛⲟⲥ ⲉⲥⲛⲕⲟ-	ⲛⲏ ⲛⲉⲛⲱⲭ	ⲙⲛϣϭ̣[ⲟⲙ
] . ϫ	ⲧ̅ⲕ̅ ⲛ̅ϩⲏⲧ̅ϥ̅	ⲡⲉⲥⲥⲟⲛ ⲡⲉ-	ⲉⲧⲣⲁϣ̣[
]ⲓ̣̈ⲛⲉ	ⳆⲠⲉϫⲁⲥ ⲛⲁϥ ϫ[ⲉ-]	[Ⲭ]ⲁⲥ̣ ⲛⲁϥ ϫⲉ-	ⲛ̅ⲕⲉⲓ̣[
]ⲧⲁ-	ⲉⲛⲱⲭ ⲡⲁ̣-	ⲉⲛⲱⲭ ⲡⲁⲥⲟ̅	ϯϫ[
ϩ]ⲣ̣ⲁⲓ̣̈	ϣⲏⲣⲉ ⲙⲁⲣ[ⲟⲛ]	[ϩ]ⲱⲛ ⲉϩⲟⲩⲛ	ⲛ̅[
]ⲁ	ⲉϩⲟⲩⲛ ⲉⲡⲕ̣[ⲟⲓ-]	ⲉ̣ⲣⲟⲓ̈ ⲛ̅ⲅ̅ϭⲱ[ϣⲧ]	ⲛ̅[
]ⲉ	[ⲧ]ⲱ̣ⲛ ⲛⲧ̣ⲛ̣[	[ⲉ]ⲃ̣ⲟⲗ ⲙ̅ⲡⲣ̣[	[

Fol. 6. *Recto*. . . . the words of the Greeks (? *ἕλλην*) . . . hear . . . . outside . . . . . the bed-chamber (*κοιτών*) of the virgin (*παρ.*), wherein she slept. She said unto him, 'Enoch, my son, let us go into the bed-chamber (? *κοι.*) and let us (?) ' . . . . .

Verso. . . . at the moment when she heard the voice (*φωνή*) of Enoch, her brother, she said unto him, 'Enoch, my brother, come in unto me and look forth. Be not . . . . .
. . . when] I took suck of my mother. It is impossible that I should [be ?] again (*or* other) ' . . . . .

1 ? the Trinity.

2 Reading ⲥⲛϩ, though as following prep. ϩⲛ would be preferable.

Fol. 7. ↑ *Recto.*		→ *Verso.* margin	
p. ⲓ̄ⲇ̄ (or ⲣ̄ⲇ̄)			
margin			
ⲉⲕϩ[ⲉ	[		[. . ⲛ]ⲛⲟ[ⲃⲉ
[. . . . .]ϥⲣ̄ ⲛ[ⲟ-]	. ⲡⲉ[	?	[ⲛ]ϥϥⲓ [ⲛⲛⲁ]ⲅⲁ-
ⲃⲉ ϩⲛⲟⲩⲙⲛⲧ-	[ⲉⲕ-]	[ⲛ]ϣⲟⲣ[ⲡ	ⲑⲟⲛ ⲛ[ϥⲧ]ⲁ-
ⲕⲟⲩ[ⲓ] ⲛϩⲏⲧ ·	ⲉϥ[ⲟ]ⲧϥ ⲉⲃⲟⲗ	[ⲥ]ϩⲁⲓ̈ ⲛ̄ⲛ̄ⲛ[ⲟ]ⲃⲉ	ⲗⲟⲟⲩ ⲉ[ⲕ]ⲉⲥⲁ
ⲙ̄ⲡⲟⲩⲙⲛ̄ⲧ-	ⲛ̄ⲕⲉⲥⲟⲡ ·	ⲙ̄ⲛⲛⲁⲅⲁⲑⲟⲛ	ⲉϥϣⲁⲛⲛⲁⲩ
ϣⲁϥⲧⲉ · ⲛ̄-	Ⲡⲉϫⲉ ⲉⲛⲱⲭ	ⲛ̄ⲛ̄ϣⲏⲣⲉ ⲛ̄-	ⲉⲛⲛⲟⲃⲉ ⲉⲩ-
ⲛⲉⲕⲥⲉϩ ⲛⲉⲩ-	ⲛⲁⲥ ϫⲉⲟⲩⲕ-	ⲛⲣⲱⲙⲉ · ⲥⲉ-	ⲥⲱⲕ ⲡⲁⲣⲁ
ⲛⲟⲃⲉ ⲛ̄ⲥⲱⲟⲩ	*sic* ⲕⲟⲩⲛ [. ⲙ]ⲡⲉⲡ-	ⲛⲁⲭ[ⲁⲣ]ⲓ̈ⲍⲉ	ⲛⲁⲅⲁⲑⲟⲛ
ⲧⲁⲭⲏ · ⲁⲗⲗ[ⲁ]	ⲛⲟⲩⲧⲉ [†] ⲛ̄ⲟⲩ-	ⲛⲁ[ⲕ] ⲙⲡⲁⲅ-	ϣⲁϥϥⲓ̈ ⲙⲡⲉϥ-
ⲉⲕⲉⲕⲱ ⲙ̄[ⲡ-]	ⲁⲅⲅⲉ[ⲗⲟ]ⲥ ϩⲛ̄-	[ⲅ]ⲉⲗⲟ[ⲥ ⲛⲧ]ⲙⲛⲧ-	ϩ[ⲣ]ⲁⲃⲇⲟⲥ ⲉⲧ-
ⲕⲁϣ ϩⲓϫ[ⲙ-]	ⲧⲡ[ⲉ] ⲛ̄ϥⲕⲁ-	ⲁϣⲁⲛⲉϩⲧⲏϥ	[ϩⲛ]ⲧⲉϥϭⲓ̈ϫ
ⲡⲕⲁⲗⲁⲙ[ⲁⲣⲓ-]	[ⲁϥ	ϭ[. . . .]ⲉⲧ[. .]	[ⲛⲟ]ⲩⲛⲁⲙ ⲛ̄ϥ-
ⲟⲛ ϭ[			ⲧ[ⲁⲗⲟ]ϥ ⲉϫⲛ-

Fol. 7 (1st fol. of quire 14).[1] *Recto.* . . . 'if] thou fi[nd (?) . . . . . he sinned through cowardice and error, thou shalt not write their sins against them hastily (ταχύ), but (ἀλλά) thou shalt put the reed into the reed-case (καλαμάριον) . . . . .

. . . delete[2] it again.' Enoch said unto her, 'Doth not God then (οὔκουν) [appoint?[3]] an angel (ἄγγ.) from heaven and (doth) he (not) [set? him' . . .

Verso. . . . 'first (*or* before [thou]) write the sins and the good-deeds (ἀγαθός) of the sons of men, thou shalt be granted (χαρίζειν) the angel (ἄγγ.) of mercy' . . . . .

. . . 'sins and he taketh the good-deeds (ἀγ.) and placeth them on another side. If he see the sins drawing (down the balance) beyond (παρά) the good-deeds (ἀγ.), he taketh his staff (ῥάβδος), that is in his right hand, and layeth it upon' . . . . .

[1] So if this is *recto*; if *verso*, it indicates p. 14, or (reading ⲣ̄ⲇ̄) p. 104.

[2] Perhaps ⲉⲕⲉϥⲟⲧϥ 'thou shalt delete'. Enoch deletes sins, *CSCO.*, vol. 42, 236.

[3] *Lit.* 'give'.]ⲛ̄, as part of a 2-rad. verb, is more difficult, though as accus., superlined before ⲟⲩ, it is also unlikely. The passage is to me quite obscure.

Fol. 8. → *Recto.* | ↑ *Verso.*

Recto		Verso	
]ⲡ̣[			
]ⲙⲉ			. ⲉ[
ⲉⲣⲉ[. . . .] ⲙ̣ⲙⲉ	ⲡ̣ⲟ̣[		ⲙⲉ[
ⲟⲛⲧⲉ ⲙ̣[ⲡ]ⲟⲩⲉï-	ⲉⲛⲱ̣[ⲭ	]ⲙ̣ⲟ	ϩ̄ⲛ̄[. . . .]ϩ̣ⲓ̣
ⲙⲉ ⲉⲣⲟⲥ̣ ⲙⲡⲟⲩ-	?	]ⲙⲏ	ⲛ̄ⲧ̣[ⲉⲧ]ⲙⲙⲁⲩ
ⲉϣⲟⲩⲟⲛϩ̄ⲥ̄ ⲉⲃⲟⲗ	ⲉⲛⲱⲭ ⲡ̣[ⲁ-]	]	ⲉïⲥ̣ ⲧⲁ[. .]ⲉⲧ ϣ̣[ⲱ-]
ⲉïⲉⲙⲏⲧⲉï	ϣⲏⲣⲉ [	]ϩ̣ⲛ̄-	ⲡⲉ ⲛⲟⲩ ⲛ̄ⲧⲁⲕ̣-
[ⲛ]ⲅ̄ⲃⲱⲕ ⲛ̄ⲅ̣̄-	ⲙ[	]	ϫⲡⲟⲥ ⲛ̄ϩⲏ[ⲧⲥ]
ⲟⲩⲟⲛϩ̄ⲥ̄ ⲉⲃⲟⲗ	ⲉⲡⲉ[	ⲉⲛ]ⲱⲭ	ⲉïⲥ ϣⲟⲙⲛ̣̄ⲧ ⲛ̣-
[ϩ]ⲛ̣̄ⲧ̣ⲙⲏⲧⲉ	ⲛⲁⲩ̣[	]ⲧⲁϫⲟ-	ⲥⲟⲡ ⲁⲥ̣ϣⲁ̣ϫ[ⲉ] [a]
[ⲙ̄]ⲡⲉⲕⲉïⲱ-	ⲛ̄ⲁ[	]ⲣ̣ⲁⲛ	ϩ̄ⲛ̄ϩⲉⲛⲛⲟ[ϭ]
[ⲧ] ⲙⲛ̄ⲧⲉⲕ ⲙ̣[ⲁⲁⲩ]	ⲧⲁ[	]ⲉ	ⲛϣⲁϫⲉ ⲕ̣ϩ̣ . [
[. . .]ϫ[	ⲭ[	]ⲉ	[.]ⲏⲛ . . ⲱ̣[

[a] ⲁϥϣⲁϫⲉ cannot be read.

Fol. 8. *Recto.* . . . 'they [1] have not known her, they have not been able to make her (? it) known, except (εἰμήτι) thou (first) go and make her (? it) known before (*lit.* in midst of) thy father and thy mo[ther' . . . . .

. . . 'Enoch [my ?] son' . . . . .

Verso. . . . En]och . . . . .

. . . 'of her. Lo, my . . . (*fem.*),[2] what shall (she ?) become (?), (she) whom thou didst beget from (her) ? Lo, three times hath she spoken great (?) words' . . . . .

Fol. 9. → *Recto.* | ↑ *Verso.*

Recto		Verso	
margin		margin	
ⲡⲛⲟⲩⲧⲉ ϭⲱ-	ⲭⲉⲟⲩⲕⲟⲩⲛ	[. .]ⲛ̣ⲁϫï ⲛ̄[ⲥ-]	ⲉⲓ̣ⲉⲙⲏⲧⲉ ⲛ-
ϣⲧ ⲉϩⲣⲁⲓ ⲉϫⲱⲕ ·	ⲡⲟ . . . ⲁ̣ⲛ̣[ⲁ-]	[ⲛⲁ]ⲩ ⲉϩⲣⲁï ⲉⲧ-	ⲡⲗⲁⲥⲥ̣ⲉ ⲛⲕ[ⲉ-]
ⲁϥⲛⲁⲩ ⲉⲣⲟⲕ	ⲗⲁⲙⲃⲁⲛⲉ [	[ⲡⲉ] ϩ̄ⲙ̄ⲡⲉⲩⲥⲱ-	ⲣⲱⲙⲉ ⲛⲑⲉ

[1] Read ? ⲟⲩⲧⲉ 'neither'.

[2]]ⲉⲧ might be completed as ⲕⲉⲧ or ⲉⲉⲧ, were they not so difficult to adapt to the context.

ϫⲉⲛⲧⲕⲟⲩⲥⲱ-
ⲧⲡ ⲁⲩⲱ ⲉⲕⲥⲁ-
ϩⲏⲩ ⲉⲃⲟⲗ ⲉⲡⲉ-
ⲑⲟⲟⲩ ⲛ[ⲓ]ⲙ · ⲡⲉ-
Ϫⲁϥ ϫⲉ[. . .]ⲉⲓⲁⲩ[a]
ⲁⲛⲟ̣[. . . .]ⲛⲉⲣ̣ .[b]
?

ⲛⲣⲱⲙⲉ [ⲉⲧ-]
ⲡⲉ ϩⲙⲡⲉϥ[ⲥⲱ-]
ⲙⲁ̣ ⲉⲓⲙⲏⲧ[ⲉⲓ]
/ ⲁ[ⲛⲟ]ⲕ̣ · ⲡⲉϫ̣[ⲁⲥ]
Ⲛ̣ⲁ[ϥ] ϫ̣ⲉ[
[ϫ]ⲟ̣ⲉ̣ⲓ̈ⲥ . . [

[ⲙⲁ] ⲟⲩⲁ ϫⲉ-
[ϩ]ⲏⲗⲓ̣̈ⲁⲥ ⲙⲛ-
[ⲕ]ⲉⲟⲩⲉⲓ ϫⲉⲧⲁ-
[ⲃⲓ]ⲑⲁ̣ ⲡ̅[. .]ⲕⲁ
]ⲙ̣ⲡⲙ̣ⲁ̣ ⲉ-
]ⲉ ⲛϩⲏ[ⲧ]ϥ̅
]ⲧ̣ⲉⲧ[

ⲙⲡⲉⲛⲉⲓ̈ⲱ[ⲧ]
ⲁⲇⲁⲙ ⲛ̅ϥϭⲱ̣-
ⲣ̅ϭ̅ ⲉⲡⲕⲁϩ
Ⲡⲉϫ[ⲁ]ⲥ ⲛⲁϥ̣
ϫⲉ[ⲡ]ⲁ̣ⲥ̣ⲟⲛ ⲁ
ⲗⲁ[. ⲡ]ⲕ̣ⲁⲣⲡⲟ̣ⲥ̣
ⲉⲧⲛ̣[ⲁⲉⲓ ⲉ]ⲃⲟⲗ
ⲛ̅ϩ[ⲏⲧⲕ

[a] Possibly ⲁⲩⲓ. [b] Possibly ⲛⲉⲛ.

Fol. 9. *Recto*. . . . 'God (did) look down upon thee and saw thee, how that thou wast a chosen one and removed from all evil.' He said, ...
. . . said,] '[Shall] not then (οὔκουν) [the Lord ?] take up (ἀναλαμβάνειν) [any ?] man to heaven in his body (? σῶμα), except (εἰμήτι) me ?' She (?) said unto [him,] ' . . . Lord (?) . . . . .

Verso. . . . shall take two up to [heaven] in their body (σῶμα): one Elias, another Tabitha . . . . . the place where . . . is . . . . .
. . . except (? εἰμήτι) by forming[1] (πλάσσειν) another man, in the fashion of our father Adam, and that he people the earth.' She said unto him, 'Mathusala (?)[2] [is the] fruit (καρ.) that [shall go] forth from [thee'. . . . .

No. 4.

From a version of the Life (?) of the Virgin, identical, in part at least, with Zoega no. cxvii, Clar. Press no. 14 (*v.* Forbes Robinson, *Apocr. Gosp.*, pp. 10, 14) and Br. Mus. no. 303.[3] In the latter of those fragments there is likewise reference to the Meletians.[4] Our fourth fragment here is perhaps wrongly associated with the other three; it may be from a different MS. and text. So too the third, which has marked differences from the others (*v.* note on text).

[1] For εἰμήτι (*cf.* the readings here *ro.* and frag. 8), perhaps ⲉⲓⲉ ⲙⲏ ⲧⲉⲛ-. But 1st pl. 'we form' seems incongruous here.

[2] Reading instead [ⲙ]ⲁⲑⲟⲩⲥⲁⲗⲁ[ⲡⲉ.

[3] *Cf.* also Revillout in *Journ. As.*, 1905, i. 412, 413.

[4] F. R., p. 2, ll. 14, 15, 'Say not as the heretics that the Virgin was a "power" (δύναμις, *cf. ib.* 108, 10); nor say as the Meletians, that she was taken up to heaven in her body.' Mr. Winstedt has kindly collated the text.

Fol. 1. ↑ *Recto.*

[ⲡⲙ]ⲁ ⲛⲛⲉϩⲟ-
ⲟⲩ ⲛⲧⲁⲕⲑⲃⲃⲓ-
ⲟⲛ ϩⲙⲡⲧⲣⲉ-
ⲡⲁϩⲏⲧ ⲙⲕⲁϩ
ⲁⲕϫⲁⲥⲧ ⲛⲑⲉ
ⲛⲟⲩⲡⲉⲧⲣⲁ ⲁⲕ-
ϫⲓ̈ ⲙⲟⲉⲓ̈ⲧ ϩⲏⲧ
ⲁⲕⲉⲛⲧ ⲉⲃⲟⲗ
ⲉⲩⲟⲩⲁⲥⲧⲛ ⲁⲕ-
ⲧⲁⲗⲟ ⲛ̄ϩⲉⲛⲣⲱ-
ⲙⲉ ⲉϫⲛⲛⲉⲛ-
[ⲁ]ⲡⲉⲩⲉ· ⲁⲕⲉⲛⲧ

margin

→ *Verso.*

margin

ⲉⲓⲛⲉ ⲛⲛⲉⲩⲧ[ⲁ-]
ⲉⲓ̈ⲟ ⲛⲓ̈ⲱⲁⲕⲉ[ⲓⲙ]
ⲁⲩⲣ ⲥⲁϣϥ ⲛ-
ϩⲟⲟⲩ ⲉⲩⲟⲩ-
ⲱⲙ ⲉⲩⲥⲱ [ⲉⲩ-]
ⲉⲩⲫⲣⲁⲛⲉ ⲉ-
ϫⲙⲡⲛⲁ ⲛ-
ⲧⲁⲡⲛⲟⲩⲧⲉ
ϫⲟⲕϥ [ⲉⲃⲟⲗ]
ⲙⲛ̄ⲓ̈ⲱⲁⲕ[ⲉⲓⲙ]
ⲙⲛⲁⲛ[ⲛⲁ

Fol. 1. *Recto.* . . . 'in [1] place of the days in which Thou didst humble us, when my heart was sad. Thou didst raise me up like a rock (πέτρα) and didst guide me and bring me forth unto a broad-place.[2] Thou didst cause men to ride over our heads and didst bring [us' . . . . .

Verso. . . . brought their gifts-of-honour unto Joakim and they spent seven days eating and drinking and rejoicing (εὐφραίνειν) over the mercy that God had fulfilled with Joakim and Anna . . . . .

Fol. 2. ↑ *Recto.*

[ⲡⲛ]ⲟⲩⲧⲉ ⲁⲁϥ
[ⲛⲙ]ⲡϣⲁ ⲉ-
[ⲧ]ⲣⲉϥϥⲓ̈ⲧⲥ
[Ⲡ]ⲗ̣ⲏⲛ ⲙⲡⲉ-
[ⲧ]ⲡⲁⲣⲑⲉⲛⲟⲥ
ϣⲓⲛⲉ ⲛⲥⲁ-
ⲛⲉⲥⲉⲓⲟⲧⲉ

margin

→ *Verso.*

margin

ⲁ[ⲩ]ⲱ [a] ⲛⲉⲧ[ⲃⲱⲕ]
ⲛⲙⲙⲁⲩ ⲉ̣ⲛ̣[ⲉⲩ-]
ⲙⲁ ⲛϣⲓ̈ⲛⲉ [ⲉⲧ-]
ⲥ̣ⲟⲟϥ ⲉⲧⲉ̣[ⲛⲉⲩ-]
ⲙⲁ ⲛϣⲱⲡ̣[ⲉ-]
ⲛⲉ· ⲟⲩⲁⲉ [ⲟⲩ-]
ⲟⲛ ⲛⲓ̈ⲙ ⲉⲧⲡⲓⲥ̣-

[a] Or ⲇⲁⲓ]ⲙⲱⲛ ⲉⲧ-.

[1] This ode is made up of various Psalm verses (*v.* F. Robinson, p. 11).

[2] F. R. ⲛⲟⲩⲱϣⲥ ⲉⲃⲟⲗ.

ⲁⲗⲗⲁ ⲛⲉⲥⲟ ⲛⲑⲉ
ⲛⲛⲉϊϭⲣⲟⲟⲙ-
ⲡⲉ ⲉⲧⲙⲟⲟⲛⲉ
ⲛⲛⲁⲩ ⲛⲓ̈ⲙ
ϩⲙⲡⲣⲡⲉ ϣⲁ-
ⲡⲉϩⲟⲟⲩ ⲛⲧⲁⲥ-
ⲙⲡϣⲁ ⲙⲡⲉϊ-
ⲛⲟϭ ⲛⲧⲁⲉϊⲟ
ⲛϩⲏⲧϥ ⲉⲧⲣⲉⲥ-
ϫⲡⲟ ⲙⲡⲉⲭ︦ⲥ︦
Ⲙⲁⲣⲟⲩϫⲓ̈ ϣⲓ̈-
ⲡⲉ ⲧⲉⲛⲟⲩ ⲛ-
ϭⲓ ⲙⲙⲉϊⲗϊⲧⲓ-
sic ⲛⲓ̈ⲁⲛⲟⲥ ⲛⲁⲓ̈
ⲉⲧϩⲩⲡⲟⲧⲉ̣ⲩⲉ̣
ⲥ̣ . [

margin

margin

ⲧⲉⲩⲉ ⲛⲙⲙⲁⲩ
ⲉⲧⲉⲩϩⲁⲓ̈ⲣⲉ-
ⲥⲓⲥ ⲉⲧⲥⲟⲟϥ
ⲛⲁⲓ̈ [ⲉⲧ]ⲥ̣ϩⲁ̣[ⲓ][a]
ⲛⲟϭ ⲛⲧⲱⲗⲙ
ⲉⲧⲙⲛⲧⲛⲟⲩ-
ⲧⲉ ⲛⲉⲙⲙⲁⲛⲟⲩ-
ⲏ̄ⲗ ⲉ̣ . . . . ⲉ̣
ⲧⲉⲧⲣⲓⲁⲥ ⲉⲧⲟⲩ-
ⲁⲁⲃ ⲡⲓ̈ⲱⲧ
ⲙⲛⲡϣⲏⲣⲉ
ⲙⲛⲡⲉⲡⲛ︦ⲁ︦
ⲉⲧⲟⲩⲁⲁⲃ ⲉⲩ-
ϥⲓ̈ ⲙⲙⲁⲩ ⲙ-
ⲡⲉⲙⲙⲏ ⲙ[b]
ⲧ̣ⲉⲛⲛⲏ ⲉⲣⲉ-

[a] Or (if space would allow) [ⲉⲧϫ]ⲉ ϩⲉ[ⲛ-. [b] ⲙⲛ- (? ⲙ̄) is required; then prob. ⲡⲉⲛⲛⲏ.

Fol. 2. *Recto.* . . . God made him (?) worthy to take her (? it). Howbeit (πλήν) the Virgin (παρ.) visited not her parents, but (ἀλλά) was like to those doves that dwelt always in the temple, until the day whereon she was worthy of this great honour, that she should bear Christ. Let the Meletians[1] be now ashamed, that cast suspicion (? ὑποπτεύειν) . . . . .

Verso. . . . and (?) they that [go] with them unto [their] filthy oracles, that is, their dwelling-places; neither (οὐδέ) any one that believeth (πιστεύειν)

[1] There is little to add to Riedel's account of the Meletians (*Can. Athanas.* xv ff. My reference there to Renaudot may now be replaced by Evetts, *Patrol. Or.*, v. 200 ff., where their magical practices are specially referred to). Their heretical tenets are condemned in the other copy of the present text (*v.* note above), their usages attacked by Damianus (Evetts *l. c.*, i. 473 = *Synax.*, 18th Sanê, *ed.* Guidi), and their survival of Siût (Br. Mus. no. 358, if by Bp. Constantine, then also of early seventh century, *v.* Br. Mus. no. 865 n.), and at Achmîm (*Mission* iv. 740; *cf.* Wüstenfeld's *Synax.*, 9th Kihak) are recorded. Athanasius, in a Festal Letter (Zoega no. cclxxvii, f. 2 = text of Paris 129^{14}, ff. 87–90, which is same MS. as Br. Mus. no. 173), refers to their trafficking in saints' relics.

with them in their filthy heresy (*αἵρ.*), who ascribe[1] great impurities unto the divinity of Emmanuel, they . . . -ing the holy Trinity (*τριάς*), the Father, the Son and the Holy Ghost (*πν.*), taking away the *mê* (*μῦ*) and the *nê* (*νῦ*)[2] . . . . .

Fol. 3. ↑ *Recto.*[a]

margin

ⲁⲩⲥⲫⲣⲁⲅ̣ⲓ̣ⲍⲉ̣ ⲙ̣-
ⲙⲟϥ ϩⲛⲟ̣ⲩⲥⲫⲣⲁ-
ⲅⲓ̈ⲥ · ⲁⲩⲱ ⲙⲛⲛ-
Ⲥⲁⲛⲁⲓ̈ ⲟⲛ ⲙⲡⲥ-
ⲥⲟⲗⲥⲗ ⲛϩⲏⲧ ⲉⲥ-
ϫⲱ̄ ⲙⲙⲟⲥ ϫⲉ-
ⲉⲓ̈ⲧⲙ̄ⲃⲱⲕ ⲧⲁ-
ⲛⲁⲩ ⲉⲡⲧⲁⲫⲟ̄ⲥ̄
ⲛⲑⲉ ⲛⲧⲁⲩⲕⲁ-
ⲁϥ ⲙⲙⲟ̄ⲥ̄ ⲛϯ-
ⲛⲁϩⲙⲟⲟ̄ⲥ̄ ⲁⲛ
Ⲉⲣⲉⲛⲁⲓ̈ ⲇⲉ ϣⲟ̄-
ⲟⲡ ⲛ̄ⲧⲉⲓ̈ϩⲉ ⲙⲁⲗ-
ⲗⲟ̄ⲛ ⲇ̄ⲉ̄ ⲛⲉ[ⲣ]ⲉ̣-
ⲟⲩⲛⲟϭ ⲛ[. .]ⲣ̣ⲃ̣
[·]ϩ̣[

[. . .]ⲧ̣ⲛⲟⲩ
[. . .] ⲉⲧⲉⲡ-
[ⲥⲁ]ⲃ̱ⲃ̱ⲁⲧⲟⲛⲡⲉ
ⲉ̣ⲥ̣ϫⲱ ⲙⲙⲟⲥ
ϫ[ⲉ]ⲙⲁⲣⲛⲧⲱ-
[ⲟ]ⲩⲛ ⲛⲧⲉⲩϣⲏ
ⲛ̣ⲧⲛⲃⲱⲕ ⲉⲃⲟⲗ
ⲛⲙⲙⲁⲥ ⲛⲧⲛ-
ϫⲓ̈ⲧⲥ ⲉⲃⲟⲗ̄ ⲛⲥ-
ⲛⲁⲩ ⲉⲡⲉϥⲥⲱ-
ⲙⲁ ϫⲉⲛⲛⲉⲥⲙⲟⲩ̄
ⲛⲧⲉϥⲁⲫⲟⲣⲙⲏ
ⲁⲩⲧⲱⲟⲩⲛ ⲁⲩ-
[ⲥ]ⲟⲃⲧⲉ ⲛ̄ϩⲉⲛ-
[ϩ]ⲏ̄ⲡ̄ⲉ̄ ⲉⲛⲁϣⲱ-
[ⲟⲩ] ⲙⲛϩⲉⲛ-
[. . .]ϣⲏⲣⲓ̣[b] . .
?

[a] The superlineation here is so peculiar and different from that on foll. 1, 2, 4, that one may doubt this leaf being from the same MS.

[b] [ⲑⲩⲙⲓ]ⲁⲧⲏⲣⲓ[ⲟⲛ is improbable.

[1] *Lit.* 'write'. Or 'speak' (grammatically preferable).

[2] I can suggest no other translation, and even for this the reading requires manipulation. I suppose the consonants of 'Emmanuel' to be intended and some magical or gnostic use of the name ⲉⲁⲟⲩⲏⲗ referred to. *Cf.* wholly vocalic forms like ⲁⲉⲏⲉⲓⲟⲩⲱⲏⲗ (*Rain. Mitth.*, v. 120). That the letters ⲙ, ⲛ were thus pronounced is seen from Hebbelynck, *Mystères*, 34, 117, Paris 131[8], f. 77 (on significance of the letters in name ⲙⲁⲣⲓⲁ).

→ *Verso.*

margin
ⲡⲉ ⲉⲧⲣ̣[ⲉⲩⲙⲟ-]
ⲟϣⲉ ⲉⲃ[ⲟⲗ ⲉ]ⲩ-
ⲣϩⲟⲧⲉⲡⲉ ⲁ[ⲩ]ⲱ
ⲉⲩϣⲧⲣⲧⲱⲣ
Ⲉⲛⲉⲣⲉⲡ̄ⲓ̈ⲟⲩ-
ⲇⲁⲓ ⲅⲁⲣ ϭⲟⲣ̣ϭ
ⲉⲡⲉⲧⲛⲁⲃⲱⲕ
ⲉⲃⲟⲗ ⲉⲡⲙϩⲁ-
ⲁⲩ ⲛⲥⲉⲉⲓ̈ⲣⲉ ⲛⲁⲩ̅
ⲛϩⲉⲛⲡⲉⲑⲟ-
ⲟⲩ· ⲛⲉⲣⲉⲛⲣⲉϥ-
ⲣⲟⲉⲓ̈ⲥ ⲣⲟⲉⲓ̈ⲥ ⲉ-
ⲣⲟϥ̅ⲡⲉ ϫⲉⲛ-
ⲛⲉⲩϥⲓ̈ ⲙⲡⲉϥ-
ⲥⲱⲙⲁ ⲛϫ[ⲓⲟ]ⲩⲉ
ⲛⲉⲣⲉⲟⲩϣⲧ[ⲟⲣ-]
ⲧⲣ ϣⲟⲟⲡ [ⲉⲧ-]
[ⲃ]ⲏⲏⲧϥ ϫ[ⲉ

ⲡ]ⲉ̣ⲭ̅ⲥ̅ (in margin)[a]
ⲉⲧϥϫⲱ ⲙⲙⲟ-
ⲟⲩ̅ ⲛⲁⲩ̅ ϫⲓ̈ⲛⲉϥ̣-
ϣⲟⲟⲡ ⲛⲙⲙⲁⲩ-
ⲡⲉ ϫ̅ⲉϩⲁ̅ⲡ̅ⲥ
ⲉⲧⲣⲁ̅ϣ̅ⲡ ⲛⲉⲓ̈-
ϩⲓⲥⲉ ⲁⲩⲱ̅ ⲛⲧⲁ-
ⲧⲱⲟⲩⲛ ⲛⲉⲣⲉ-
sic ⲕⲁ
ⲟⲩⲕⲉ ⲛⲃⲟⲗ ⲙⲛ-
ⲟⲩ̅ϣⲧⲟⲣⲧⲣ
ⲁⲩⲱ ⲁⲩ̅ⲕⲱ̅ ⲛ-
ⲥⲱⲟⲩ̅ ⲛⲛⲁⲓ̈
ⲧⲏⲣⲟⲩ̅ ⲁⲩⲙⲟ̅-
ⲟϣⲉ· ⲡ̅ⲙⲙⲁⲥ
[ⲉ]ⲧⲃⲉⲧⲉⲥ̅ ⲙⲛⲧ̅-
ⲁⲛⲁⲅⲕⲏ ⲙⲡ̅-
[ⲡⲉⲥϣⲧⲟ]ⲣⲧⲣ

[a] This being the *verso*, the formula [ⲓ̅ⲥ̅ ⲡ]ⲉⲭ̅ⲥ̅ would indicate the last fol. of a quire. (More usually ⲓ̅ⲥ̅ on the last, ⲡⲉⲭ̅ⲥ̅ on first of following quire.)

Fol. 3. *Recto.* . . . they sealed (σφραγίζειν) it with a seal (σφραγίς). And after this also she was not comforted at heart, saying, 'If I go not and see the tomb (τάφος), how they have laid Him, I will not sit down.' But (δέ) these things being so, and moreover (μᾶλλον δέ) as there was a great . . . . .
. . . which as the Sabbath, she saying, 'Let us arise at night and go forth with her and take her out and she see His body (σῶ.), lest she die on His account (ἀφορμή).' They arose and prepared much spices and . . . (*plur.*) . .

Verso. . . . that they should go forward, being afraid and trembling. For (γάρ) the Jews were lying in wait for whoso should go forth to the grave, that they might do them evil; and the watchers were watching it, lest His body (σῶ.) should be taken by stealth; and there was a disturbance on His (?) account, because that . . . . .

. . . words] that He spake unto them, while He was with them, 'Needs must that I should suffer these things and should arise, there being (still) darkness and disturbance.'[1] And they left all these things behind them and went with her, by reason of her need (ἀνάγκη) and her trouble . . . . .

Fol. 4. → *Recto.*

margin

ⲛⲁ[
ϣⲁ[
ⲉⲛⲉϩ ⲓ̣[ⲉⲧ-]
ϩⲓ̈ϫⲙ̅ⲙ̅ⲡⲕⲁϩ ⲕ[
ⲉⲣⲉⲡⲉⲩ̣ϩⲏⲧ[a] ⲥ̣[. .]
ⲛⲑⲉ ⲛⲧⲛⲉⲓ̣[. .]
ⲉⲩⲥⲟⲫⲟⲥⲡ[ⲉ] ⲉ-
ⲡⲉϩⲟⲩⲟ (*sic* ⲛ) ⲉⲛⲧⲁⲩ-
ϣⲱⲡⲉ ⲧⲏⲣⲟⲩ
ϩⲓ̈ϫⲙⲙⲡⲕⲁϩ
ⲕⲁⲛ ⲉⲁϥϫⲓ̈ ⲡⲛⲟ-
[ⲙⲟ]ⲥ ⲛⲑⲉ ⲙⲙⲱ-
[ⲩⲥⲏⲥ] ⲕⲁⲛ ⲉⲁϥ-
]ⲙⲡ-

↑ *Verso.*

]ⲱ
ⲡⲉ]ϥ̣ⲟⲩⲟ-
[ⲉⲓⲛ] ⲁⲛⲥⲓⲟⲩ
ⲁⲛⲁⲭⲱⲣⲉⲓ
ⲛ̣ⲁⲩ ⲁⲧⲕⲁⲕⲉ
ϣⲱⲡⲉ ⲛⲧⲡⲁ-
ϣⲉ ⲙⲡⲉϩⲟⲟⲩ
ⲁⲛⲉⲧⲙⲟⲟⲩⲧ
ⲧⲱⲟⲩⲛ ⲁⲩⲉⲓ ⲉ-
ⲃⲟⲗ ϩⲛⲛⲉⲙ-
ϩⲁⲁⲩ
ⲁⲡⲕⲁⲧ[ⲁⲡⲉⲧⲁⲥⲙⲁ][b]
ⲙⲡⲣ̣[ⲡⲉ
?

margin

[a] ⲡⲉϥϩⲏⲧ more probable. [b] Inevitable, if not too long. Last letters perhaps above the line.

Fol. 4. *Recto.* . . . ever . . . on the earth . . ., his (?) heart being . . . like . . . . ., he being wise (σοφός) beyond all them that had been upon earth, whether (κἄν) when he received[2] the law (νόμ.) like Moses, or (κἄν) when he . . . . .

Verso. . . . his (?) light; the stars departed (ἀναχωρεῖν); darkness was at midday; the dead arose and came forth from the graves. The veil (? καταπέτασμα[3]) of the temple (?) . . . . .

[1] *Cf.* Lemm, *Misc.* lix. [2] 'accepted', if this refers to Christ. [3] *V.* note [b].

No. 5.

Presumably from a Sermon (or Encomium), with reference, on *verso*, to the death of the Virgin. *Cf.* the passages in Forbes Robinson's *Apocr. Gospels*, pp. 65, 83, and in *PSBA*. xxix. 304. The narrative would appear not to be related here by an apostle.

→ *Recto.*

margin

ⲁϥϯ ⲛⲁϥ̄ ⲛ[ϩⲉⲛ-]	
ⲧⲁⲉⲓⲟ ϩⲱⲱ̄[ϥ]	
ⲙⲛ̄ϩⲉⲛ̄ⲇⲱ[ⲣⲟⲛ]	
ⲉⲛⲁϣⲱⲟⲩ —	ϣ[
Ⲁϥϫⲟⲟⲥ ⲛⲓ̈ⲱ̄	ⲅⲉⲓ̣[
ⲥⲏⲫ ϫⲉⲉⲓ̈ⲥ ⲡⲁ-	ⲱⲡ̣[
ⲕⲁϩ ⲧⲏⲣϥ̄ ⲙⲡⲉⲙ̄-	ⲥ̣ⲛⲁⲩ ⲁ̣[
ⲧⲟ ⲉⲃⲟⲗ ⲙⲡⲉⲕ-	ⲁⲩⲙ̣ⲡ̣[
ⲉⲓⲱⲧ ⲙⲛⲛⲉ̣[ⲕ-]	ⲁ̣ϥⲧ̣ⲛ[
ⲥⲛⲏⲩ ⲙⲁⲣⲟⲩ-	
ⲟⲩⲱϩ̄ ϩⲙⲡⲕⲁϩ	
ⲉⲧⲛ̄ⲁⲛⲟⲩϥ	
ⲛⲥⲉϫⲓ ⲛ̄ⲥⲉϯ	
ⲛ̣̄ⲥ̣ⲉϣⲱⲡⲉ	
ϩ̣ⲙⲡⲉ̣ⲟ̣ⲟ̣ⲩ ⲛ̣-	
ⲧⲁⲙⲛ̄ⲧⲉⲣ[ⲟ]	
ⲙⲛ̄ⲛⲁⲅⲁ[ⲑⲟⲛ]	
ⲙⲡⲕⲁϩ·	
Ⲉϣϫⲉ ⲁⲛ̣[	

↑ *Verso.*

margin

	[ⲡ]ⲏⲩⲉ ⲉⲣⲉⲛ̄ⲃⲁ̣[ⲗ]
	[ⲛ]ⲛ̄ⲁⲡⲟⲥⲧⲟⲗ̣-[a]
	[ⲗ]ⲟⲥ ϭⲱϣⲧ̄ ⲛ̄-
]ⲃⲱⲕ	ⲥⲱⲥ̆ ⲉⲩ̣ⲑⲉⲱⲣⲉ̣ⲓ̣
ⲙ]ⲡⲏⲩⲉ	ⲙⲙⲟⲥ ⲙⲛ̄ⲡⲉⲥ-
]ⲧ̣ⲛⲟⲩ	ⲉⲟⲟⲩ ⲛⲁⲧϣⲁ-
]ⲛⲟⲥ̣	ϫⲉ ⲉⲣⲟϥ· ⲁⲩⲱ
]ⲁ̣ⲥⲱϣ	ⲛⲧⲉⲣⲟⲩⲡⲱϩ̄
]ϫⲁⲉ̣ⲙ	ⲛⲙⲙⲁⲥ ⲉⲙⲡⲩ-
]ⲥϩ	ⲗⲏ ⲛ̄ⲙⲡⲏⲩⲉ
	ⲁⲛⲉⲑⲩ̄ⲣⲟⲩⲣⲟⲥ̆
	ⲛ̄ⲙⲡⲏⲩⲉ ⲣⲁ-
	ϣⲉ ⲁⲩⲱϣ̄ ⲉ-
	ⲃⲟⲗ̄ ⲉⲩϫⲱ ⲙ-
	ⲙⲟⲥ ϩⲓ̈ⲧⲛ̄ⲧⲉ-
	[ⲥ]ⲙⲏ ⲛ̄ⲧⲁⲥϣⲱ-
	[ⲡⲉ] ⲙⲙⲟⲥ̆ ⲙ-
	[ⲡⲛ]ⲁⲩ ⲛ̄ⲧⲁⲡⲉⲥ̆-
	[ϣⲏ]ⲣⲉ ⲃⲱⲕ̄ ⲉ-
	[ϩⲣⲁⲓ] ⲉⲙⲡⲏⲩⲉ
	[. . . .]ⲱⲛ̣[

[a] Perhaps nothing instead of ⲗ.

Recto. . . . he gave unto him also (?) honours and many gifts (*δῶρον*). He said unto Joseph,[1] 'Behold, my whole land is before thy father and thy

[1] *V.* Gen. xlvii. 6.

brethren. Let them dwell in the good land and buy and sell and share (*lit.* be) in the honour of my kingdom and the good-things (ἀγαθός) of the land.'[1] If we (?) . . . . .

Verso. . . . to] heaven, the eyes of the apostles (ἀπ.) looking after her, beholding her and her unspeakable glory. And when they[2] had attained with her unto the gates (πύλη) of heaven, the door-keepers (θυρωρός) of heaven rejoiced and cried out, saying, with the voice that had reached her[3] at the time when her Son had gone up to heaven . . . . .

No. 6.

We have here the last words of one Sermon, followed by the title and opening of another; also (fol. 2) a passage, relating to Acts i. 3 ff., which may belong to either or to neither of the preceding. That with its title preserved was pronounced at Christmas, and might be attributed to Basil of Caesarea, if that town's name could be read in the second lacuna. The text, however, does not resemble that of any published sermon by Basil.

Fol. 1. ↑ *Recto.*

margin

ϫⲟⲉⲓⲥ ⲛⲁï ⲉ-	ⲱⲧ ⲙ̅ⲡⲛ[ⲉⲡⲛ̅ⲁ]
ⲃⲟⲗ ϩⲓⲧⲟⲟⲧϥ	ⲉⲧⲟⲩⲁⲁⲃ [ϣⲁⲉⲛⲉϩ]
ⲡⲉⲟⲟⲩ ⲙ̅ⲡⲉⲓ-	ⲛ̅ⲉⲛⲉϩ ϩ[ⲁⲙⲏⲛ·]

— — — — — — — —

7 ⲟⲩⲉⲝⲏⲅⲏⲥⲓⲥ ⲛ̅ⲧⲉ [
ⲡⲉⲡⲓⲥⲕⲟⲡⲟⲥ ⲛ̅ⲧⲡ̣[
ⲛ̅ⲧϣⲟⲣⲡ ⲛ̅ⲕⲁⲡⲡⲁ[ⲇⲟⲕⲓⲁ
ⲉϥϣⲁϫⲉ ⲉⲧⲃⲉⲡ[ϩⲟⲩⲙⲓⲥⲉ ⲙ̅ⲡⲉⲛ-]

→ *Verso.*

margin

[. . .]ⲥ̣ ⲛ̅ⲥⲉϩⲱ-	ⲗⲟⲟⲗⲉ' ⲉⲥⲱⲗ̅ⲡ
[ⲃⲥ][a] ⲙ̅ⲡⲁⲏⲣ ⲉⲩ-	ⲙ̅ⲡϣⲗ̅ϩ ⲉⲧⲉ-
]ϫⲙ̅ ϩⲛ̅-	ⲛ̅ϥⲛⲁϯ ⲕⲁⲣⲡⲟⲥ
]ⲧⲡⲉ	ⲁⲛ· ⲛ̅ϥⲧⲃ̅ⲃⲟ
]ⲙ̣ⲙ̣ⲁ ⲛⲏⲩ	ⲙ̅ⲡⲉⲧⲛⲁϯ ⲕⲁⲣ-
] ?	ⲡⲟⲥ ϩ̅ⲛⲟⲩⲟⲩ-
] ⲉ̣ⲃⲟⲗ	ⲣⲟⲧ · ⲧⲟⲧⲉ
]ⲕⲁⲗⲏ	ϣⲁⲣⲉⲡⲟⲩⲟⲉⲓⲉ
]ⲟⲩ	ϫⲱⲣ ⲙ̅ⲡⲉϥⲟϩ̅ⲉ
]ⲟ̣ⲟⲩ	ⲉⲱϩ̅ⲉ ⲛ̅ⲛⲉⲛ-
]ⲛⲟϥ	ⲧⲁⲩϫⲁⲁⲧⲉ ϩⲛ̅-
]ⲛ̣ⲥⲉ	ⲟⲩⲧⲉⲗ̣[ⲏⲗ] ⲧⲟ-
] ?	ⲧⲉ ϣⲁ[

[a] ϩⲱⲗ ϩⲙ̅- less probable because of the division ϩⲱ-ⲗ.

[1] Perhaps the supposed quotation does not end here. [2] *Sc.* the angels. [3] *Lit.* 'been for her'.

. [ⲥⲱⲧ]ⲏⲣ ⲓ̅ⲥ̅ ⲡⲉⲭ̅ⲥ̅ [ⲛⲥⲟ̀ⲩϫⲟⲩⲧⲯⲓⲥ ⲙ-]
[ⲡⲉⲃⲟⲧ ⲭⲟ]ⲓⲁⲭⲕ: [ϩⲛⲟⲩⲉⲓⲣⲏⲛⲏ ?
]— — — —

[Ⲉ]ⲣϣⲁⲛⲡⲉⲭⲓ-
ⲙⲱⲛ ⲟⲩⲉⲓⲛⲉ·
ⲛ̄ⲧⲉⲡϩⲟⲩⲙ-
ⲡⲉ ⲁⲛⲁⲭⲱⲣⲉⲓ·
ⲕⲁⲧⲁ ⲡϣⲁϫⲉ
ⲙ̄ⲡⲥⲟⲫⲟⲥ ⲥⲟ-
ⲗⲟⲙⲱⲛ ⲛ̄ⲧⲉ
ⲡⲁⲏⲣ ⲛⲟⲩⲧϥ·
ⲛ̄ⲧⲉⲡⲣⲏ ϣⲁ·
ⲧⲟⲧⲉ ϣⲁⲣⲉ-
ⲡⲕⲁϩ ⲧⲁⲩⲟ ⲉ-

ϩⲣⲁï ⲛ̄ⲟ[ⲩϣ-]
ⲏⲏ ⲛ̄ⲭⲟⲣ[ⲧⲟⲥ]
ϣⲁⲣⲉⲛ̄ϣ[ⲏⲛ]
ϩ̣ⲓ ⲣⲁϣⲉ ⲉⲃ[ⲟⲗ ⲙ̄-]
ⲡϯⲱ’·[a] ϣⲁ[ⲣⲉ-]
ⲡⲣⲏ’ ⲃⲟⲩⲃ̣[ⲟⲩ]
ϩ̄ⲛ̄[b][
ⲛ̄[
ⲛ̄ⲓ̣[. ⲁⲩ]ⲱ ⲟ̣ⲛ̣
ϣⲁⲣⲉⲛϩⲁⲗ[ⲁⲧⲉ]
ⲉⲓ’ ⲉⲃⲟⲗ ϩ̄ⲛ̄[.]

margin

]ϩⲉ
]ϣ̣ⲃⲛⲟ-[c]
]ⲣⲁϣⲉ
]ⲟⲩϩ̣ⲗ̣ⲟ̣ⲟⲩ
ⲟ]ⲩⲏϩ ⲛ̄ⲥ̣ⲁ-
]ⲉϣ̄ⲛ̄ⲧⲁϭ-
[ⲥⲉ] ϩ̄ⲛ̄ⲟⲩⲟⲩ-
[ⲣⲟ]ⲧ ⲉⲩⲥⲕⲓ̣ⲣ-
[ⲧⲁ] ϩ̄ⲛ̄ⲙ̄ⲙ̄ⲙⲁ ⲙ̄-
[ⲙⲟ]ⲟⲛⲉ’ ⲉⲧⲉ-
]ⲩ̣ ⲧⲟⲧⲉ
ⲥ̣ⲏϥ[ⲉ[d] . .]ϥ̣ⲙⲟ- (? ?)
ⲟ̣ϣⲉ ⲉⲃⲟⲗ ⲉ-
ⲧⲉϥⲃⲱ ⲛ̄ⲉ-

ⲁⲁ[·
ⲡⲉⲥ̣[
ϩⲣⲏⲣⲉ [?ⲧⲟⲩ-]
ⲣⲏⲥ ⲙ̄ⲡⲉⲧⲛⲓ-
ϥⲉ ⲉϩⲟⲩⲛ’ ϩ̄ⲙ̄-
ⲡⲕⲩⲡⲟⲥ ⲛ̄ⲧ-
ⲛⲩⲙⲫⲏ ϣⲁⲛ-
ⲧⲉⲛⲉϥϣⲏⲛ
ϯ ⲛ̄ⲛⲉⲩⲥϯ-
ⲛⲟⲩϥⲉ· ⲁⲩⲱ
ⲛ̄ⲟⲩⲱϩⲉ ϣⲁⲩ-
ϯ ⲛ̣ⲛⲉⲩϣⲏⲛⲩ
ⲉⲑⲁⲗⲁⲥⲁ (*sic*) ⲛ̄-
ⲥⲉⲉⲓⲣⲉ ⲛ̄ⲧⲉⲩ-
ⲉⲣⲅⲁⲥⲓⲁ’ ϩ̄ⲛ̄-

margin

[a] Read ϯⲟⲩⲱ. [b] ? ϩⲛ[ⲡⲉϥⲁⲕⲧⲓⲛ]. [c] ? ⲧⲃ̄ⲛⲟⲟⲩⲉ. [d] Must be ⲧⲥⲏϥⲉ.

Fol. 1. *Recto*. . . . our] Lord, He through whom (be) glory to the Father and the Holy [Ghost (πν.)] [for ever] and ever. A[men.]

A Sermon (ἐξήγησις) *of . . ., the bishop* (ἐπ.) *of . . ., of Cappa[docia] Prima, discoursing upon the [Birthday of our Sav]iour* (σω.) *Jesus Christ, [on the 29th day of the month Cho]iahk. [? In peace* (εἰρ.). *Amen ?]*

When[1] the winter (χιών) is gone by and the rain hath past (ἀναχωρεῖν), according to (κατά) the words of the wise (σοφός) Solomon, and the air (ἀήρ) is pleasant, and the sun doth shine; then (τότε) doth the earth put forth a garden of herbs (χόρτος), the trees burst forth in gladness[2] at budding, the sun is fervid in . . . . And the birds likewise (?) go forth from . . .

(*Verso*) and cover (?) the air while they . . . . . the sky . . . . following . . . footsteps gladly, skipping (σκιρτᾶν) in the . . . pastures. Then (τότε) doth [the] knife (*lit.* sword) go forth unto its vine, to cut off the

[1] *Cf.* Cant. ii. 11. [2] *Lit.* 'throw out gladness'.

branch that shall not bear fruit (*καρ.*) and to dress (*lit.* cleanse) that which is about to bear fruit in gladness. Then (*τότε*) doth the husbandman sharpen his sickle to reap those that have made progress joyfully. Then (*τότε*) doth (?) . . . . flower . . . southwind of that (?) which[1] bloweth upon the orchard (*κῆπος*) of the bride[2] (*νύμφη*), that its trees may give their perfume. And the fishermen put their nets into the sea (*θάλ.*) and do their business (*ἐργασία*) in . . . . .

Fol. 2. → *Recto* (?).		↑ *Verso* (?).	
	2 illegible lines.	margin	
	] ? ⲉⲩ-	ⲧⲉ ⲛ̄ⲧ̣[ⲙⲛ̄ⲧ-]	
[ⲟⲩⲱⲛϩ] ⲉⲃⲟⲗ	ϫⲛⲟⲩϭⲉ ⲙ̄ⲙⲟϥ	ⲉⲣⲟ ⲙⲛ̄[ⲧ]ⲉ-	[
[ⲛϩⲙⲉ] ⲛ̄ϩⲟⲟⲩ	ⲛ̄ϭⲓ ⲛⲉⲛⲧⲁⲩ-	ⲍⲟⲩⲥⲓⲁ ⲛ̄ⲧⲙⲛ̄ⲧ-	ⲉϩⲱ[
[ⲉϥⲉⲓ]ⲣ̣ⲉ ⲛ̄ϩⲉⲛ-	ⲥⲱⲧⲙ ⲉⲩ-	ⲛⲟⲩⲧⲉ· ⲟⲩ-	ⲧⲙ ⲡⲉ̣[
]ϭ̣[a] ⲁⲩⲱ	ϫⲱ ⲙ̄ⲙⲟⲥ	ϭⲉ ⲡⲉⲛⲧⲁϥ-	ⲁⲩⲱ ⲟ̣[
[ⲉϥϣ]ⲁ̣ϫⲉ ⲛⲙ-	ϫⲉⲡϫⲟⲉⲓⲥ	ⲟⲩⲱϣ̣ⲃ ⲛⲁⲩ	ⲧⲉⲡϣ̣[ⲏⲣⲉ ⲧⲉ-]
[ⲙⲁⲩ ⲉⲧⲃ]ⲉ̣ⲧ̣ⲙⲧ-	ⲙⲏ ϩⲣⲁï ϩ̣[ⲙⲡⲓ-]	ⲛ̄ϩⲏⲧϥ ⲛ̄ϭⲓ	ⲍⲟⲩⲥⲓ[ⲁ
[ⲉⲣⲟ ⲙ̄]ⲡⲛⲟⲩ-	ⲟ̣ⲩ̣ⲟ̣[? ⲧⲙⲛ̄]ⲧⲉ-[c]	ⲡϫⲟⲉⲓⲥ ⲡⲉ-	ⲛ̣ϫ̣ⲱ̣ⲕ̣[? ⲉ-]
[ⲧⲉ] ⲁⲩⲱ ⲉ̣ϥ-	[ⲣ]ⲟ̣ ⲙ̄ⲡ̣ⲓ̣ⲏⲗ	[ⲭⲥ·] ⲛ̄ⲧⲱⲧⲛ	ⲃⲟⲗ ⲉ[ϥϫⲱ ⲙ-]
[ⲟⲩⲱⲙ] ⲛ̣ⲙⲙⲁⲩ̣	ⲛ̄ⲁϣ ⲇⲉ ⲛ̄ϩⲉ	ⲙ̣[? ⲟⲩⲟⲉⲓϣ[d]]	ⲙ̣ⲟⲥ̣ ϫ̣[ⲉⲟⲩⲛ-]
[ⲁⲩⲱ] ⲛⲉϥⲡⲁ-	ϥⲛⲁϯ ⲛ̄ⲧⲙⲛ̄ⲧ-	ⲙⲛ̄ⲛⲉⲭⲣⲟ̣[ⲛⲟⲥ]	ⲧ̣ⲁ̣ị̈ [ⲧⲉⲍⲟⲩⲥⲓⲁ]
ⲣⲁⲅⲅⲉⲓⲗⲉ ⲛⲁⲩ	ⲉⲣⲟ ⲛ̄ϭⲓ ⲡⲉ-	ϫⲉⲕⲁⲥ ⲛ̄ⲛⲉϥ-	ⲉ̣ⲕⲱ ⲛ̄ⲧⲁⲯ[ⲩ-]
ⲉⲧⲙⲉⲓ ⲉⲃⲟⲗ	ⲧⲉⲙⲛ̄ⲧⲁϥ ⲙ̄-	ⲧⲱϭⲉ ⲛ̄ⲟⲩ-	ⲭⲏ· ⲁⲩⲱ ⲟⲩⲛ-
ϩ̣ⲛ̣ⲑⲓⲗⲙ ⲁⲗⲗ=[b]	ⲙⲁⲩ ⲛ̄ⲧⲁⲩⲑⲉ-	ⲙⲛ̄ⲧⲁⲧⲥⲟⲟⲩ	ⲧⲁï ⲧⲉⲍⲟⲩⲥ[ⲓⲁ]
ⲉ̣ϭ̣ⲱ̣ ⲉⲡⲉⲣⲏⲧ	ⲧⲓⲁ ⲙⲛ̄ⲧϭⲟⲙ·	ⲉⲡϣⲏⲣⲉ·	ⲉϫⲓⲧⲥ· ⲁⲩⲱ
ⲙ̄ⲡⲉⲓⲱⲧ	ⲡϫⲟⲉⲓⲥ ⲉⲛ̣ⲉ̣	ⲙ̄ⲡⲱⲧⲛ̄ ⲁⲛⲡⲉ	ⲙ̄ⲡⲣ̄ⲣ̄ϣⲡⲏⲣ[ⲉ]
ⲡ̣ⲁï ⲛ̄ⲧⲁⲧⲉ̣-	ϩⲣⲁï ϩ̣ⲙ̄ⲡⲉ̣ⲟ̣ⲩ̣-	ⲥⲟⲩⲛ̄ ⲛⲉⲟⲩⲟ-	ⲱ̄ ⲡⲙⲉⲣⲓⲧ
ⲧ̣ⲛ̣ⲥ̣ⲟⲧⲙⲉϥ	ⲟⲉⲓϣ ⲕⲛ̣[ⲁϯ]	ⲉⲓϣ ⲙⲛ̄ⲛⲉ-	ϫ[ⲉ]ⲁϥⲕⲱ ⲙ̄-
ⲛ̣̄ⲧⲟⲟⲧ ⲡ̣ⲉ-	ⲛ̄ⲧⲙⲛ̣ⲧ̣ⲉ̣[ⲣⲟ]	ⲭⲣⲟⲛⲟⲥ ⲛⲁï	ⲡⲥ̣ⲟ̣ⲟⲩⲛ ⲛ̄ⲛⲉ-
ϫ̣ⲁ̣ϥ ϫⲉïⲱ-	ⲙ̄ⲡ̣ⲓ̣ⲏⲗ ⲉϥϫ̣[ⲱ]	ⲛ̄ⲧⲁⲡⲉⲓⲱⲧ	ⲭⲣⲟⲛⲟⲥ [ϩⲁ]ⲧⲉ-

[a] One expects ⲙⲁⲉⲓ]ⲛ. [b] *Sic.* A strange abbreviation; recurs in col. 2, penult. [c] This line may begin ⲥϫ. [Either MS. or copy is faulty. The proper text of v. 6 follows below. [d] Here again more space seems indispensable to the sense. In preceding line ? ⲡⲉϫⲁϥ.

[1] ⲙ is difficult: possibly 'of Him that'. [2] *Cf.* Cant. iv. 16.

ϩⲁⲛⲛⲏⲥ ⲙⲉ̄	ⲙ̄ⲙⲟⲥ̣ [ⲛⲁⲩ ϫⲉ-]	ⲕⲁⲁⲩ ϩⲁⲧⲉϥⲉ-	ⲍⲟⲩⲥⲓⲁ ⲙ̄ⲡϣⲏ̣-
ⲁ̣ϥⲃⲁⲡⲧⲓⲍⲉ	ⲡⲉⲓⲱⲧ ⲛⲁ-	ⲍⲟⲩⲥⲓ̈ⲁ ⲙⲁⲩ[ⲁ-]	ⲣⲉ ⲉϣϫⲉⲡ̄-
]	ϯ ⲛⲧⲙ̄ⲛ̄ⲧⲉ̣-	ⲁϥ · ⲁⲛⲟⲕ ⲉ[ⲓ-]	ⲕⲁ ⲛⲓⲙ ⲉⲧⲥ̣-
	[ⲣ]ⲟ̣ · ⲁⲗ̣ⲗ̣= ⲉⲩ-	ⲑⲉⲱⲣⲉⲓ ⲛ̄[	ⲉ̣ϫ̣ⲛ̄ . . [
	[ϣⲁ]ϫⲉ ⲉⲡⲉ̣-	ϣⲏ̣ⲣⲉ [	

Fol. 2. *Recto*. . . . appearing[1] during forty days, doing signs (?) and speaking with them concerning the kingdom of God; and, eating with them, He charged (*παράγγ.*) them not to go forth from Jerusalem, but (*ἀλλά*) to wait for the promise of the Father, 'the which ye have heard from me.' He said, 'John indeed (*μέν*) did baptize (*βαπτ.*) . . . . .

they then, that had heard him asking Him, saying,[2] 'Lord, dost Thou (*μή*) at this time (?) . . . . . the kingdom to Israel?' But (*δέ*) in what manner shall he that hath not the authority (*αὐθεντία*) and the power give the kingdom? 'Lord, wilt thou, at this time, give the kingdom to Israel?' When He said unto them, 'The Father shall give the kingdom,' they rather (*ἀλλά*) spake of the . . . . .

Verso. . . . the kingdom and the power (*ἐξουσία*) of divinity. What, then, was it that the Lord [Christ?] answered them? 'Ye[3] . . . . . times] and the seasons (*χρόνος*),' that He might not impute ignorance unto the Son. 'It is not yours to know the times and the seasons (*χρ.*) which the Father hath set within His own power (*ἐξ.*).' I behold (*θεωρεῖν*) . . . Son . . . . .

. . . the Son . . . power (*ἐξ.*), . . . to fulfil . . ., saying,[4] 'I have power (*ἐξ.*) to lay down my life (*ψυ.*) and I have power (*ἐξ.*) to take it up.' And be not astonished, O beloved, that He placed the knowledge of the seasons (*χρ.*) within the power (*ἐξ.*) of the Son, when everything that . . . on . . . . .

No. 7.

This Sermon has an unusual interest from containing the mention—so rare in Coptic literature—of contemporary historical persons and events. Not only was it pronounced at Alexandria in the cathedral church[5] by the patriarch Damianus,[6] its author, but this in presence of the emperor Maurice's

[1] Acts i. 3.

[2] Text of following clause not in order.

[3] Nor of this one.

[4] John x. 18.

[5] *καθολικὴ ἐκκλ.* *V.* Rossi, *Papiri*, ii. IV. 59 c (*v.* below on these texts). *Cf. PSBA.* xxvii. 171.

[6] Damianus, 578–605. See my notes *Copt. Ostr.* no. 18, and Krüger in *PRE*³. iv. 439.

envoy, Constantine *Λάδρυς*.[1] With him was Amantius, apparently a prominent eunuch.[2] Constantine's mission to Alexandria is mentioned, though without year, by John of Nikiou.[3] If it were but possible to identify, among the various earthquakes of this period, one shortly previous to that mission, we might arrive at the date of the latter. It was one, at any rate, which shook Syria (*v.* below), and, to judge by the title of the present sermon, presumably Egypt also. Evagrius records an earthquake, affecting Antioch and its suburbs, in Oct. 589.[4] In the foregoing (or same?) year Agapius mentions one, likewise at Antioch, and in 591 and 599 others, not localized[5]; while John of Nikiou describes one which devastated Antioch, the east and 'the isles' in this reign.[6] The title of our sermon is but a fragment—that a considerable part of it is lost may be estimated from a comparison between the length of gaps in fol. 10 and in the parallel passage in the Turin MS. (*v.* below)—so that the effects of the earthquake, to which it no doubt made reference, are unknown. Nor can it be decided whether the words here used as to Constantine and the Egyptian magnates are to be connected with those disturbances to which he, according to John of Nikiou, put an end.[7]

This text has further value in being the means of ascribing certain of the Turin fragments to their true author. F. Rossi, *I Papiri*, ii. IV. 56–62 have been assumed[8] to belong to the sermon of Athanasius, *ib.* ii. I. 5 ff.; but their identity in several passages with our text now shows them to be due to Damianus. And besides the passages actually identical, there are among Rossi's fragments others, which (though neither facsimiles nor descriptions of this group are given) it is tolerably certain must belong to the same work. One of these[9] has importance in that it names four places which suffered through the earthquake—doubtless that referred to in the title of our present text: Berytus and Aradus with [ ]**ϥⲉⲛⲏ** and **ⲁⲅⲣⲓⲛⲏ**. These Lemm seeks[10] (as *Στεφάνη* and the island *'Ορεινή*) in

[1] Theoph. Simoc. viii. 9 and 13, *Chron. Pasc.* an. 602 (*PG.* 92, 972). The latter has variant Λάρδις. The three titles here given him are a usual combination in that age, *e.g.* Cairo Pap. 67002 (*ed.* J. Maspero in the *Catal. Gén.*); the two first in Pap. Oxyrh. 138.

[2] A strange coincidence: Amantius had been the name of a powerful eunuch executed by Justin I. When one finds this eunuch (or yet another namesake?) reappearing as Theodora's envoy to Egypt (Zoega clxvi), one suspects that the name had grown legendary.

[3] Pp. 298, 532. What his office in Egypt was is not clearly stated: three words (*masfen, makuanen, šeyûm*) are indiscriminately used by the translator, sometimes (as on pp. 295, 296) to designate the same official. De Ricci, *PSBA.* xxiv. 107, and M. Gelzer, *Leipz. Hist. Abh.* xiii. 33, take him for the prefect.

[4] vi. 8. *Cf. Chron. de Michel* ii. 359, and others on pp. 351, 352, 373.

[5] *Ed.* A. Vasiliev in *Patr. Or.*, pp. 180, 187.

[6] P. 536.

[7] P. 532. The Coptic verb here, literally 'receive', is not often found as 'take into custody', which seems to be the present meaning.

[8] By O. von Lemm, *KKS.* 280, 321 ff. That the Turin collection once included still another homily on the Nativity, and that by Cyril, is clear from the fragment Rossi, ii. II. 5 = III. 2. Presumably to this belongs the fragment ii. IV. 77 b, referring to Nestorius as the speaker's opponent 'in the midst of the *σύνοδος*'. It may be noted that Rylands, no. 73, is a text very similar to these. (In its 2nd line read **ϫⲉⲗⲡⲟⲩⲩⲟⲥ**, *cf.* Rossi, ii. IV. 57 c.)

[9] Rossi, ii. IV. 60 c.

[10] *L. c.* 324.

Paphlagonia and Ethiopia respectively; but one would here rather expect localities not so far distant from the Syrian coast. I would propose either for the first name Sophene, and for the second Auranitis[1] (whether the district south of Damascus or that between Palmyra and the Euphrates); or merely *ὀρεινή*, 'the highlands,' for the latter, and *σεφενη* = ? *σεφηλά*, 'the low country, coast,' for the former.[2]

Fol. I. ↑ *Recto.*

—— . . . —— . . . —— . . . ——

Ⲟⲩⲗⲟⲅⲟ[ⲥ] ⲉⲁϥⲧⲁⲩⲟϥ ⲛ̄ϭⲓ ⲡϩⲁ-
ⲕⲓⲟⲥ ⲁⲡⲁ ⲇⲁⲙⲓⲁⲛⲟⲥ ⲡⲁⲣⲭⲏ̄-
ⲉⲡⲓⲥⲕⲟⲡⲟⲥ ⲛ̄ⲣⲁⲕⲟⲧⲉ· ⲉⲧⲃⲉ-
ⲡⲉϫⲡⲟ ⲙ̄ⲡⲉⲛⲥⲱⲧⲏ̄ⲣ̄ ⲓ̄ⲥ̄ ⲡⲉⲭ̄ⲥ̄
ⲡⲉⲛϫⲟⲉⲓⲥ ⲛ̄ⲥⲟⲩϫⲟⲩⲧⲯⲓⲥ ⲙ̄-
ⲡⲉⲃⲟⲧ ⲭⲟⲓ̈ⲁ̄ⲕ̄ϩ̄· ⲁⲩⲱ ⲉⲧⲃⲉⲡϣⲁ̣-
ⲁⲛ̣ ⲙ̣̄ⲡⲙⲟⲩ· ⲙⲛ̄ⲡⲕⲙ̄ⲧⲟ ⲛ̄ⲧⲁϥ-
[. . . . . ⲛϩ]ⲏ̣ⲡⲥ̣ⲓ̣ⲥ̣[ⲧ]ⲱ̣ⲥ ⲛ̄ⲙ̄ⲡⲟⲗⲓ̣-
[ⲧⲉⲩⲟⲙ]ⲉ̣ⲛ̣ⲟ̣ⲥ̣ ⲉ . [ⲁⲛ]ⲁ̣ⲅⲕⲁⲍⲉ
[. . . . .]ⲁⲓ̈ ⲉⲧⲱⲣ̄ⲡ̄ [ⲛ]ⲛⲕⲁ ⲛ̄ⲛ̄ⲁ̣-
ⲉ]ⲙ̣̄ⲛ̄ⲧⲟⲩ ⲛ̣[ⲁ]ⲩ ⲛ̄ⲓ̣ⲱ̣ⲧ ⲙ̣̄ⲛ̣̄-
]ⲉⲧⲡ̣ . [

→ *Verso.*

margin

ƶ [. .]ϣⲏⲙ ϩⲓ̣[ⲕ]ⲱⲥ[ⲧⲁⲛ]ⲧ̣ⲓⲛⲟⲥ ⲡⲡ[ⲁⲧ-]
ƶ ⲣⲓⲕⲓⲟⲥ ⲡⲉⲧⲉϣⲁⲩⲙⲟⲩⲧⲉ ⲉⲣⲟϥ
ƶ ϫⲉⲡⲗⲁⲣ̄ⲧⲏⲥ· ϩⲙ̄ⲡⲧⲣⲉϥⲧⲛ-
ƶ ⲛⲟⲟⲩϥ ⲛϭⲓ ⲙⲁⲩⲣⲓⲕⲓⲟⲥ ⲡⲣ̄ⲣⲟ̄
ƶ ⲉⲣⲁⲕⲟⲧⲉ ⲉⲧⲣⲉϥϫⲓ ⲛ̄ⲛ̄ⲁⲣⲭ̄ⲱ̄
ƶ ⲧⲏⲣⲟⲩ ⲛⲕⲏⲙⲉ· ⲁⲩⲱ ⲉϥⲙ̄ⲙⲁⲩ
ƶ ⲛϭⲓ ⲡⲡⲁⲧⲣⲓⲕⲓⲟⲥ ⲙⲛ̄ⲡϩⲩ̄ⲡⲁ-
ƶ ⲧⲟⲥ· [ⲙ]ⲛ̄ⲡⲉⲥⲧⲣⲁⲧ[ⲏⲗⲁ]-
ⲧⲏⲥ· ⲙⲛⲁⲙⲁⲛⲧⲓ̈ⲟ[ⲥ . . . . ⲥⲓ-]
ⲟ̣ⲩⲣ̄ ⲙ̄ⲛ̄ⲛ̄ⲁⲣⲭⲱⲛ ⲧⲏⲣ[ⲟⲩ ⲛⲕⲏ-]
ⲙ̣ⲉ ⲁⲩⲱ ⲡⲇⲏⲙⲟⲥ ⲧⲏ[ⲣϥ
[.]ⲙ̣ ⲛⲧⲡⲟⲗⲓⲥ ⲧⲏⲣⲥ̣ [
[.]ⲩⲁ̣ ——————〈ο[

Fol. I. *Recto.* A discourse (λόγος) which the holy (ἅγιος) Apa Damianus, the archbishop (ἀρχιεπ.) of Alexandria, pronounced concerning the Birth of Our Saviour (σωτ.) Jesus Christ, Our Lord, upon the 29th day of Choiahk; and concerning the terror (?) of death[3] and the earthquake, that did . . . the most exalted (?? ὕψιστος) of the citizens (? πολιτευόμενος[4]), compelling (? ἀναγκάζειν) . . . . . to seize the goods of . . . . . that had not any (?) . . . . .

[1] It will be objected that ⲥⲟⲫⲉⲛⲏ (even with possibly preceding article ⲧ-) is a word too short to fill the line, and that the other is an unauthenticated equivalent for Αὐρανῖτις.

[2] Or again ⲇⲁ]ⲫⲉⲛⲏ for Δάφνη (of Antioch) might be geographically possible, though orthographically improbable, besides being too short for the gap.

[3] Reading ϣⲗⲁϩ, though hitherto not found in Sa'idic.

[4] Πόλις would, in the context, seem more likely. The sense is utterly obscure.

Verso. . . . the Younger (?)[1] and Constantine the patrician (*πατρ.*), who was called Lartês[2]; when Maurice the king sent him unto Alexandria, to take (into custody ?) all the magnates (*ἄρχων*) of Egypt. And the patrician (*πατρ.*) and consul (*ὕπατος*) and general[3] (*στρατηλάτης*) was present, and Amantius the . . . eunuch[4] and all the magnates (*ἄρχ.*) of Egypt and all the populace (*δῆμος*) . . . . . of the whole city (*πόλις*) . . . . .

Fol. 2. ↑ *Recto* (?).		→ *Verso* (?).	
margin		margin	
ϩⲟⲛ[a] ⲧⲏⲣⲟⲩ	ⲡⲉⲩⲁⲅⲅⲉⲗⲓⲥ-	ⲧⲏⲣⲟⲩ ⲛ̄ⲧⲉⲕ-	ⲃⲉ ⲙ̄ⲡⲙⲉⲕⲉ-
ⲙ̄ⲛⲛⲉⲕⲧⲁⲓ̈ⲟ	ⲧⲏⲥ ·	ⲕⲗⲏⲥⲓ̈ⲁ ϣⲁ-	ⲑⲟⲥ ⲛ̄ⲧⲉⲕ-
▽Ⲱ̄ ⲓ̄ⲥ̄ ⲡⲉⲧⲉⲡⲱϥ-	ⲁⲩⲱ ⲡⲙⲁⲣ̄ⲧⲩ-	ϩⲣⲁⲓ̈ ⲉⲧⲉⲛ-	ⲙⲛ̄ⲧⲛⲟⲩⲧⲉ
ⲡⲉ ⲧⲁⲓ̈ⲟ ⲛⲓⲙ	ⲣⲟⲥ ·	ⲙⲛ̄ⲧⲣⲉϥⲣ̄-	Ⲛⲓⲙ ⲡⲉⲧⲛⲁⲣ̄-
ϩⲓⲥⲙⲟⲩ ⲛⲓⲙ	ⲙ̄ⲡⲁⲛϫⲱ̄ϫ	ⲛⲟⲃⲉ · ⲁⲩⲱ	*sic* ▽ⲡⲉϥⲛⲟⲩⲥ
ⲉ̣ⲓ̈ⲛⲁⲣ̄ϩⲉ ⲛ̄ⲟⲩⲁ̣	ⲡⲉⲧⲣⲟⲥ ·	ⲙⲡⲟⲩϭ[ⲛ ϭⲉ ⲛ-]	ⲛ̄ⲣⲙ̄ⲙ̄ⲡⲉ
]	ⲁⲩⲱ ⲡⲙⲁⲧⲩ (*sic*)	ϫⲱⲕ ⲙ[ⲡⲉⲕ-]	?
	ⲣⲟⲥ ·	ⲧ̣ⲁⲓ̈ⲟ ⲙⲙ̣[	
	[. . .]ⲉ̣ϫ̣ⲁⲛ[b]		

[a] ⲁⲟϩⲟⲛ.   [b] ? ⲁⲩⲱ ⲡ]ⲉⲩⲁⲅ[ⲅⲉⲗⲓⲥⲧⲏⲥ.

Fol. 2. *Recto* (?). . . . all [Thy] glory (? *δόξον*[5]) and Thy honours. O Jesus, whose is all honour and all blessing, I shall be like unto one . . . . .

. . . the evangelist (*εὐαγ.*), and the martyr (*μάρτυρος*) and head, Peter, and the martyr (*μάρ.*) . . . . .

Verso (?). . . . all [the . . .] of the church (*ἐκ.*), down to our sinfulness.[6] And they did not find [means to] complete the . . . honour of . . . . .

. . . of the greatness (*μέγεθος*) of Thy divinity? Who shall make his understanding (*νοῦς*) celestial . . . . .

[1] I do not know whether ϣⲏⲙ (like ϩⲣⲣⲉ), with a name preceding it, can = *junior*. Whether in Lepsius, *Denkm.* vi. 102, nos. 9, 10, 19 &c., Murray, *Osireion*, pll. 26, 31, it has this meaning or is mere humility, may be doubted. Perhaps read ⲟⲩϣⲏⲙ, the town of Ausîm.

[2] *Lit.* 'the Lartês'.

[3] These complimentary titles designate merely Constantine.

[4] Space would allow ⲡⲛⲟϭ ⲛ- or ⲡⲁⲣⲭⲓ- 'the chief eunuch'.

[5] I cannot find this form in literary use, though it had acquired a legal meaning. *V.* Rylands Catal., no. 139.

[6] *I.e.* 'to me, Damianus'.

Fol. 3. → *Recto* (?).		↑ *Verso* (?).	
margin		margin	
ⲡⲁϣⲧⲉⲭⲛⲉ-	ⲡⲉⲧⲛⲁϣ[ϩⲓⲥ-]	[ⲧ]ⲙⲛ̄ⲧⲛⲟⲩ-	Ⲁϣ ⲛϣⲟⲩⲱ-
ⲁ̣ⲗⲟⲕⲉⲓ ⲛ̄ⲧ-	ⲧⲟⲣⲓⲍⲉ·	[ⲧ]ⲉ· ⲡⲕⲟⲩⲓ̈	ⲃⲉ ⲧⲉⲧⲛⲁϣ-
ⲉⲕϭⲓⲛⲉⲓ ϣⲁ̄-	ⲏ̄ ⲛϥ̄ⲭⲗⲟⲛⲟ[ⲅ-]	[ϩ]ⲛⲟⲩⲗⲏⲕⲓ̈ⲁ	ⲱϣ ⲉⲃⲟⲗ ⲛ̄-
ⲣⲟⲛ·	ⲣⲁⲫⲟⲩ·	[ⲁ]ⲩⲱ ⲡⲛⲟϭ	ⲑⲉ ⲛ̄ⲟⲩⲥⲁⲗ-
⳩Ⲱ ⲉ̄ⲙⲙⲁⲛⲟⲩⲏⲗ	ⲏ̄ ⲛϥ̄ⲅⲉⲛⲉⲁ-	ϩⲛⲛⲉϥϩⲟⲟⲩ·	ⲡⲓⲅ̄ⲝ ⲛ̄ⲥⲉⲉⲅ̄-
ⲡϣⲏⲣⲉ ⲙ̄-	ⲗⲟⲅⲉⲓ ⲛ̄ⲧⲉⲕ-	[ⲁ]ϣ ⲛ̄ⲥⲡⲟⲧⲟⲩ	ⲕⲱⲙⲓ̈ⲁⲍⲉ
ⲡⲛⲟⲩⲧⲉ	ϭⲓⲛϫⲡⲟ̄ ⲱ̄	[. . .]ⲡⲕⲁⲣⲱ̄ϥ	ⲛ̄ⲧⲉⲕⲉⲡⲓ̈ⲇⲏ-
ⲕⲁⲧⲁ ⲧⲉϥ-	ⲉ̄ⲙⲙⲁ[ⲛⲟⲩⲏⲗ]	[ⲛⲉⲧⲛ]ⲁϣϣⲁ-	ⲙⲓ̈ⲁ ϣⲁⲣⲟⲛ̄
ⲙⲛ̄ⲧⲛⲟⲩⲧⲉ	ⲡⲛⲟ̣[ⲩⲧⲉ ⲙ̄-]	[ϫⲉ . . .]ⲩ̣ⲥ	⳩Ⲡϣⲱⲥ ⲙ̄ⲙⲉ
⳩Ⲉⲙⲉϥϣⲓ̈ⲃⲉ	ⲙⲉ̣ [	]ⲛ̣	ⲛⲧⲁϥⲕⲱ̄ ⲛ̄-
ⲉⲙⲉϥⲡⲱ-	ⲡⲣⲱ[ⲙⲉ	?	ⲧⲉϥⲯⲩⲭⲏ
ⲱⲛⲉ· ..	ⲗ̣ⲱ̣ⲧ[		[ϩ]ⲁ̣ⲛ̣ⲉϥ[ⲉⲥⲟⲟⲩ]
]ⲉ̣ⲕⲱ̣			

Fol. 3. *Recto* (?). . . . shall be able fitly to account for (τεχνεαλογίζειν [1]) Thy coming unto us, O Emmanuel, Son of God according to His divinity? It (?) altereth not, it is not transformed . . . . .

. . . Who] shall be able to narrate (ἱστορίζειν) or (ἤ) who shall record (χρονογράφειν) or (ἤ) who shall trace (γενεαλογεῖν) Thy birth, O Emmanuel, true (?) God . . . man . . . . .

Verso (?). . . . divinity; the young in age (ἡλικία) and the old (*lit.* great [2]) in His days? What lips . . . silence . . . . shall be able to speak . . . . .? What throat shall be able to cry out like a trumpet (σάλ.) and belaud (ἐγκωμιάζειν) Thy sojourn (ἐπιδημία) with us, true shepherd, that did lay down His life (ψυ.) for His [sheep . . . . .

Fol. 4. ↑ *Recto.*		→ *Verso.*	
margin		margin	
ⲉⲓⲙⲉ ϩⲓⲧⲛ̄-	ⲧ[	]ⲓ̈	⳩ϩⲟⲙⲟⲗⲟⲅⲉⲓ̈
ⲛⲓⲙ ⲙ̄ⲛϣϭⲙ (ⲟ above)	ⲙ[	]ⲧ̣ⲉ	ⲛⲁⲛ ⲙ̄ⲡⲉⲛ-

[1] Could τεχνολογίζω have such a meaning? The verb Rossi ii, I. 34 c would scarcely be the same. [2] Not the phrase of Dan. vii. 9.

ⲛ̄ⲗⲁⲥ ⲛ̄ⲥⲁⲣⲝ̄	ⲡ[	]ⲟⲛ	ⲧⲁϥ ϣⲱ-
ⲉⲅⲉⲛⲉⲁⲗⲟ-	⁊ⲡⲉ[	]ⲱ	ⲡⲉ ·
ⲅⲉⲓ ⲙ̄ⲡⲉϫⲡⲟ̄	ⲁⲗ[ⲏⲑⲱⲥ	]ⲱⲣ	⁊ϯⲛⲁⲕⲁⲁⲕ
ⲙ̄ⲡⲉⲛ̄ⲥⲱ-	ⲡⲉ[	?	ⲉⲃⲟⲗ ⲁⲛ ⲱ̄
ⲧⲏⲣ̄ ·	ⲉ[	?	ⲅⲁⲃⲣⲓⲏⲗ
ⲁⲗⲏⲑⲱⲥ ⲡⲁ-	ⲡ[		ⲟⲩⲇⲉ ⲛ̄ⲧ-
]ⲣⲁⲥ			ⲛ̣[ⲛⲁ

Fol. 4. *Recto.* . . . learn (it?) through whom? Fleshly (-*σάρξ*) tongue hath not power to trace (*γενεαλογεῖν*) the birth of our Saviour (*σωτήρ*). Verily (*ἀληθῶς*) my . . . . . grow old . . . . .

Verso. . . . confess (*ὁμολογεῖν*) unto us what befell. I will not release thee, O Gabriel, neither (*οὐδέ*) will we . . . . .

Fol. 5. → *Recto.*		↑ *Verso.*	
	[ⲡϫⲟ]ⲉⲓⲥ ⲛ̄ⲙ-	ⲭⲁⲓ̈ⲣⲉ [ⲙⲁⲣⲓⲁ]	
	ⲙⲉ ·	ⲧⲥ̣ⲱϣⲉ̣ ⲉⲧ-	
	Χⲁⲓ̈ⲣⲉ ⲙⲁⲣⲓ̈ⲁ	ⲧⲃⲃⲏⲩ ⲉⲧ̣ⲉ-	
	ⲧⲉⲕⲗⲟⲟⲗⲉ	ⲣⲉⲡⲙⲁ[ⲣ]ⲕⲁ-	[
]ⲉ	ⲉⲧⲁⲥⲱⲟⲩ	ⲣⲓⲧⲓⲥ ⲛ̄ϩⲏ-	ⲙ[
[Χⲁⲓⲣⲉ ⲙⲁ]ⲣⲓ̈ⲁ	ⲉⲧⲣ̄ⲟⲩⲟⲉⲓⲛ̄	ⲧⲉ ⲉⲧⲉⲡⲁⲓ̈-	⁊ⲭⲁ[ⲓⲣⲉ
]ⲁ̣	ⲉⲛⲉⲧϩⲙⲟ-	ⲡⲉ ⲡⲉⲛϫⲟ-	? [
] ⲉⲧⲧⲟ	ⲟⲥ ϩⲙⲡⲕⲁ-	ⲉⲓⲥ ⲓ̄ⲥ̄ ⲡⲉⲭ̄ⲥ̄	ⲛ̣ⲟⲩⲃ[
[ϩⲓⲱ] ⲉⲧⲉⲡⲉⲩ-	ⲕⲉ ⲙ̄ⲡⲑⲁⲓ̈-	?	?
]ⲟ̣ⲩⲱⲛⲉ [a]	ⲃⲉⲥ ⲙ̄ⲡⲙⲟⲩ		
]ⲡⲉⲧⲩͦ-	ⲭⲁⲓ̈ⲣⲉ ⲧⲉⲛ-		
]ⲉ ⲛ̄ⲓⲁ-	ⲧⲁⲥϭⲛ [ϩⲙⲟⲧ]		
[ⲕⲱⲃ	ⲡ̣ϫ̣[ⲟⲉⲓⲥ ⲛⲙ-]		
	[ⲙⲉ		

[a] Or]ⲟⲩⲱ ⲡⲉ (*fem.*).

Fol. 5. (*Possibly not a part of this MS.*) *Recto.* . . . Hail (*χαῖρε*)]

Mary .... [garment (?)] that is [on thee ?], which is their ... stone [1] ... which they ... Ja[cob [2] .....

..., the Lord is with thee. Hail (χ.) Mary, light (*levis*) cloud [3] which illumineth them that sit in darkness and the shadow of death. Hail (χ.) thou that hast found [grace], the Lord [is with thee .....

Verso. ... Hail (χ.) (Mary), pure meadow, wherein is the pearl (μαργ.) [4] which is our Lord Jesus Christ .....
... Hail (χ.) ..... gold (?) .....

Fol. 6. ↑ *Recto* (?).

ⲡⲉⲛⲧⲁⲥϫⲡⲟ[ϥ]
ⲡⲁⲣⲁ ⲡ[ⲉⲭⲣⲟ-]
ⲛⲟⲥ ⲛ̄ⲧⲙⲛ̄ⲧ-
ⲣⲉϥⲙⲓⲥⲉ ·
▽Ⲁϫⲓⲥ ⲉⲣⲟⲓ̈ ⲱ̄ ⲧ-
ⲡⲁⲣⲑⲉⲛⲟⲥ ⲉ-
ⲧⲟⲩⲁⲁⲃ ϫⲉⲉⲣ̄-
ⲃⲏⲕ ⲉⲧⲱⲛ
ⲙ̄ⲡⲉⲓⲛⲟϭ ⲛ̄-
[ⲁⲡ]ⲁ[ⲛⲧ]ⲏⲙⲁ
[. . . . .]ⲉⲓⲛⲟϭ

[ⲧⲉⲧ]ⲉ̣ⲙ[ⲉⲥ]ⲉ-
ⲡ̣ⲉⲓⲑⲩ[ⲙ]ⲉ̣ⲓ ⲉ-
ⲛⲉϩ ⲉⲡⲥⲟⲗⲥⲗ̅
ⲛ̄ⲛⲁⲅⲟⲣⲁ ⲙ̄ⲡ̄-
ⲛ̄ϫⲟⲗⲙⲉⲥ ⲛ̄ⲙ̄-
ⲙⲁ ⲛ̄ⲥⲱ · ⲙ̄ⲛ̄-
ⲛⲥⲱⲛⲧⲉⲭⲓ̈ⲁ
ⲛ̄ϫⲓ ϩⲣⲁϥ̄ · ⲧⲉ-
▽Ⲧⲉⲙⲉⲥⲃⲱⲕ ⲉ-
ϩⲟⲩⲛ ⲁⲩⲏⲓ̈ (*sic*) ⲉⲡ-
ⲧⲏⲣ̄ϥ̄ ⲉϥϩⲙ̄ⲛ
ⲉϩⲟⲩⲛ ⲉⲡⲣ̣ⲡ̣[ⲉ]
Ⲧⲉⲧⲉⲙⲉⲥ[
[. .]ⲏ ⲉϣ[

→ *Verso* (?).

ⲧⲏ [ⲧⲡ]ⲁ[ⲣⲑⲉ-]
ⲛⲟ̣[ⲥ ⲉ]ⲧⲟⲩⲁ[ⲁⲃ]
ⲙⲁⲣⲓⲁ ⲉⲥⲕⲟⲥ-
ⲙⲉⲓ ϩⲛ̄ⲉⲡⲓⲥ-
ⲧⲏⲙⲉ (*sic*) ⲛⲓⲙ ·
ⲉ̣ⲥϩⲟⲗϭ ϩⲙ̄ⲡ-
ⲉⲥⲗⲁⲥ ⲉⲥⲧⲟⲩ-
ϫⲏⲩ [a] ϩⲛ̄ⲛⲉⲥ-
ⲃⲁⲗ ⲉⲧϭⲓⲛϭⲱ-
ϣⲧ ⲉⲧϣⲟⲩ-
ⲉⲓⲧ · ⲁ[ⲩⲱ]
ⲙⲉⲥⲣ̄ϩⲱⲃ ϩⲛ̣-
ⲛⲉⲥϭⲓϫ ⲛ̄ϭⲓ
[ⲧⲡⲁⲣ]ⲑⲉ[ⲛ]ⲟ̣ⲥ

ⲧ[ⲡ]ⲁⲣⲑⲉⲛⲟ[ⲥ]
[ϫⲉⲉ]ⲣ̣ⲃⲏⲕ ⲉ-
ⲧⲱⲛ ⲙⲡⲉⲓ-
ⲛⲟϭ ⲛⲟⲩⲉ ⲉ-
ⲧⲟⲣⲓⲛ̄ⲏ̄ ⲉⲧϭⲉ-
ⲡⲏ ⲉⲃⲱⲕ
ⲡⲉϫⲁⲥ ⲉⲛⲁⲩ
ⲉⲧⲉϣⲡⲏⲣⲉ
ⲛ̄ⲧⲁⲥϣⲱ-
ⲡⲉ [
?

[a] Here Rossi, 62 c.

[1] Or '... to thee' (*fem.*), ⲟⲩⲱ being a verb.

[2] Or 'jasper stone' ⲱⲛ]ⲉ ⲛⲓⲁ[ⲥⲡⲓⲥ.

[3] *Cf.* Cairo, *Theotokia* 195 (= Tuki 100) and Isa. xix. 1, which verse is similarly used in χαιρετισμοί, though differently interpreted, by Joh. Damas. (*PG.* 96, 693) and Theod. Stud. (*ib.* 99, 725). It is remarkable that the Ethiopic (Fries, *Weddâsê Mâryâm*, 38), renders خفيفة by *za-ba-'aman* 'true', taking it for حقيقة: a contribution towards proof of translation from the Arabic. Nothing can of course be deduced from these coincidences as to the early existence of a Sa'idic *Theotokia*; the specimens in Samannûdî's *Scala* (Paris MS. 44, f. 21) show indeed true Sa. forms, but may point (in the 13th century) to a version from Bo. But if Simeon Ḳuḳaya (*ca.* 520) be, as Euringer (*Or. Christ.* 1911, 215 ff.) plausibly suggests, author of the *Theotokia*, the present passages, in a work dating only some 80 years later, and by a writer of Syrian origin, have an added interest.

[4] *Cf.* Cairo *Theot.*, 178; also, besides Usener's article (in *Theol. Abh. f. Weizsäcker*), Rossi, *l. c.* 58 b; Rylands Cat., no. 72; *Kebra Nagast, ed.* Bezold, p. xl and § 68; and Lagarde, *Aeg.* 48, 22 (= F. Robinson, p. 53) where read ⲱⲛⲓ for ⲟⲩⲱⲓⲛⲓ.

Fol. 6. *Recto.* . . . . 'him whom she hath borne, out of (*παρά*) the time (*χρ.*) of bearing.' Tell me, O holy Virgin (*παρ.*), whither thou goest for (?) this great meeting[1] [and] this great . . . . .

. . . She who never desired (*ἐπιθυμεῖν*) the distractions (*lit.* consolations) of the market-place (*ἀγορά*) nor the festivities[2] of the drinking-place, nor meetings (*συντυχία*) for merrymaking. She who never entered a house that was near to the[3] . . . . . She who did not . . . . .

Verso. . . . holy Virgin (? *παρ.*) Mary, adorned (*κοσμεῖν*) with all knowledge (*ἐπιστήμη*), sweet in her tongue, preserving her eyes[4] from vain glances. And the Virgin doth not work with her hands . . . . .

. . . Tell me, O] Virgin, whither goest thou, this great distance, to the hill-country (*ὀρεινή*)?[5] 'I hasten and go,' saith she, 'to see the marvel that hath happened . . . . .

Fol. 7. → *Recto.*

. margin

ⲧⲁϭⲣⲏⲛ ⲉⲧⲉ̅ⲓ̅	ϥⲱⲱ̅ⲣⲉ ⲉⲃⲟⲗ
ⲕⲉⲥⲟⲟⲩ ⲛⲉ-	ϯⲛⲁⲛⲁⲩ ϫⲉⲛ̅ⲕⲓ̈- (*sic*)
ⲃⲟⲧⲛⲉ ·	ⲃⲉ ⲛⲧⲁⲩϣⲟⲟⲩⲉ
ϣⲁ̣ⲛⲉ̣. ⲁ̣ⲙ̣ⲙ̣ϫⲉ	ⲙ̅ⲛ̅ⲛ̅ⲥⲁⲛⲉ-
	ⲭⲣⲟⲛⲟⲥ ⲁⲩⲙ̣[ⲟ̊ⲩϩ]
	ⲛⲉⲣⲱⲧⲉ ·
	Ⲁⲣⲏⲩ[a] ⲣⲱ̅ ⲉⲩⲣ̅-
	ϩⲁⲗ ⲙ̅ⲙⲟⲓ̣
	[ϩⲙⲡ]ⲛ̅ⲧⲁ̣[ⲩ-]

↑ *Verso.*

margin

ⲙ̅ⲡⲉϥ̅ϫⲟⲉⲓⲥ	⁊ ⲛⲁϣ[
ⲉⲥⲛⲏⲩ ⲉⲣⲁⲧϥ[b]	ⲛⲁⲥ̣ . . .
ⲛ̅ⲧⲉϥⲙⲁⲁⲩ	ⲁⲛ ⲉⲓ ⲛⲁ[ⲓ
ⲁ̣ϥϫⲓ ϥⲟ̅ϭⲥ̅	ϫⲟⲉⲓⲥ ⲁⲩⲱ
ⲁϥⲥⲕⲓ̈ⲣⲧⲁ	ⲧⲙ̣ⲁⲁⲩ ⲙⲡⲁ-
ⲁϥϫⲓ ϥⲟ̅ϭⲥ̅	ϫⲟ[ⲉⲓⲥ ⲉⲓ]
[ϩⲓⲑ]ⲏ ⲙ̅ⲡ̣ . . .	

[a] Here Rossi, 62 c.

[b] Read ⲉⲣⲁⲧⲥ.

[1] Ἀπάντημα is rare apparently. Διανόημα would fit, though less appropriate. Or ? ⲁⲡⲁⲛⲧⲏ ⲙⲁ-.

[2] *V. Can. Athan.*, p. 66 n. To the instances there add *Triadon*, *ed.* Lemm, § 368 = تنعم (parallel to *εὐφραίνειν*), and Paris 131[6], f. 9 (? same MS. as Br. Mus., no. 362): ⲁⲥϣⲱⲡⲉ ⲙⲙⲟⲓ ⲉⲓⲁⲛⲁⲭⲱⲣⲉⲓ ⲙⲁⲩⲁⲁⲧ ⲁⲓϫⲱⲗⲙ ⲙⲡⲟⲩⲥⲟⲛ ⲉϥϩⲓⲧⲟⲩⲱⲓ ⲁⲩⲱ ⲁⲓⲕⲁⲁⲥ ϩⲙⲡⲁϩⲏⲧ ⲉⲧⲙⲧⲣⲁⲃⲱⲗ ⲛⲙⲙⲁϥ. Thereupon a saint appears, bidding ⲟⲛⲧⲱⲥ ⲕⲛⲁⲙⲟⲩⲣ ⲙⲡⲉⲧϩⲓⲧⲟⲩⲱⲕ ϫⲉⲁϥϯ ⲙⲧⲟⲛ ⲛⲁⲕ, and quoting 1 Pet. ii. 23. In this latter passage, and in Brit. Mus. Cat., no. 217 n., the meaning can hardly be the same as in the others. In Mingarelli 295 it is equally obscure (*cf.* Stern, *Gram.*, p. 388).

[3] 'Temple' seems unlikely, though my copy suggests it.

[4] *Lit.* 'preserved in her eyes'. *Cf.* Ps. cxviii. 37.

[5] *Cf.* Luke i. 39.

Fol. 7. *Recto.* . . . the barren woman. Yet (ἔτι) other six months is it,[1] until . . . . womb] swollen.[2] I shall see how that the breasts, which were dried up, after the (proper) time (χρ.) have become full of milk.' Perchance [3] indeed they have deceived me [in that] which [they . . . . .

Verso. . . . of (?) his Lord, when she came up to his mother, he leaped [4] and jumped (σκιρτᾶν), he leaped [in the] womb (?), ere (?) . . . . .

. . . 'How (? what) . . . . . come unto me (?) [my ?] Lord and the mother of my Lord' [5] . . . . .

Fol. 8. → *Recto.*

ⲉⲣⲁⲧϥ ⲙ̅ⲡⲉϥ-	ⲧⲓ̈ⲁ ⲙ̅ⲡϩⲩ̣[ⲙⲛⲱ-]
ⲥⲧⲣⲁⲧⲏⲣⲁ-	ⲇⲟⲥ ⲇⲁⲩ[ⲉⲓⲇ]
ⲧⲏⲥ ·	ϫⲉⲁⲛⲛ̅ⲁ̅ [ⲙⲛ̅-]
Ⲟⲩⲥⲧⲣⲁⲧⲱⲣ	ⲧⲙⲉ ⲧⲱⲙ[ⲛⲧ]
ⲉϥⲛⲏⲩ ⲉⲣⲁ-	ⲉⲛⲉⲩⲉⲣⲏ[ⲩ ·]
ⲧϥ ⲙⲡⲉϥϯ-	ⲁⲧⲇⲓⲕⲁⲓ̈[ⲟⲥⲩ-]
ⲣⲱⲛ ·	ⲛⲏ ⲙⲛ̅ϯ[ⲣⲏ-]
Ⲟⲩϣⲱⲥ ⲉϥ	ⲛⲏ ϯⲡⲓ̈ ⲉ-
ⲛⲏⲩ [ⲉⲣⲁⲧ]ϥ	ⲛⲉⲩⲉⲣ[ⲏⲩ
[ⲙⲡ]ⲉϥⲉⲥⲟⲩ (*sic*)	ⲛⲧⲡ̣[
[ⲧ]ⲉ̣ⲱⲥ ⲱ̅ ⲛⲁ-	?
[ⲙ]ⲉⲣⲁ̣ⲧⲉ ⲟⲩ-	
[ϣ]ⲡⲏⲣⲉⲧⲉ	
[ⲧⲟ]ⲓ̈ⲕⲟⲛⲟⲙⲓ̈ⲁ	

↑ *Verso.*

[. .]ⲛ ϣⲁϫⲉ ⲙⲛ̅-	ϣⲱⲡⲉ[a] ⲛⲁⲓ̈ ⲛ̅-
[ⲛⲉⲩ]ⲉⲣⲏⲩ ⲁⲓ̈-	ϩⲩⲡⲉⲣⲉⲧ[ⲏⲥ ·]
[ⲧ]ⲉ̣ⲓ̣ ⲉⲩϩⲛⲑⲏ ·	Ⲁⲛⲟⲕ ⲁⲓϥⲓ ⲙ̅-
[Ⲡⲉ]ϫⲁϥ ⲛ̅ϭⲓ ⲡϩⲓⲉ-	ⲙⲁⲩ ⲛⲧⲙ̅ⲛ̅-
[ⲣⲟ]ⲯⲁⲗⲧⲏⲥ	ⲧⲁϭⲣⲏⲛ ⲛ̅-
[ⲇⲁⲩ]ⲉⲓⲇ ϫⲉⲡⲛⲩ̊ⲛ	ⲧⲉⲕⲙⲁⲁⲩ
[ⲛⲁ]ⲟⲩⲱϣ̅ϥ̅ (*sic*) ⲟⲩ-	ϫⲉⲉⲥⲛⲁϫ-
[ⲃⲉ]ⲡⲛⲟⲩⲛ ⲉⲡⲉ-	ⲡⲟⲕ ⲛ̅ⲡ̅ⲥⲟϥ-
[ϩⲣⲟⲟⲩ] ⲛ̅ⲛⲉⲕ-	ⲧⲉ ⲛ̅ⲛⲉϩⲓⲱ̅-
[ⲕⲁⲧⲁϩⲣⲁ]ⲕⲧⲏⲥ	ⲟⲩⲉ ϩⲓⲑⲏ ⲙ-
] ?	ⲡⲉⲕϫⲟ̣[ⲉⲓⲥ]
]ϣⲉ	ⲛ̣[ⲧⲟⲕⲡⲉ ⲓⲱ-]
	ϩⲁⲛⲛⲏⲥ̣ [ⲡⲁ]-
	ⲙⲉⲣⲓⲧ

[a] Here Rossi, 61 c.

Fol. 8. *Recto.* . . . coming] to his general (στρατηλάτης); a . . . . .[6] (στράτωρ) coming to his recruit (τίρων); a shepherd coming to his sheep. Howbeit (τέως),[7] O my beloved, a marvel is the dispensation (οἰκονομία) [of God . . . .] of the singer (ὑμνῳδός) David,[8] 'Mercy and truth are met

[1] Luke i. 36.

[2] *Cf.* the phrases in Rossi, ii. 1. 10 b.

[3] Here, I assume, the preacher resumes.

[4] Luke i. 44.

[5] *Ib.* 43.

[6] 'Groom' is the sole meaning offered for this. Probably a mistake for a high military title.

[7] 'Meanwhile' seems unsuitable. Perhaps read ὅμως.

[8] Ps. lxxxiv. 10.

together; righteousness (δικαιοσύνη) and peace (εἰρ.) have kissed one another'[1].....

Verso. ... talked one with another, whilst yet (ἔτι) they were in the womb. The hieropsalt (ἱεροψ.) David said,[2] 'Deep answereth unto deep at the voice of Thy cataracts (κατ.)'.....

... be unto me servant (ὑπηρέτης). It is I have taken away the barrenness of thy mother; for she shall bear thee and thou shalt prepare the ways before thy Lord..... John, my beloved.....

Fol. 9. ↑ *Recto.*		→ *Verso.*	
margin		margin	
Ⲕⲁⲑⲁⲣⲓⲍⲉ ⲛ̄ⲛⲉ-	ⲱⲧ[	]ⲉⲛ	ⲧⲁϩⲟ[c] · ⲙ̄ⲡⲉ-
ϩⲓⲟⲟⲩⲉ ⲉⲧϭⲟ-	▽Ⲡⲉⲛ[	] ⲙⲁⲣⲛ̄-	ⲧⲁⲕⲟⲛⲓ̈ⲁ ⲛⲛ-
ⲟⲙⲉ ϩⲓⲑⲏ ⲙ̄-	ⲛⲁⲛ[	] ⲙⲡⲉⲛ-	ϣⲁⲙⲓⲥⲉ ⲧⲁϩⲟ
ⲡⲉⲕϫⲟⲉⲓⲥ ·	▽Ⲛ̄ⲧⲟⲕ ⲡ̣[ⲉ	]ⲁ̣ⲙ̣ⲛ̣ⲥⲛ-	ⲱ̄ ⲙⲁⲣⲓⲁ ⲧⲡⲁⲣ-
▽Ⲛ̄ⲧⲟⲕⲡⲉ ϯⲛⲁ-	ⲡⲉϥϣⲁ[	ⲥⲛ]ⲙⲁⲛⲉ	ⲑⲉⲛⲟⲥ ·
ⲃⲁⲡⲧⲓ̈ⲍⲉ[a] ⲉⲃⲟⲗ	ϭⲓϫ ⲉϥ[	ⲉ]ⲧⲃⲉⲡⲉⲓ-	▽Ⲁⲣⲙⲓⲥⲉ ⲛ̄ⲧⲟ
ϩⲓⲧⲟⲟⲧⲕ̄ ·	ⲙ̄ⲡⲉϥ[	[ϣⲁⲙⲓ]ⲥⲉ ⲉⲧ-	ⲟⲩⲡⲁⲣⲑⲉⲛⲟⲥ
▽Ⲁⲙⲟⲩ ⲧⲉⲛⲟⲩ	▽Ⲛ̄ⲧⲟⲕ ⲡ[ⲉ	] ⲉⲃⲟⲗ ⲙ̄-	▽Ⲁⲣⲙⲉⲥⲓⲱ̄ ⲙ̄ⲙⲟ̄
ⲡⲃⲁⲓ̈ϣⲙ̄ⲛⲟⲩ-	ⲁⲥⲡⲉ[	]ⲡⲉⲓ̄	ⲙⲁⲩⲁⲁⲧⲉ ·
ϥⲉ ⲉⲧⲧⲁⲓ̈ⲏⲩ	ⲛ̄ⲧⲉⲡⲁ[	ⲉⲛⲥⲙⲟⲩ	ⲛ̣ⲧⲟ̣ ⲟⲩⲡⲁⲣⲑⲉ-
ⲛ̄ⲅ̄ⲕⲁⲑⲁⲣⲓ̈ⲍⲉ	ⲁⲩ[	]ⲛ̣	ⲛⲟⲥ ?
[ⲛ̄]ⲛⲉϩⲓ̈ⲟⲟⲩⲉ	▽		
[ϩⲓ]ⲑ̣ⲏ ⲙ̄ⲡ-[b]			

[a] Here Rossi, 61 c. [b] ⲡⲉⲕϫⲟⲉⲓⲥ. [c] Here Rossi, 58 c.

Fol. 9. *Recto.* ... Make clean (καθαρίζειν) the crooked paths before thy Lord.[3] Thou it is by whom I shall be baptized (βαπτ.). Come now, honoured bearer of good-tidings, make clean (καθ.) the paths before the.....

... Thou........ Thou........

Verso. ... signify (σημαίνειν)[4] ... because of this first-born (?) that ... out from .....

[1] Rossi, ii. IV. 94, Fr. vi ⲙ̄ⲙⲟ appears to expatiate on this.

[2] Ps. xli. 8.

[3] The verb used recalls Isa. lvii. 14.

[4] Occurs in Rossi, 62 c, but I cannot identify the two passages.

. . . reached thee (not). The pangs (ἀγωνία) of the first-born[1] befell thee not, O Maria the Virgin (παρ.). Thou didst bring forth, thou a virgin. Thou didst deliver[2] thyself, thou a virgin . . . . .

Fol. 10. → *Recto.*	
margin	
ⲃⲱⲗ[a] ⲉⲃⲟⲗ · ⲧ̄ⲉ̄-	ⲟⲙ̣[
Ⲗⲟⲟⲗⲉ ⲙ̄ⲡⲉⲧ-	ⲟⲛ ⲙ̣̄[
ⲙⲟⲟⲛⲉ ⲙ̄ⲡⲥⲱ-	ⲛⲟⲥ̣[? ϭⲗⲟⲙ-]
ⲛ̄ⲧ ⲧⲏⲣϥ̄ ·	Ⲗⲙ̄ ⲙ̄ⲙⲟϥ [ⲛϩⲉⲛ-]
Ⲡⲉⲧϯϩⲣⲉ ⲙ̄-	ⲧⲟⲉⲓⲥ ϥ[
ⲡⲥⲱⲛⲧ ⲧⲏ-	ϩⲓ̈ⲱⲟⲩ ⲛ̣[
ⲣϥ ⲁⲣϯⲉⲣⲱⲧⲉ	ⲛⲁⲙⲓⲥ̣[ⲉ
ⲛⲁϥ ϩⲱⲥ ⲕⲟⲩⲓ̈	Ϣ̄[c] ⲡⲉⲓⲟⲩ[ⲟⲙϥ]
ϩⲓⲧⲛⲧⲟⲩⲉⲣⲱ̄-	ⲙ̄ⲙⲁⲕⲁ̣[ⲣⲓⲟⲥ]
ⲧⲉ ⲛ̄ⲗⲟⲕⲓⲕⲏ	Ϣ̄ ⲛ̣ⲛ̣ⲏ̣ⲥ[[d]
Ⲡⲉⲧⲉ̣ⲙⲉⲣⲉ-	
ⲙⲁ ϣⲟⲡ̄ϥ̄[b] ⲁϥⲱ-	
[ⲣ]ⲃ̣ ⲉϩⲟⲩ̄ⲛ̄ ϩⲛ̄-	

↑ *Verso.*	
margin	
]ⲛ̄	ⲙ̄ⲛ̄ⲛ̄ⲥⲉⲣⲁⲫⲓⲙ
]ⲅⲏ	ⲛ̄ⲇⲩⲛⲁⲙⲓⲥ
] · ⲩ[e]	ⲙ̄ⲛ̄ⲛⲉⲭⲣⲟⲛⲟⲥ
[ⲙⲛⲛ]ⲥⲓⲃⲧ	ⲛ̄ⲁⲣⲭⲏ ⲙ̄ⲛ̄-
[ⲙⲛ]ⲡ̣ⲣⲏ ·	ⲛⲉⲝⲟⲩⲥⲓ̈ⲁ
[ⲙⲛ]ⲡ̣ⲟⲟϩ ⲙ̄ⲛ̄-	ⲙⲛ̄ⲛ̄ⲕⲟⲥⲙⲟⲕ-
[ⲛ̄ⲥⲓⲟ]ⲩ · ⲙ̄ⲛ̄-	ⲣⲁⲧⲱⲣ̄ ⲛ̄ⲧⲟⲕ-
[ⲛϣⲏ]ⲛ *sic* ⲛ̄ ⲧⲥⲱ-	ⲡⲉ ⲡⲉⲩⲇⲏⲙⲓ̈-
[ϣⲉ] ⲡ̣ϣⲱⲙ	Ⲟⲣⲅⲟⲥ ⲧⲏⲣⲟⲩ ·
[ⲙⲛⲡⲉ]ⲁⲣ̄	Ⲁⲩⲱ ⲡⲉϫⲁϥ
[ⲡⲉⲭⲓⲱ]ⲛ ⲁⲩⲱ̄	ϫⲉⲙⲛⲙ̣ⲁ ϣⲟ-
[ⲡⲉⲕⲣⲩⲥ]ⲧⲁⲣⲥ[o]	ⲟⲡ ⲛⲁⲩ ϩ̄ⲙ̄ⲡ̄-
	ⲙⲁ [ⲛϭ]ⲟ̣ⲓ̣[ⲗⲉ]

[a] Here Rossi, 58 c. [b] *Cf.* ⲡⲉⲧⲉⲙⲉⲣⲉⲡⲧⲏⲣϥ ϣⲟⲡϥ ⲟⲩⲇⲉ ⲙⲉⲩⲉϣⲟⲣⲃϥ ⲉϩⲟⲩⲛ ⲉⲩⲙⲁ ⲛⲟⲩⲱⲧ in Damianus' *Synodikon*, *Miss.* i. 38, line 7. I propose to re-edit this text shortly, having identified it with that in Chabot's *Chron. de Michel* ii. 325 ff. *Cf.* my *Ostraca*, no. 18 n. [c] Here Rossi, 59 a, b. [d] Perhaps with Rossi ⲛⲉⲓⲧⲟ[ⲉⲓⲥ. [e] Here Rossi, 56 a, b.

Fol. 10. *Recto.* . . . dissolved. Thou (*fem.*) dost nurse[3] Him that shepherdeth all creation. He that giveth food unto all creation, thou gavedst Him milk when (ὡς) a child, with thy reasonable (λογικός) milk. He whom no place may hold was confined within . . . . .

. . . swathed Him in bandages . . . . O this blessed (μακ.) manger, O these[4] . . . . .

Verso. . . . the] hills [and] the sun and the moon and the stars and the

[1] So far recorded only as a Bohairic form, though Peyron (280 b) knew the Sa'idic.

[2] *Lit.* (reading ⲁⲣⲙⲙⲉⲥⲓⲱ) 'didst act midwife'. *Pap. Bruce*, p. 259, uses the verb as here. Perhaps for ⲧⲙⲉⲥⲓⲟ (*cf.* Steindorff, *Gram.*[2], § 262).

[3] Reading ϩⲗⲟⲟⲗⲉ with Rossi.

[4] 'Incorruptible bandages' (Rossi).

trees of the field; the summer and the spring (ἔαρ), snow (χιών) and ice (κρύσταλλος) . . . . .

. . . the Cherubim] and the Seraphim, the powers (δύναμις) and the seasons (χρόνος)[1] the principalities (ἀρχή) and the powers (ἐξ.) and the rulers (κοσμοκράτωρ), Thou it is art the Creator (δημιουργός) of them all. And he saith, 'There was not place for them in the lodging' . . . . .

Fol. 11. ↑ *Recto.*

margin	
ⳁ[a] ϩⲓⲱⲟⲩ ⲛ̄ϩⲉⲛ-	ⲉⲃⲟⲗ · ⲙ[ⲁⲣⲟⲩ-]
ϩⲟⲓ̈ⲧⲉ ⲉⲛⲁϣⲉ	ⲭⲓ[b] ϣⲓ̈ⲡⲉ [ⲧⲉⲛⲟⲩ]
ⲥⲟⲩⲉⲛⲧⲟⲩ ⲉⲩⲟ	ⲛϭⲓ ⲛ̄ⲟⲩ[ⲱⲛϣ]
ⲙ̄ⲙⲓ̈ⲛⲉ ⲙⲓ̈ⲛⲉ	ⲉⲑⲟⲟⲩ ⲛ̄[ϩⲁⲓⲣⲉ-]
ϩⲟⲓ̈ⲛⲉ ⲉⲧⲃⲉ-	ⲧⲓⲕⲟⲥ . [[c]
ⲡϣⲱⲙ ϩⲉⲛⲕⲟ-	ⲑⲏⲡ ϩⲛ[ⲧⲡⲟ-]
ⲟⲩⲉ ⲉⲧⲃⲉⲧⲉⲡ-	ⲗⲓⲥ[d] ⲉⲧⲥ[ⲱⲧⲙ ⲉ-]
ⲣⲱ̄ · ⲡⲛⲟⲩⲧⲉ	ⲣⲟⲛ ⲙ̄ⲡ̣[ⲟⲟⲩ ·]
ⲇⲉ ⲡⲇⲏⲙⲓⲟⲣ̄-	Ⲡⲁⲣⲉϥϫ[ⲓ ϣⲓ̈ⲡⲉ]
ⲅⲟⲥ ϭ̄ⲗ̄ⲙ̄ⲗ̄ⲱ̄ⲙ̄	ⲛϭⲓ [
[ⲛ̄]ϩⲉⲛⲧⲟⲉⲓⲥ	ⲡ[
? ?	?

→ *Verso.*

margin	
]ⲧⲁⲕⲟ ⲛ̄ϭⲓ	ⲭⲉ ⲛ̄ϭⲓ ⲡⲡⲉⲧⲩ̊-
[ⲛⲡⲁ]ⲣⲁⲛⲟⲙⲟⲥ	ⲁⲁⲃ ⲛ̄ⲉⲩⲁⲅⲅⲉ-
]ⲓ̣ⲑⲁⲧⲏⲥ[e]	ⲗⲓⲥⲧⲏⲥ ⲉϥ-
[ⲛⲁⲓ] ⲉⲧⲟⲛⲟ-	ϫⲱ ⲙ̄ⲙⲟⲥ ϫⲉ-
]ⲛⲉ[f] ⲛ̄ϣⲟ̄ⲙ̄-	ⲛⲉⲙ̄ⲛ̄ⲙⲁ ϣⲟ-
sic [ⲛⲧ ⲙⲙ]ⲛⲧⲛⲟⲩ-[g]	ⲟⲡ ⲛⲁⲩ ϩ̄ⲙ̄ⲡ-
[ⲧⲉ ⲉ]ⲩ̣ⲡⲱⲣϫ̄	ⲙⲁ ⲛϭⲟⲓ̈ⲗⲉ
[ⲙ̄ⲡⲉⲓ]ⲱⲧ ⲉⲃⲟⲗ	ⲁⲩⲱ ϫⲉⲁⲩϭⲗⲙ-
[ⲙ̄ⲡϣⲏ]ⲣⲉ ⲙⲛ-	ⲗⲱ̄ⲙ̄ϥ̄ ⲛ̄ϩⲉⲛ-
[ⲡⲉⲡ̄ⲛ̄ⲁ̄ ⲉ]ⲧⲟⲩ[ⲁ̄-]	ⲧⲟ̣ⲉⲓⲥ ⲁⲩϫ̣[ⲧⲟϥ]
[ⲁⲃ ⲙⲁ]ⲣⲟⲩ-	ϩⲛ̄ⲟⲩⲟⲙϥ [
ⲛ̄]ϭⲓ	ⲉⲣⲉⲡⲟⲩⲟⲙ[ϥ
	ⲁⲣϫⲓ ⲙ̄ⲡ[
	[. .]ⲥ̣ ⲛⲑ[ⲉ ⲛ

[a] Here Rossi, 56 c. [b] Probably = Rossi, 57 b. [c] ? ⲛ[ⲁⲓ ⲉ-]. [d] 'Hidden for us' (Rossi). [e] First visible letter not very like ⲩ. [f] ? ⲉⲧ[ⲟⲛⲟⲙⲁ]ⲍⲉ. [g] The prolonged stroke over ⲛ demanding ⲙ, one cannot read ϣⲟⲙⲛⲧ ⲛⲟⲩ[ⲥⲓⲁ.

Fol. 11. *Recto.* . . . clothe them[selves?] in garments of great price, of divers sorts, some because of the summer, others because of the winter. But (δέ) God, the Creator (δημιουργός), is swathed in bandages . . . . .

. . . Let [them] be shamed [now], the evil wolves of [here]tics (αἱρετικός)

[1] Read θρόνος with Rossi.

[that are] hidden in the city (? πόλις), that hear us to-day. Let him be [shamed] . . . . .

Verso. . . . [Let them] perish, the presumptuous (? αὐθάδης) transgressors (παράνομος), [they] that name (? ὀνομάζειν) three divinities, dividing the Father from the Son and [the] Holy [Ghost (πν.).[1] Let] them . . . . .
. . . the holy evangelist (εὐαγγ.) . . .,[2] saying,[3] 'There was not place for them in the lodging,' and 'they swathed Him in bandages and laid Him in a manger.' [Him whom] the manger did . . ., thou (*fem.*) didst take . . . . . like . . . . .

No. 8.

From a Sermon, treating here of the Last Judgement. The inability of the righteous to aid the wicked in that day is similarly alluded to in Homilies by John *Jejunator* and Theophilus.[4]

Fol. 1. → *Recto.*	↑ *Verso.*
ⲙⲙⲛⲧⲉϥⲓⲏⲛ	ⲓ̈ⲱⲧ ⲛⲁⲛⲟⲩϥ̣
ϫⲉⲟⲩⲟⲓ ⲛⲁ̈ⲓ	ⲉⲛⲉⲛⲡ̣ⲉⲕ-
[ⲡⲁ]ⲓ̈ⲱⲧ ⲉⲕ-	ϫⲡⲟⲓ ϫⲉ[
ⲛ̣[ⲁ]ⲕⲁⲁⲧ ⲛ-	ⲉⲛⲁ̣ⲩ [ⲉⲣⲟⲕ]
ⲥⲱⲕ ⲛⲧⲉ-	ϩⲛ̄ⲛⲉⲓϩⲓⲥⲉ
ⲡⲉϥⲓⲱⲧ ⲟⲩ-	ⲱ ⲡ[ⲁ]ⲓⲱⲧ ⲙ̄ⲛ-
ⲱϣⲃ̄ ϩⲛ̄ⲟⲩ-	ϣϭⲟⲙ ⲙ̄ⲙⲟⲓ̈
ⲣⲓ̈ⲙⲉ ⲙ̄ⲡⲟⲩ-	ⲉⲃⲟⲏⲑⲉⲓ̈ⲁ
ⲁϣⲁϩⲟⲙ·	ⲉⲣⲟⲕ ⲙ̄ⲡⲉⲓ-
ϫⲉⲟⲩⲟⲓ ⲛⲁ̈ⲓ	ⲙⲁ· ⲉⲃⲟⲗ
ⲡⲁϣⲏⲣⲉ	ϫⲉ ⲁⲓϩⲓⲥⲉ
ⲙ̄ⲡϣϭⲟⲙ ⲙ̄-[a]	ⲉⲓϯⲥⲃⲱ ⲛⲁⲕ
margin	margin

(margin at left of Recto and at right of Verso)

[a] ⲙⲙⲟⲓ.

[1] What relation this heresy bears towards the distinctive position of Damianus himself (*v.* Krüger's article, *PRE.*) is not clear. In Rossi, 57 b c (if parallel here) the sect in question are named Πλατωνίτης.

[2] A Greek verb.

[3] Luke ii. 7.

[4] Budge, *Copt. Hom.*, 38 *inf.*, 71 *inf.*

Fol. 1. *Recto.* . . . . wretchedness, (saying,) 'Woe is me, my father! Thou wilt leave me behind thee?' And his father shall make answer, with weeping and groaning, 'Woe is me, my son! [I] have not power [to' . . . . .

Verso. . . . 'my] father, it were good if thou hadst not begotten me. For . . . to see [thee?] in these distresses. O my father, I have not power to help (βοηθεῖν[1]) thee here. Because I was at pains and taught thee' . . . . .

Fol. 2. ↑ *Recto.*	→ *Verso.*
ϣⲁϩⲟⲙ ⲛ̄ⲧ̄-	ⲛ̄ⲧⲉⲥϣ[ⲉⲉ-]
ϩ̣ⲉ̣ ⲉⲩⲙⲁⲁⲩ	ⲣⲉ ϫⲉⲉⲩⲛⲁ-
[ⲛⲇ]ⲓⲕⲁⲓⲟⲥ	ⲛⲟϫⲥ ⲉⲛ̣[ⲕⲟ-]
ϩ̣[ⲙⲡ]ⲙ̣ⲁ ⲉⲧⲙ-	ⲗⲁⲥⲓ̄ⲥ̄ [. .]ⲉ
ⲙⲁⲩ ⲉⲥⲁ-	ϣⲁⲥⲱϣ ⲉⲃⲟⲗ
ⲙⲁϩⲧⲉ ⲛⲧ-	ⲛ̄ϭⲓ ⲧⲉⲥϣⲉ-
ϭⲓϫ ⲛ̄ⲧⲉⲥ-	ⲉⲣⲉ ϫⲉⲟⲩⲟⲓ̈
ϣⲉⲉⲣⲉ ⲛⲣ̄ϥ̄-	ⲛⲁⲓ̈ ⲧⲁⲙⲁⲁⲩ
ⲉⲣⲛⲟⲃⲉ ⲛⲧⲉ-	ⲙⲛ̄ϣϭⲟⲙ ⲙ̄
ⲧⲁⲡⲟⲫⲁⲥⲓ̈ⲥ	ⲙⲟⲓ̈ ⲉⲃⲟⲏ-
ⲉⲓ̈ ⲉⲃⲟⲗ ϩⲓⲧⲙ-	ⲑⲉⲓⲁ ⲉⲣⲟ· ⲉ-
ⲡϫⲟⲉⲓ̈ⲥ ⲓ̄ⲥ̄	ⲃⲟⲗ ϫⲉⲁⲓϩⲓⲥⲉ
margin (left and bottom)	margin (right and bottom)

Fol. 2. *Recto.* . . . groaning and thou shalt (?) find a righteous (δίκαιος) mother there, clasping the hand of her ill-doing daughter and the judgement (ἀπόφασις) coming forth from the Lord Jesus . . . . .

Verso. . . . her daughter, because they are about to cast her to the torments (κόλασις) . . .[2] her daughter will cry out, 'Woe is me, my mother! I have not power to help (βο.) thee. Because I was at pains' . . . . .

[1] Nominal for verbal forms are not uncommon; of this same verb, *e.g.* Brit. Mus. no. 370, Rylands no. 340.

[2] ⲧⲟⲧⲉ probably too long for the gap.

Fol. 3. → *Recto.*

margin

ⲣⲓ]ⲙ̣ⲉ ϩⲓⲁ-
[ϣⲁ]ϩ̣ⲟⲙ ⲙ-
[ⲡⲉ]ⲟⲩⲟⲛ ϣⲱ-
ⲡ̣[ⲉ ⲛⲧ]ⲉⲥϩⲉ
ⲉⲛⲉϩ[a] ⲛ̄ⲧ̄-
ϩⲉ ⲉⲩⲟⲟⲛ ⲛ̄-
ⲇⲓⲕⲁⲓⲟⲥ ⲉϥ-
ⲁⲙⲁϩⲧⲉ ⲛ̄ⲧ-
ϭⲓϫ ⲙ̄ⲡⲉϥ-
ⲥⲟⲛ ⲛ̄ⲣⲉϥⲉⲣ-
ⲛⲟⲃⲉ · ⲛ̄ⲧⲉ-
ⲧⲁⲡⲟⲫⲁⲥⲓ̄ⲥ̄

margin

↑ *Verso.*

ⲡⲱ̣[ⲙ-]
ⲡⲉⲟⲩ[ⲟⲛ ϣⲱ-]
ⲡⲉ ⲛ̄ⲧⲉ̣[ⲥ̣ϩⲉ]
ⲉⲛⲉϩ [
} Ⲟⲩⲟⲓ̣ [ⲛⲁⲛ]
ⲙⲁⲣⲉⲛⲧⲱ-
ⲟⲩⲛ ⲧⲛⲣⲓⲙⲉ
ⲉⲣⲟⲛ ⲙ̄ⲙⲁⲩ-
ⲁⲁⲛ ⲧⲛⲡⲱϩ
ⲛ̄ⲛⲉⲛϩⲏⲧ
ⲧⲛϣⲏϣ ⲕⲏⲣ-
ⲙⲉⲥ ⲉϫⲱⲛ
ⲙ̄ⲡⲁ̣ⲧⲉⲡⲉ-

margin

margin

[a] *Cf.* Mark xiii. 19.

Fol. 3. *Recto.* . . . weeping and groaning, the like of which never was. And thou shalt find a righteous (*δίκαιος*) brother clasping the hand of his ill-doing brother and the judgement (*ἀπόφ.*) . . . . .

Verso. . . . the like of which never was. Woe [unto us]! Let us arise and weep over ourselves and break our hearts and scatter ashes upon us, ere the . . . . .

Fol. 4. ↑ *Recto.*

margin

ϩⲛ[ⲧ]ⲙ̣ⲏⲧⲉ
ⲛ̄ⲛ̣ⲉⲧⲟⲩⲁⲁⲃ
[ⲙⲛ̄ⲛ]ⲁⲡⲟⲥ-
ⲧⲟⲗⲟⲥ ⲉⲩ-
ϫⲡⲓ̈ⲟ ⲙ̄ⲙⲟⲛ
ϩⲁⲛⲉⲛⲧⲁⲛ-
ⲁⲁⲩ · ⲙⲏ ⲛ̄-

→ *Verso.*

mostly
illegible

ϫⲉⲧⲉⲛⲉⲣ̣-

margin

ⲣⲱⲛ ⲛⲁⲧⲱⲙ
ⲁⲛ ⲧ̄ⲛ̄ⲧⲙ-
ϭⲛ ϣⲁϫⲉ ⲉ-
ϫⲱ· ⲉⲩϫⲡ̈ⲓⲟ
ⲙⲙⲟⲛ ϫⲉⲉⲧ-

ϩⲟⲧⲉ ⲉϩⲏ- (sic)
ⲧⲟⲩ ⲛ̄ⲛⲣⲱⲙⲉ
ⲡⲁⲣⲁ ⲡⲛⲟⲩ
ⲧⲉ· ⲉⲕ-
ϣⲁⲛϫⲟⲟⲥ
margin

Fol. 4. *Recto.* ... in the midst of the saints [and] the apostles (ἀπ.), upbraiding us for the things we have done. Shall not (μή) our mouths be shut and we find not a word to say, whilst they upbraid us for that .....

Verso. ... because we fear men more than (παρά) God. If thou say....

No. 9.

This Homily does not appear among the works ascribed to Gregory Nazianzen.[1] The connected foll. 5, 6, 7 contain the author's name; they belong therefore to the title-page, fol. 1; while foll. 3, 4, connected by their subject-matter, appear immediately to precede fol. 5. But since the title relates to Rom. iv. 15, therefore foll. 11, 12, 13 must belong to this same text, dealing as they also do with that verse. Again, repentance being the subject of foll. 3, 4, 5, therefore fol. 2 probably comes near these. Finally, I have noted (on my copy) that foll. 8, 10 appear, from their present shape, to lie near to fol. 7; they too, then, should belong to this sermon; while fol. 9, dealing, like the last, with charity,[2] should probably be placed close to them.

Cf. also No. 1.

Fol. 1. → *Recto.*

[ⲟⲩϩⲟ]ⲙⲉⲗⲓⲁ'[a] ⲛ̄ⲧⲉ ⲡϩⲁⲅⲓⲟⲥ' ⲅⲣⲏⲅⲱ-
[ⲣⲓⲟⲥ] ⲡⲑⲉⲟⲗ̄ⲟⲅⲟⲥ' ⲡⲉⲡⲓⲥⲕⲟⲡⲟⲥ'
[ⲛⲛⲁ]ⲍⲓⲁⲛⲍⲟⲥ' ⲉⲁϥⲧⲁⲩⲟⲥ' ⲉⲧⲃⲉ-
] ? ⲉⲧ . ⲩϩ . . [ⲡ]ⲁⲡⲟⲥⲧ[ⲟ-]

↑ *Verso.*

[+]]ⲙⲉ· ⲡⲁⲩⲗⲟ[ⲥ ⲉϥ-]
ⲉⲧⲃⲉⲟ̄ⲩ ϯⲛⲁ- ϫⲱ' [ⲛ̄ⲙⲟⲥ']
ϫⲟⲟⲥ' ϫⲉⲉⲩ- +ϫⲉⲡ[ⲙⲁ' ⲉⲧⲉ-]
ϣⲁⲛⲉⲓ ⲉⲃⲟⲗ' ⲙ̄ⲡⲛ[ⲟⲙⲟⲥ']

[a] Above this line another, or an ornament. The six lines of title are in a sloping script.

[1] Nor among those of his namesakes.
[2] On Zoega p. 19 is the title of a homily by Gregory on charity. Its text is unpublished.

[ⲗⲟⲥ] ⲉⲧⲟⲩⲁⲁⲃ' ϫⲉⲡⲙⲁ' ⲉⲧⲉⲙ̄ⲛ̄ⲛ̄[ⲟ-]
[ⲙ]ⲟⲥ' ⲛ̄ϩⲏⲧϥ' ⲙ̄ⲙ̄ⲛ̄ⲡⲁⲣⲁⲃⲁⲥⲓⲥ [a]

ⲛⲁ]ⲛⲟⲩⲥ'	ⲡⲉⲩϩⲱⲃ̣ [
]ⲉⲧⲣⲉ-	ⲙⲁⲧⲉ̣ ⲡϩ̣[
]ⲧⲡϣⲁ-	ⲛⲉϫ ⲕ̣ⲣⲁ̣ⲩⲅ̣ⲏ̣
[ϫⲉⲛ]ⲧⲏⲥ̣ⲏ-	ⲛ̄ⲥⲱⲥ' · ⲉⲩ-
[ⲙⲁⲛ]ⲛⲉⲓ	+ϫⲱ' ⲙ̄ⲙⲟ̣ⲥ̣
]ⲧϥ	ϫⲉⲧⲛ̄ϯ
?	ϩ̣ⲧⲏ̣ⲛ ⲉⲧ̣-
	. ⲱ̣ ?

ϩⲛ̄ⲧⲉⲕⲕⲗⲏ-	ⲛ̄ϩⲏⲧ[ϥ]' ⲙ̄ⲛ̄-]
ⲥⲓⲁ' · ⲁⲗⲗⲁ' ϫⲓⲛ-	ⲡⲁⲣⲁ[ⲃⲁⲥⲓⲥ'·]
ⲧⲉⲩ̄ⲛⲟⲩ' ⲉⲩ-	+ⲉⲕϫⲱ' [ⲙ̄ⲙⲟⲥ']
ϩⲙⲟⲟⲥ' ϩⲛ̄-	ϫⲉⲟⲩ̄ [ⲱ̄ ⲡⲁⲩ-]
ⲧⲉ̄ⲩⲛⲁⲝⲓⲥ' ·	ⲗⲟⲥ' · [
[+ⲉ]ⲩϣⲁⲛⲥⲱ-	ϩⲙ̄ⲧ̣ⲗⲟ̣[
ⲧⲙ̄' ⲉⲧⲗⲉⲝⲓⲥ'	ⲉⲣⲟⲛ [
ⲛ̄ⲧⲉⲕⲉⲟⲩⲉⲓ̈	ⲥⲟⲛ[
ⲉ̣ⲓ̈ ⲙ̄ⲛ̄ⲛ̄ⲥⲱⲥ'	+ⲉⲓⲙⲉ[
ϣⲁⲩⲣ̄ⲡⲱⲃϣ̄'	ⲛ̄ⲧⲛ̄[
ⲙ̣ⲡⲉⲛⲧⲁⲩ-	ϫⲉ[
[ⲥ]ⲟ̣ⲧ̣ⲙⲉϥ' ⲛ̄-	?
[ⲧ]ⲉⲩⲛⲟⲩ ·	?
[. .]ⲛⲁ̣ⲥⲱⲧⲙ̄'	

[a] After this I read ⲛ ., very doubtfully. It did not seem to be ⲁⲙⲏⲛ.

Fol. I. *Recto. A Homily* (ὁμιλία) *of St.* (ἅγιος) *Gregory the Theologian* (θεόλ.), *the bishop* (ἐπ.) *of Nazianzus, which he pronounced concerning* .... *the holy apostle* (ἀπ.), *namely, 'The place wherein there is not law* (νό.), *there is not transgression* (παράβασις).'[1]

. . . good (?) . . . that . . . the word (?) whereby (?) we point out (? σημαίνειν) .....

....., cried (-κραυγή) after her, saying, We give heed unto .....

Verso. ... Wherefore? I will tell. (It is because) whenever they come forth from the church, nay (ἀλλά) from the moment that they are seated at service (σύναξις), if they hear the lesson (λέξις) and there follow another (lesson) after it, straightway they forget what they have heard. Let them (?) hear .....

... Paul, [who] saith, 'the place wherein there is not law, there is not transgression.' What sayest thou, O Paul? .....

[1] Rom. iv. 15.

Fol. 2. ↑ *Recto.*		→ *Verso.*	
ⲙⲱⲩⲥⲏⲥ			ⲛ̄ⲥ̣ⲡⲟⲗⲓⲧⲉⲩ[ⲉ]
ⲁϥϯ ⲡⲛⲟⲙⲟⲥ			ⲛ̄ϣⲟⲣⲡ̄ʼ ·
ⲁϥϫⲟⲟⲩ ⲛ̄-		]ⲡⲁ-	+ⲁⲗⲗⲁʼ ⲉϣⲁϥ-
ⲛⲉⲡⲣⲟⲫⲏ-		[ⲡⲁϩⲃ] ⲅⲁⲣ ϩⲟ-	ϫⲟⲟⲥʼ ϫⲉ-
ⲧⲏⲥʼ ⲁⲩⲱʼ	ⲡⲉ[	[ⲗϭ ⲁ]ⲩⲱ ⲥⲁⲥⲱ-	ⲉⲓⲥ ϩⲏⲏⲧⲉʼ
ⲙ̄ⲡⲟⲩⲡⲓⲥ-	+ⲉⲓⲥ ϩⲏⲏ[ⲧⲉ]	[ⲟⲩ] ⲛϭⲓ ⲧⲁⲉⲧⲡⲱ	ⲁⲕⲟⲩϫⲁⲓ̈
ⲧⲉⲩⲉ · ⲙ̄ⲛ̄-	ϯϫⲓ ϣ[ⲓⲡⲉ	]ⲟ̣ ⲟⲩⲛⲁ [b]	ⲙ̄ⲡⲣ̄ⲕⲟⲧⲕ̄ʼ
+ⲛ̄ⲥⲱⲥʼ ⲁⲡϣⲏ-	ⲉⲃⲟⲗ [	ⲛ]ϭⲓ̣ ⲧ̣ⲉⲧⲡⲱ	ⲉⲣ̄ⲛⲟⲃⲉʼ
ⲣⲉʼ ⲙ̄ⲡⲛⲟⲩ-	ⲙⲏ[	?	ϫⲉⲉⲛⲉⲡⲉ-
ⲧⲉʼ ⲧⲱⲟⲩⲛ̄ʼ	ϣⲁⲣ[	[ⲉⲣϣ]ⲁⲛⲟⲩⲁʼ	ⲑⲟⲟⲩʼ ⲉⲡⲁⲓ̈
ϩⲓⲟⲩⲛⲁⲙ	ⲟⲛ̄ ⲛⲥ̣[ⲛ-]	[ϯ]ⲡⲉϥⲟⲩⲟ̈ⲓ	ϣⲱⲡⲉʼ ⲙ̄-
ⲙ̄ⲡⲉϥⲉⲓⲱⲧʼ	ⲧⲁⲩⲣ[	[ⲉⲡⲉ]ⲭ̣ⲥ̄ ⲉⲧⲃⲉ-	ⲙⲟⲕʼ · ⲉⲧⲉ-
+ⲁϥⲉⲓ ⲉϥϣⲁ-	ⲁⲛⲟⲕ [	]ⲛ̣ⲟ̣ⲃ̣ⲉ̣	+ⲡⲁⲓ̈ⲡⲉʼ ϫⲉ-
ϫⲉʼ ⲛ̄ⲙⲙⲁⲛ	ⲧⲉ ⲉⲧ[ⲛ-]	?	ⲧⲉⲕⲡⲟⲗⲓ-
ⲉϥϫⲱʼ ⲙⲙⲟⲥʼ ·	ⲧⲁϥⲉ[	?	ⲧⲓ̈ⲁʼ ⲧⲏⲣⲥ̄ʼ-
+ϫⲉⲉϣϫⲉⲁⲓ̈-	ⲛ̄ⲕⲁ ⲛ[ⲓⲙ	] ⲉ̣ⲃ̣ⲟ̣ⲗ	ⲡⲉ ⲧⲙ̄ⲕⲟ-
ϫⲟⲟⲩ ⲛ̄ⲛⲁ-	ⲉⲃⲟⲗ ⲁ[[a]	?	ⲧⲕ̄ʼ ⲉⲡⲛⲟ-
ⲡⲣⲟⲫⲏⲧⲏⲥʼ	ⲥⲉⲡⲏⲧ̣ [ⲉ-]	]ϥϣⲱⲛⲉʼ	ⲃⲉʼ ⲛ̄ⲕⲉⲥⲟⲡ ·
ⲉⲧⲟⲩⲁⲁⲃʼ	ⲃⲟⲗʼ ⲙ̄[ⲙⲟⲓ]	]ⲟⲩⲱϣʼ	+ⲧⲙⲉⲧⲁⲛⲟⲓ̈ⲁʼ
ⲛⲏⲧⲛ̄ʼ ⲁⲩⲱʼ	+ⲛ̄ⲧⲁϥ[ϫⲟⲟⲥ]	[ⲉⲧ]ⲣⲉϥⲧⲁⲗ-	ⲙ̄ⲡⲛⲟⲃⲉʼ-
ⲁⲩϣⲁϫⲉʼ ⲛ̄ⲙ̄-	ⲁⲛʼ ⲛ̄ϭⲓ̣ [ⲡⲛⲟⲩ-]	[ϭⲟⲟ]ⲩʼ · ⲙⲉϥ-	ⲡⲉ ⲧⲙ̄ⲕⲟⲧⲕ̄ʼ
ⲙⲛ̄ⲧⲛ̄ʼ ⲉϫⲙ̄-	ⲧⲉʼ ϫ[ⲉⲙⲏⲛ-]	ⲟⲩ]ⲛⲟϭʼ	ⲉⲣⲟϥʼ · ⲉⲣ-
ⲡⲁⲣⲁⲛ · ⲡⲉ-	ⲉⲓⲧ[ⲛ ϣⲁⲣⲟⲓ]	[ⲛⲉⲧⲡ]ⲱʼ ⲉϥ- [c]	+ϣⲁⲛⲡⲣⲱⲙⲉʼ
margin	margin	ⲉ]ϫⲱϥʼ	ⲕⲟⲧϥʼ. ⲉⲡ$\overset{ⲟ}{\underset{ⲩ}{ⲛ̄}}$-
		margin	margin

[a] ⲁⲩⲱ or ⲁⲗⲗⲁ. [b] ⲡⲁϣⲧ? [c] Not an epithet of ⲉⲧⲡⲱ.

Fol. 2. *Recto.* . . . Moses. He gave the law (*νόμ.*), He sent the prophets (*πρ.*) and they believed (*πίστ.*) not. Afterward the Son of God arose upon His Father's right, and came and spake with us, saying, 'If I have sent my holy prophets (*πρ.*) unto you and they have spoken with you in my name . . . . .

. . . Lo, I am put to shame (?) through . . . . all things . . . . . they flee from [me']. Hath not God said, 'Come unto me[1] . . . . .

Verso. . . . for (*γάρ*) my [yoke] is easy and my burden is light' . . . . . . the burden . . . . [If] one betake him to Christ by reason of . . . sin (?) . . . . disease(d ?) [and ?] desire that He would heal them, He doth not [lay a heavy ? bur]den . . . . .

. . . 'and first thou live strictly (*πολιτεύειν*).' But (*ἀλλά*) He saith,[2] 'Behold, thou hast been made whole; turn not again to commit sin, lest a worse thing than this befall thee,' which is (to say,) 'Thy whole way-of-life (*πολιτεία*) is (that) thou turn not unto sin again.' Repentance (*μετ.*) of sin is not returning thereto. If a man turn unto God . . . . .

Fol. 3. ↑ *Recto.*		→ *Verso.*	
ⲧⲉ' ⲉϥⲟⲩ-			ⲛ̄ⲥⲱϥ' ·
ⲱϣ' ⲉⲙⲉⲧⲁ-			+ϩⲉⲛⲕⲟⲟⲩⲉ'
ⲛⲟⲉⲓ · ⲉϥϫⲓ̈			ⲁⲩϭⲱ' ϩ̄ⲙ̄-
+ⲙ̄ⲡ̄ⲧ̄ⲩⲡⲟⲥ'	ⲣ̄ⲡ̄[	]ⲛⲁ	ⲡⲙⲟⲟⲩ'
ⲛ̄ⲟ̣[ⲩϭⲗⲟ]ⲟ̄ϭⲉ'	ⲛⲟ[	]ⲧⲃⲗ̣-	ⲉⲩⲁϣⲉ' ⲛ̄-
ⲉⲣⲉⲣⲁⲧ̄ⲥ̄	ⲕⲟ[	]ϣ̣̄ⲕ̄'	ⲥⲁⲡϫⲟⲓ̈ ·
ⲧⲁϫⲣⲏⲩ'	ⲃⲉ' [	] ⲉⲧϩⲓ-	+ϩⲉⲛⲕⲟⲟⲩⲉ'
ⲉϫ̄ⲙ̄ⲡⲕⲁϩ'	+Ⲉⲓⲱ[	]ⲁⲧⲉ̣	ⲉⲩϩⲙⲟⲟⲥ'
ⲉⲣⲉⲧⲉⲥⲁⲡⲉ'	ⲧ̄ⲛ̄[	]ⲡ̣ⲟϭⲉ̣	ⲉⲃⲟⲗ' ϩ̄ⲙ̄-
ⲡⲏϩ' ⲉϩⲣⲁⲓ̈	ⲛⲁ[	?	ⲡϫⲟⲓ̈ · ϩⲉⲛ-
ⲉⲧⲡⲉ ⲉⲣⲉ-	ϫⲉ[	]ⲥⲱⲧ̄ⲙ̄	+ⲕⲟⲟⲩⲉ' ⲉⲩ-
ⲛⲉⲥⲡⲟⲉⲓϣ'	ϫⲉ[	?	ⲁϩ'ⲉ ⲣⲁⲧⲟⲩ'
ϫⲟⲥⲉ' ⲉⲛⲉⲩ-	ϩ̣ⲙ̣[	]ⲟⲣ ⲉϥ-	ϩⲓⲡϫⲟⲓ̈ ⲙ̄-
ⲉⲣⲏⲩ' · ⲛ̄ⲑⲉ'	ⲧ[	?	ⲡⲟⲩϭⲛ̄ ⲙⲁ
+ⲙ̄ⲡⲣⲱⲙⲉ'	ϭ[	]ⲉⲙⲛ-	ⲛ̄ϩⲙⲟⲟⲥ'
ⲉϥⲛⲁϥⲓ' ⲧⲉϥ-	ⲡⲉ̣[	]. ⲉⲥ̣ⲉ	ϣⲁⲛⲧⲟⲩ-

[1] Matt. xi. 28–30.

[2] John v. 14.

ⲟⲩⲉⲣⲏⲧⲉ'	ⲉⲡ[	]ⲣⲱⲙⲉ'	ⲡⲱϩ' ⲉⲡⲉ-
ⲙ̄ⲙⲁⲩ' ϩⲓϫⲙ̄-	+ⲕⲁ[	] ⲛ̄ⲧⲉ-	ⲕⲣⲟ̄'· ⲉⲩ-
ⲡⲕⲁϩ' ⲛ̄ϥⲟⲩ-	ϣⲙ̣[	]ⲉⲓ	+ϣⲁⲛⲡⲱϩ'
+ⲁϥⲥ̄' ⲉϫⲙ̄ⲡϣⲟ-	+ⲕⲁⲛ[	]ϣ'	ϫⲉ' ⲉⲡⲉⲕⲣⲟ̄
ⲣⲡ' ⲙ̄ⲡⲟⲉⲓϣ'	ⲧⲛ̄[	] ⲉ̣ⲣⲟϥ'	ⲛ̄ⲧⲉⲡϫⲟⲓ̈
ⲛ̄ⲧⲉϭⲗⲟⲟ̄ϭⲉ·	?	]ⲩ	ⲙⲟⲟ̄ⲛⲉ'·
+ⲧⲁⲓ̈ ϩⲱⲱϥ'-	+ⲙ[	ⲡ]ϫⲟⲓ̈·	+ϣⲁⲩⲉⲓ̄ ϫⲉ'
ⲧⲉ ⲑⲉ' ⲙ̄ⲡⲣⲱ-		]ⲉ̄·	ⲉϩⲣⲁⲓ̈ ϩⲙ̄-
margin		]ⲧⲟⲩ'	margin

Fol. 3. *Recto*. . . . desiring to repent (μετανοεῖν) he hath the type (τύπος) of a ladder, the foot thereof fixed upon the earth, its head reaching up to heaven and its steps[1] raised one (above) the other. Like as a man lifteth his foot from the earth and setteth it upon the first step of the ladder, even thus the man . . . . .

Verso. . . . others[2] stay in the water, hanging upon the ship; others sit on the outside of (?)[3] the ship; others stand upon the ship and have not found place to sit, until they attain unto the shore. But (δέ) when they attain unto the shore and the ship is in port, they come (+ δέ) up from (?) [the ship . . . . .

Fol. 4. → *Recto*.		↑ *Verso*.	
ⲛ̣ . ⲟⲓ̣ⲛ ⲉⲩ-			ϩⲓⲧⲉ' · ⲁⲕ-
ϩⲙⲟⲟⲥ' ⲕⲁ-			+ⲧⲱⲟⲩⲛ̄' ϫⲉ-
ⲗⲱⲥ' ⲙ̄ⲛ̄-			ⲉⲓⲛⲁⲉⲥⲕⲣⲁ-
ⲛⲉⲧϩⲙ̄ⲡⲙⲟ-			ⲧⲉⲩⲉ' ⲙ̄ⲙⲟⲓ̈
ⲟⲩ' ⲛ̄ⲥⲉⲉ̄ⲓ̄			ⲛ̄ⲧⲁⲙⲉⲧⲁ-
ⲧⲏⲣⲟⲩ' ⲉϫⲙ̄-			ⲛⲟⲉⲓ̄ · ⲛ̄ⲧⲉ̄-
ⲡⲉⲧϣⲟⲩ-			ⲥⲟⲟⲩⲛ̄' ⲁⲛ'
ⲱ̄ⲟⲩ' ⲛ̄ⲥⲉ-	ϩ[	]ⲓ̣ⲕⲟⲥ[a]	ϫⲉⲛ̄ⲛⲁⲱ̄ⲛϩ'

[a] ⲕⲟⲥⲙⲓⲕⲟⲥ, ⲕⲗⲏⲣⲓⲕⲟⲥ, ϩⲁⲓⲣⲉⲧⲓⲕⲟⲥ?

[1] ⲡⲟⲉⲓϣ is a new word.

[2] The preceding column too dealt with the shipwreck: ϫⲟⲓ is legible.

[3] I can find no instance of ϩⲙⲟⲟⲥ so constructed. Brit. Mus. *Gk. Cat.* iv, no. 1609 is too uncertain; Crum, *Ostr.* no. 351 still more so.

ⲟⲩϫⲁⲓ̈ ⲧⲏ-
ⲣⲟⲩ · ⲧⲁⲓ̈-
+ⲧⲉ ⲑⲉ' ⲙ̄ⲡⲉ-
ⲧⲟⲩⲛⲁϩⲉ'
ⲉⲩⲃ̄ⲗ̄ⲃⲓⲗⲉ'
ⲛ̄ⲟⲩⲱⲧ'
ϩ̄ⲙ̄ⲡⲉϥⲥⲙⲁϩ'
ⲉⲧⲉⲡⲁⲓ̈-
ⲡⲉ ⲟⲩⲙⲉ-
ⲣⲟⲥ' ⲙ̄ⲙⲉ-
ⲧⲁⲛⲟⲓⲁ' ·
+ϣⲁⲣⲉⲧⲙⲛ̄ⲧ-
ϣⲁⲛϩⲧⲏϥ'
ⲙ̄ⲡⲛⲟⲩⲧⲉ'
ⲧⲁϩⲟⲟⲩ'
ⲧⲏⲣⲟⲩ' ⲛ̄-
margin

ⲥⲉ[
ⲟⲩ[
ⲥⲓ̣[
ⲧ[
ⲁⲩ[
ⲑ̣ⲉ[
ⲟⲛ̣[
ϫ̣ⲁ̣[
?
ϫ[
ⲕⲁ[
ϩⲁⲥ̣[
+ⲉⲣⲟ̣[

]ϣ̣ⲁⲣⲉ-
]ⲕⲛ
ⲟ]ⲩⲁ ⲉⲓ
?
]ⲉϥ-
[. ⲣ̄ϩⲗ]ⲗ̣ⲟ' [a] ⲛ̄ϥ-
[ⲉⲅⲕⲣⲁ]ⲧⲉⲩⲉ'
[ⲙ̄ⲙⲟ]ϥ ⲛ̄ⲥⲉ-
]ⲥ̣ ⲉⲣⲟϥ'
]ⲉⲅⲕⲣⲁ-
[ⲧⲉⲩⲉ ⲁⲗ]ⲗⲁ' ⲟⲩ-
[ⲙⲛ̄ⲧⲁ]ⲧϭⲟⲙ'
ⲡ]ⲥⲱⲙⲁ'
ⲥ]ⲛⲁⲩ'
?
]ⲓⲁ
margin

ϣⲁⲛⲧⲕ̄ⲣ̄-
ϩ̄ⲗ̄ⲗⲟ' ⲛ̄ⲅⲙⲉ-
ⲧⲁⲛⲟⲉⲓ ·
+ⲙⲏ ⲁⲕⲥⲙ̄ⲛ̄
ⲇⲓⲁⲑⲏⲕⲏ
ⲙⲛ̄ⲡⲙⲟⲩ'
ⲁⲛ' ϩⲛ̄ⲧⲉⲕ-
ⲙⲛ̄ⲧⲕⲟⲩⲓ̈ ·
+ⲟⲩⲣⲱⲙⲉ' ⲉϥ-
ⲣ̄ⲛⲟⲃⲉ' ⲉϥ-
ⲕⲱ' ⲛ̄ϩⲧⲏϥ'
ⲉⲡⲛⲁ' ⲙ̄ⲡⲛⲟⲩ-
ⲧⲉ' ⲉϥϫⲱ'
ⲙ̄ⲙⲟⲥ' ϫⲉ-
margin

[a] ⲉϥⲉⲣ- or ⲉϥⲛⲁⲣ-.

Fol. 4. *Recto.* . . . they remaining (*lit.* sitting) placidly (καλῶς) with them that are in the water, and all come on to dry-land and are all saved. This is the manner of him who shall find a single grape in his cluster,[1] that is to say, a portion (μέρος) of repentance (μετ.). God's pitifulness reacheth all of them . . . . .

Verso. . . . when] he [shall] grow old and be temperate (ἐγκρατεύειν) and they . . . him . . . be temperate (ἐγκ.). But (ἀλλά) [it is] an impossi-[bility that ? the] body (σῶμα) . . . two (?) . . . . .

. . . torment and didst arise (saying,) 'I will be temperate (ἐγκ.) and will repent (μετ.).' Thou knowest not that thou shalt live till thou be old and (then) repent (μετ.). Hast thou (μή) established a covenant (διαθ.) with death[2] in thy youth? A man that, sinning, turneth his thoughts to God's mercy, saying, ...

[1] *Cf.* Isa. lxv. 8 (Sa'id. *ed.* Schleifer).

[2] *Cf.* Isa. xxviii. 15, 18.

Fol. 5. ↑ p. ⲓ̄ⲉ̄.

margin

[ⲉⲓϣⲁ]ⲛⲙⲟ̊ⲩ'
[ⲉⲣⲉⲡⲛ]ⲁⲏⲧ'
[ⲡ̄]ⲛⲟⲩⲧⲉ' [a]
[ⲛ]ⲁⲣ̣̄ⲟⲩⲛⲁ'
[ⲛ]ⲙ̄ⲙⲁⲓ̈ ⲛ̄ϥ-
[ⲕⲱ'] ⲛⲁⲛⲟⲃⲉ'
[ⲉⲃ]ⲟⲗ ⲛ̄ϥϭⲱ'
[. .]ⲓ̣ⲟⲩⲉϩ [b] ⲛⲟ-
[ⲃⲉ] ⲉϫⲛ̄ⲛⲉϥ-
[ⲛⲟ]ⲃ̣ⲉ ⲛ̄ϥ-
[ⲧ]ⲙ̄ ⲙⲉⲧⲁ-
ⲛⲟⲉⲓ̄· ⲡⲁⲓ̈
ⲛ̄ⲧⲉⲓⲙⲓⲛⲉ'
ⲟ̄ ⲛ̄ϣⲙ̄ⲙⲟ̄
ⲉⲡⲛⲁ' ⲙ̄ⲡⲛ̄ⲟ̊-
ⲩ̣ⲧ̣ⲉ' ⲡ̄ⲡⲁⲛ-
[ⲧⲟⲕⲣⲁ]ⲧⲱⲣ'
[. . . .]ⲡ̣ⲕⲟⲥ .

margin

+ⲛ̄ϩⲏⲧⲟⲩ ⲉϥⲟ̄
ⲙ̄ⲙⲁⲅⲟⲥ'·
ⲡⲁⲓ̈ ⲛ̄ⲧⲓⲙ̣ⲓ̣ⲛ̣ⲉ̣'
ⲉϥϣⲁⲛⲙⲟⲩ'
ⲙ̄ⲡⲁⲧⲉϥⲙⲉ-
ⲧⲁⲛⲟⲉⲓ̄· ϥ̄ⲛⲁ-
+ⲕⲁⲧⲁⲛⲧⲁ'
ⲉⲁⲙⲛ̄ⲧⲉ' ⲙ̣̄-
ⲡⲉⲥⲏⲧ'· ⲡⲙ[ⲁ']
+ⲉⲧⲉⲙⲙ̄ⲛ̄ⲗⲁⲁⲩ
ⲛ̄ⲟⲩⲟ̄ⲉⲓⲛ'
ⲛ̄ϩⲏⲧϥ· [ⲟⲩ-]
+ϫⲉ ⲡⲛⲟⲩⲧⲉ
ⲛⲁⲣ̄ⲡ[ⲙⲉ]ⲉⲩⲉ̣
ⲁⲛ' ⲛ̄[ⲛⲉⲧ-]
ϩⲙ̄ⲡⲙⲁ' ⲉ[ⲧⲙ̄-]
ⲙⲁⲩ' ϣⲁⲉ-
ⲛⲉϩ· ⲟ̣[ⲩⲭⲣⲏⲥ-]
ⲧ̣ⲓⲁⲛⲟⲥ [ⲉϥ-]
[ⲛⲁ]ϫⲓ̣ⲥ̣[

→ p. ⲓ̄ⲋ̄.

ⲓ̄ⲥ̄ ⳨ ⲭ̄ⲥ̄

ⲧⲉ ⲛⲧⲁϥⲁⲁⲥ'·
+ⲟⲩⲭⲣⲏⲥⲧⲓⲁ-
ⲛⲟⲥ' ⲉϥⲛⲁϫⲓ
ϭⲟⲗ' ϩⲛ̄ⲗⲁⲁⲩ'
ⲛ̄ϩⲱⲃ' ⲛ̄ⲟⲩ-
ⲭⲣⲏⲥⲧⲓⲁⲛⲟⲥ'
ⲁⲛ'ⲡⲉ· ⲟⲩ-
+ⲣⲱⲙⲉ ⲉϥⲱ̄-
ⲣ̄ⲕ' ⲙ̄ⲡⲣⲁⲛ' ⲙ̄-
ⲡⲛⲟⲩⲧⲉ' ⲛ-
ⲛⲟⲩϫ' ⲉϥⲧⲁ-
ⲕⲉ' ⲙ̄ⲙⲟϥ ⲛ̄-
ϩⲁϩ ⲛ̄ⲥⲟⲡ'
ⲡⲛⲟⲩⲧⲉ ⲛⲁ-
ⲧⲁⲕⲟϥ' ⲛ̄ϥⲣ̄
ϭⲣⲱϭ' [c] ⲙ̄ⲡⲟⲉⲓⲕ'
[ⲙ̄]ⲡ̣ⲁⲧ̣ϥⲙⲟⲩ·
[+ⲟⲩⲭ]ⲣ̣ⲏ[ⲥ]ⲧ[ⲓⲁ-]
[ⲛⲟⲥ

ⲫⲩⲗ[ⲁⲕⲧⲏ-]
ⲣⲓⲟⲛ̣ [
ⲛ̄ⲟⲩⲙ[
ⲛ̣ⲥⲉ[
ⲉϫⲱϥ' [
ⲟⲩⲛⲉ[
ⲥ̄ⲉ̄ϥ'· ⲛ̄ [ⲉϥ-]
ⲛⲁⲃⲱ̣[ⲕ
ϩⲟⲗⲱ[ⲥ']
ⲉⲡⲙⲁ̣' [ⲛⲟⲩ-]
ⲣⲉϥⲙ[ⲟⲩⲧⲉ]
ⲏ̄ ⲟⲩⲣⲉϥ-
ⲕⲁ ⲟⲩⲛⲟⲩ'·
+ⲡⲁⲓ̈ ⲛ̄ⲧⲉⲓ-
ⲙⲓⲛⲉ' ⲁⲩ-
ⲟⲩⲱ' ⲉⲩⲕⲱ
ⲙ̄ⲙⲟϥ' ⲛ̣[ⲁ-]
ϩⲏ[ⲩ

[a] Perhaps too little, but grammar forbids ⲙⲡⲛⲟⲩⲧⲉ. [b] Should be ⲉϥⲟⲩⲉϩ.
[c] So copy, but must be ϭⲣⲱϩ.

Fol. 5. P. 15. . . . 'If I] die, the merciful God shall have mercy with me and forgive my sins,' and he continueth adding sin to his sin and repenting (*μετ.*) not; such an one as this is estranged from the mercy of God Almighty (*παντοκρ.*) . . . . .

. . . therein, being a magician (*μάγος*). Such an one as this, if he die ere he have repented (*μετ.*), shall reach (*καταντᾶν*) the nether hell,[1] the place

[1] *Cf.* Ps. lxxxv. 13.

where no light is, neither (*οὐδέ*) shall God remember them that are in that place for ever. A Christian (χρ.) that shall . . . . .

P. 16 (*last of a quire*). . . . that he hath done. A Christian (χρ.) that shall lie in anything is not a Christian. A man that sweareth by God's name falsely destroyeth himself many times. God shall destroy him, and he shall be in want of bread ere he die. A Christian . . . . .

. . . amulet (*φυλακτήριον*) . . . . shall go (?) . . . at all (*ὅλως*) to the place of a wizard or (*ἤ*) a soothsayer, such an one hath already been stripped [of baptism (?)[1] . . . . .

Fol. 6. → p. ⲓ̅ⲍ̅.	ⲓ̅ⲥ̅ ⳨ ⲭ̅ⲥ̅	↑ p. ⲓ̅ⲏ̅.	
]ⲟ̣ⲩⲥϩⲓ-	+ⲉⲛϣⲁⲛⲣⲛⲉ-	ⲕⲁⲗⲱⲥ ⲕ̄ⲡⲓⲥ-	ⲧⲓⲥⲙ̣[ⲁ
[ⲙⲉ ⲉ]ⲥⲡⲟⲣ-	ϩⲃⲏⲩⲉ' ⲙ̄-	ⲧⲉⲩⲉ' ⲉⲡⲙⲟⲩ'	ϥⲉⲧ[ⲧⲉϥ-]
[ⲛⲉⲩ]ⲉ' ⲉⲩⲛ̄-	ⲡⲃⲁⲡⲧⲓⲥⲙⲁ	ⲛ̄ⲓ̅ⲥ̅' ⲙ̅ⲛ̅ⲧⲉϥ-	ⲥⲫⲣⲁ[ⲅⲓⲥ]
[ⲧⲥ ϩ]ⲁⲓ̈ ⲁⲩ-	ⲉⲓⲉ ⲕⲁⲗⲱⲥ	ⲁⲛⲁⲥⲧⲁⲥⲓ̅ⲥ̅:	ⲉⲃⲟⲗ̣ [ϩⲛⲧ-]
]ⲡⲉ̣ ⲁⲛ'	ⲁⲛϫⲓ ⲡⲃⲁⲡ-	+ⲁⲕϫⲓ ⲡⲃⲁⲡ-	ⲧⲉϩⲛ[ⲉ
]ⲓ̣ ⲉⲃⲟⲗ'	ⲧⲓⲥⲙⲁ'· ⲙ̄-	ⲧⲓⲥⲙⲁ ⲁⲕϯ	ⲡⲱϩ' ⲉ̣[
[ϩⲛ]ⲧ̣̅ⲙ̅ⲛ̅ⲧ-	+ⲡ̄ⲣ̄ⲧⲣⲉⲛϣⲟⲩ-	ⲡⲉⲭ̅ⲥ̅ ϩⲓⲱ̄ⲱⲕ'	ⲉⲧⲙ̄[
[ⲭⲣⲏ]ⲥⲧⲓⲁ-	ϣⲟⲩ' ⲙ̄ⲙⲟⲛ'	ⲉⲕϣⲁⲛⲕⲁ-	ⲛ̄ⲥⲉⲡ̣[
[ⲛⲟⲥ]· ⲁⲛⲟⲕ'	ϫⲉⲁⲛⲫⲟⲣⲉⲓ̈	ⲁⲕ' ⲕⲁϩⲏⲩ ⲙ̄-	ⲗⲁⲁⲩ [ⲙ̄ⲙⲁ-]
[ⲅⲣⲏ]ⲅⲱⲣⲓⲟⲥ'	ⲙ̄ⲡⲉⲥⲭⲏⲙⲁ'	ⲙⲟϥ' ϩⲓⲧ̅ⲛ̅-	ⲉⲓⲛ' ⲙ̄[ⲙ̅ⲛ̅ⲧ-]
[ⲙⲡ]ⲉⲓϫⲱ'	ⲛ̄ⲧⲡⲓⲥⲧⲓⲥ'	ⲛⲉⲕϩⲃⲏⲩⲉ'	ⲭⲣⲏⲥ[ⲧⲓⲁ-]
[ⲙⲡⲁⲓ] ⲁⲛ'ϩⲁ-	ⲛ̄ⲧⲛ̄ϭⲛ̄ ⲧⲡⲓⲥ-	ⲉⲑⲟⲟⲩ' ⲉⲓⲉ	ⲛⲟⲥ' [
[ⲣⲟⲓ ⲙ]ⲁⲩⲁ-	+ⲧⲓⲥ' ⲉⲥⲟ̄ ⲛ̄-	ⲁⲕⲁⲁⲕ' ⲛ̄ⲁⲣ-	+Ⲟⲩⲟ̣[ⲓ ⲛⲁⲕ]
[ⲁⲧ ⲁⲓ]ⲙ̣ⲟⲩ-	ⲁⲣⲅⲟⲛ'· ⲧⲡⲓⲥ-	ⲅⲟⲛ'· ⲉϣⲁⲩ-	ⲉⲩⲧ̅ⲙ̅[ϭⲛ]
[ϣ]ⲧ̣' ϩⲛ̄ⲛ̄ⲛⲟ-	ⲧⲓⲥ' ⲉϫ̅ⲛ̅ⲛⲉ-	+ⲙⲟⲩⲧⲉ' ⲉϩⲛⲟ̄	ⲡⲙⲁⲉ[ⲓⲛ]
[ⲙ]ⲟ̣ⲥ' ⲛ̄ⲧⲁ-	ϩⲃⲏⲩⲉ' ⲥⲟ̄	ⲛⲓⲙ ⲉϥⲛⲁⲣ̄	ⲙ̄ⲡⲙⲟ[ⲩ]
[ⲛⲉ]ⲛⲉⲓⲟⲧⲉ'	ⲛ̄ⲁⲣⲅⲟⲛ'·	ⲁⲥ' ⲛ̄ⲥⲉⲧⲁ-	ⲙ̄ⲡⲉⲭ̅ⲥ̅ [ϩⲓ-]
[ⲉ]ⲧⲟⲩⲁⲁⲃ'	+ⲕⲁⲗⲱⲥ ⲕ̄ⲡⲓⲥ-	ⲕⲟ̄' ϫⲉⲁⲣⲅⲟⲛ'·	ⲱ̄ⲱⲕ' ⲉ-
[ⲛ̄]ⲁⲡⲟⲥⲧⲟ-	ⲧⲉⲩⲉ' ⲉⲡⲛⲟⲩ-	+ⲉⲛⲧ̅ⲙ̅ⲣ̄ⲛⲉ-	ⲡⲉϥⲥ̅⳨̅[ⲟ̅ⲥ̅-]

[1] *Cf.* p. ⲓ̅ⲏ̅.

[ⲗ]ⲟⲥ ⲕⲁⲛⲱ-
[ⲛ]ϊϫⲉ ⲙ̄ⲙⲟ-
[ⲟⲩ ⲛⲛⲉ]ⲧⲛ̣ⲁ-

ⲧⲉ' · ⲛ̄ⲕⲉ-
ⲇⲁⲓⲙⲟⲛⲓⲟⲛ'
ϩⲱⲟⲩ ⲟⲛ'
ⲡⲓⲥⲧⲉⲩⲉ'
[ⲁ]ⲩⲱ' ⲥⲉⲥⲧ[ⲱⲧ']

ϩⲃⲏⲩⲉ' ⲙ̄ⲡⲃⲁⲡ-
ⲧⲓⲥⲙⲁ' ⲁⲕ-
ⲧⲁⲕⲟ̄ ⲙ̄ⲡⲃⲁⲡ-
ⲧⲓⲥⲙⲁ · ⲥⲉ̣-
[ⲛⲁ]ⲕⲁⲁⲕ' ⲕ[ⲁϩⲏⲩ]

ⲡⲉ' ϫⲉ[ⲕ-]
ⲛⲁⲣ̄ⲟⲩ [

Fol. 6. P. 17 (*first of a quire*). . . . a woman that fornicateth (*πορνεύειν*), she having an husband . . . . out from Christianity (-*χρηστιανός*). I, Gregory, I have not said this of myself alone; I have studied (?) the laws (*νόμ.*) which our fathers the apostles (*ἀπ.*) did fix (*κανονίζειν*) [for them ?] that should . . . . .

. . . If we do the deeds of baptism (*βάπτισμα*), then (is it) well (*καλῶς*) that we have received baptism (*βάπ.*). Let us not boast ourselves that we wear (*φορεῖν*) the habit (*σχῆμα*) of faith (*πίσ.*), and (then) find faith barren (*ἀργός*). 'Faith without works is barren (*ἀρ.*).'[1] (It is) well (*καλῶς*) thou believe (*πιστεύειν*) in God; the devils (*δαιμόνιον*) also believe and tremble[2] . . . . .

P. 18. (It is) well (*καλῶς*) thou believe (*πιστ.*) in the death of Jesus and His resurrection (*ἀνάστ.*). Thou hast received baptism (*βάπτ.*) and hast clothed thee with Christ. If thou strip thyself of Him through thy evil deeds, then hast thou made thyself barren (*ἀργός*), every vessel that is becoming old and perished being called barren (useless *ἀρ.*). If thou do not the deeds of baptism (*βάπ.*), thou hast destroyed baptism: thou shalt be stripped . . . . .

. . . wipe off its (?) seal (*σφραγίς*) from the brow . . . . . and they . . . no sign of Christianity (-*χρ.*). Woe [unto thee], if the sign of Christ's death be not [found] upon thee, which is His cross (*στ.*). For what wilt thou do? . . . . .

Fol. 7. ↑ p. ⲓ̄ⲑ̄.

margin
ⲧ̄ⲕ ⲉⲧⲃⲉⲛⲉⲕ-
ϩⲃⲏⲩⲉ' ⲉⲑⲟ-
ⲟⲩ' · ⲧⲡⲓⲥⲧⲓⲥ'

→ p. ⲕ̄.

margin
ⲉⲣⲟⲟⲩ' ϫⲉ-
ⲛⲉⲧⲧⲁⲕⲟ̄
ⲛ̄ ⲛⲉⲛⲧⲁⲩ- +ϩ[

[1] Jas. ii. 20.

[2] *Ib.* 19.

]ⲉ̣ⲧⲙ
]ⲉⲣⲉ-
]ⲉ
]ⲉⲡⲉⲕ-
]ⲉⲕ-
]ⲱϣ'
[ⲉⲃⲟⲗ] ϫ̣ⲉⲁⲛⲅ̄-
[ⲟⲩⲭⲣⲏⲥ]ⲧⲓⲁ-
[ⲛⲟⲥ ϩⲱ]ⲱⲧ
[ⲁⲓϫⲓ] ⲙ̣ⲡⲃⲁⲡ-
[ⲧⲓ]ⲥⲙⲁ'
[ⲉⲡ]ⲣⲁⲛ' ⲙ̄-
[ⲡ]ⲉⲭ̄ⲥ̄ · ⲁⲓ̈ϫⲓ
ⲡⲉⲕⲥⲱⲙⲁ'
[ⲛ]ⲛⲟⲩⲧⲉ'
[ⲙⲛ]ⲡⲉⲕⲥⲛⲟϥ'
ⲛ]ⲁϫⲟⲟⲥ
]ⲧ .

+ⲉϫⲙ̄ⲡⲉϩⲃⲏⲩⲉ'
ⲥⲟ̄ ⲛ̄ⲁⲣⲅⲟⲛ' ·
+ⲁⲓ̈ϫⲟⲟⲥ' ⲛ̄ⲕⲉ-
ⲥⲟⲡ' · ϫⲉⲉϣⲁⲩ-
ⲙⲟⲩⲧⲉ' ⲉϩⲛⲟ̄
ⲛⲓⲙ' ⲉϥⲛⲁⲣ̄
ⲁⲥ ⲛ̄ⲥⲉⲧⲁⲕⲟ̄
ϫⲉⲁⲣⲅⲟⲛ' ·
+ⲉⲓⲧⲉ' ϩⲛⲟ̄' ⲛ̄-
ϩⲟⲙ̄ⲛ̄ⲧ : ⲉⲓ-
ⲧⲉ' ϩⲛⲟ̄' ⲛϩⲁⲧ'
ⲉⲓⲧⲉ' ⲛⲟⲩⲃ'
+ⲉⲥϣⲁⲛϣⲱ-
ⲡⲉ ⲛ̄ⲥⲉⲣ̄ⲁⲥ
ⲛ̄ⲥⲉⲧⲁⲕⲟ̄
+ϣⲁⲩⲟⲩⲟⲧϩⲟ[ⲩ]
ⲛ̄ⲕⲉⲥⲟⲡ' ⲛ̄-
ⲥⲉⲁⲁⲩ' ⲛ̄ⲃⲣ̄-
sic ⲃⲉ' ⲛ̄ⲥⲉⲗⲟ̄
ⲉ̣ⲩ̣[ⲙ]ⲟⲩⲧⲉ
margin

ⲧⲁⲕⲟ̄ · ⲛ̄ⲧⲟⲕ'
+ϩⲱⲱⲕ' ⲉⲕ-
ϣⲁⲛⲉⲓⲙⲉ'
ϫⲉⲁⲕⲣ̄ⲁⲧ-
ϣⲁⲩ' ⲛ̄ⲥⲁ'ⲥⲁ'
ⲛⲓⲙ' · ϭⲉⲡⲏ
ⲡⲱⲧ' ⲉⲣⲁⲧϥ̄
ⲙ̄ⲡⲉⲑⲏⲥⲓ-
ⲁⲥⲧⲩⲣⲓⲟⲛ' ·
+ⲡⲱϩ̄ⲧ ⲙ̄ⲡⲉⲕ-
ⲣ̄ⲙⲉⲓⲟ̄ⲟⲩⲉ'
ϩⲓⲟⲛ' ⲙ̄ⲡⲉ-
ⲭ̄ⲥ̄' · ϩⲓⲟⲩⲉ'
ⲉϩⲟⲩⲛ' ϩⲙ̄ⲧⲉⲕ-
ⲙⲉⲥⲑ̄ⲏⲧ' ·
ⲉⲕϫⲱ' ⲙ̄ⲙⲟⲥ
ϫⲉⲁⲓ̈ⲣ̄ⲛⲟⲃⲉ'
ⲡϫⲟⲉⲓⲥ'
ⲕⲱ' ⲛⲁⲓ̈ ⲉⲃⲟⲗ'
ⲛ̄ⲛⲛⲟⲃⲉ'
ⲙ̄ⲡⲁϩⲟⲩ'
ⲛ̄ϯⲛⲁⲟⲩⲱϩ
[ⲁⲛ ⲉⲧⲟⲟ]ⲧ

ⲏ̣[
ⲧ[
ⲛ̄ⲓ̣[
ⲉⲣ̣[
+ⲱ ⲁ[ⲕⲁϣⲁ-]
ϩⲟⲙ [
ϩⲓⲑⲏ̣ [ⲙ̄ⲡⲉ-]
ⲑⲏ[ⲥⲓⲁⲥⲧⲩ-]
ⲣ[ⲓⲟⲛ
ⲥⲁϩⲱ̣[ⲱⲕ]
ⲉⲃⲟⲗ' [ⲛⲛⲉⲕ-]
ⲛⲟⲃⲉ' [ⲛ̄ⲧ-]
ⲧ̄ⲙ̄ⲕ[ⲧⲟⲕ]
ⲉⲣⲟⲟⲩ [ⲁⲩⲱ]
+ⲁⲛⲟⲕ' [ϯⲛⲁ-]
ϣ̄ⲡ̄ ⲧⲱ̣[ⲣⲉ]
ⲛⲁⲕ' ϫ̣[ⲉⲛ-]
ⲛⲉⲕ[

Fol. 7. P. 19. . . . thou . . . cry out, 'I too am a Christian (χρ.); I have received baptism (βάπ.) in the name of Christ; I have received Thy divine body (σῶμα) [and] Thy blood . . . . . shall say . . . . .

. . . thee because of thy evil deeds. Faith without works is barren (ἀργός).[1] I say once more that every vessel that is becoming old and perished is called useless (ἀργ.), be it (εἴτε) vessel of bronze or (εἴτε) vessel

[1] Jas. ii. 20.

of silver or (εἴτε) gold. If so be that they grow old and perished, they are molten again and made new and cease to be called

P. 20. perishable or (ἤ) perished.[1] Thou likewise, if thou know that thou art useless altogether (*lit.* on every side), hasten, flee unto the altar (θυσιαστήριον); pour forth thy tears before Christ; beat thy breast, saying, 'I have sinned; Lord, forgive me the sins of the past (*lit.* of behind); I will not continue' . . . . .

. . . hast] groaned . . . before the altar (? θυσ.) . . . departed far from [thy] sins [and tu]rned not again unto them, I it is will go surety for thee, that thou do [not . . .

Fol. 8. → *Recto*,[a] p. ?		↑ *Verso*, p. ?	
	margin	margin	
	✝ ⲁⲅⲁⲡ̄ⲏ̄’ ⲛⲁⲩ’	ⲉⲡⲉⲥⲏⲧ’	
	ⲣ̄ⲭⲣⲓⲁ’ ⲁⲛ’·	ⲉϫⲙ̄ⲡⲟⲉⲓⲕ’	
]ⲡⲛ̊	+ⲟⲩⲛ̄ϩⲟⲉⲓⲛⲉ’	ⲙ̄ⲛ̄ⲡ̄ⲡⲟⲁⲏ-	
	ⲉⲩϯⲡⲣⲟⲥ-	ⲣⲓⲟⲛ’ ⲛ̄ϥⲥⲱ-	+ⲉ[
	ⲫⲟⲣⲁ’ ⲉⲡⲏⲓ̈	ⲧⲙ̄ ⲛ̄ⲥⲱⲟⲩ’	
]ⲙ̄	ⲙ̄ⲡⲛⲟⲩⲧⲉ’	ⲛ̄ϥⲉⲓ’· ⲉⲓϫⲉ-	ϩ[
]ⲡⲛ̊ⲩ-	ⲉⲣⲉⲡⲉⲩϩⲏⲧ’	+ⲣⲟⲕ’ ⲛ̄ⲧⲟⲕ’	ⲉⲓ̣[
[ⲧⲉ . ϩ̄ⲙ̄]ϩⲁⲗ’	ϭⲛ̄ ⲁⲣⲓⲕⲉ’	ⲱ̄ ⲡⲗⲁⲓ̈ⲕⲟⲥ’	ⲧⲁ[
]ϩⲱ	ⲉⲣⲟⲟⲩ’ ϫⲉ-	ⲙ̄ⲡⲣ̄ⲕⲣⲓⲛⲉ	ⲉⲣ[
]ⲕ̣ⲟⲩ	ⲛⲉⲧⲛ̄ϯ	ⲛ̄ⲛⲉⲧⲉⲣⲉ-	+ϣⲁ̣[
]ⲡⲛⲁ’	ⲡⲣⲟⲥⲫⲟⲣⲁ’	ⲡⲛⲟⲩⲧⲉ’	ⲟ̣ⲓ̣[
	ⲛⲁⲩ’ ϩⲉⲛⲣⲉϥ-	ⲥⲱⲧⲙ̄’ ⲉⲣⲟ-	ⲧ̣[
	ⲣ̄ⲛⲟⲃⲉ’ⲛⲉ’	ⲟⲩ’· ⲕⲁⲛ’ ϩⲉ̄-	ⲧ̣[
ⲗ]ⲁⲁⲩ’ ⲛⲁ-	ⲛ̄ⲧⲉⲛϩⲉ’ ⲉⲧⲉ-	+ⲣⲉϥⲣ̄ⲛⲟⲃⲉ’-	ⲧⲙ[
[ⲛⲟ]ⲩϩ̣ⲙ̄’ ⲡⲣⲱ-	ⲛⲁⲉⲧⲟⲥ’ⲛⲉ’	ⲛⲉ’ ⲙ̄ⲛ̄ⲧⲁⲕ-	ⲧⲉⲧⲱ̣[

[a] The traces of pagination here might be ⲗ̄ and a second letter; not ⲗ̄ and ⲗ̄ⲁ̄, since these would not, by rights, fall upon the same leaf.

[1] *Lit.* 'they that perish or that have perished'. It is not easy to reproduce this in idiomatic English.

[ⲙⲉ] ⲛ̄ⲥⲁⲧⲁ-	ⲉⲧⲟⲩⲁⲁⲃ'	ϩⲱⲃ' ⲛ̄ⲧⲟⲕ'	ⲛ̄ⲓ̈ⲉⲍ̣ⲉ[ⲕⲓⲏⲗ]
[ⲅⲁ]ⲡⲏ̄ · ⲧⲁ-	ⲛ̄ⲕⲗⲏⲣⲓⲕⲟⲥ	ⲛ̄ⲧⲁⲩⲧⲁⲛ-	ⲉⲓ ⲉϫⲛ̄[ⲧⲏⲩ-]
[ⲅⲁⲡ]ⲏ̄ · ⲙⲉⲥ-	+ⲡⲁï ⲉϣⲁⲩ-	ϩⲟⲩⲧⲕ̄' ⲁⲛ'	ⲧⲛ̄' · ⲉ[ⲣⲉ-]
[ϣⲓ]ⲛⲉ' ⲛ̄ⲥⲁ-	ϫⲟⲟⲥ' ⲙ̄ⲡⲛ̄ⲟⲩ-	ⲉⲣⲟⲟⲩ' ⲉⲧⲣⲉⲕ-	+ⲡⲉⲥⲛⲟ[ϥ ⲙ̄-]
[ⲛ]ⲉ̣ⲧⲉⲛⲟⲩⲥ-	ⲧⲉ' ϩⲓⲧⲙ̄-	ⲡⲣⲉⲥⲃⲉⲩⲉ'	ⲡⲟⲩⲁ' [ⲡⲟⲩⲁ']
[ⲛⲉ ·] ⲟⲩⲛ̄-	ⲡϣⲁϫⲉ' ⲛ̄-	ϩⲁⲛⲉⲩⲛⲟⲃⲉ'	ⲛⲁⲉⲓ ⲉ[ϫⲛ̄-]
[ϩⲟⲉⲓⲛ]ⲉ ⲉⲩ-	ⲧⲉⲩⲧⲁⲡⲣⲟ	ⲁⲗⲗⲁ ⲛ̄ⲧⲁⲩ-	ⲧⲉϥ̣[
]ⲛ̣ ⲉⲣⲉ-	ⲙ̄ⲙⲁⲧⲉ' ϫⲉ-	ⲧⲁⲛϩⲟⲩⲧⲟ̣ⲩ'	+ⲉⲧ̣[
	ⲕⲁⲧⲁⲍ̄ⲓⲟⲩ	ⲉⲛⲉⲧⲙ̄ⲯⲩ-	
	ⲙ̣̄ⲙ̣ⲟⲕ' ⲁⲙ-	ⲭ̄ⲏ' ⲉⲧⲣⲉⲩ-	
	[ⲟⲩ]		

Fol. 8. *Recto.* . . . nought shall save (?) [1] a man except charity (ἀγάπη). 'Charity seeketh not the things that are her own.' [2] There are [some] do . . . . .

. . . to whom charity (ἀγ.) is given that need (-χρεία) it not. There are some do make offering (προσφορά) at the house of God, whose heart accuseth them (saying,) 'Those unto whom we give offerings (πρ.) are sinful men like unto us,' that is, the holy eagles (ἀετός) [3] the clergy (κληρικός), that do say unto God, with the mere words of their mouth, 'Be favourable (καταξιοῦν), come

(*Verso*) down upon the bread and the cup (ποτήριον),' and He heareth them and doth come. I say unto thee,[4] O layman (λαικός), judge (κρίνειν) not them whom God heareth,[5] even (κἄν) be they sinful men: thou hast nought (to do with that). Hast thou been entrusted with them, that thou shouldest intercede (πρεσβεύειν) for their sins? Rather (ἀλλά) have they been entrusted with your souls (ψυ.), that they may . . . . .

. . . to (?) Ezekiel [shall] come upon you.[6] The blood of [each] one shall come u[pon] his [[7] . . . . .

[1] If so, ⲛⲉϩⲙ is required. But this scribe is not very accurate. [2] 1 Cor. xiii. 5.

[3] *Cf. Can. Athanas.* p. 16, where the same simile is used. A sermon on Epiphany (Paris 131[4], 114 = MS. of Br. Mus. no. 257 &c.) refers to the deacons at the sacrament as 'the eagles flapping (ⲧⲁⲁⲧⲉ) their wings around the body (σῶμα)'.

[4] *V.* p. 65 note.

[5] The difference achieved by the varying preposition is between mere *hearing* here and *acquiescing, obeying* in the preceding sentence.

[6] *V.* Ezek. iii. 18.

[7] ? 'hand'; *cf.* Ezek., *l. c.*

Fol. 9. ↑ *Recto.*		→ *Verso.*	
	ϫⲉ [ⲙ̄ⲡⲉϥϫⲟ-]	]ϥⲧⲁ-	
ⲟⲩ]ⲕⲟⲩⲛ̄	ⲟⲥ’ ϫⲉ[ⲁⲕⲁϩ-]	]ϥ̣ⲥⲙⲟⲩ’	ⲙⲁ̣[
[ⲁⲧⲉ]ⲧⲛ̄ⲉⲓ-	ⲉⲣⲁⲧⲕ̣ [ⲛ̄ⲥⲁ-]	]’ · ⲉⲓⲉ	⳨ⲡⲁⲛⲟ̣[ⲩ ⲅⲁⲣ]
ⲙⲉ [a] ⲱ̄ ⲛⲁ-	ϩⲃⲟⲩ[ⲣ ⲙ̄ⲡϩⲏ-]	[ⲡⲉⲥ]ⲱ̣ⲧⲙ’ ⲁⲛ’	†’ ⲁⲅⲁⲡⲏ̣ [
ⲙⲉⲣⲁⲧⲉ’ ϫⲉ-	ⲕⲉ’ · ⲁ[ⲗⲗⲁ]	[ϫⲉϣⲁ]ⲣⲉⲡⲉⲧ-	ⲛ̄ⲟⲩⲁ’ ⲛ̄ϩ[ⲟⲩⲟ]
ⲧ̣ⲉⲧⲉⲣⲧ̣[.]	⳨[ⲁ]ϥϫⲟⲟ̣ⲥ̣ [d]	[† ⲛ]ⲟⲩϩ[ⲏⲕⲉ]’	ⲉⲣⲟⲥ’ ⲉⲕ̣[ϣⲁⲛ-]
ⲟⲙ̣ⲡⲟⲩⲁ̣	[ϫⲉ]ⲁⲕⲁϩ’-	† ϩⲁⲧ’ ⲉ[ⲙ]ⲏ-	ϫⲓ̄ ⲛ̄ⲧⲟ[ⲟⲧ [e]
]ⲙⲟϥ’	[ⲉⲣ]ⲁⲧⲕ ⲛ̄ⲥⲁ-	ⲥⲉ’ ⲙ̄ⲡⲛ[ⲟⲩ-]	ⲛ̄ⲕⲟ̣ⲧ̣[
] ⲙ̣̄ⲙⲟϥ’ ·	[ⲟ]ⲩⲛⲁⲙ’ ⲙ̄-	ⲧⲉ’ · ⲉⲓⲉ [ⲉⲓ-]	⳨ⲉⲓⲉ ⲛ̣[
] ⲉⲧϭⲓϫ’	ⲡϩⲏⲕⲉ’ ·	ⲥ̣ⲱⲧⲙ ⲁⲛⲟⲕ	ϩⲁⲙ̣[
[ⲙⲡⲉ]ⲭ︦ⲥ︦ ⲓ︦ⲥ︦ ·	⳨[ⲉ]ⲡⲉⲓⲇ︦ⲏ︦ ⲣⲱ-	ϫⲉⲉⲫ ⲟⲥⲱⲛ	ϫⲉ[
[ⲡⲉⲛ]ϫⲟⲉⲓⲥ̣ [b]	ⲙⲉ’ ⲛⲓⲙ’ ⲉϥ†	ⲁⲧⲉⲧⲛ̄ⲁⲁ̣[ⲥ]	ⲧⲉ’ ⲧ[
]ⲥ̣ⲱⲧⲙ̄	ϩ̄[ⲛ̄]ⲧⲉϥϭⲓϫ	ⲛ̄ⲟⲩⲁ’ ⲛ̄[ⲛ]ⲉⲓ-	ⲁⲩ . [
]ⲡ̣ⲉⲓⲁ [c]	[ⲛⲟⲩ]ⲛⲁⲙ’	ⲕⲟ̣ⲩⲓ̣ [ⲁⲛⲟⲕ]	ⲥ̣[
[ⲉϥϫⲱ] ⲙ̣̄ⲙⲟⲥ’	⳨ϩ[ⲙ̄ⲡ]ⲧⲣⲉϩⲏ- *sic*	ⲡⲉⲛⲧ[ⲁⲧ]ⲉⲧⲛ-	ⲉⲕ̣[
[? ⲛⲧⲉⲓ]ϩⲉ	ⲕⲉ ⲥⲟⲟⲩⲧⲛ̄	ⲁⲁⲥ’ ⲛ[ⲁϊ]	⳨ⲉⲓ̣[ⲉ
]ⲟⲩ	ⲉⲃⲟⲗ ⲛ̄ⲧⲉ[ϥ-]	[⳨ⲉ]ⲧⲃⲉⲡⲁϊ ⲉⲕ-	ϫⲉ̣[
margin	ϭⲓϫ’ ⲉϫⲓ ·	ϣⲁⲛⲣⲟⲩⲡⲉⲧ-	ⲉ̣[
	margin	ϩⲟⲟⲩ’ ⲛ̄ⲟⲩ-	ⲁ[
		margin	

[a] Or ⲙⲡⲉⲧⲛⲉⲓⲙⲉ. [b] This reading unlikely if the stop after ⲓ︦ⲥ︦ is correct. *Cf. vo.*, col. 1, ll. 3, 4 ⲉⲓⲉ. [c] ? ϫⲁ]ⲩⲉⲓⲁ. [d] Or ⲁ[ⲗⲗⲁ ⲛ][ⲧⲁϥ-. [e] Or ⲛⲧⲟⲕ.

Fol. 9. *Recto.* . . . Do ye then not (*οὐκουν*) know, O my beloved, that . . . . the hand of Christ Jesus [our] Lord . . . . . hear David (?), speaking thus, ...

. . . [He hath not] said, 'Thou hast stood at the left of the poor,' but (*ἀλλά*) he said,[1] 'Thou hast stood at the right of the poor.' Since (*ἐπειδή*) every man that giveth with his right hand, when the poor stretcheth forth his hand to receive . . . . .

[1] Ps. cviii. 31. But no text or version that I can find reads 2nd pers. thus, for 3rd.

Verso. . . . bless(ing ?) . . . Dost thou then not hear that[1] 'He that giveth unto a poor (man), lendeth at usury unto God ?' I indeed do (?) hear that[2] 'Inasmuch as (ἐφ' ὅσον) ye have done it unto one of these little ones, it is unto me ye have done it.' Wherefore if thou do evil unto a (?) . . . . .

. . . [? For (γάρ)] it is better to give charity (ἀγ.) than if thou receive from (?)[3] . . . . .

Fol. 10.	→ *Recto.*	↑ *Verso.*	
margin		margin	
	ⲙ̣ⲛⲧ’ ⲛ̄ϩⲟⲗⲟ-	ⲕⲁⲛ’ ⲟⲩⲣ̄ⲙ̄[ⲙⲁⲟ-]	
	ⲕⲟⲧⲓⲛⲟⲥ’	ⲡⲉ’ ϣⲁϥⲧⲁ-	
	ⲛ̄ⲁⲅⲁⲡ̄ⲏ̄ ⲧ̄ⲣ̄-	ⲁϥ’ ⲛⲁϥ · ⲁϥ-	
	ⲣⲟⲙⲡⲉ’ ⲟⲩⲁ’	+ⲧⲱⲟⲩ̄ⲛ̄’ ⲙ̄-	
	ⲕⲁⲧⲁ ⲟⲩⲟⲉⲓϣ’ ·	ⲡⲉⲓ̣ϩⲟⲟⲩ’ ⲁϥ-	
	+ⲁϥⲥⲱⲧ̄ⲙ̄’	ⲁⲡⲁⲛⲧⲁ’ ⲉⲩ̣-	
	ⲉⲡⲁⲩⲗⲟⲥ’	ⲛⲟϭ’ ⲛ̄ⲣ̄ⲙ̄ⲙ̄ⲙⲁⲟ	
	ⲉϥϫⲱ’ ⲙ̄ⲙͦⲥ	ϩ̄ⲛ̄ⲧⲡⲟⲗⲓⲥ’	
]ⲁⲅ-	ϫⲉⲙⲉⲣⲉⲧⲁ-	ⲁϥⲙⲟⲟϣⲉ’	
[ⲁⲡⲏ ⲁ]ⲗⲗⲁ’	ⲅⲁⲡ̄ⲏ̄’ ϣⲓⲛⲉ’	ⲉⲣⲟϥ’ ⲛ̄ϩⲱⲡ’	
] ?	ⲛ̄ⲥⲁⲛⲉⲧⲉ-	ⲁϥⲧⲁⲁϥ’	
	ⲛⲟⲩ̄ⲥ̄ⲛⲉ ·	ⲛⲁϥ’ · ⲙ̄ⲛ̄-	
	+ϣⲁϥⲧⲱⲟⲩ · (*sic*)	+ⲛ̄ⲥⲁⲧⲣⲉϥ-	
]ⲥ	ⲉϩⲧⲟⲟⲩⲉ’	ⲧⲁⲁϥ ⲛⲁϥ’	[
ⲛ]ϥⲣ̄ⲭⲣⲓⲁ’	ϩ̄ⲙ̄ⲡⲉϩⲟⲟⲩ’	ⲁϥⲥⲟⲩⲱⲛ̄ϥ̄’ ·	+ⲁϥⲥⲟ̣[
[ⲁⲛ] ⲥⲱⲧⲙ’	ⲉⲧ̄ϥ̄ⲛⲁϯ-	+ⲁϥϭⲱ’ ⲉϥϫⲓ̈-	ⲟⲛ’ · ⲁ[ⲩⲱ]
ⲧⲁⲧⲁⲙⲟⲕ’	ⲁⲅⲁⲡⲏ̄ ⲛ̄-	ⲁⲕⲣⲓⲛⲉ’ ϩ̄ⲙ̄-	+ⲉⲣⲉⲛⲉⲓ̣[ⲙⲉ-]
[ⲙ]ⲡⲉⲓϩⲱⲃ’	ϩⲏⲧ̄ϥ̄’ ϣⲁϥ-	ⲡⲉϥϩⲏⲧ’	ⲉⲩⲉ’ ϯ [ⲛ̄ⲙ̄-]
[ⲛ]ϣⲟⲩⲣ̄-	+ⲃⲱⲕ’ ⲉⲃⲟⲗ’	ϫⲉⲟⲩ̄ⲣ̄ⲙ̄ⲙⲁⲟ̄-	ⲙⲁϥ’ · ϩ̣[ⲟ-]
[ϣⲡⲏ]ⲣⲉ’ ⲙ̄-	ϩ̄ⲙ̄ⲡⲉϥⲏⲓ̈’	ⲡⲉ ⲡⲁⲓ̈ ⲡⲁ-	+ⲙⲟⲓⲱ̣[ⲥ
[ⲙⲟϥ ·] ⲛⲉⲩ-	+ⲡϣⲟ̄ⲣ̄ⲡ̄’ ⲛ̄-	ⲣⲁⲣⲟⲓ̈ · ⲁⲛⲟⲕ’	ⲁϥϯ [ⲡⲉϥ-]

[1] ? Prov. xix. 17.

[2] Matt. xxv. 40. Note the reading.

[3] Or 'if thou thyself receive' . . . . .

[ⲛⲟⲩⲣ]ⲱⲙⲉ'	ⲣⲱⲙⲉ' ⲉⲧϥ̣-	[+]ⲉⲧⲣ̄ⲭⲣⲓⲁ' ⲛ̄-	ⲟⲩ[ⲟⲓ
]ⲏ̣ⲥ̣'	ⲛⲁⲁⲡⲁⲛⲧⲁ	ϫⲓ ⲁⲅⲁⲡⲏ̄' ⲛ̄-	[
	ⲉⲣⲟϥ' ⲕⲁⲛ	ⲧⲟⲟ̄ⲧϥ̄ ·	
☩ ϣⲟ-]	[ⲟ]ⲩϩⲏⲕⲉ'ⲡ[ⲉ']	[+]ⲙ̄ⲛ̄ⲛ̄ⲥⲱⲥ [	
margin		margin	

Fol. 10. *Recto*. . . . hath [not] need (χρεία). Hearken and I will tell thee this thing, worthy of wonder. There was a man . . . . . ? was wont to give] three *solidi* (ὁλοκ.) in charity (ἀγάπη) yearly, one at (κατά) a time. He heard Paul saying,[1] 'Charity (ἀγ.) seeketh not the things that are her own.' He would arise in the morning on the day whereon he should do charity (ἀγ.), and would go forth from his house; the first man that he should meet (ἀπαντᾶν), whether (κἄν) he were a poor man, (*Verso*) or (κἄν) a rich, he would give it (*sc.* the *solidus*) unto him. He arose that day and met (ἀπ.) a great rich man of the city (πόλις) and he went toward him stealthily and gave it unto him. After that he had given it unto him he knew him, and stayed doubting (διακρίνειν) in his heart (saying), 'This man is richer than (παρά) I. It is I have need (χρεία) to receive charity (ἀγ.) at his hands.' Afterwards . . . . .

. . . and these thoughts contended with him. Likewise (ὁμοίως[2]) he betook himself (?) . . . . .

Fol. 11. → *Recto*.		↑ *Verso*.	
	margin	margin	
]ⲥ̣ⲟ̣[	ϫⲉⲧⲅⲉⲛⲏⲥ[ⲓⲥ']	ⲉⲛⲓⲙ' · ϫⲉ-	[
] ⲉⲣⲟⲥ' ⲁϥ-	ⲙ̄ⲙⲱⲩ̈ⲥⲏⲥ'	+ⲡⲙⲁ' ⲉⲧⲉⲙ̄ⲛ̄-	
	+ⲕⲁⲓ ⲅⲁⲣ' ⲛ̄ⲕⲉ-	ⲛⲟⲙⲟⲥ' ⲙ̄ⲛ̄-	
	ⲉⲓⲟ̄ⲧⲉ' ⲛ̄ⲧⲁⲩ-	ⲡⲁⲣⲁⲃⲁⲥⲓⲥ' ·	
	ϫⲡⲉ ⲙⲱⲩ̈-	+ⲡⲉϫⲁϥ' ϫⲉ-	
	ⲥⲏⲥ' ⲙ̄ⲡⲟⲩ-	ⲙ̄ⲙⲟⲛ ⲛ̄-	
	ϣⲱⲡⲉ' ϩ̄ⲛ̄-	ⲧⲉⲓϩⲉ' ⲁⲛ'-	
	ⲧⲅⲉⲛⲏⲥⲓⲥ'	ⲧⲉ ⲧⲡⲁⲣⲁ-	
	[. .]ⲗⲙ̣ⲡⲉⲧϣⲱ	ⲃⲁⲥⲓⲥ [	
	]ⲧⲏⲣ̄ⲥ̄	+ⲉ.ⲁⲥ ⲛ̄ⲧ[	

[1] 1 Cor. xiii. 5.

[2] Ὅμως 'however' would seem more suitable.

Fol. 11. *Recto.* . . . the Genesis (*γέν.*) of Moses. For (*καὶ γάρ*) the parents too that begat Moses were not in Genesis, but (? *ἀλλά*) all that . . . . .

Verso. . . . to (?) whom? 'Where there is not law, there is not transgression.' He said, 'Nay[1]; the transgression (*παράβασις*) is not of this sort . . . . .

Fol. 12. → *Recto.*

margin

ⲧ̅ⲥ̅’ ⲁⲛⲡⲉ
+ⲉⲧⲃⲉⲡⲁϊ
ⲁⲡⲁⲩⲗⲟⲥ’
ⲱϣ ⲉⲃⲟⲗ’
ϫⲉⲡⲙⲁ’ ⲉⲧⲉ-
ⲙ̅ⲛ̅ⲛⲟⲙⲟⲥ
ⲙ̅ⲛ̅ⲡⲁⲣⲁⲃⲁ-
ⲥⲓⲥ’ · ϩⲟⲙⲟⲓ-
+ⲱⲥ’ ⲟⲛ’ ϩⲣⲟⲩ-
ⲃⲏⲛ’ ⲛ̄ⲧⲁϥ-
ⲉⲛⲕⲟⲧ̅ⲕ̅
ⲙ̅ⲛ̅ⲑ(sic)ⲁⲙⲁ̣[ⲣ]
ⲑⲓⲙⲉ’ ⲙ̄[ⲡⲉϥ-]
ⲉⲓⲱⲧ [ⲁⲩⲱ]
ⲁ̣ⲃ̣ⲓⲙⲉⲗ̣[ⲉⲭ]
ⲛ̄ⲧⲁϥⲉ[ⲡⲓ-]
ⲑ̅ⲩ̅ⲙⲉⲓ̈ · [ⲁⲩⲱ]
+ⲡⲕ’ⲉⲥⲉ[ⲉⲡⲉ]
ⲛ̄ⲧⲁⲩ[
\+ ?

↑ *Verso.*

+[. . .]ⲛⲛⲟⲃⲉ ·
ⲉⲧⲃⲉϫⲉⲁⲩ-
ϯ ⲡⲛⲟⲙⲟⲥ’
ⲛⲁϥ’ ⲁϥⲡⲁⲣⲁ’-
ⲃⲁ’ ⲙ̄ⲙⲟϥ ·
+ⲡⲙⲁ’ ⲉⲧⲉ-
ⲙ̅ⲛ̅ⲛⲟⲙⲟⲥ’
ⲙ̅ⲛ̅ⲡⲁⲣⲁⲃⲁ-
ⲥⲓⲥ · ⲉⲓⲥ ⲟⲩ-
+ⲏ̅ⲣ̅ ⲛⲉⲧⲛⲁ-
ϣⲱⲡⲉ’ ⲙ̄-
ⲙⲟⲛ’ ⲁⲛⲟⲛ’
ⲛⲉⲭⲣⲏⲥⲧⲓ̈-
[ⲁⲛ]ⲟⲥ’ · ⲉⲓⲥ
[ⲛ]ⲉⲩⲁⲅⲅⲉⲗⲓ-
ⲟⲛ’ ⲁⲩⲧⲁⲁⲩ’
ⲉⲧⲟⲟⲧ̅ⲛ̅ ·
[ⲉ]ⲓ̣ⲥ ⲛⲉⲥⲃⲟ-
[ⲟ]ⲩⲉ’ ⲛ̄ⲛⲉⲛ-
[ⲉⲓ]ⲟ̄ⲧⲉ ⲉⲧⲟⲩ-
[ⲁⲁ]ⲃ’ ⲛⲁⲡⲟⲥ-
[ⲧⲟⲗⲟⲥ

margin

Fol. 12. *Recto.* . . . not . . . it. For this cause did Paul cry out, 'Where there is not law, there is not transgression (*παρ.*).' Likewise (*ὁμοίως*) also

[1] Or 'Verily'.

Reuben, when he lay with Thamar,[1] his father's wife, [and] Abimelek, when he coveted [2] (ἐπιθυμεῖν), and the rest, when they . . . . .

Verso. . . . sin, because the law (νόμ.) hath (had?) been given him and he hath (had?) transgressed (παραβαίνειν) it. 'Where there is not law, there is not transgression (παρ.).' Lo, how much shall not be ours,[3] we Christians (χρ.)? Lo, the Gospels (εὐ.) have been given unto us; lo, the teachings of our holy fathers the apostles (ἀπ.) . . . . .

Fol. 13. → *Recto* (?).

ⲛⲟϫⲟⲩ ⲛ̄ⲥⲁ'-	
ⲃⲟⲗ' ⲙ̄ⲙⲟⲛ ·	
+ⲟⲩⲟ̄ⲉⲓ · ⲟⲩⲟ̄ⲓ̈	ϣⲁ[
ⲟⲩⲏ̄ⲣ'ⲛⲉ ⲛ̄-	ⲉϫ[
ϩⲓⲥⲉ' ⲉⲧϭⲉ-	ϭⲓⲛ[
ⲉⲧ' ⲉⲣⲟⲛ ·	+ⲁⲛⲟ[
+ⲉϣϫⲉ ⲁⲩⲙⲟⲩ-	ϩⲓⲥ̣[
ⲟⲩⲧ ⲙ̄ⲡⲁⲓ̈	ⲛⲁⲛ[
ⲛ̄ⲧⲁⲩϭⲛ̄ⲧϥ	ⲟⲩⲟ̣[
ⲉϥϭ̄ⲗϣⲉ' ϩⲛ̄-	ⲛ̣ⲧ̣[
ⲧⲥⲱϣⲉ ·	ⲟ̣ϣ[
+ⲉⲓⲉ ⲟⲩⲙⲟⲩ'	ⲟⲛ̣'[
ⲛ̄ⲁϣ' ⲛ̄ϭⲟⲧ'	ⲧⲁ̣[
ⲡⲉⲧⲛⲁⲧⲁ-	ⲟⲩ[
ϩⲟⲛ' · ⲟⲩⲟ̄ⲓ̈	ⲉⲧ[
+ⲟⲩⲟ̄ⲉⲓ ϫⲉⲧⲛ-	ⲡⲣⲁ[ⲛ ⲙ̄ⲡⲛⲟⲩ-]
ⲫⲟⲣⲉⲓ ⲛ̄ⲟⲩ-	ⲧⲉ[
ⲥⲭⲏⲙⲁ' ⲛ̄-	
ⲁⲅⲅⲉⲗⲓⲕⲟⲛ'	
ⲁⲛⲣ̄ ⲛⲉϩⲃⲏⲩⲉ'	

↑ *Verso* (?).

	ⲡⲱⲛ ⲁ[ⲛⲡⲉ ·]
]ⲡ̣ⲱⲟⲩ	+ⲁⲗⲏⲑⲱⲥ'
]ⲡϭⲱⲙ'	ⲛⲁⲙⲉⲣⲁⲧⲉ'
]ⲧ̣ⲁⲁϥ'	ⲉⲣⲉⲧⲙ̄ⲡⲛ̄ⲩ̊-
]ⲁⲩϥⲓ̈	ⲧⲉ' ⲕⲱ̄' ⲛⲁⲛ'
]ⲟⲩ' ⲁⲩ-	ⲉⲃⲟⲗ' ⲙ̄ⲡ-
]ϫ̣ⲉⲙ̄-	ⲟⲩⲁ' ⲛ̄ⲟⲩⲱⲧ'
]ⲁ̣ϩⲉ'	ϩⲛ̄ⲧⲉⲓⲅⲉⲛⲉⲁ'
] . . . ⲩ	ⲛⲁⲟⲩϫⲁⲓ
]ⲡ̣ⲉⲉⲩ [a]	ⲉⲛⲕⲟⲗⲁⲥⲓⲥ'
ⲛ̄ⲁ]ϣ ⲛ̄ϭⲧ̊	ⲙ̄ⲡϣⲏⲣⲉ'
[ⲡⲉⲧⲛⲁ]ⲧⲁϩ̄ⲟ̄ ·	ⲙ̄ⲡⲛⲟⲩⲧⲉ ·
]ⲟⲗ' ϫⲓⲛ-	+ⲡⲙⲁ' ⲉⲧⲉⲙ̄ⲛ̄-
[ϩⲧⲟⲟⲩ]ⲉ' ϣⲁ-	ⲛⲟⲙⲟⲥ ⲙ̄ⲛ̄-
[ⲣⲟⲩϩⲉ] ⲙ̄ⲙⲏ-	ⲡⲁⲣⲁⲃⲁⲥⲓⲥ' ·
[ⲛⲉ] ⲉϣϫⲉ-	+ⲉⲛⲉ ⲙ̄ⲡⲉⲓⲉⲓ
]ⲟⲩ'	ⲧⲁϣⲁϫⲉ'
]ⲩ' ⲣⲱ̄'	ⲙ̄ⲡⲕⲟⲥ-
	ⲙⲟⲥ' ⲛⲉⲙ̄ⲡ-
	ⲛⲟⲃⲉ' ⲉⲣⲟⲟⲩ'
	margin

[a] Perhaps ⲟ]ⲩ̣[ⲣⲡ]ⲙⲉⲉⲩ[ⲉ.

[1] A mistake for Bilhah; *v.* Gen. xxxv. 22 (21). Yet palaeographically ⲃⲁⲗⲗⲁ and ⲑⲁⲙⲁ[ⲣ] might well be confused.

[2] Gen. xx. 2.

[3] I suppose this to mean, 'How great punishments shall not be ours?'

Fol. 13. *Recto* (?). . . . cast them forth from us. Woe, woe! How great are the troubles that await us. If they slew this (man) whom they had found gathering wood[1] in the field, what manner of death, then, is it shall overtake us? Woe, woe! For we wear (φορεῖν) an angelic (ἀγγελικός) habit (σχῆμα) and have done the deeds [of . . . . .

Verso (?). . . . the garden . . . . What manner of [remembr]ance (?) [is it shall] overtake us? . . . . . .[2] from . . . till . . ., da[ily.] If . . . . .
. . . that are] not ours (?). Verily (ἀληθῶς), my beloved, unless God forgive us, there shall not a single one from this generation (γενεά) be saved from the punishment (κόλασις) of the Son of God. 'Where there is not law, there is not transgression.' 'If[3] I had not come and talked with the world (κόσ), they had been guilty of no sin' . . . . . .

No. 10.

From a Sermon, treating here of repentance, as exemplified by Nebuchadnezzar. Repentance is apostrophized similarly in a sermon by Theophilus (Budge, *Copt. Hom.* 69).

Fol. 1. → *Recto.*		↑ *Verso.*	
ⲧ[			]ⲧⲉⲧ̣ⲛ-
ϣ[			]ⲁ
ⲙⲡⲉⲣ[			]ⲧ̣ⲥ
ⲭⲱⲣⲓ̣̈ⲥ̣ [			]ⲁⲗ ⲙ̣ⲙ-
ⲥⲱⲧⲙ [ⲉⲧⲙⲉⲧⲁⲛⲟⲓⲁ]			]ⲛ̣ⲧ . . ⲧ
? [			]ⲣ
ϩⲣⲁⲓ̈ ϣⲁ̣ⲧ[			[. .]ⲛ . ⲣⲟ̣ . . ⲙ̣ ·
ⲛⲛⲉⲧ̣ⲡⲏ[ⲧ ⲉ]ⲣ̣ⲁⲧⲥ̣			[. .]ⲁⲩ . ⲛ . . ⲁ̣ⲓ̈ ϥ-
ⲥⲱⲧⲙ ⲉⲧⲙⲉⲧⲁⲛⲟⲓⲁ		]ⲃⲟ̣ .	[. .]ⲧⲟ[ⲗ]ⲙⲏⲣⲟⲥ̄
ⲧⲉⲧϥ̣ⲱⲧⲉ ⲉⲃⲟⲗ ⲛ-	ⲉ[	] ?	ⲉⲓ̈ ⲟⲩⲱ̣[ⲛ]ϩ̣ ⲉⲃⲟⲗ
ⲛⲉⲛⲧⲁⲩⲣⲁⲁⲥ ϩⲛ-	ϩⲟ̣[	]ⲟⲥ ⲉⲓ	ⲛⲛⲉⲛⲧ̣ⲁ̣ⲕϣⲱ-

[1] Num. xv. 30 (32). ϭⲗϣⲉ in Zoega, 337 = συλλέγειν ξύλα in *PG.* 65, 256. *Cf.* Deut. xxix. 11 = ξυλοκόπος, also Zoega 487 *ult.*

[2] Perhaps 'We lie (ϫⲓϭⲟⲗ) from morn till evening'.

[3] John xv. 22. Note the reading.

ⲧⲕⲁⲕⲓ̈ⲁ · ⲥⲱⲧⲙ
ⲉⲧⲙⲉⲧⲁⲛⲟⲓ̈ⲁ ⲉⲧⲟ
ⲛϣⲃⲏⲣ ⲉⲛⲁⲅⲅⲉ-
ⲗⲟⲥ ⲙⲡⲛⲟⲩⲧⲉ
Ⲱ ⲧⲙⲉⲧⲁⲛⲟⲓ̈ⲁ ⲡⲟ-
ⲉⲓ̈ⲕ ⲛⲕⲁⲑⲁⲣⲱⲛ
[ⲉ]ⲧ̣ⲥⲁⲁⲛϣ ⲛ[. . . .
]ⲏ̣ⲩ̣[

ⲛ[
Ⲱ ⲧ[ⲙⲉⲧⲁⲛⲟⲓⲁ
ⲧⲣ̣[
ϩ[
ⲫ[
ⲟⲩ[
ⲡ̣ⲟ̣[

]ⲁⲩⲣϩⲗ-
[ⲗⲟ ϩⲛⲛⲉⲩⲛ]ⲟⲃⲉ
ⲛ]ⲕⲉⲥⲟⲡ
[Ⲱ ⲧⲙⲉⲧⲁⲛⲟ]ⲓ̈ⲁ
]ⲉⲛ
ⲡⲏ]ⲧ ⲉⲣⲁⲧⲥ
]ⲡⲛ . .

ⲡⲉ ⲛϩⲏⲧⲟⲩ ⲙ-
ⲙⲟⲛ ⲛⲛⲉⲥϣⲱ-
ⲡⲉ · ⲁⲗⲗⲁ ⲉⲓ̈ⲧⲁ-
ⲙⲟ ⲛⲟⲩⲟⲛ ⲛⲓⲙ
ⲉⲧⲟⲩⲱϣ ⲉⲱ-
ⲛϩ ⲛⲕⲉⲥⲟⲡ ϩⲓ̈-
ⲧⲛⲧⲙⲉⲧⲁⲛⲟⲓ̈ⲁ
[.]ⲧ̣ⲛⲛⲉ̣[
ϣ[

Fol. 1. *Recto*. . . . Hearken [unto Repentance (*μετ.*) . . . . them that betake themselves to her. Hearken unto Repentance, she that cleanseth (*lit.* wipeth out) such as are old in wickedness (*κακία*). Hearken unto Repentance, that is a fellow unto the angels (*ἄγγ.*) of God. O Repentance, pure (*καθαρός*) bread which nourisheth . . . . .

. . . O Repentance, ...

Verso. . . . that] are grown old [in their] sins . . . once more. [O Repentan]ce . . . . . flee unto . . . . .

. . . bold (*τολμηρός*), whilst I show forth the state that thou wast in. Nay; so shall it not be. Rather (*ἀλλά*) I tell every one that would live again through Repentance . . . . .

Fol. 2. ↑ *Recto*.

margin

ⲁⲁϥ [
ⲛⲁⲓ̈ · ⲁ[ⲧⲉⲧⲛ-]
ⲥⲱⲧⲙ ⲉⲡⲥⲟ-
ⲡⲥ ⲛⲇⲁⲛⲓ̈ⲏⲗ
ⲉⲧⲃⲉⲧϫⲟⲩⲧⲟⲩⲉ
ⲛⲣⲟⲙⲡⲉ ⲛ-
[ⲧⲁⲩ]ϩⲟⲣⲓ̈ⲍⲉ ⲙ-
[ⲙⲟⲥ ⲛ]ⲁ̣ϥ ⲉⲛ-
[. . . . .]ⲧ̣ⲟⲩⲥ̣

margin

→ *Verso*.

margin

margin

[. . . . .] ⲙⲛⲛⲁ-
[. . .]ϭⲟⲙ ⲙⲡⲛⲟⲩ-
ⲧⲉ ⲁⲩⲱ ⲁϥⲡⲱⲧ
ⲉⲣⲁⲧⲥ ⲛⲧⲙⲉⲧⲁⲛⲟ[ⲓ-]
ⲁ · ⲁϥⲟⲩⲱⲛϩ ⲉ-
ⲃⲟⲗ ⲛⲧⲉϥⲙⲛ[ⲧⲁⲧ-]
ϭⲟⲙ · ⲁⲩⲱ̣ [
ⲥ̣ⲙ̣ⲓ̣ⲛ̣[
ⲙ[

Fol. 2. *Recto.* . . . [Ye] have heard the prayer of Daniel concerning the one and twenty years[1] that had been fixed (*ὁρίζειν*) for him . . . . .

Verso. . . . power of God, and he betook himself unto Repentance (*μετ.*) and displayed his weakness. And . . . . .

Fol. 3. ↑ *Recto.*

margin

ⲁ]ϥⲧⲣⲉⲧⲟⲓ-
ⲕ[ⲟⲩ]ⲙⲉⲛⲏ ⲧⲏⲣ̅ⲥ̅
ⲟⲩⲱϣⲧ ⲛⲁϥ
ϩⲱⲥ ⲛⲟⲩⲧⲉ ⲁⲩ[ⲱ]
ⲡⲁ̈ⲓ ⲛⲧⲉ̈ⲓⲙⲓⲛ[ⲉ]
Ⲛⲧⲉⲣⲉⲡⲉϥϩⲏ̣[ⲧ]
ⲉⲛϣⲟ̣ⲧ ⲉⲣⲟϥ
ⲛⲑⲉ̣ ⲙⲡϩ̣ⲏⲧ
ⲛ[

→ *Verso.*

ϫⲓ-]
ⲧϥ [ⲉⲃⲟⲗ[a] ϩⲙ-]
ⲡⲙⲁ ⲉⲧϥⲟⲧⲡ
ⲉϩⲟⲩⲛ ⲉⲣⲟϥ
ⲁϥϯ ⲛⲁϥ ⲙ-
ⲡⲉϥⲉ̣ⲟⲟⲩ ⲛ-
ϣⲟⲣⲡ ⲁⲩⲟⲡϥ
ⲙⲛⲛⲉϥⲉⲓⲟⲧⲉ
Ⲁⲧⲉⲧⲛⲛⲁⲩ ⲱ
[ⲛⲁⲥⲛⲏⲩ] ϫⲉⲟⲩ-

margin

[a] Or ⲛⲧϥ ⲉϩⲣⲁⲓ.

Fol. 3. *Recto.* . . . caused all the world (*οἰκουμένη*) to worship him as (*ὡς*) God. And the aforesaid (king), after that his heart had been hardened, like the heart of . . . . .

Verso. . . . he brought ?] him [forth from] the place wherein he was confined and gave unto him his former honour, and he was reckoned unto his fathers. Ye have seen, O [my brethren ?,] how . . . . .

[1] I cannot identify this reference. 'Twenty-one' occurs in Daniel only in x. 13, but in an apparently apocryphal reference to this book it recurs in the Eulogy on Victor (*Miss.* viii. 195).

Fol. 4. ↑ *Recto.*

margin

ϫⲉ[ⲛⲧⲟⲕ ⲡϫⲟ-]
]ⲛ̣ⲟⲩ ⲉⲓⲥ ⲡ̣[
ⲥⲉ· ⲛϣⲁⲛϩⲧⲏϥ
ⲁⲩⲱ ⲛϩⲁⲣϣ
ϩⲏⲧ ⲉⲛⲁϣⲉ
ⲡⲉⲕⲛⲁ· ⲉⲕϯ
ⲙⲉⲧⲁⲛⲟⲓ̈ⲁ ⲛⲛ̄-[a]
ⲣⲉ̣[ϥⲣ]ⲛⲟ̣[ⲃⲉ] ⲧⲏ-
ⲣⲟ̣[ⲩ

margin

→ *Verso.*

margin

ϣ *sic*
ⲙ]ⲛϭⲟⲙ
ⲙⲙⲟⲓ̈ ⲉϭⲱϣⲧ
ⲉϩⲣⲁⲓ̈ ⲉⲧⲡⲉ ⲉⲧ-
ⲃⲉⲡⲁϣⲁⲓ̈ ⲛ̣[ⲛⲁ-]
ϫⲓ̈ⲛϭⲟⲛⲥ [ϩⲛ-]
ⲟⲩⲙⲉ ⲁⲓϯ ϭⲱ-
ⲛⲧ ⲛⲁⲕ ϯⲥⲟⲡ[ⲥ]
ⲙⲙⲟⲕ ⲉⲓ̈ⲙ̣[
ϩⲛⲟⲩⲙⲏⲏ̣[ϣⲉ

margin

[a] A 3rd ⲛ precludes the proposed restitution.

Fol. 4. *Recto.* . . . (saying,) [Thou] Lord, . . . merciful and longsuffering, whose mercy is great. Thou givest repentance (*μετ.*) unto all sinners (?) . . . . .

Verso. . . . I am not able to look up to heaven by reason of the multitude of my iniquities. Verily I have angered Thee. I entreat Thee, . . . -ing with many . . . . .

Fol. 5. ↑ *Recto.*

margin

margin

ⲙⲙⲟϥ ϩⲱⲧⲧⲏⲩ-
ⲧⲛ ϫⲉⲛϩ̣ⲟⲥⲟⲛ
ⲉⲣⲉⲡⲣⲙⲙⲁⲟ ϫⲓ̈
ⲛϩⲣⲁϥ ϩⲛⲛⲉⲓ̈ϫⲓ̈
ϩⲣⲁϥ ⲧⲏⲣⲟⲩ —
)ϣⲁⲣⲉⲣⲟⲩϩⲉ ϣⲱ-
ⲡⲉ ⲉⲣⲟϥ ⲉⲧⲉⲧⲁⲓ̈-
ⲧⲉ ⲑⲁⲛ [ⲙ]ⲡⲉϥⲁ-
ϩⲉ ⲛϥϯ ⲟⲥⲉ ⲙⲡⲉϥ-
ⲱⲛϩ ⲧⲏⲣϥ —
)Ⲟⲩⲛ ϩⲟⲉⲓ̈ⲛ *sic* ϩⲛⲛ-
ϩⲁⲗⲁⲁⲧⲉ ⲙⲡⲕⲟⲥ-
[ⲙ]ⲟⲥ ⲉⲣⲉⲛⲉⲩ[

→ *Verso.*

margin

ϣⲁϥϩⲱ .[a] ⲉⲙⲁⲩ
sic ⲧ
ⲛ̣ⲁⲗⲁⲁⲩ ⲛⲉⲧ-
ⲡⲱ —
)Ⲡⲣⲙⲙⲁⲟ ϩⲱⲱϥ
ⲉϥⲧⲛⲧⲱⲛ ⲉⲩ-
]ⲕⲉ ⲛⲟϭ ⲛϫⲟⲓ̈ ⲉⲣⲉⲡⲉϥ-
]ⲁⲧ̣ ⲁⲩⲉⲓ̈ⲛ ϩⲟⲣϣ ⲉⲙⲉϥ-
]ⲕ [. . . . .] ϩⲛ̄ⲗⲁⲁⲩ
[ⲙ]ⲙ̣ⲁ ⲉⲓⲙⲏⲧⲉⲓ
ϩⲙ̣ⲡⲡⲉⲗⲁⲅⲟⲥ
ⲉⲧϣ̣ⲏⲕ ⲉϣⲁϥ-
ⲕⲓⲛⲇⲩⲛⲉⲩⲉ ⲛⲟⲩ-
. ⲡ̣ . ⲙ̣ⲱ̣ⲉ[b] ⲛⲥ[

[a] ϩⲱⲛ or ϩⲱⲗ.

[b] ? ⲙⲏⲏϣⲉ.

Fol. 5. *Recto.* . . . ye also. For whilst (ὅσον) the rich man disporteth himself in all these sports, evening cometh upon him, which is the end of his lifetime, and he doth forfeit his whole life. There be some of the birds of the world (κόσ.) whose . . . are . . . . .

Verso. . . . will draw nigh (*or* fly) there, without any burden. But the rich man is like unto a great ship, whose freight is heavy, ⟨so that⟩ it doth not . . . anywhere, except (εἰμήτι) in the deep sea (πέλαγος) and is in danger (κινδυνεύειν) of a . . . . .

No. 11.

From a Sermon, treating here of charity and of the Good Samaritan.

→ *Recto.*

[ⲡⲧ̄]ⲙ̣ⲉⲣⲉ̣[ⲡⲉⲧϩⲓ-]
ⲧⲟⲩⲱⲱϥ [ⲛ̄ⲧⲉⲕ-]
ϩⲉ ⲉ̣ϥⲧⲁⲙ[ⲟ ⲙ-]
Ⲙⲟⲛ ϫⲉϣϣ[ⲉ ⲉϯ]
ϩⲧⲏⲕ ⲉϫⲛ̄[ⲟⲩⲟⲛ]
ⲛⲓⲙ ⲉⲧⲕ̄ⲛⲁⲛⲁⲩ
ⲉⲣⲟⲟⲩ ϩⲙ̄ⲡⲉⲩⲁ-
ⲛⲁⲅⲕⲏ ϩⲓⲧⲛ̄ⲛⲉⲓ-
Ⲉⲛⲧⲟⲗⲏ ⲅⲁⲣ ⲉⲕ-
ⲛⲁⲟⲩⲱⲛ̄ϩ̣ ⲉⲃⲟⲗ
ϫⲉⲕⲙ̄ⲙⲉ ⲙ̄ⲡϫⲟ-
ⲉⲓⲥ ⲡⲉⲕⲛ̄ⲟⲩⲧⲉ
ϩⲙ̄ⲡⲉⲕϩⲏⲧ ⲧⲏⲣϥ
Ⲉ[ⲃⲟ]ⲗ ϫⲉⲉⲩⲛ̄ ϩⲁϩ
[ⲉⲩ]ϣⲁⲛ̄ⲛⲁⲩ ⲉ̀ⲟⲩⲁ̄
[ⲉϥϣ]ⲟⲟⲡ ϩⲛ̄ϩⲉⲛ— *sic*
[. .][a] ⲉⲩⲟϣ' ⲉⲓⲧⲉ
[ⲟⲩϣ]ⲱⲛⲉ ⲉⲓⲧⲉ ⲟⲩ-

ⲡ̣ⲧⲩ[ⲡⲟⲥ ⲙ̄ⲡⲟⲩⲏ-]
ⲏⲃ [b] ⲙ̄[ⲛ̄ⲡⲗⲉⲩⲓ-]
ⲧⲏⲥ ⲛ[
ⲡⲉⲛⲧ̣ⲁⲩ[
ⲙ̣ⲉⲓ ⲙ̄ⲡ[
ⲉⲁⲩⲛⲁⲩ ⲉⲣ[ⲟϥ ⲁⲩ-]
ⲥⲁⲁⲧϥ ⲙ̄ⲡⲟ[ⲩϣⲛ-]
ϩⲧⲏⲩ ϩⲁⲣⲟϥ [ⲟⲩ-]
ϫⲉ ⲙ̄ⲡⲟⲩⲙ[ⲟⲩⲣ]
ⲛ̄ⲛⲉϥⲥⲁϣ [

margin

↑ *Verso.*

] ?
] . ϩⲓⲧⲛ̄-
[ⲧⲙⲛ̄ⲧϣⲁ]ⲛ̄ϩⲧⲏϥ
[ⲉⲧⲛ̄ϩⲏ]ⲧϥⲡⲉ [c]
]ⲉⲁϥⲙⲟⲩⲣ
[ⲛ̄ⲛⲉ]ϥⲥⲁϣ ⲁϥ-
[ⲡⲱ]ϩⲧ ⲛ̄ⲟⲩⲛⲉϩ
[ⲙ̄ⲛ̄]ⲟⲩⲏⲣⲡ̄ ⲉϩⲣⲁⲓ
[ⲉϫ]ⲱϥ ⲁϥⲧⲁⲗϥ
[ⲉϫ]ⲙ̄ⲡⲉϥⲧⲃ̄ⲛⲏ
[ⲙ]ⲙⲓⲛ ⲙ̄ⲙⲟϥ

] . ⲗⲉ ⲙ̄[
] . . ⲙ̄ⲡⲡⲁ̣- [d]
[ⲧⲟⲭ]ⲉ̣ⲩⲥ̣' ⲁⲩⲱ ⲁϥ-
[ϩⲱ]ⲛ̣ ⲉⲧⲟⲟⲧϥ
ϫⲉϥⲓ ⲡⲉϥⲣⲟⲟⲩϣ
ⲕⲁⲗⲱⲥ ⲡⲉⲧⲕ̄-
ⲛⲁϫⲟϥ' ⲉⲃⲟⲗ ⲉⲣϥ
ⲉ̣ⲓ̣ ϣⲁⲛⲕⲧⲟⲓ ϯⲛⲁ-
ⲧⲁⲁϥ ⲛⲁⲕ·
Ⲁⲕⲛ̄ⲛⲁⲩ ⲱ ⲡⲙⲉⲣ[ⲓⲧ]
ⲉⲧⲙⲛ̄ⲧϣⲁⲛϩⲧ̣[ⲏϥ]
ϫⲉϣⲁⲥϫⲱⲕ [ⲉ-]
ⲃⲟⲗ ϩⲓⲧⲛ̄ⲟⲩⲏⲣⲡ
ⲛ̄ϩⲱⲃ· ⲟ[ⲩⲛⲟϭ]
Ⲛ̄ⲕⲉⲫⲁⲗ[ⲁⲓⲟⲛ-]
ⲧⲉ ⲧⲙⲛⲧ[ϣⲁⲛ-]
ϩⲧⲏϥ ϣⲁ̣[

margin

[a] ⲛ[ϣⲟⲧ], if the space would permit it.

[b] *V.* Luke x. 31 ff.

[c] Or ⲡⲉ[ϫⲁϥ], parenthetically, or ⲡⲉ[ϫⲁϥ ϫ]ⲉ-. *V.* Luke x. 33, 34.

[d] Probably ⲡⲁ̄ = ⲡⲁⲛ.

Recto. . . . and thou] love thy neighbour as thyself,'[1] while he telleth us, 'Thou oughtest to give heed to every [one] whom thou seest in trouble (ἀνάγκη).'[2] For (γάρ) by means of these commandments (ἐντολή) shalt thou make manifest that thou dost love the Lord thy God with all thy heart. Because many there be that, when they see one in heavy difficulties (?), whether (εἴτε) an illness or (εἴτε) a . . . . .

. . . the manner (τύπος) of the priest and the Levite . . . ., when they had beheld him, they passed him by; they had not pity on him, neither (οὐδέ) did they bind up his wounds . . . . .

Verso. . . . through the compassion that was in him, sai[th ? he,] having bound up his wounds, he poured oil and wine upon him and set him upon his own beast . . . . .

. . . the innkeeper (πανδοχεύς). And he bade him, saying, 'Take well (καλῶς) care of him; whatever thou spendest, when I shall return, I will give it thee.' Thou hast seen, O beloved, by how many means (*lit.* things) compassion may be fulfilled. Compassion is a great matter (κεφάλαιον) . . . . .

No. 12.

Apparently from a Dialogue or ἐρωταπόκρισις concerning the interpretation of various passages in the Gospels.[3] The problems are stated by Anatolius (tolerably certain, *v.* fol. 2 *ro.*) and Militius (3 *ro.*, uncertain, for Meletius ?), and solved by Ba . . . . (perhaps Bachius[4]). The bible texts incidental are for the most part paraphrased or loosely quoted. The sequence in foll. 2 and 3 is certain; the position of fol. 1 doubtful.

Fol. 1. ↑ *Recto.*		→ *Verso.*	
]ϫⲉ[ⲕ-]		]ⲛϩⲁⲙ̣ . [[b]	ⲛⲁ̣[
ⲁⲥ ⲛϩⲟ]ⲩ̣ⲟ ⲛⲧⲉ-	ϥϫⲱ ⲙ̣[ⲙⲟⲥ]	ⲙ]ⲡ̣ⲉⲕϩⲟ̄ ⲉⲃⲟⲗ	ⲡⲉⲛ̣[
[ⲛϩⲃⲏ]ⲩ̣ⲉ[a] ⲙⲡⲁ-	ϫⲉⲡⲉⲧⲛ[ⲁⲛⲟⲩϭⲥ]	[ϩⲙ]ⲡⲙⲁ ⲉⲧⲙⲙⲁⲩ	ⲡⲉⲡⲟ̣ⲥ̣[

[a] My copy]ⲡ̣ⲉ.

[b] ⲉⲓⲱ ⲙ]ⲡⲉⲕ- or ⲉⲓⲁ]ⲡⲉⲕ-.

[1] Matt. xix. 19, xxii. 39, or Mark xii. 31.

[2] *Lit.* 'their troubles'.

[3] The literature of such dialogues is described by R. Nachtigall in *Arch. f. Slav. Philol.* xxiii, xxiv; Berendts in *T. u. U.*, N. F. xi. 34 ff.; and Heinrici in the Leipzig *Abhandl.*, Phil. hist. Kl., xxviii. But I have found nothing resembling the present fragments, either in names or contents.

[4] The obvious Basilius seems too long for the gap, fol. 2 *ro.*, l. 1, though not for *ib. vo.*, l. 8. Bachius is the name (1) of a writer of sermons (Zoega cclxv) and ? of an encomium on James the Persian martyr (to be presumed from the words quoted by Zoega cclxiv. The martyr's relics were in Egypt; *v. Synax.*, 27th Hathor); (2) of a priest in Palestine who converts a Samaritan in a λόγος of Pseudo-Cyril of Jerusalem (Brit. Mus. Or. 6799, abstract in *Synax.*, 17th Thot).

ⲉⲓⲱⲧ ⲟⲩⲱⲛ̄ϩ	ⲉⲡⲉϥⲥⲟⲛ [ⲉⲓⲕⲏ]	[ⲁⲩ]ⲱ ⲕⲛⲁⲛⲁⲩ ⲉ-	ⲡⲕⲁϩ ⲙ̄ⲡϣ[ⲟ-]
ⲉⲃⲟⲗ ϩⲣⲁï ⲛϩⲏ̄-	ϥⲟ ⲛⲉⲛⲟⲭ[ⲟⲥ ⲉⲧⲉⲕ-]	[ⲃⲟⲗ] · ⳁϫⲱ ⲙ̄ⲙⲟⲥ	ⲣ̄ⲡ ⲛⲥⲟⲡ ⲙ̣[ⲛ̄-]
ⲧϥ̄ · ⲟⲛⲧⲱⲥ ⳁ-	ⲣⲓⲥⲓ̈ⲥ [	[ϫⲉ]ⲥⲓ̈ⲗⲱ̄-	ⲛⲥⲱⲥ ⲛ̄ⲅ̣[ⲓⲅⲁⲥ]
ⲁ̣ⲡⲟⲣⲉï ⲉïϫⲱ	ⲟⲛ ϫ[ⲉ	[ϩⲁⲙⲡⲉ] ⲧⲉⲕⲕⲗⲏ-	÷ⲙ̄ⲛ̄ⲛⲥⲱⲥ [ⲡⲕⲁ-
ⲙ̄ⲡⲉïϣⲁϫⲉ	ⲛⲟⲩ[	[ⲥⲓⲁ ⲙ̄ⲙ]ⲙ̣ⲟⲟⲩ ⲟⲛ̄	ⲧⲁⲕⲗⲩⲥⲙⲟⲥ
[ⲉ]ⲣⲉⲡⲛⲟⲩⲧⲉ ⲣⲙ̣ⲉ̣[a]	ⲡⲕⲁ[	[ⲉⲧⲉⲙⲙⲟ]ⲟⲩ ⲙ-	÷ⲙ̄ⲛ̄ⲛⲥⲱⲥ ϩ̣[ⲛ]
[ⲣ]ⲙ̣ⲛ̄ⲧⲣⲉ ϩⲁⲡⲉï-	ⲛ[	[ⲡⲃⲁⲡⲧⲓⲥ]ⲙⲁ	ⲡⲕⲁϩ ⲛⲧⲁϥ[ϭⲱ-]
ⲣⲱⲙⲉ ϫⲉⲙⲙ̄ⲡⲉ̣-	ϩ[	[ⲉⲧⲟⲩⲁⲁⲃ]ⲡ̣ⲉ	ⲣ̄ϭ ⲙ̄ⲡⲙⲉϩ-
[ⲡ]ⲁ̣ⲓ̣ ⲣⲛⲟⲃⲉ ⲟⲩ-	[	]	ⲥⲟⲡ ⲥⲛⲁⲩ [ⲙⲛ̄-]
ⲇ̣ⲉ̣ ⲙ̄ⲡⲉⲛⲉϥⲉï-	ϫⲉ[	]ⲡ̣ⲛⲟⲩ-	ⲛⲥⲱⲥ ⲡ̣ⲛ̣[ⲟⲙⲟⲥ]
ⲟⲧⲉ̣ ⲉ̣ⲓⲣⲉ	ϫⲁ̣[	[ⲧⲉ]ϫ̣ ⲟⲩⲱ-	ⲛⲧⲁϥⲧⲁ̣ⲩⲟ̣[ϥ]
Ⲡⲉϫⲉ ⲁⲡ[ⲁ] ⲃ̣ⲁ̣-	ⲛⲉⲛⲉ[	[ⲛϩ ⲉⲃ]ⲟⲗ ϩⲙ̄-	ⲙ̄ⲙⲱⲩⲥ[ⲏⲥ]
	ⲧⲁⲩϫ̣[		ϩⲓϫⲙ̄ⲡⲧⲟ̣[ⲟⲩ]

[a] Possibly ⲣⲱ.

Fol. 1. *Recto.* . . . rather that the works (?) of my Father may be manifested in him.'[1] Verily (ὄντως) I am perplexed (ἀπορεῖσθαι) when I say these words, God Himself (?) testifying concerning this man that 'Neither did this (man) sin nor (οὔτε) did his parents do (so).' Apa Ba[. . . .] said [. . . . . saying,[2] 'He that shall be [wroth] against his brother without cause (εἰκῇ), is in danger of the judgement (ἔνοχος, κρίσις) . . . . .

Verso. . . . wash] thy face there and thou shalt see.'[3] I say . . .[4] Siloam is the church (ἐκκλ.). The waters are [the wate]rs of [holy baptis]m (βαπ.)[5], manifested in . . . . the earth, the first time; afterward the giants (γίγας)[6]; afterward the flood (κατακλυσμός); afterward the earth that was peopled for the second time; afterward the law (νόμος) that He committed unto Moses upon the mount . . . . .

[1] *Cf.* John ix. 3.

[2] Matt. v. 22.

[3] *Cf.* John ix. 7.

[4] Some particle or 'to thee'.

[5] *Cf.* Cyril's interpretation in Lagarde, *Catenae*, 201, 36.

[6] Gen. vi. 4.

Fol. 2. → *Recto.*

] ⲙⲛⲟⲩⲡⲓⲥ-
[ⲧⲓⲥ ⲛ]ⲟⲩⲱⲧ ⲉⲥ-
[ϫⲏⲕ] ⲉⲃⲟⲗ ϩⲙ-
[ⲡ]ϣⲱϣ ⲛⲁⲧ-
[ⲣ̄ⲛⲟ]ⲃⲉ ⲛⲁⲧⲥⲕⲁⲛ̄-
[ⲇⲁⲗ]ⲓⲍⲉ · ⲛⲁïⲛⲉ
[ⲛⲉϩ]ⲃⲏⲩⲉ ⲛⲧⲁⲡⲛⲟⲩ-
[ⲧⲉ ⲟ]ⲩⲟⲛϩⲟⲩ ⲉⲃⲟⲗ
[ⲙ]ⲡⲉⲛⲉïⲱⲧ ⲁ-
[ⲇⲁ]ⲙ̣ ⲡⲉϫⲉ ⲁⲛⲁ-
[Ⲧⲟⲗ]ïⲟⲥ ϫⲉⲙ-
[ⲡⲛⲁ]ⲩ ⲛ̣ⲧ̣ⲁⲩⲧⲉ-

Ⲡⲉϫⲉ ⲁ[ⲡⲁ Ⲃ
ϫⲉⲛⲧⲁⲩ[
ϩⲱⲥ ⲣⲱ[ⲙⲉ ·]
÷Ⲡⲉϫⲉ ⲁⲛ̣[ⲁⲧⲟ-]
ⲗⲓⲟⲥ ϫⲉⲙ[
ⲛⲧⲁϥⲧⲣ̣[ⲉⲡⲙⲟ-]
ⲟⲩ ⲣⲏⲣⲡ [
ⲉïⲣⲉ ϩⲱ[ⲥ ⲣⲱ-]
ⲙⲉ ϫⲉ[ⲛϩⲱⲥ ⲛⲟⲩ-]
ⲧⲉ · ⲡⲉ[ϫⲉ ⲁⲡⲁ]
÷Ⲃⲁ[ϫⲉⲛ-]
ⲧⲁ[ϥ
ϩⲱ̣[ⲥ
÷Ⲡⲉ̣[ϫⲉ

margin

↑ *Verso.*

]ⲉⲛ
]ⲧⲣⲉⲡⲙ̣ⲟ̣-
[ⲟⲩ ⲣⲏ]ⲣ̄ⲡ ⲛϩⲏⲧⲥ
[ϫⲛ]ⲙⲙⲟⲛ ⲉⲣⲉ-
[ϩⲉ]ⲛⲟⲩⲛⲟⲟⲩⲉ
[ⲛ]ⲧⲟⲟⲧϥ ⲉϥⲣϩⲱⲃ
[ⲛϩ]ⲏⲧⲟⲩ ·
[Ⲡⲉ]ϫⲉ ⲁⲡⲁ Ⲃⲁ-
[. . .]ⲥ ϫⲉⲙⲙⲟⲛ̄
[ⲛⲧⲉⲓ]ϩⲉ ⲁⲛⲧⲉ
ⲥⲱ]ⲧⲙ ⲉⲣⲟï
ϯ ϩ]ⲧⲏϥ ⲁⲩⲱ
]ⲡ̣ⲭⲟⲣⲏ-
[ⲅⲉⲓ ⲙ̄]ⲡⲉⲡ̄ⲛ̄ⲁ

ⲧⲅⲁ-]
ⲗï[ⲗⲁⲓⲁ
ⲣ̣ⲏⲙⲁⲥ̣ [a] [
ⲙⲙⲁⲩ [
ⲟⲛ ⲛⲓ̄ⲥ̄ ⲙ[ⲛⲛⲉϥ-
ⲙⲁⲑⲏⲧⲏ[ⲥ ⲉⲧϣⲉ·
ⲗⲉⲉⲧ ⲛ[ⲉⲓⲟⲧⲉ [b]]
÷Ⲇⲉ ⲛⲧϣⲉ̣[ⲗⲉⲉⲧ]
ⲛⲥⲩⲅⲅⲉ̣[ⲛⲏⲥⲛⲉ]
ⲙⲙⲁⲣïⲁ [ⲧⲙⲁⲁ
ⲛⲓ̄ⲥ̄ ⲁⲩⲱ̣ [ⲛⲣⲱ-]
ⲙⲉ ⲉⲧⲙⲙ[ⲁⲩ

margin

[a] For ⲥ perhaps ⲟ or ⲱ.

[b] Or ⲣⲱⲙⲉ.

Fol. 2. *Recto.* . . . with a single faith (πίσ.), perfect in equality, sinless and without offence (σκανδαλίζειν). These are the things that God revealed unto our father A[da]m'.[1] Ana[tol]ius said, ' . . . . .

. . . A[pa B . . . . .] said, ' They [2] . . . . . as (ὡς) man.' An[ato]lius said, ' At [the time] when He caused the water become wine,[3] [did He] do (this) as (ὡς) man or (?) [as (ὡς)] God ?' [Apa] Ba[. . . . .] said, ' . . . . [He] did . . . . as (ὡς) . . . . .' . . . . . said, '

Verso. . . . wherewith [He ?] cause[d ?] the water become wine ; or hath He times (*or* seasons) in His hand,[4] wherewith He worketh ?' Apa Ba . . . s said, ' Nay, not thus is it . . . . . heard one . . . . . [payeth] heed ? (and) . . . furnisheth (χορηγεῖν [5]) the Spirit (πν.) . . . . .

[1] Space scarcely allows ⲁ[ⲃⲣⲁϩⲁ]ⲙ, but is Adam probable?

[2] One is tempted to read ϫⲉⲛⲧⲁϥ[, ' He . . .

[3] *Cf.* John ii. 1 ff.

[4] *I.e.* 'at His disposal'. Perhaps a reference to some accusation of magical processes.

[5] Perhaps χορηγός preferable. Πνεῦμα could not be subject unless there were space for ⲛϭⲓ.

. . . Ga]li[lee . . . . there . . . . . also Jesus and His disciples (*μαθ.*) to the marriage. But (*δέ*) the [parents [1] ?] of the bride were kinsmen (*συγγενής*) of Mary [the mother] of Jesus, and the people there . . . . .

Fol. 3. ↑ *Recto.*

margin

] ⲉⲧⲃⲉⲡⲁⲓ̈ ⲁϥ-	ⲁⲃⲟⲗⲟⲥ ⲛϩⲙ̣[ⲉ]
[ϫⲟⲟ]ⲥ ⲛⲁⲥ ϫⲉⲙ-	ⲛϩⲟⲟⲩ ⲙⲡ̄ϩⲙ̣[ⲉ]
[ⲡⲁ]ⲧⲉⲧⲁⲟⲩⲛⲟⲩ	ⲛⲟⲩϣⲏ ⲛⲁⲧⲟⲩ-
[ⲉⲓ·] ⲡⲉϫⲉ ⲙⲓ̈ⲗⲓ̈-	ⲱⲙ ⲛⲁⲧⲥⲱ
ⲓⲟⲥ] ϫⲉⲉⲛⲟⲩ-	Ⲛⲧⲉⲣⲉⲡⲇⲓ̈ⲁⲃⲟ-
[ⲱϣ] ⲱ ⲡⲉⲛⲉⲓ̈-	ⲗⲟⲥ ⲉⲓ̈ⲙⲉ ϫⲉⲁϥ-
[ⲱⲧ ⲉ]ⲧⲣⲉⲕⲃⲱⲗ	ϩⲕⲟ̄ ⲁϥϯ ⲡⲉϥⲟⲩ-
[ⲛⲁⲛ] ⲙⲡⲉⲓ̈ⲕⲉ-	ⲟⲉⲓ̈ ⲉⲣⲟϥ ⲉϥϫⲱ
[ⲍⲏⲧ]ⲏⲙⲁ ⲉϥϫⲱ	ⲙⲙⲟⲥ ϫⲉⲉϣ-
[ⲙⲙⲟⲥ] ϫⲉⲛⲧⲉⲣⲉ-	ϫⲉⲛⲧⲟⲕⲡⲉ [ⲡⲉ-]
[ⲓ̅ⲥ̅ ⲉⲓ ⲉϩⲣ]ⲁⲓ̈ ϩⲙ-	ⲭ̅ⲥ̅ ⲁϫⲓ̈ⲥ ⲉⲛⲉⲓ[ⲱ-]
[ⲡⲙⲟⲟⲩ] ⲙⲡⲛⲥⲁ- [a]	ⲛⲉ ⲙⲁⲣⲟⲩⲣⲟⲉⲓ̈ⲕ
[. . . .]ⲡ̣ⲃⲁⲡ-	÷Ⲡⲉϫⲉ ⲓ̅ⲥ̅ ⲛⲁϥ ϫ[ⲉ-]
[ⲧⲓⲥⲙⲁ . .]ⲁ̣ϥ	ⲙⲉⲣⲉⲣⲱⲙⲉ ⲱⲛ[ϩ]
]ϫⲓ̈	ⲉⲟⲉⲓ̈ⲕ ⲙⲁⲩⲁⲁϥ
?	ⲁⲗⲗⲁ ⲉϣⲁϫⲉ ⲛ[ⲓ̈ⲙ]
	[ⲉ]ⲧⲛⲏⲩ ⲉⲃⲟⲗ ϩⲛ-
	ⲧ[ⲧⲁ]ⲡⲣⲟ ⲙⲡⲛ[ⲟⲩⲧⲉ]
ⲡϫⲓ-]	[Ⲁⲩ]ⲱ̣ ⲛⲧⲉⲣ[ⲉ-]

margin

→ *Verso.*

margin

[ⲡ]ϫⲁϫⲉ ϫⲱⲕ	ⲣ̄ⲡ ⲉⲩⲱⲛ[ⲉ ⲛ-]
ⲉⲃⲟⲗ ⲙⲡⲓ̈ⲣⲁⲥⲙⲟⲥ	ⲧⲉⲕⲟⲩⲉⲣⲏ[ⲧⲉ]
ⲛⲓ̈ⲙ ⲁⲡϫⲁϫⲉ ϫⲓ̈-	÷ⲡⲉϫⲉ ⲓ̅ⲥ̅ ⲛ[ⲁϥ ϫⲉ-]
ⲧ̅ϥ̅ ⲉϩⲟⲩⲛ ⲉⲧⲡⲟ-	ⲛⲛⲉⲕⲡ[ⲓⲣⲁⲍⲉ]
ⲗⲓ̈ⲥ ⲉⲧⲟⲩⲁⲁⲃ ⲑⲓ̈-	ⲙⲡϫⲟ[ⲉⲓⲥ ⲡⲉⲕ-]
ⲉⲗⲏ̅ⲙ̅ ⲁϥⲧⲁⲗⲟϥ	ⲛⲟⲩⲧ[ⲉ ⲁⲩⲱ]
ⲉϫⲙⲡⲧⲡ̅ϩ̅ ⲙ-	ⲡϫⲟⲉ[ⲓⲥ ⲡⲉⲕ-]
ⲡⲣⲡⲉ· ⲡⲉϫⲁϥ ⲛ̄ⲁϥ	ⲛⲟⲩⲧ[ⲉ ⲡⲉⲧⲕ-]
ϫⲉⲉϣϫⲉ ⲛⲧⲟⲕ-	ⲛⲁϣⲗ[ⲏⲗ ⲉⲣⲟϥ·]
ⲡⲉ ⲡϣⲏⲣⲉ ⲙ-	÷Ⲁⲩⲱ ⲛ[ⲧⲉⲣⲉϥ-]
ⲡⲛⲟⲩⲧⲉ ⲛⲟϫ̅ⲕ̅	ϫⲱⲕ [ⲉⲃⲟⲗ ⲙ̄-]
ⲉⲡⲉⲥⲏⲧ ϩⲓ̈ϫⲙ̅-	ⲡⲓ̈ⲣⲁ̣[ⲥⲙⲟⲥ ⲛⲓⲙ]
ⲡⲉⲓ̈ⲙⲁ· ϥⲥⲏϩ	ⲡⲉϫ[ⲉ ⲓ̅ⲥ̅ ⲛⲁϥ]
ⲅⲁⲣ ϫⲉϥⲛⲁϩⲱⲛ̄	ϫⲉⲥⲁ̣[ϩⲱⲕ ⲉⲡⲁ-]
ⲉⲧⲟⲟⲧⲟⲩ ⲛⲛⲉϥ-	ϩ[ⲟⲩ ⲙⲙⲟⲓ]
ⲁⲅⲅⲉⲗⲟⲥ ⲉⲧⲃⲏ-	ⲡ[ⲥⲁⲧⲁⲛⲁⲥ·]
ⲏⲧⲕ ⲛⲥⲉϥⲓ̈ⲧⲕ	Ⲁ[
ⲉϫⲛ̄ⲛⲉⲩϭ[ⲓϫ]	?
ⲙⲏⲡⲟⲧ[ⲉ ⲛⲅϫⲱ-]	

margin

[a] Perhaps ⲙⲡⲛⲥⲁ[ⲧⲣⲉϥ]ϫⲓ ⲃ̄.

[1] Or 'people'. This tradition referred to in F. Robinson, *Ap. Gosp.*, 165.

Fol. 3. *Recto.* ... Wherefore He said unto her,[1] 'Not yet is my hour [come].' Mili[tius?] said, 'We des[ire], O our father, that thou wouldest explain [unto us] this other question (*ζήτημα?*), when he[2] saith, 'When [Jesus was come] up from [the water], after that [He had had?] baptism (*βάπτισμα*) ..... take (took?) .....

... the] devil (*διάβ.*)[3], forty days and forty nights, neither eating nor drinking. When the devil (*διάβ.*) knew that He was an hungered, he betook him unto Him, saying, 'If thou art the Christ, say unto these stones that they may become bread.' Jesus said unto him, 'Man useth not to live by bread alone, but (*ἀλλά*) by every word that cometh forth from the mouth of God.' And when

(*Verso*) [the] enemy had fulfilled every temptation (*πειρασμός*)[4], the enemy brought Him in unto the holy city (*πόλις*) Jerusalem and set Him upon the wing of the temple. He said unto Him, 'If thou it is art the son of God, cast thyself down from hence. For (*γάρ*) it is written, He shall bid His angels (*ἄγγ.*) concerning thee, and they shall bear thee upon their hands, lest at any time (*μήποτε*) thou dash against a stone thy foot.' Jesus said unto him, 'Thou shalt not tempt (*πειράζειν*) the Lord thy God, [and] the Lord [thy] God [it is to whom] thou shalt pray.'[5] And when he had fulfilled [every] temptation (*πει.*), [Jesus] said [unto him], 'Withdraw [thyself be]hind [me.] [Satan .....

No. 13.

Fragments of a version from the Greek of anecdotes embodied by John of Maiuma in his *Πληροφορίαι*, whereof hitherto only a Syriac translation was known.[6] That this Coptic text is not a translation of the latter is clear from divergences in detail which even its dilapidated condition allows us to recognize.[7] The former existence of a Coptic version of the *Testimonies* is known from its occurrence in a 6th or 7th century book list,[8] and its mention in the *Antiphonary*.[9] As in both these the work is definitely ascribed to Peter the Iberian, it may be assumed that John's collection was made from one already existing, and due to that saint himself.

[1] John ii. 4.

[2] *I. e.* the evangelist. *Cf.* Matt. iii. 16.

[3] *Cf.* Matt. iv. 2-4.

[4] *Cf.* Luke iv. 13.

[5] ϣⲙ[ϣⲉ 'serve' (Matt. iv. 10) would be preferable.

[6] *Ed.* Nau in *Patr. Or.* viii (1). Our passages are parallel with the end of cap. xxvi and beginning of xxvii (= *l.c.*, pp. 67, 68). Fol. 2 is not identified; it seems to be absent from John's collection.

[7] *Recto*: 'blessed Timotheus', 'his treatises'; *Verso*: 'rank', 'to-day'.

[8] *V.* my *Coptic Ostr.*, no. 459: 'The Pler. of Apa Peter the Iberian'.

[9] *V.* Rylands *Catal.*, p. 212. The context is: 'Those that would forsake the treachery of Chalcedon, let them take the Book of Testimonies (ϫⲱⲙ ⲛⲧⲉ ⲛⲓⲙⲉⲧⲙⲉⲑⲣⲉⲩ) of Peter and the *συντάγματα* of Timothy the *ὁμολογητής* and the Letters of Severus.'

Fol. 1. → *Recto.*	↑ *Verso.*
margin	margin
ⲁⲩ]ⲱ̣ ⲁⲓⲥⲟⲧⲙⲉ[ⲥ]	[ⲍ]ⲏⲛⲱⲛ · ⲛ̣[ⲧⲡⲁ-]
]ⲥ̣ⲟⲟⲩⲛ ⲙ̄ⲙⲟϥ	ⲗ̣ⲁⲓⲥⲧⲓⲛⲏ̣ ⲛ̣[
]ⲃ̣ⲉ ⲉⲡⲁⲣⲭⲓⲉⲡ[ⲓ]-	ⲡⲉⲛⲙⲁⲕⲁⲣⲓ[ⲟⲥ ⲛⲉⲓⲱⲧ ϩⲁ-]
ⲕⲟⲡⲟⲥ ⲁⲡⲁ ⲧⲓⲙⲟ]ⲑⲉⲟⲥ · ⲉⲧⲓ ⲇⲉ ⲟⲛ	ϩⲧⲏϥ ϫⲉⲁⲟ̣ⲩ[ⲁ ⲉⲡⲉϥⲣⲁⲛⲡⲉ ⲡⲉ-]
]ⲟⲩⲁ̄ ⲛ̄ⲛⲉⲛⲧⲁⲩ-	ⲧⲣⲟⲥ, ⲉⲩⲥⲭⲟⲗ[ⲁⲣⲓⲟⲥⲡⲉ ϩⲙ̄ⲡⲉϥⲁ-]
ⲛ]ⲥⲩ́ⲅⲕⲉⲗⲗⲟⲥ (margin)	(margin) ⲝⲓⲱⲙⲁ · ⲡ[
ⲛⲥⲉϩ]ⲩⲡⲏⲣⲉⲧⲉⲓ ⲙ̄-	ⲡⲟⲟⲩ ⲛⲉⲓ̈ⲙⲉ [ⲛ̄ⲛⲉⲥⲧⲱⲣⲓⲟⲥ
ⲙⲟϥ ⲉϥϩⲛ̄ⲧ]ⲉⲝⲱⲣⲓⲥⲧⲉⲓⲁ · ⲉⲧⲃⲉ-	ⲡⲉ · ⲁⲩⲱ ϯⲭ̣[ⲧⲉⲥⲩⲛϩⲟⲇⲟⲥ]
ⲁⲓ ϩ]ⲱ̣ⲥ ⲉⲁϥⲉⲓⲙⲉ ⲉⲧ[	[ⲛ̄]ⲭⲁⲗⲕⲏⲇⲱⲛ ⲙ̄ⲛ̄[ⲣ̄ⲣⲟ ⲙⲁⲣ-]
ⲡ]ⲙⲁⲕⲁⲣⲓⲟⲥ ⲧⲓⲙⲟⲑ[ⲉⲟⲥ]	[ⲕⲓ]ⲁⲛⲟⲥ · ⲁⲩⲱ ϩⲁϩ [ⲛ̄ⲥⲟⲡ
ⲛϩⲁ]ϩ̣ ⲛ̄ⲥⲟⲡ ϩⲛ̄ⲛⲉϥ[ⲉⲡⲓⲥ-]	[. .]ⲁⲓ̈ϯ ⲟⲩⲃⲉⲛⲉⲧⲕ[ⲁⲧⲏⲅⲟⲣⲉⲓ ⲙ̄-]
ⲟⲗⲏ ⲁⲩⲱ ϩ]ⲛ̣̄ⲛⲉϥⲕⲉⲥⲩⲛⲧⲁ[ⲅⲙⲁ]	[ⲙⲟ]ⲟⲩ · ⲙ̄ⲛ̄ⲛ̄ⲥⲱⲥ [
ⲧⲉⲥⲩ]ⲛϩⲟⲇⲟⲥ ⲛ̄ⲭⲁⲗⲕ[ⲏⲇⲱⲛ]	[ⲟⲩ]ϣ̣ⲏ̄ ⲉⲟⲩⲁ̄ ⲉϥⲁ̣ⲙ̣[
]ⲱ̣[	]ⲧⲛ[

Fol. 1. *Recto.* . . . and I heard it . . . . . knew him . . . . . to the arch[bishop Apa Tim]otheus. And while (ἔτι δέ) yet . . . . . one of them that had . . . . . *syncellus*[1] . . . . and had] served (ὑπηρετεῖν) [him while he was in] exile (ἐξοριστία). Wherefore . . . . . since (ὡς) he had known the . . . . ., the blessed (μακ.) Timotheus[2] . . . . . many a time in his [epistles (ἐπ.) and] also in his treatises (σύνταγμα) . . . . . the synod (σύνοδος) of Chalcedon . . . . .

Verso. . . . the king] Zeno . . . . . Palestine . . . . our blessed (μακ.) [father] . . . . . with him,[3] saying, 'One [whose name was Pe]ter, being a σχολ[άριος in his] rank (ἀξίωμα) . . . . . to-day, I loved [Nestorius] . . . . . And I . . . . . of Chalcedon and . . . . . [the king Mar]cian. And many [times] . . . . . I opposed them that did ac[cuse] (κατηγορεῖν) them. Afterwards . . . . . night, one that . . . . .

[1] This is accented in the MS.: a very rare feature in Coptic (*e.g.* Brit. Mus. Pap. v, *ed.* Winstedt, *Coptic Texts*, 1910, p. 175).

[2] Or 'Timotheus' might (with preceding ⲛϭⲓ) be subject of 'known'.

[3] *I.e.* in his presence.

Fol. 2. ↑ *Recto* (?).	→ *Verso* (?).
]ⲣⲣⲟ ⲑⲉⲟ[ⲇⲟⲥⲓⲟⲥ	]ⲙ̣ⲟ [
]ⲁϣ ⲛ̄ϩ[[a]	ⲁ]ⲩⲱ ⲛⲧ[
]ⲁ̣ϥ [b] ϫⲉⲉϥ[	ⲛ]ⲧⲁϥϣ[
]ⲉ ⲛ̄[	]ⲁⲡⲟⲥⲧⲟ[ⲗⲟⲥ
]ⲧ̣ⲟ[	ϫ]ⲡ̣ⲟⲓ̈ⲛⲉ ⲡ̣[
	?
	]ⲁϩ[

[a] ⲡ]ⲁϣ ⲛϩ[ⲉ, or ⲡ]ⲁϣⲛϩ[ⲧⲏϥ, or ⲁⲛ]ⲁϣ. [b] ⲡⲉϫ]ⲁϥ, or ⲡⲉϫⲁϥ ⲛ]ⲁϥ, or ϫⲟⲟⲥ ⲛ]ⲁϥ.

Fol. 2. *Recto.* ... king Theo[dosius ..... in what manner [1] (?) ..... said ?] unto him, '.....

Verso. ... and .... he had ..... apostles (ἀπ.) .....

No. 14.

This is presumably from apocryphal Acts, in which Andrew plays a part; but it is difficult to say to which story it belongs. Passages on pp. 70, 73–75 of Bonnet's *Acta Apost. Apocr.* ii [1] relate to sea voyages, and the last of them to the appearance of Christ as a ship's master, whom the apostle accosts [2]; but none of these is sufficiently like to be identified with what is discernible here.

Sequence of *Recto* and *Verso* is uncertain.

Fol. 1. ↑ *Recto* (?).		→ *Verso* (?).	
	ⲉⲧⲉⲛ[	]ⲃ̣ⲓ̣ⲥ̣ ϩⲛ-	
]ⲛⲡ̣-	ⲁⲛ ⲛ[ⲕⲓⲛ-]	]ⲛⲉ ⲥ	ⲙⲁ[
] ⲡⲣⲟⲥ	ⲇⲩⲛ[ⲟⲥ ⲛⲑⲁ-]	]ⲛⲣⲁϩⲧ̣	Ⲏⲧ[
]ⲉⲕⲁⲥ ⲟ̣ⲩ̣ [a]	ⲗⲁⲥⲥⲁ	]ϯⲃⲱⲕ	ⲛ[
] ⲛϭⲓ ⲙ̄-	Ⲍⲑⲉⲗⲡⲓⲥ ⲛ-	]ⲡ̣ ⲉⲡⲙⲁ	ϫ . [
[ⲙⲁⲑⲏ]ⲧⲏⲥ	ⲧⲁⲩⲣⲁ̣ⲫ̣[[b]	] ⲙⲡⲉ̣ⲓ̣ⲛⲓ [c]	ⲑⲏ[

[a] Perhaps ϫ]ⲉⲕⲁⲥ ⲉⲩ[ⲉ-. [b] This cannot be correct. Perhaps ⲛ[ⲡⲉⲛ]ⲧⲁⲩ-, followed by a Greek verb. [c] ? ⲛⲓ[ϥⲉ ⲛ].

[1] Several alternatives are possible here.

[2] *Cf.* the Coptic in Guidi's *Frammenti*, pp. 55, 56 (Nota iv); Lemm, *Kopt. Apokr. Apost.* (= *Mélanges Asiatiques* x), p. 156; Ethiopic in Budge, *Contendings* ii. 189, 270, 374.

[ϣⲁⲛⲧⲟ]ⲩⲡⲱϩ
ⲉ[ⲧⲡⲟ]ⲗⲓⲥ ⲉⲧⲟⲩ-
ⲛⲁⲃⲱⲕ[a] ⲉⲣⲟⲥ
ϫⲉⲕⲁⲥ ⲛⲛⲉⲩ-
ϣⲧⲟⲣⲧⲣ ⲛⲑⲁⲗ-
ⲗⲁⲥⲥⲁ·
Ⲁϥϣⲗⲏⲗ ⲛⲧⲉⲓ-
ϩⲉ ⲉϥϫⲱ ⲙ-
ⲙⲟⲥ ϫⲉϯⲧⲱ-
ⲃϩ ⲙⲙ[ⲟⲛ

ⲍⲉ ⲉⲧⲉⲁ[ⲛⲟⲛ-]
ⲡⲉ ⲛⲧⲁ[ⲛⲕⲱ]
ⲛ[ⲥ]ⲱⲛ [ⲛⲑⲉⲗ-]
ⲡⲓⲥ ⲙⲡⲉⲡ̣[
ϫⲉⲕⲁⲥ ⲉⲛⲉϫ[ⲡⲟ]
ⲛⲁⲛ ⲛⲧⲉⲕ-
sic ϩⲗⲡⲓⲥ ⲉⲧⲉ-
ⲧⲱⲕⲧ̣ⲉ
ⲡ̣ⲁ̣[

]ϩ̣ⲏⲧ ϫⲉ-
[ⲕⲁⲥ] ⲉⲩⲉⲟⲩϫⲁⲓ
]ⲛⲟϭ ⲛⲥⲟ-
]ⲉⲣ̣̅ ?
? ?
ⲛϭⲓ ⲁⲛⲇⲣⲉⲁⲥ
ⲉⲓⲥ ϩⲏⲏⲧⲉ ⲁⲩ-

ⲧⲕⲁ[
?
ⲡⲕ[
ⲡϫⲟⲓ ⲉⲧⲙ[ⲣⲱ]
ⲡⲉ ? [
Ⲡⲉϫⲁϥ ϫⲉⲉⲓ-
ϫⲉⲣⲟⲕ ⲛⲧⲟⲕ
ⲡⲛⲉⲉϥ ⲙ̣-
ⲡϫⲟⲉⲓⲥ[b] ⲁⲧ̣ⲁ-
]ⲧⲉⲕ-

[a] My copy has ⲓⲧⲟⲩ-. [b] Or ⲡϫⲟⲉⲓ. But the form ϫⲟⲓ above makes this unlikely.

Recto (?). . : . so that (?) the disciples ($\mu\alpha\theta.$) should . . . [until] they reached the city ($\pi\acute{o}\lambda\iota\varsigma$) whither they were going, so that they might not disturb[1] the sea ($\theta\acute{\alpha}\lambda.$). Thus did he pray, saying, 'I beseech [Thee' . . . . .
. . . 'the perils ($\kappa\acute{\iota}\nu\delta\upsilon\nu o\varsigma$) of the sea ($\theta\acute{\alpha}\lambda.$). The hope ($\grave{\epsilon}\lambda\pi\acute{\iota}\varsigma$) of them that have[2] (?) . . ., that is [us] who have [forsaken] . . . . . the hope ($\grave{\epsilon}\lambda.$) of th[is ? world] . . ., so that we may [get] for ourselves Thy hope ($\grave{\epsilon}\lambda.$) which is Thine' . . . . .

Verso (?). . . . I go [to . . .] the place . . . ., so that they be saved . . . . Andrew [said,] 'Behold,' . . . . .
. . . the ship to the sho[re (?) . . . . . He said, 'I say (?) unto thee,[3] thou sailor of the Lord,[4] my . . . hath . . . . . thy' . . . . .

No. 15.

The date in the title and the words of fol. 1 point to the martyrdom of Mark the Evangelist. We have, therefore, it may be assumed, an Encomium upon him. Those known in Greek, whereof the initial words are published, do not appear to correspond with this text.[5]

[1] Grammar demands this. The subject may be 'winds', or the like, in the earlier, lost part of the sentence.

[2] This assumes an emendation of my copy.

[3] A doubtful locution; *v.* Steindorff, *Gram.*[2] 43*, also no. 9 above, f. 8 *vo.*, *BKU.*, no. 183, 1. Peyron 47 and Stern § 26 took it for $\epsilon\tilde{\iota}\gamma\epsilon$. But Mk. v. 41 ($\sigma o\grave{\iota}\ \lambda\acute{\epsilon}\gamma\omega$) confirms Steindorff's suggestion. In Bo. it appears as ⲁⲓϭⲉⲣⲟⲕ ⲛⲑⲟⲕ (*Test. Abr.*, Rendic. 1900, 164, 10), but also ϫⲉ-, *CSCO.*, vol. 41. 17, 47.

[4] 'Of the ship' is less likely.

[5] *V.* the Bollandist inventories. Fragments of Coptic texts, *v.* Br. Mus., nos. 299, 300.

Fol. I. ↑ *Recto.*

, ⲁⲗⲕⲉ ⲙⲡⲉ̣[ⲃⲟⲧ ⲡⲁⲣⲙⲟⲩⲧⲉ]
; ϩⲛⲟⲩⲉⲓⲣⲏ[ⲛⲏ ⲛⲧⲉ ⲡⲛⲟⲩⲧⲉ]
; ϩⲁⲙⲏⲛ
• ——— • ——— • • ——— • •
• ——— • • ——— • • ——— • •

ⲧ̄ⲭⲣⲉⲱⲥⲧⲉⲓ̄	ⲧⲁⲃ̣[
ⲛⲁⲕ ⲱ̄ ⲡϩⲁⲅⲓ-	ⲅⲁⲣ ⲓ̣[
ⲟⲥ ⲙⲁⲣⲕⲟⲥ ⲛ̄ⲟⲩ-	ⲥⲁⲣ[
ⲛⲟϭ̄ ⲛ̄ⲭⲣⲉ-	ⲕⲁ[
ⲱⲥ̄ · ϯϩⲟⲙⲟⲗⲟ-	ⲡ̣ⲱ̣[
ⲅⲉⲓ̈ ϫⲉϯⲭⲣⲉ-	ⲅⲁⲣ̣ [
ⲱⲥⲧⲉⲓ ⲛⲁⲕ̄	ⲡⲙ̣[
ⲛ̄ⲟⲩϩⲟⲟⲩ̄ ⲁⲛ̄	ⲉⲣ[
ⲟⲩⲇⲉ̄ ⲥⲛⲁⲩ	ⲡⲣ̣[
ⲁⲗⲗⲁ̄ ⲙⲡⲉⲓ̣̈-	ⲡ . [
ⲟⲩⲟⲉⲓϣ̄ ⲧⲏ-	. ⲱ̣[
ⲣϥ ⲙ̄ⲡⲁⲱⲛ̄ϩ	?
ⲧⲁⲧ̣ⲁ̣[	
ⲱⲥ̣[	
ⲙ̄ⲙⲛ̄[	
ⲛϩⲉⲛⲛ̣[	
margin	

→ *Verso.*

	]ϫⲱ̣
	ⲁⲩ ⲛ̣ⲥ̣ⲉ̣ⲁⲡⲁⲧ̣ⲏ̣
	ⲧⲏⲣⲟⲩ ϩⲁⲑⲏ
	ⲛ̄ⲛⲉⲓⲟⲩⲟⲉⲓϣ
]ⲡ̣̄	ⲁϥϫⲟⲟⲩⲕ̄
] ⲁⲩⲱ̄	ⲇⲉ ⲉⲣⲁⲕⲟⲧⲉ
]ϭⲱⲧⲡ̄	ⲙ̄ⲙⲁⲧⲉ ⲁⲛ
]ⲡⲟⲗⲩⲙⲉⲓ̄	ⲁⲗⲗⲁ ⲁϥϫⲟ-
]ⲕⲉ	ⲟⲩⲕ̄ ⲟⲛ̄ ⲉⲧⲉ-
]ⲧⲡ̣ⲓ̣ⲥ-	ⲭⲱⲣⲁ ⲛ̄ⲕⲏⲙⲉ
]ⲛ̣ⲉ	ⲉⲧⲗⲟⲃⲉ̄ ϩⲁ-
?	ⲑⲛ̄ ⲙⲡⲟⲟⲩ
] . ⲥ̣ⲟ̣̄	ϩⲙ̄ⲡⲗⲓⲃⲉ
]ⲉⲡ . . ̄	ⲛ̄ⲛⲉⲓⲁⲱ-
]ⲟⲗ .	ⲗⲟⲛ̄ ⲛⲓⲙ̄
]ⲥⲁϥ	ⲡⲉⲧⲛⲁϣⲡⲓ-
]ⲁ	ⲑⲉ̄ ⲛⲛⲓⲗⲁⲟ[ⲥ]
]ⲁ̄	. . . ⲧ̣ⲏⲓ̣ⲡⲉ ⲉ-
]ⲁⲓ̣	[ⲕⲁ]ⲧⲁⲫⲣⲟ[ⲛⲉⲓ]
	ⲛⲛⲁⲁⲓⲙⲱⲛ
	margin

Fol. I. *Recto.* . . . on] the last day of the month [Parmoute]. In peace (εἰρ.) [of God]. Amen :—

I owe (χρεωστεῖν) thee, O holy (ἅγ.) Mark, a great debt (χρέως). I confess (ὁμολογεῖν) that I owe (χρ.) thee not one day nor (οὐδέ) two, but rather (ἀλλά) all the (*lit.* this) time of my life, that I may . . . as (? ὡς) . . . . .

Verso. . . . conquer . . . contend (πολεμεῖν) . . . . .

. . . all,[1] before this age (*lit.* these times). And (δέ) He sent thee not to

[1] The preceding word perhaps ἀπάτη for ἀπατᾶ(ν) 'deceive'.

Rakote (Alexandria) alone, but (ἀλλά) He sent thee also to the land (χώρα) of Egypt, that was mad until to-day, with the madness of the idols (εἴδ.).[1] Who shall be able to persuade (πείθειν) the peoples (λαός) . . . to despise (καταφρονεῖν) the demons (δαίμων) . . . . .

Fol. 2. ↑ *Recto* (?).

[ⲡⲁ]ϩⲣⲉ ⲉⲣⲟⲟⲩ ⲉϣ̣[
ϩⲛⲧⲉϥⲡⲁϭ- ⲛⲉ[
ⲥⲉ̄ · ⲛⲉϯⲛⲁ̄ϣⲟ-
ⲟϭⲟⲩ̄ ϩⲛⲛⲁ̄-
ⲥⲟⲧⲉ̄ ϥⲛⲁ̄-
ⲧⲁⲗ̄ϭⲟⲟⲩ ϩⲙ̄-
ⲡⲉϥϣⲁϫⲉ̄
ⲛⲉϯⲛⲁ̄ϥⲓ-
ⲧⲟⲩ̄ ⲉⲛⲉⲥ̆ⲡⲛ̄-
ⲗⲁⲓ̈ⲟⲛ ⲛⲕⲁ-
ⲕⲉ ϥ̄ⲛⲁⲣⲟⲩⲟ̄-
ⲉⲓⲛ̄ ⲉⲣⲟⲟⲩ̄
ϩⲛⲧⲗⲁⲙ̄ⲡⲁⲥ̆
ⲙⲡⲉ̣[ⲩ]ⲁ̣ⲅⲅⲉ̄-
ⲗ̣[ⲓⲟⲛ .]ϥ ⲛ̄-
ⲧ[
ⲁϥ̣[
ⲥⲓ[
margin

→ *Verso* (?).

ⲙ̣ⲡ̣[ⲉⲩⲁⲅⲅⲉ-]
]ϫⲙ̄ ⲗⲓⲟⲛ ϫ̣[
]ϥ ⲁϥϫⲓ̣ϣ̣ⲓ̣ⲡ̣ⲉ̣
ⲛϭⲓ̈ ⲡϫⲁϫⲉ̄
ⲁϥⲙⲟⲩ̄ ⲙⲉⲛ̄
ⲅⲁⲣ̄ ⲁⲗⲗⲁ̄
ⲡⲉϥ̄ⲙⲟⲩ ⲡⲣⲟ̄-
ⲧⲣⲉⲡⲉ̄ ⲛⲟⲩ̄-
ⲙⲏ̄ⲛϣⲉ ⲁⲩⲣ̄-
ⲙⲁⲣⲧⲩⲣⲟⲥ
ⲁϥϩⲱⲡ̄ ⲙⲉ̄
ϩⲁⲡⲕⲁϩ̄ ⲁⲗ̄-
ⲗⲁ ⲛⲉϥⲕⲗⲟ̣ⲙ̣
ⲣⲟⲩⲟⲉⲓⲛ̄ ⲙ-
ⲙⲏⲛⲉ̄ ⲛϩⲩ̊ⲟ
ⲉⲧⲁⲥ̣[ⲧⲣⲁⲡ]ⲛ̄
]
] ?
ⲥ]ⲱ̣ⲙⲁ̣̄
margin

Fol. 2. *Recto* (?). . . . 'give] healing[2] unto them by his spittle.[3] Them that I shall wound with my darts he will make whole with his word;

[1] *Cf.* εἰδωλομανία.   [2] The devil *loq.*   [3] A reference to the healing of Anianus' hand.

them that I shall lead into dark caverns (*σπήλαιον*), he will enlighten with the lamp (*λαμπάς*) of the gospel (*εὐαγ.*)'[1] . . . . .

Verso (?). . . . of (?) the gospel (*εὐαγ.*) . . . the enemy was shamed. He died indeed (*μὲν γάρ*), yet (*ἀλλά*) his death incited (*προτρέπειν*) a multitude and they became martyrs (*μάρτυρος*). He was (+ *μέν*) hidden below the earth, yet (*ἀλλά*) do his crowns[2] shine forth daily, more than the li[ghtning] (*ἀστραπή*) . . . . body . . . . .

No. 16.

From the Martyrdom of Philotheus of Antioch. The story was apparently similar to that abbreviated in the *Synaxarium*, 16th Tubah.[3] Other remnants of the Sa'idic version are among the copies of papyri made by A. des Rivières[4] and in a Borgian MS.,[5] Brit. Mus., no. 330 being another copy of the latter passage. His Martyrdom appears in a 6th or 7th century library catalogue.[6] It is presumably this martyr[7] who is invoked, with other Antiochene military saints, upon grave stelae[8] and in the diptychs.[9] He too appears once as a dragon slayer.[10] The Encomium, attributed to Severus of Antioch, for the building (? بنيان) of his church and 'invention' (ظهور) of his relics, on the 16th Abîb, appears to relate various miracles, but no facts.[11]

→ *Recto.*

]ⲛⲁ[

ϣⲏⲣⲉ] ⲕⲟⲩⲓ̈ ⲇⲉ ϩⲛ̣[

[. .]ⲣ̣ⲓⲧⲉ[a] ⲛⲣⲱⲙⲡⲉ ⲉⲡⲉϥⲣⲁⲛ̣[ⲡⲉ ⲫⲓⲗⲟⲑⲉⲟⲥ]

[a] One might more easily emend to ⲯⲓⲧⲉ than ⲙⲏⲧⲉ which Ar. requires.

[1] *Cf.* the phrases in Paris 129[14], f. 136 (encom. on Mark): ⲕⲁⲓ ⲅⲁⲣ ϩⲁⲑⲏ ⲙⲡⲁⲧⲉⲙⲁⲣⲕⲟⲥ ⲉⲓ ⲡⲉⲙⲛϩⲟⲟⲩ ϣⲟⲟⲡ ⲉⲡⲧⲏⲣϥⲡⲉ ϩⲛⲕⲏⲙⲉ ⲁⲗⲗⲁ ⲟⲩⲟⲩϣⲏⲡⲉ ⲉⲥⲙⲏⲛ ⲉⲃⲟⲗ ⲛⲧⲉⲣⲉϥⲉⲓ ⲇⲉ ⲛϭⲓ ⲙⲁⲣⲕⲟⲥ ⲡⲟⲩⲟⲉⲓⲛ ⲁⲡϩⲟⲟⲩ ⲁⲣⲭⲉⲓ . . . *Cf.* here the very similar phraseology in the Encomium of Severus (9th cent.), *ed.* Bargès, p. 6.

[2] Those granted to martyrs for their virginity, piety, sufferings &c.

[3] Forget, i. 213 = Wüstenfeld, *Synax.* 241; Amélineau, *Actes*, 193.

[4] Munich, Landesbibl., MS. Copt. no. 3, fragg. lxxiv–lxxvii. The first fragment gives the calf's name, ⲥⲙⲁⲣⲁⲅⲇⲟⲛ, with the epithet ⲡϣⲟⲩⲙⲉⲣⲓⲧϥ = *ἀγαπητός*.

[5] *Ed.* Balestri, *Sacr. Bibl. Fragm.*, xxxix ff.

[6] *Recueil*, xi. 133.

[7] And not him of Oxyrhynchus (Hyvernat, *Actes*, 100). Philotheus of Dronkah (Forget, *Synax.* ii. 100) suffered in A.D. 1380.

[8] Quibell-Thompson, *Saqqara*, no. 203. *Cf.* Clédat, *Baouit*, i, pl. xxxi.

[9] Tuki's *Theotokia*, 41; Cairo *do.* 289; Leyden Museum, MS. copte no. 41; Brit. Mus. no. 865.

[10] *Bull. Soc. Nat. d. Antiq. de France*, 1898, Novembre = G. Lefebvre, *Rec. des Inscr.*, no. 778.

[11] Paris, MS. arabe 153, 243b, almost wholly illegible.

margin

Ⲛⲉϥⲉⲓⲟⲧⲉ̈ ϫⲉ ⲛⲉϩⲉⲛϩⲉⲗ[ⲗⲏⲛⲛⲉ ⲉⲩⲥⲟⲟⲩⲛ]
ⲁⲛ ⲙ̄ⲡⲛⲟⲩⲧⲉ · ⲁⲗⲗⲁ ⲉⲩ[ϣⲙ̄ϣⲉ ⲛⲟⲩ-]
ⲙⲁⲥⲉ ⲛⲁⲙ̄ⲭⲟ́ⲣⲧⲟⲥ (*sic*) ⲁ̣[
ⲛⲉϥⲉⲓⲟⲧⲉ ⲉⲓⲣⲉ̈ ⲙ̄ⲙⲟⲟⲩ ⲙ̄[
ⲛⲁϥ ⲙ̄ⲙⲏⲛⲉ (*sic*) ϣⲟⲙⲛⲧ ⲛ̄ϣⲓ̣ [ⲛ̄ⲥⲁⲙⲓⲧ ⲉⲩⲟⲩ-]
ⲱϣⲙ̄ ⲛ̣[. . .] ⲛⲛⲉϩ[a] · ϩⲛ̣ϩⲱ[[b]
Ⲧⲣⲉϥⲛ̣[. . . ⲉ]ⲃⲟⲗ ⲛ̄ϩⲏⲧⲟⲩ ⲁⲩⲱ [
]ⲛ̄ⲥ[ⲟ]ϭⲛ ⲛ̄ϣⲟⲙⲛⲧ ⲛ̄[ⲥⲟⲡ
]ⲛⲉϥⲥⲱ ⲉⲃⲟⲗ ϩⲛⲟⲩⲏ́ⲣ[ⲡ
] ⲙ̄ⲛⲟⲩϩⲣⲱⲥⲁⲧⲟⲛ · ⲁⲩ̣[ⲱ
]ⲡ̣ⲏⲩⲉ̣ . . . [
]ϣ̣ⲱⲙ̣ · ⲁⲩⲱ ⲕ[ⲉ
]ⲛⲉ ⲁⲩⲱ . [
] ⲛ̣ⲛⲟⲩⲃ · ⲁⲩⲱ [
] . ⲧⲉ[

[a] The constant phrase is ⲟⲩⲟϣⲙ ϩⲙⲛⲉϩ (*e.g.* Lev. vii. 12, ix. 4), rarely ϩⲛⲟⲩⲛⲉϩ (ii. 4). My copy makes either of these difficult here.   [b] ? ϩⲓϩⲣⲱ[ⲥⲁⲧⲟⲛ, following Ar. بزيت وسيرج.

↑ *Verso.*

]ⲛϩ̣ . ⲙ̣ⲟ : ⲛⲉ . [
ⲛⲉϥⲙⲁⲁ]ϫⲉ ⲥⲛⲧⲉ ⲟ ⲛⲑⲉ̣ [ⲛ
ⲧ]ⲉϥⲧⲁⲡⲣⲟ́ : ⲉⲣⲉⲛⲉϥⲟⲩⲉ̣ⲣⲏ̣[ⲧⲉ]
ϩⲉⲛⲥⲧⲩⲗ]ⲗⲟⲥ ⲛ̄ϩⲁⲧ · ϩⲓϫⲛ̄ϩⲉⲛ̄ⲃⲁⲥⲓ́ⲥ
ⲉⲩⲧⲁ]ϫⲣⲏⲩ · ⲉϥⲟ ⲛ̄ⲣⲙ̄ⲣⲁϣ ⲛⲁϭⲁ-
[ⲑⲟⲥ]ⲙⲙⲛⲧⲥⲁïⲏ ⲛⲓⲙ ⲛⲑⲉ ⲛ̄-
[ⲓⲱⲥⲏⲫ]ⲕⲏⲙⲉ ⲉϥⲟ ⲛ̄ⲣⲙ̄ⲣⲁϣ ⲛ̄ⲛⲁⲩ̇ ⲛⲓⲙ
]ⲛⲛⲉϥϩⲙ̄ϩⲁⲗ ⲙ̣̄ⲛ̣ⲛⲁⲡⲉϥⲏⲧ · ⲙ̄ⲛ̄-
ⲛ]ⲉ̣ⲧϩⲓⲃⲟⲗ · ⲛⲉⲩⲙⲉ [ⲙⲙⲟ]ⲟϥ ⲧⲏⲣⲟⲩ ⲉⲧ-
[ⲃⲉ ⲡⲉ]ϥⲟⲩⲣⲟⲧ̇ ⲙ̄ⲡⲉϥ . [. . . .] ⲛ̣ⲉⲣⲉⲛ .
]ϥ ⲙ̣̄ⲙ̣ⲏⲛⲉ ⲛ̣ⲉⲧⲉ̣[. . . . .]ⲛ̣ⲧⲉ

margin

]ϫ̄ⲙⲡⲙⲁⲥⲉ ϫⲉⲛⲉⲩⲟⲩⲁ̣[ϣϥ

]ⲛ ⲉϥϫⲱϭⲉ̣ [ⲙⲙⲟ]ⲥ [

]ⲡⲉ [a] ⲡⲛⲟⲩⲧⲉ ⲛⲧ[ⲡⲉ

]ⲛⲛⲉⲧⲛϩⲏ[ⲧⲟⲩ

ϣⲁ]ϫⲉ ⲛϭⲓ ⲡϣⲏ̣ⲣ̣[ⲉ ϣⲏⲙ

]ⲙ[. .]ⲙⲩⲥⲧ[ⲏⲣⲓⲟⲛ

[a] ? ⲛⲧⲟⲕ]ⲡⲉ.

Recto. . . . But (δέ) a young boy . . . . . [of] . . .[1] years, whose name was [Philotheus]. And (δέ) his parents [were] pag[ans (ἕλλην), knowing] not God, but rather (ἀλλά) [worshipping (?) a] grass-eating (-χόρτος) calf . . . . . that his parents did, [giving ?] him daily three measures [of flour] kneaded [with ?] oil . . . . .[2] they . . . from them and . . . . of ointment three [times daily. And] he used to drink of . . . . . wine and . . . and rose-wine (ῥόσατον). And . . . . summer and another . . . . and . . . . of gold. And . . . . .

Verso. . . . his[3] two ears were like . . . . his mouth, while his feet were . . . . . pillars (στῦλος) of silver upon bases (βάσις) of . . . . . firmly fixed; and he was mild and good (ἀγαθός) [and adorned with] every beauty, even as [Joseph[4] . . .] Egypt, being mild[5] at all times [toward] his servants and those of his house and . . . . . those without. They used all to love him be[cause of his] joyous . . . and his . . . . him (?) daily . . . . upon (?) the calf, for they loved [him ?] . . . . saying (?), ...[6] the God of [heaven and earth and all] that are in [them] . . . . . the boy . . . . . [his ?] words (?) . . . . mysteries (μυστ.) . . . . .

No. 17.

From the Martyrdom of Philotheus. Nothing parallel to the incidents here related is found in the *Synaxarium's* abbreviated story. It will be observed that Brit. Mus. no. 330 (*v.* above) gives Raphael as the angel who attended the saint. The last of A. des Rivières' fragments (lxxvii) tells of the emperor's dismay at the destruction of his gods.[7]

[1] It is difficult to read 'ten' with Ar.; 'nine' were more possible.

[2] Perhaps here 'and rose-wine'. This would, here and below, = Ar. 'sesame oil'. *Cf.* the mixture described by Lane, *Mod. Eg.* (1836), ii. 274.

[3] *I.e.* Philotheus.

[4] *Cf.* Gen. xxxix. 6.

[5] The epithet applied to Moses (= πραύς), Num. xii. 3.

[6] Perhaps 'Art thou the God?' *Cf.* Arabic.

[7] 'Thou hast destroyed', he says, 'the great god that gave me victory and hast enchanted my three generals and all my army. By the might of the Romans, I will cause thy flesh to . . .'

Fol. I. → *Recto.*

margin

[.]ⲉϩⲣⲁⲫⲁⲏⲗ
[ⲡⲁⲅ]ⲅⲉⲗⲟⲥ ⲁϩ-
ⲉⲣ]ⲁⲧϥ ⲛ̄ⲥⲁⲟⲩ-
ⲥⲁ] ⲙ̄ⲙⲟϥ ⲡ̄-
]ⲛ̣ⲁ̣ⲛ̣ ⲡⲉ̣-
ϫⲁϥ] ⲉϩⲟⲩⲛ ϩ̄ⲛ̄-
ⲇⲓⲟ]ⲕⲗⲏ [ϫ]ⲉⲱ̄
ⲡⲉ]ⲑⲩⲣⲓⲟⲛ ⲉ-
ⲑⲟⲟ]ⲩ · ⲉⲉⲓⲉϩⲉ̄-
]ⲁⲛⲉ ⲛⲉⲕ-
] ⲛ̄ⲧⲉⲓϩⲉ
ⲡ]ⲉⲓⲙⲏ-
ⲏϣⲉ . .] . . ϩ̣ⲁ̣
. . . .] . ⲉ . ⲛ̣ⲁ̣
]ⲙⲟⲟ̣-
ϣⲉ]ⲟ̣ϥ

[. .]ⲛ̄ⲡ̣[
[. .]ⲉⲓ̣ⲡ̣[
ⲙⲛⲧⲯ[ⲓⲥ ⲛ̄-]
ⲧⲟⲩⲱⲧ [
[.]ⲉⲁ̣ . ⲙ[
[.]ⲡ[.]ⲕ̣ⲉ[
ⲛ̄ⲟⲩ[.]ⲏ̣[. .]ⲧ
ⲧⲁϩ[ⲟ]ⲓ̈ ⲛ̣ . ⲉⲓⲙ
ϩ̄ⲛ̄ⲟⲩϭⲉⲡⲏ ·
ⲧ̣[ⲁ]ⲣⲉⲧϭⲟⲙ ⲙ̄-
ⲡⲁϫⲟⲉⲓⲥ ⲟⲩⲱ-
ⲛ̄ϩ̄ [ⲉ]ⲃⲟ[ⲗ] ϩ̄ⲛ̄-
ⲧⲙⲏⲧⲉ ⲙ̄ⲡⲉⲓ-
ⲙⲏⲏϣⲉ · ⲁⲩⲱ
ⲁⲡⲉⲧⲟⲩⲱⲧ
ⲡⲱⲧ [ϩ̄ⲛ̄]ⲟⲩϭⲉ-
ⲡ[ⲏ . . .]ⲧ ⲙ̣̄-
ⲙⲟ[ϥ . . .]ⲛ[a] ⲉ̣-
ⲡⲣ̄ⲡ[ⲉ
ⲉϩⲟⲩ[ⲛ

↑ *Verso.*

margin

ⲇⲓⲟ]ⲕⲗⲏ [ ]
]ⲁⲙ[. .]
]ϥⲙ . ⲧ̣
]ⲁϥϯ ⲣ̣ .
] ϫⲉ[ⲉ]ⲓⲥ [
[. . . .]ⲟ[. .]ⲉⲁⲛ
. ⲉ[. . ⲡ]ϩⲙϩⲁⲗ
ⲙ̄ⲡ[ⲛⲟⲩ]ⲧⲉ
[ⲫ]ⲓⲗ[ⲟⲑ]ⲉⲟⲥ
ϩ̄ⲛ̄ⲟⲩϭⲉⲡⲏ ·
ⲁⲩⲱ ⲛ̄ⲧⲉⲩⲛⲟⲩ
ⲁⲩϥⲟϭⲟⲩ [ⲉ]ⲡⲉ-
ⲥⲏⲧ ϩⲓϫⲛ̄ⲛⲉⲩ-
ⲃ[ⲁ]ⲥⲓⲥ ϫⲉⲉⲛⲉϩⲣⲁ-
ⲫⲁⲏ[ⲗ ⲡⲁ]ⲣⲭⲁⲅ-
ⲅⲉⲗⲟ[ⲥ
ⲉ]ⲃⲟⲗ
]ⲛ̄ϭⲓ

ⲙ̄ⲙ[ⲟⲟ]ⲩ [. .]
ⲧⲟⲩ ⲉⲓ ⲉϩⲣ̣[ⲁⲓ ⲉ-]
ⲡⲉⲑⲉⲁⲧⲣ[ⲟⲛ]
ⲛ̄ⲥⲉⲁϩⲉⲣ[ⲁⲧⲟⲩ]
ⲙ̄ⲡⲉⲙⲧⲟ [ⲉⲃⲟⲗ]
ⲙ̄ⲡϩⲁⲅⲓⲟⲥ[b]
ⲫⲓⲗⲟ[ⲑ]ⲉⲟⲥ ϩ[ⲛ̄ⲟⲩ-]
ⲛⲟϭ ⲛ̄ϩⲟⲧ[ⲉ ⲁⲩⲱ]
ⲡⲉϫⲁⲩ ⲧⲏ̣[ⲣⲟⲩ]
ⲛ̄ⲑⲉ ⲉⲃⲟⲗ [ϩ̄ⲛ̄ⲟⲩ-]
ⲧⲁⲡⲣⲟ ⲛ̄[ⲟⲩⲱⲧ]
ϫⲉⲉⲓⲥ ϩⲏ[ⲏⲧⲉ]
ⲁⲛⲉⲓ̈ ⲡ̣[ϩⲙϩⲁⲗ]
ⲙ̄ⲡ̣ⲛⲟ[ⲩⲧⲉ ϫⲉ-]
ⲁⲛⲙⲟⲩ[ⲧⲉ ⲉⲣⲟⲛ]
ⲏⲧ[ⲉ]ⲣⲉ̣[

[a] ? ⲉϩⲟⲩ]ⲛ ⲉ-.   [b] Space for ⲁⲡⲁ.

Fol. I. *Recto.* . . . Raphael the angel (*ἄγ.*) standing be[side] him . . . He said unto Diocletian,[1] 'O evil beast (*θηρίον*), are then . . . . . thy (*pl.*) . . . like this . . . . . this mul[titude (?)] . . . . .

. . . 'nineteen idols[2] . . . . quickly, that the power of my Lord

[1] Here (as in *PSBA*. xxxii. 246 ff.) always 'Dioclê', a form due presumably to the ⲇⲓⲟⲕⲗⲏ/ frequently used in Sa'idic dated colophons (Brit. Mus. nos. 162, 398, 490; Paris 132[1], ff. 66, 74 &c.) and represented in Arabic as ديقلا (Sever. Ashm. in *Patr. Or.* vi. 126, 127).

[2] Diocletian is usually given seventy idols: Hyvernat, *Actes*, 78, 202; Winstedt, *Theodore*, 58; *CSCO*. vol. 44, pp. 78, 123; *Ib.* 38, pp. 16, 120 &c.

may be manifested in the midst of this multitude.' And the idol ran quickly . . . . . in (*or* into) the temple . . . . .

Verso. . . . Diocletian . . . . [saying,[1]] 'Lo . . . . the servant of God Philotheus quickly.' And straightway they leapt down from their pedestals (*βάσις*), for the archangel (*ἀρχάγ.*) Raphael was . . . . .

. . . then . . . . . come in unto the theatre (*θέατρον*) and stood before Saint (*ἅγιος*) Philotheus[2] in great fear [and] they all said, as if with a [single] voice, 'Lo, we are come, servant of God, [for] thou didst call [us.'] When . . . . .

Fol. 2. ↑ *Recto.*

margin

]ⲁϩⲧⲥ̣
ϫ]ⲟⲉⲓⲥ · ⲁⲛⲛⲁⲩ
[ⲉ]ⲛ̄ⲭⲣⲓⲥⲧⲓⲁⲛⲟⲥ
]ϩⲓⲑⲏ ⲱ̄
] ϩⲛ̄ϩⲉⲛⲙⲁ
]ⲙ̄ⲡⲛ . . ⲥ̣ⲉ
]ⲓⲁ̣ ⲉϥ[ⲟ] ⲛ̄ⲑⲉ
[ⲛ̄ⲟⲩⲕ]ⲟⲩⲓ̣ [a] ϣⲏⲣⲉ
] . ⲉⲧϩⲛⲁⲙ̄ⲛ̄ⲧⲏ
[ⲛ̄ⲣⲱⲙ]ⲡⲉ · ⲡⲉ-
[ϫⲉ ⲇ]ⲓⲟⲕⲗⲏ ⲉϩⲟⲩⲛ̣
[ϩⲛ̄ϩⲣ]ⲱⲙⲁⲛⲟⲥ
[ⲙⲛ̄ⲛ]ⲉϥⲛⲟϭ ⲧⲏⲣⲟⲩ
[ϫⲉ] . . ⲡⲉⲕ̣-
[. . . ⲡⲁⲓ]ⲇ̣ⲉⲩⲥⲓⲥ
]ⲥ̣ ⲛ̣ⲁϥ

[. .]ⲙⲉϣ[
ⲛ[ⲣ]ⲟⲕϩⲟ[ⲩ ϩⲛ̄-]
ⲟⲩⲥⲁⲧⲉ [ϣⲁⲛⲧ-]
ⲟ[ⲩ]ⲱϫ̄ⲛ̄ [
[. .]ⲧ[.]ⲕ[
ⲛ̣̄ϭ̄ⲛ[ⲟ]ϫ[ϥ
ⲉⲑⲁⲗ[ⲗ]ⲁ[ⲥⲥⲁ] (*sic*)
ϩⲱⲥⲧⲉ ⲉ[ⲧ̄ⲙ̄]ⲧⲣ[ⲉⲩ-]
[ϩ]ⲉ̣ ⲉ̣ⲡ̣ⲉ[ϥ]ⲕ̣ⲉ̣ⲥⲱⲙ[ⲁ]
[ϩ]ⲟⲗⲱⲥ ⲉⲕⲱⲧ
ⲉⲣⲟϥ ⲛ̄ⲟ[ⲩ]ⲙⲁⲣⲧⲩ-
ⲣⲓⲟⲛ ϫⲉⲥ̣ⲉⲛⲁ-
ⲕⲱⲧ ⲉⲣⲟⲟⲩ ⲛ̄ⲟⲩ-
ⲙⲁⲣⲧⲩⲣⲓⲟⲛ ϩⲛ̄-
ⲑⲁⲛ · ⲛ̄[
ⲛ̄ⲧ[
ϭ[
ⲃⲟⲗ ⲛ̄[
[.]ⲟⲩ̣[

→ *Verso.*

margin

[. . .]ⲡ̣ⲣ̄ⲣⲟ [
[. . . .]ⲣⲉⲛ[
[. . .]ⲡⲓϣⲁϫⲉ[
[. . .]ⲛ̣ϭⲓ ⲙ̄ⲙ̣[ⲁⲧⲟⲓ]
[. . . .]ϥ . ⲙⲡ̣ϣ̣ .
[. . . . .]· ⲉⲧⲉⲩ-
ⲁ̣[. . .] ⲛⲁϥ ⲕⲁⲧⲁ
ⲧⲕ[ⲉⲗ]ⲉⲩⲥⲓⲥ ⲙ̄-
ⲡⲣ̄[ⲣⲟ ⲁⲩϫⲟⲟⲥ] [b]
ⲛⲁϥ ⲛϭⲓ ⲙ̄ⲙⲁ[ⲧ]ⲟⲓ̈
ϫⲉⲧⲛ[ⲟ]ⲩⲱϣ · (*sic*)
ⲉϯⲥⲟ̄ ⲉⲣⲟⲕ ⲉⲧⲃⲉ-
ⲡⲉⲕⲥⲁ ⲱ̄ ⲫⲓⲗⲟ-
[ⲑ]ⲉⲟⲥ · ⲁⲗⲗⲁ ⲧ̄ⲛ̄ⲡ̄-
[. . .]ⲧ̣ⲥ [c] ⲛ̄ⲧⲕⲉ-
[ⲗⲉⲩⲥⲓⲥ ⲙ̄ⲡⲣ̄ⲣ]ⲟ
]ⲉⲛ
]ϫ̣ⲉⲙⲓϣ-

ⲁ̣ⲗ̣ⲗ[ⲁ] ⲡ̣ⲉ[ⲧⲟⲩⲛⲁ-
ⲭ[ⲁ]ⲣ̣ⲓ̣ⲍⲉ ⲛⲧ̣[ⲟⲟ-]
ⲧⲛ ϣⲁⲛϫⲱ[ⲕ]
ⲉⲃⲟⲗ · ⲙ̄ⲡⲟⲩ[ⲉϩ-]
ⲥⲁϩⲛⲉ [ⲙ̄ⲡ-]
ⲣ̄ⲣⲟ̄ ⲁϥⲥⲫⲣ[ⲁⲅⲓⲍⲉ]
ⲙ̄ⲙ[ⲟ]ϥ ϩⲙ̄ⲡ̣[ⲣⲁⲛ]
ⲙ̄ⲡⲉⲭ̄ⲥ̄ · ⲡ̣[ⲉϫⲁϥ]
ϫⲉⲡⲁϫⲟⲉ[ⲓⲥ ⲓ̄ⲥ̄]
ⲡⲉⲭ̄ⲥ̄ · ⲉϣ[ϫⲉ]
ⲡⲁ̈ⲓⲡⲉ ⲡⲉⲕ̣[ⲟⲩⲱϣ]
ⲉⲧⲣⲁϫⲱⲕ̣ [ⲉ-]
ⲃⲟⲗ ⲙ̄ⲡⲁ[ⲁⲅⲱⲛ]
ϩⲛ̄ⲧⲉⲓⲕⲟⲗ̣[ⲁⲥⲓⲥ]
ⲧ̣ⲁ[ⲓ] ⲉ̣ⲓ̣ⲉ [[d]
?

[a] Or [ⲙⲛⲓⲕ]. [b] My copy does not admit of ⲡⲉϫⲁⲩ. [c] There should be space for [ϩⲟⲧⲉ ϩⲏ]ⲧⲥ. [d] My copy allows ⲧⲁⲉⲓ ⲉ[.

[1] Raphael *loq.*? [2] Possibly 'the saintly [Apa] Ph.'

Fol. 2. *Recto.* . . . 'lord. We beheld the Christians (χρ.) . . . before . . . . . in places . . . ., he being like unto a youth[1] . . . of about fifteen years.' Diocletian said unto Romanus and all his great (men), '. . . . . thy (?) . . . [com]mand (? κέλευσις[2]) . . . to him . . . . .

. . . burn them[3] [in] fire, [until they] cease . . . . then cast [him in]to the sea (θάλ.), so that (ὥστε) they may not even find (?) his body (σῶ.) at all (ὅλως), to build for it a shrine (μαρτύριον)'; for a shrine (μ.) shall be built for them at the last . . . . .

Verso. . . . the king . . . . this word . . . the so[ldiers ?] . . . . their . . . according to (κατά) the command (κέλευσις) of the king. The soldiers [said] unto him, 'We would spare thee for thy beauty's sake, O Philotheus, but (ἀλλά) we [fear ?] the com[mand (κέλ.) of the kin]g . . . . .

. . . but (ἀλλά) whoso is delivered (χαρίζεσθαι) unto us, we fulfil the king's bidding.' He signed (σφραγίζειν) himself in Christ's [name] and said, 'My Lord [Jesus] Christ, if this be Thy [will], that I should finish my [fight (ἀγών)] in this torture (κόλασις), and that I go (?)[4] . . . . .

No. 18.

From the Martyrdom of Psate, bishop of Psoi (Ptolemais).[5] The same incident, of the devil, in the guise of a serpent, inspiring the young Diocletian, then still known as Agripidos,[6] is found in the *Synaxarium*.[7] The only new feature is the name of the saint's native village.[8]

[1] Or 'this youth'.

[2] Or possibly 'instruction, chastisement', παίδευσις.

[3] The *number* of this and several following pronouns is quite uncertain.

[4] Or possibly 'then' (*apodosis*) . . . . .

[5] *Synax.*, 27 Kihak. The name is as often Psote. Fragments of the text: Brit. Mus. no. 347; Winstedt in *PSBA*. xxxii. 195, 246, 283.

[6] Written ⲁⲕⲣⲓⲡⲡⲓⲧⲁ Zoega 60 = Winstedt, *Theod.* 57, *Synax. l. c.* Aḳribîdâ, Ethiop. (*CSCO.*, vol. 37, 133) Agripâdâ, ⲁⲅⲣⲓⲡⲓⲇⲟⲥ (*CSCO.*, vol. 42, 36), Balaizah frag. (Petrie, *Gizeh* 41) ⲁⲅⲣⲓⲡⲓⲧⲟⲥ.

[7] Basset p. 456. The Copts had also a befitting legend of the persecutor's miserable end: Joh. Nikiou 418, *CSCO.*, vol. 38, 80; *B. Kopt. U.* no. 32, 9.

[8] Doubtless منجوج Mangûg, opposite Psoi (Menshîyah). In our fragment ⲧⲙⲟⲩ- is scarcely possible, though most such names have the article (ⲧⲙⲟⲩⲛϭⲣⲏϭⲉ, ⲧⲙⲟⲩⲛⲁϩⲓ, ⲧⲙⲟⲩⲛϩⲁϭⲉ), rarely not (Μουναχθη). The full form, though without gen. ⲛ-, is in ⲧⲙⲟⲩⲓⲟⲩⲃⲁⲥⲧⲓ (Brit. Mus. no. 529). Mangûg is 'in the district of ابسو' (Amél. *Géog.* 238), in a Cairo *Synax.* (my copy) ابسو ابصاى, though transcribed in another (Forget ii. 270) ⲡⲥⲱ, *i.e.* ⲡⲥⲟⲓ. Note that either ⲡⲥⲱⲟⲩ, Zoega 34 (= *CSCO.*, vol. 41, 11), should be read ⲡⲥⲱⲟⲩⲛ, to agree with ابصونة, *Synax.* 5 Mechîr (Forget i. 452), now باصونة, S. of Marâghah (probably the same too as ⲡⲥⲟⲟⲩⲛ, *Miss.* iv. 737); or that *Synax.* here is mistaken and the Arabic of Zoega *l.c.* is right in reading this as ابصاى.

→ *Recto.*

] ⲛⲟⲩⲱⲧ̣
] ⲉϣⲁⲩ-
[ⲙⲟⲩⲧ]ⲉ ⲉⲣⲟϥ
[ϫⲉ]ⲙ̣ⲟⲩⲛϭⲟⲩϭ
]ϩⲣϣⲓⲣⲉ

[. . .]ⲱ ⲛⲟⲩⲉϣ-
[ϭ]ⲱⲗⲡ ⲉⲃⲟⲗ
[ⲙ]ⲡ̣ⲉ̣ⲩⲃⲓⲟⲥ ⲉ-
[. . . . .]ⲏ̣ⲩ
[ⲡⲇⲓⲕ]ⲁ̣ⲓⲟⲥ ⲙ̄ⲛ-
[ⲡⲁ]ⲇ̣ⲓ̣ⲕⲟⲥ ·
[.]ⲙ̣ⲡⲉⲩⲥⲉⲃⲏⲥ
[ⲙⲛ]ⲡⲁⲥⲉⲃⲏ̣ⲥ̣
]ⲟⲩⲥⲙⲟⲧ ⲛ-
ⲧⲉⲓⲙⲓⲛⲉ ·
[ⲁ]ⲥϣⲱⲡⲉ ⲇ̣ⲉ̣
ⲛⲟⲩϩⲟⲟⲩ ⲁ-
ⲡϣⲱⲥ ⲕⲁⲁⲩ
ⲙⲡⲉⲥⲛⲁⲩ
ϩⲁϩⲧⲛⲛⲧⲃ-
ⲛⲟⲟⲩⲉ ⲁϥ-
ⲃⲱⲕ ⲉⲡⲉϥ-
ⲏⲓ ⲁϥⲛⲕⲟⲧ[ⲕ]
ⲙⲡⲉϩⲟⲟⲩ ⲉ-

↑ *Verso.*

ⲙⲛⲡϩ̣ⲣ[ϣⲓⲣⲉ]
ⲙⲙⲁⲛ̄ⲉ[ⲃⲁⲁⲙ-]
ⲡⲉ ⲡⲁⲓ ⲉ[ⲧⲉ-]
ϣⲁⲩⲙⲟ[ⲩⲧⲉ]
ⲉⲣⲟϥ ϫⲉ[ⲁⲕⲣⲓ-]
ⲡⲓⲧⲁ ·
ⲁⲡⲛⲟⲩⲧⲉ ϭ[ⲱ-]
ⲗⲡ ⲉⲃⲟⲗ ⲛ̣[ⲟⲩ-]
ϩⲱⲣⲱ[ⲙⲁ
ⲑⲁⲩⲙ̄ⲁⲥⲉ ⲛ̣[ⲡⲉ-]
ⲧⲟⲩⲁ̄ⲁⲃ ⲁⲡ[ⲁ]
ⲯⲁⲧⲉ ⲁϥ-
ϭⲱϣⲧ ⲁϥⲛⲁⲩ
ⲉⲡⲉⲓⲛⲟϭ ⲛ̄-
ⲇⲣⲁ̄ⲕⲱⲛ ⲛ̄-
ϩⲟϥ ⲛⲕⲁ̄ⲙ[ⲉ]
ⲉϥⲛⲕⲟⲧⲕ [ϩⲁ-]
ⲧⲁⲡⲉ ⲛⲁⲕ[ⲣⲓ-]
ⲡⲓⲧⲁ̄ ⲡⲕ[ⲟⲩⲓ

ⲡⲉϫⲁ[ϥ ⲛⲁϥ]
ϫⲉⲡⲁ̣[ϣⲏⲣⲉ]
ⲁⲕⲣⲓ[ⲡⲓⲧⲁ]
ⲁⲟⲩⲱ̣[ⲛ ⲛⲧⲉⲕ-]
ⲧⲁⲡⲣ̣[ⲟ

Recto. . . . the] same [village], which they call Mounġouġ . . . youth (? youths) . . . . .

. . . without displaying their life (*βίος*) . . . . . the just (*δίκ.*) and the unjust (*ἄδικος*), . . . the godly (*εὐσεβής*) and the ungodly (*ἀσεβ.*), in a fashion such as this. It befell, on a day, that the shepherd left them both with the beasts and went to his house and lay down, [that] day . . . . .

Verso. . . . and the goat-herd boy, him that was called [Akri]pita. God revealed a vision (*ὅραμα*) . . . wonder (? *θαῦμα*)[1] . . . the holy Apa Psate beheld and saw this (*sic*) great black dragon (*δράκων*) serpent lying beneath the head of the boy (?) Ak[ri]pita . . . . .

. . . He said [unto him], 'My [son] Akri[pita], open [thy] mouth' . . . . .

[1] I cannot offer a satisfactory reading here.

No. 19.

The Martyrdom of Apa Moui seems to be otherwise unrecorded, though the name, sometimes with 'Apa' prefixed, is frequent.[1] He appears to have suffered at Alexandria, presumably just before his companion, Apa Herwoj,[2] here mentioned. The story is apparently narrated by a certain Pġôl,[3] in presence of other 'saints'; but this narrative again is embedded in an Encomium, pronounced at the martyr's shrine upon his festival day.

Fol. 1. → *Recto.*

ⲗⲁⲕⲏ[a] ⲛ̣[ⲣⲁⲕⲟ-]
ⲧⲉ' ⲁⲥⲱϣ ⲉⲃ[ⲟⲗ]
ϫⲉⲡϩⲁⲅⲓⲟⲥ . ⲉ[ⲧⲟⲩ]ⲁⲁ̣ⲃ
ⲡϣⲏⲣⲉ ϣⲏⲙ ⲛⲁⲫⲟ̣[ⲁⲣ-]
ⲧⲟⲥ' ⲃⲟⲏ̄ⲑⲉⲓ ⲉⲧⲁⲙ̄ⲛ̄ⲧⲁⲧ-
ⲣⲱⲙⲉ' ⲛ̄ⲅ̄ⲡⲁⲣⲁⲕⲁⲗⲉⲓ
ⲙ̄ⲡⲉⲭ̄ⲥ̄ ⲛ̄ϥ̄ⲭⲁⲣⲓⲍⲉ ⲛⲁⲓ ⲛ-
ⲟⲩϣⲏⲣⲉ' ⲙ̄ⲙⲟⲛ ⲉⲓⲥ ϩⲏⲛ-
ⲧⲉ' ⲉⲓⲥ ⲡⲉⲙⲕⲁϩ' ⲛ̄ϩⲏⲧ
ⲛ̄ⲙⲙⲁϊ ⲛ̄ϩⲟⲩⲟ' ⲉⲟⲩⲁ' ⲉϥ̣-
ϩ̄ⲛ̄ⲟⲩⲛⲟϭ ⲛ̄ⲉⲍⲱⲣⲏ̣ⲥ-
ⲧⲓⲁ · ϩ̣ⲛ̄ⲧⲉⲩⲛⲟⲩ ⲇⲉ

↑ *Verso.*

[Ⲁⲩⲱ ⲁⲥ]ϣⲱⲡⲉ̣ ⲁⲡⲛⲟ̊ⲩ-
[ⲧⲉ ⲥⲙⲟⲩ ⲉ]ⲣ̣ⲟⲥ ⲁⲥⲱ' ⲁⲥϫⲡⲟ'
[ⲛ̄ⲟ]ⲩϣⲏⲣⲉ [ⲁ]ⲥⲙⲟⲩⲧⲉ' ⲉⲡⲉϥ-
[ⲣⲁ]ⲛ ⲙ̄ⲡⲣⲁⲛ ⲙ̄ⲡⲙⲁⲣⲧⲩ-
[ⲣⲟ]ⲥ ⲉⲧⲟⲩⲁⲁⲃ' ⲁⲡⲁ ⲙⲟⲩϊ :
Ⲁⲥϣⲱⲡⲉ ⲇⲉ ⲡⲉϫⲁϥ' ⲙ̄ⲛ̄-
ⲛ̄ⲥⲁⲧⲣⲉⲡϩⲏⲅ̄ⲉⲙⲱⲛ
ϣⲓⲛⲉ ⲛ̄ⲥⲱϥ ⲕⲁⲧⲁ ⲡⲟⲣ-
ⲇ̣ⲓ̣ⲛⲟⲛ' ⲁϥϣⲁϫⲉ' ⲙ̄ⲛ̄ⲡⲙⲁⲣ-
ⲧⲩⲣⲟⲥ ⲉⲧⲟⲩⲁⲁⲃ' ⲉϥϫⲱ' ⲙ̄-
ⲙⲟⲥ ϫⲉⲟⲩ̄ⲛⲉ ⲛⲉϊϩⲃⲏⲩⲉ' ⲉ-
ⲧ̄ⲕⲉⲓⲣⲉ ⲙ̄ⲙⲟⲟⲩ ϩ̄ⲛ̄ⲧⲉⲫⲩⲗ-

[a] ⲫⲩ̣ⲗ]ⲗⲁⲕⲏ.

[1] With ⲁⲡⲁ, Brit. Mus. nos. 1027, 1228; *Saqqara* no. 73; without, Brit. Mus. no. 1102; Gayet pl. lviii; Hall *Copt. and Gr. Texts*, 113; Rylands no. 122 &c. Krall no. viii cites Μούη (whence ?), *cf.* 'Αμμώης of the *Apophthegmata*. The بموية of *Synax.*, 20 Bâbeh = ⲁⲙⲟⲓ (*Mus. Guim.* xxv. 327). Μωβεῖ *Vit. Pachom.* § 72 is اموى in the Cairo edition 136 (*v.* Appendix below), though in Paris MS. 261, f. 218 امون.

[2] Reading uncertain. A martyr thus named, هرواج, 16 Kihak. His church, at ? Aphrodito, *Pap. Gr. Byz.* (J. Maspero) no. 67094. Scarcely the saint هرودة Abû Sâlih, 90 b = Makrizi, *Churches* no. 31 مارروطا (? ظا), with church at Sumustâ. The name 'Ωρουώγχιος, 'Αρ- (*v.* Brit. Mus. no. 1028) is particularly frequent in Aphrodito documents (*v.* Brit. Mus. *Gr. Pap. Cat.* iv). Abû 'l-Barakât's Calendar (Paris arabe 203, f. 258 v.) transcribes this رواخياس.

[3] Whether this is Shenoute's predecessor, and the latter the same as the ⲡϫⲟⲗ بجول of certain Diptychs (Cairo *Theotokia* 82, Leyden MS. no. 41, named with the martyrs ⲕⲗⲟϫ Coluthus and ⲕⲁⲩ) we cannot tell; nor whether ⲡϭⲱⲗ invoked on stelae (Petrie *Memphis* i, pll. liii, liv; *Ann. du Serv.* viii. 83) is distinct from these.

Ⲉⲧⲙ̄ⲙⲁⲩ ⲁⲡⲙⲁⲣⲧⲩⲣ[ⲟⲥ]
ⲉⲧⲟⲩⲁⲁⲃ ϣ̄ⲡ̄ϩⲧⲏϥ ⲉ̣ϫ̣ⲱ̣[ⲥ]
ⲁϥⲥⲙⲟⲩ' ⲉⲣⲟⲥ ⲁⲥⲟⲩϫⲁï
ⲁⲥⲃⲱⲕ ⲉⲡⲉⲥⲏï ⲉⲥϯ ⲉⲟ[ⲟⲩ]
ⲙ̄ⲡⲛⲟⲩⲧⲉ' ⲙⲛ̄ⲡⲙⲁⲣ-
ⲧⲩⲣⲟⲥ ⲉⲧⲟⲩⲁⲁⲃ·
margin

ⲗⲁⲕⲏ· ⲁⲩⲱ ϩ̄ⲛ̄ⲟⲩⲛⲟϭ ⲛ̄-
Ⲑⲩⲙⲟⲥ' ⲁϥⲕⲉⲗⲉⲩⲉ ⲉⲧⲣⲉⲩ-
ⲃⲁⲥⲁⲛⲓⲍⲉ ⲙ̄ⲡⲡⲉⲧⲟⲩⲁⲁⲃ'
ϩ̄ⲛ̄ϩⲉⲛⲃⲁⲥⲁⲛⲟⲥ' ⲉⲩⲟϣ'
ⲙⲛ̄ϩⲉⲛⲕⲟⲗⲁⲥⲧⲏⲣⲓⲟⲛ'
ⲉⲛⲁϣⲱⲟⲩ ⲉⲁϥⲧⲁⲗⲟϥ'[a] ⲉ-
margin

[a] Apparently not ⲉⲁⲩ-; therefore ⲁϥϩⲓⲧⲉ in next line.

Fol. 1. *Recto.* ... 'prison (*φυλακή*) of [? Rako]te (Alexandria) and she cried out, "Holy (*ἅγιος*) saint, un[blemish]ed (? *ἄφθαρτος*[1]) youth, help (*βοηθεῖν*) my forlornness, and entreat (*παρακαλεῖν*) the Christ that He grant (*χαρίζειν*) me a child. Verily behold, grief is mine (*lit.* is with me) more than (were I) one in distant (*lit.* great) exile (*ἐξοριστία*)." And (*δέ*) thereupon the saintly martyr (*μάρτυρος*) had pity upon her and blessed her, and she was made whole and went unto her house, giving glory unto God and the saintly martyr (*μαρ.*).[2]

(*Verso.*) [And it] befell that God [blessed] her and she conceived and bare a son, and called his name (as) the name of the saintly martyr (*μαρ.*) Apa Moui. But (*δέ*) it befell,' said he, 'after that the *praeses* (*ἡγεμών*) had required him in (*κατά*) his turn (*ὄρδινον*), that he spake with the saintly martyr (*μαρ.*), saying, "What be these things which thou doest in the prison (*φυλ.*)?" And in great wrath (*θυμός*) he bade (*κελ.*) them torment (*βασανίζειν*) the saint with heavy torments (*βάσανος*) and many punishments (*κολαστήριον*), and having raised him upon

Fol. 2. → *Recto.*

margin

ⲡϩⲉⲣⲙⲏⲛⲧⲁ[ⲣⲓⲟⲛ ⲁϥϩⲓⲧⲉ]
ⲙ̄ⲙⲟϥ' ϣⲁⲛ[ⲧⲉⲡⲉϥⲥⲛⲟϥ]
ϣⲟⲩⲟ ⲉϫⲙ̄ⲡⲕⲁϩ ⲁϥⲕ[ⲉ-]

↑ *Verso.*

margin

]ⲟ̣ⲟⲩ ϩⲙ̄ⲡⲧⲣⲉϥ-
]ⲧⲉϩⲉ' ⲛ̄ϩⲟⲙⲛ̄ⲧ
ⲛⲥⲉⲥⲁϩⲧⲉ ϩⲁⲣⲟϥ ⲛ̄ϥⲧⲣⲉⲩ-

[1] Sophocles *s. v.* gives an instance of such a usage.

[2] Presumably no gap between the columns.

ⲗⲉⲩⲉ̄ ⲇⲉ' ⲟⲛ' ⲉⲧⲣⲉⲩϯ' ⲛ̄ϩⲉⲛ-
ⲕⲁⲥⲓⲥ' ⲉⲩⲗⲟⲃϣ̄ ⲉϫⲛ̄ⲧⲉϥⲁ-
ⲡⲉ' ϣⲁⲛⲧⲉⲧⲥⲟⲟⲩϩⲉ' ⲛ̄ϫⲱ[ϥ]
ⲕⲱ' ⲉⲃⲟⲗ' ⲙ̄ⲛ̄ⲛ̄ⲥⲱⲥ' ⲁϥ-
ⲧⲣⲉⲩϩⲱⲧⲉ ⲙ̄ⲡⲉϥϯⲃⲥ̄
ⲛ̄ⲟⲩⲥⲁϩ' ⲉϥⲗⲟⲃϣ̄' ⲙⲛ̄ⲛ̄-
ⲕⲉⲃⲁⲥⲁⲛⲟⲥ ⲧⲏⲣⲟⲩ ⲛ̄ⲧⲁϥ-
ϩⲩⲡⲟⲙⲓⲛⲉ' ⲉⲣⲟⲟⲩ ⲛ̄ϭⲓ ⲡϣⲏ-
ⲣⲉ ϣⲏⲙ' ⲛ̄ϫⲱⲱⲣⲉ' ⲗⲟⲓ-
Ⲡⲟⲛ ⲛ̄ⲧⲉⲣⲉϥⲇⲟⲕⲓⲙⲁⲍⲉ
ⲙ̄ⲙⲟ[ϥ ϩ]ⲛ̄ϩⲁϩ' ⲛ̄ⲧⲓⲙⲱ-
ⲣⲓⲁ' ⲛ̄ϭⲓ ⲡⲁⲛⲟⲙⲟⲥ ⲛ̄ϩⲏⲅⲉ-
ⲙⲱⲛ' ⲉⲁϥⲉⲓⲙⲉ ϫⲉⲛϥ-
ⲛⲁⲥⲱⲧⲙ̄ ⲛ̄ⲥⲱϥ' ⲁⲛ
ⲉⲑⲩⲥⲓⲁ[ⲍⲉ] ⲛ̄ⲛⲉϥⲉⲓⲇⲱⲗⲟ[ⲛ]
margin

ⲛⲟⲩϫⲉ ⲛ̄ⲛⲉϥϭⲓϫ' ⲉϩⲟⲩⲛ ϩⲁ-
ⲡϭ̄ⲗϭⲓⲗ ⲛ̄ⲥⲉⲱϣⲉ' ⲉϫⲱϥ· ⲁⲩⲱ
ⲙ̄ⲛ̄ⲛ̄ⲥⲁⲧⲣⲉⲩⲛⲱⲧⲉ ⲛ̄ϩⲉ-
ⲙⲟⲩⲥ' ⲉⲃⲟⲗ' ϩⲓⲡⲉϥⲥⲟⲓ̈ ⲛ̄ⲥⲉ-
ϭⲱϭ ⲙ̄ⲙⲟⲟⲩ ϩⲛ̄ⲟⲩⲕⲱϩ̄ⲧ
ⲙ̄ⲛⲟⲩⲛⲉϩ' ⲙ̄ⲡⲥ̄ⲣ̄ⲣⲟⲟⲩϣ'
ⲛⲁϥ' ϩⲟⲗⲱⲥ' ϩⲁⲛⲉⲓⲃⲁⲥⲁⲛⲟⲥ
ϫⲉⲛⲉⲣⲉⲙⲓⲭⲁⲏⲗ' ⲡⲁⲣⲭⲁⲅⲅⲉ-
ⲗⲟⲥ' ⲥⲕⲉⲡⲁⲍⲉ' ⲙ̄ⲙⲟϥ' ⲉϥϯ
ϭⲟⲙ' ⲛⲁϥ' ⲁⲩⲱ ⲛⲉⲣⲉⲡ̄ⲡⲉⲧ-
ⲟⲩⲁⲁⲃ' ⲁⲡⲁ ϩⲉⲣⲟ̣ⲩ̣ⲟ̣[ϫ] ϯ ⲧⲱⲕ
ⲛ̄ϩⲏⲧ' ⲛⲁϥ
Ⲛⲧⲉⲣⲉϥⲛⲁⲩ ⲇⲉ' ⲛ̄ϭⲓ ⲡϩⲏ-
ⲅⲉⲙⲱⲛ' ϫⲉⲛϥⲛⲁⲥⲱⲧⲙ̄
ⲁⲛ' ⲛ̄ⲥⲱϥ' ⲉⲑ[ⲩⲥⲓ]ⲁⲍⲉ' ⲁϥ-
ϭⲱⲛⲧ' ⲁϥϯ [ⲛ̄ⲧ]ⲉϥⲁⲡⲟ-
margin

(Fol. 2. *Recto.*) the rack (ἑρμητάριον), [he tortured] him, until [his blood] flowed upon the ground. And (δέ) he bade (κελ.) them moreover set glowing helmets (κασσίς[1]) upon his head, till the crown of his head was loosed. Afterward he caused them to pierce his heels[2] with a glowing awl,[3] besides (*lit.* and) all the other torments (βάσ.) that the brave youth bare (ὑπομένειν). Howbeit (λοιπόν) after the wicked (ἄνομος) *praeses* (ἡγ.) had proved (δοκιμάζειν) him with many punishments (τιμωρία), when he knew that he would not hearken unto him, to sacrifice (θυσιάζειν) unto his idols (εἴδ.)

(*Verso.*) . . . . . as he . . . the cow of bronze and that they should kindle fire beneath it[4]; and he had them lay his (*sc.* martyr's) hands in beneath

[1] This torture in Rossi *Pap.* i. v. 28; *CSCO.*, vol. 42, 131 (περικεφάλαιον); Budge *St. George*, 24 (*sic* for ⲃⲁⲥⲓⲥ), 91.

[2] This often, *e.g. CSCO., l.c.* 79, 151; Hyvernat *Actes*, 147. For ϩⲱⲧⲉ I read ϫⲱⲧⲉ.

[3] Hitherto only ⲥⲁϩϥ (*v.* my *Ostr.*, no. 468).

[4] The cow (*sic* fem.) as here *CSCO., l.c.* 5; Budge, *l.c.* 13 (ⲙⲁⲥⲓ), 121. For ⲥⲱⲇⲓⲟⲛ, Hyvernat *Actes*, 103 ? σαίτιον.

the wheel[1] and press thereon. And after that they had cut out[2] strips from off his back and had boiled them[3] with fire and oil, it caused him not to pay heed[4] at all (*ὅλως*) under these torments (*βάσ.*), for Michael the archangel (*ἀρχ.*) protected (*σκεπάζειν*) him, strengthening him, and the saintly Apa Herwoj (?) did encourage him. But (*δέ*) when the *praeses* (*ἡγ.*) saw how that he would not hearken unto him to sacrifice (*θυσ.*), he was wroth and gave his sentence (*ἀπόφασις*).

Fol. 3. ↑ *Recto.*

ϩⲫⲁⲥⲓⲥ’ ⲗⲟⲓ[ⲡⲟⲛ’ ϩⲙ̄ⲡ-]
ⲧⲣⲉⲡϩⲏⲅⲉⲙ[ⲱⲛ ϯ ⲁⲡⲟⲫⲁ-]
ⲥⲓⲥ’ ⲉⲣⲟϥ’ ⲁϥ[ϣⲁ]ϫⲉ ⲛ̣[ϭⲓ ⲁⲡⲁ]
ⲡϭⲱⲗ’ ⲉⲧⲃⲉⲛϭⲟⲙ ⲙ̣̄[ⲡⲛⲟⲩ-]
ⲧⲉ’ ⲛ̄ⲧⲁⲩϣⲱⲡⲉ ⲉⲃ[ⲟⲗ’ ϩⲓⲧⲟ-]
ⲟⲧϥ̄ ⲙ̄ⲡ̄ⲡⲉⲧⲟⲩⲁⲁⲃ’ ⲁⲡⲁ
ⲙⲟⲩ̈ⲓ · ⲁⲩⲟⲩⲱϣ̄ⲃ ⲛ̄ϭⲓ ⲛ̄ⲉ-
ⲧⲟⲩⲁⲁⲃ’ ⲉⲩϫⲱ̄ ⲙ̄ⲙⲟⲥ’ ϫⲉ-
ϩⲁϩ’ ⲛ̄ⲥⲟⲡ’ ⲁⲡⲉⲭ̄ⲥ̄ ϣⲁϫⲉ
ⲙ̄ⲛ̄ⲡⲅⲉⲛⲛⲁⲓⲟⲥ’ ⲙ̄ⲡⲉⲭ̄ⲥ̄
ⲛⲁⲙⲉ’ ⲉϥϫⲱ’ ⲙ̄ⲙⲟⲥ ⲉⲛⲥⲱ-
ⲧⲙ̄ ϫⲉⲁⲗⲏⲑⲱⲥ’ ⲡⲁⲥⲱ-
ⲧⲡ̄ ⲣⲱⲙⲉ’ ⲛⲓⲙ’ ⲉϥⲛⲁⲟⲛⲟ-
ⲙⲁⲍ[ⲉ] ⲙ̄[ⲡ]ⲉⲕⲣⲁⲛ’ ⲉⲧⲟⲩⲁⲁⲃ’
ⲛ̄ⲥⲉϫⲟⲟⲥ ϫⲉⲡⲛⲟⲩⲧⲉ ⲙ̄-
ⲡⲙⲁⲣⲧⲩⲣⲟⲥ’ ⲉⲧⲟⲩⲁⲁⲃ
ⲁⲡⲁ ⲙⲟⲩ[ⲓ̈ ⲉ]ⲕⲉⲥⲱⲧⲙ̄ ⲉⲣⲟ̄
ϩⲙ̄ⲡⲉⲓ̣[ϩ]ⲱϣ [a] ⲛ̄ⲧⲉⲩⲛⲟ[ⲩ]

margin

→ *Verso.*

[ϯⲛⲁⲥⲱⲧⲙ ⲉⲣ]ⲟⲟⲩ ϩⲛⲟⲩϭⲉ-
[ⲡⲏ · (*blank*)
[Ⲡⲛⲟⲩⲧⲉ ⲡⲁ]ⲅⲁⲑⲟⲥ’ ⲡⲉⲧⲣ̄-
[ϩⲙ̄ⲙ]ⲉ̣ ⲙ̣ⲡⲧⲏⲣϥ̄ ⲱ̄ ⲛⲁⲙⲉ-
[ⲣⲁⲧ]ⲉ’ ⲛ̄ⲧⲟϥ’ ⲟⲛ ⲧⲉⲛⲟⲩ ⲡⲉ-
ⲧⲣ̄ϩⲙ̄ⲙⲉ ⲙ̄ⲙⲟⲛ’ ⲉⲧⲣⲉⲛ-
ⲃⲱⲕ ⲉⲡⲙⲁⲣⲧⲩⲣⲓⲟⲛ’ ⲙ̄-
[ⲡ]ⲙⲁⲣⲧⲩⲣⲟⲥ’ ⲉⲧⲟⲩⲁⲁⲃ’ ⲁⲡⲁ
ⲙⲟⲩ̈ⲓ ⲛ̄ⲧⲛⲱϣ’ ⲉⲃⲟⲗ’ ϩⲓ-
ⲟⲩⲥⲟⲡ’ ϫⲉⲡⲛⲟⲩⲧⲉ ⲙ̄ⲡϩⲁ-
ⲅⲓⲟⲥ’ ⲙ̄ⲙⲁⲣⲧⲩⲣⲟⲥ’ ⲙ̄ⲡⲉⲭ̄ⲥ̄
ⲉⲕⲉⲥⲱⲧⲙ̄ ⲉⲣⲟⲛ’ ⲛ̄ⲅϩⲁⲣⲉϩ’
ⲉⲣⲟⲛ’ ⲉⲛϭⲟⲣϭ̄ⲥ̄ ⲙ̄ⲡⲇⲓⲁⲃⲟ-
ⲗⲟⲥ’ ⲡⲙⲁⲣⲧ[ⲩⲣⲟⲥ] ⲙ̄ⲡⲉ-
ⲭ̄ⲥ̄ ⲉⲕⲉⲥⲟⲟⲩⲧⲛ̄ ⲛⲛⲉⲛϩⲓⲟ-
ⲟⲩⲉ’ ⲛ̄ⲅϩⲁⲣⲉϩ’ ⲉⲣⲟⲛ’ ⲉⲡⲡⲟ-
ⲗⲩⲙⲟ̣ⲥ’ ⲉⲑⲏⲡ ⲛ̄ⲧⲉ ⲡⲁⲛ-
ⲧⲓⲕⲓⲙⲉⲛⲟⲥ’

Ⲡⲉⲓⲙ̣ⲁⲣⲧ̣ⲩ[ⲣⲟⲥ ⲉ]ⲧⲟⲩⲁⲁⲃ

margin

[a] Or ϩⲙ̄ⲡⲉⲛ[.

[1] The wheel, *CSCO.*, *l.c.* 13, 26, 113, 218; Budge, *l.c.* 113, 178; Rylands *Cat.* no. 94. *Cf.* the remarks of Peeters, *An. Boll.* xxviii. 490, and the text *ib.* xxvi. 27, 28.

[2] *Lit.* 'divide, separate'. *Cf.* ⲥⲱⲗⲡ ⲉⲃⲟⲗ. *CSCO.*, *l.c.* 73.

[3] *Sc.* the places thus bared.

[4] The same phrase, Zoega 361. *Cf.* Brit. Mus. no. 344, ⲛⲥⲙⲉⲗⲉⲓ ⲛⲁⲓ ⲁⲛ.

(Fol. 3. *Recto.*) Howbeit (λοιπόν), as the *praeses* (ἡγ.) [gave senten]ce (? ἀπ.) upon him, [Apa] Pġôl [spa]ke[1] concerning the mighty (works) of God that had come about through the saintly Apa Moui. The saints made answer saying, 'Many a time did Christ talk with the truly noble one (γενναῖος) of Christ, saying, whilst we heard, "Of a truth (ἀληθῶς), my chosen one, every man that shall pronounce (ὀνομάζειν) thy saintly name and say, God of the saintly martyr (μαρ.) Apa Moui, do Thou hear us in this (*or* our) need; straightway

(*Verso.*) [I will hear] them quickly."'

[The] good (ἀγαθός) God, He that guideth all, O my beloved, He it is also that now guideth us, that we should go to the shrine (μαρτύριον) of the saintly martyr (μαρ.) Apa Moui, and that we should cry out together, 'God of Christ's holy (ἅγιος) martyr, do Thou hear us and preserve us from the snares of the devil (διάβ.). Martyr of Christ, do Thou make straight our ways and preserve us from the hidden war (πόλεμος) of the adversary (ἀντικείμενος).' This saintly martyr

Fol. 4. ↑ *Recto.*

margin

ⲉⲧⲛ[ⲣ]ϣⲁ ⲛ[ⲁϥ ⲙ̄ⲡⲟⲟⲩ ⲟⲩ-]
ⲕⲟⲩïⲡⲉ’ ϩⲛ̄ⲧ[ϩⲏⲗⲓⲕⲓⲁ ⲁⲗ-]
ⲗⲁ’ ⲟⲩⲛⲟϭⲡⲉ’ ϩⲛ̄ⲧⲥⲟⲫⲓⲁ [ⲛ̄-]
ⲁⲗⲏⲑⲓⲛⲟⲛ · ⲁⲩϫⲟⲟⲥ ⲇⲉ ⲟ̣ⲛ̣ [a]
Ϫⲉϩⲁϩ ⲛ̄ⲥⲟⲡ’ ⲁⲡⲉⲡ̅ⲛ̅ⲁ̅ ⲙ̄[ⲡ̣ϫⲟ-]
ⲉⲓⲥ ⲧⲟⲣⲡ̅ϥ̅ ⲉⲛⲉⲡⲟⲩⲣⲁⲛⲓⲟ[ⲛ]
ⲙ̄ⲡⲟⲩⲟⲉⲓⲛ’ ϩⲓⲧⲙ̄ⲡⲉϥⲧ̅ⲃ̅-
ⲃⲟ’ · ⲁⲩϯ ⲛⲁϥ’ ⲙ̄ⲡⲉϥ[ⲱ-]
ⲧⲓⲥⲙⲁ’ ⲛ̄ⲙ̄ⲡⲏⲩⲉ’ ϩⲓⲧⲛ̄-
ⲧⲛⲟϭ ⲛ̄ⲇⲩⲛⲁⲙⲓⲥ’ ⲉⲧⲙⲟⲟ-
ϣⲉ’ ⲛ̅ⲙ̅ⲙ̅ⲁϥ’ ⲛ̄ⲟⲩⲟⲉⲓϣ’
ⲛⲓⲙ’ ⲉⲓⲧⲁ’ ⲙⲛ̄ⲛ̄ⲥⲁⲛⲁï
Ⲏϯⲛⲁⲕⲁ ⲣⲱï ⲁⲛ’ ⲉⲡⲣ̄ⲡⲙⲉ-

→ *Verso.*

[ⲛϣⲁ ⲉⲧⲧⲁⲉⲓ]ⲏⲩ ⲛ[ⲧ]ⲉⲡⲁ-
[ⲑⲗⲏⲧⲏⲥ ⲛ̄ⲅ̄ⲉ]ⲛⲛⲁⲓⲟⲥ’ ⲡⲁⲣⲁ-
[ⲕ]ⲁⲗⲉⲓ ⲙ̄ⲡⲛⲟⲩⲧⲉ’ ⲡⲁϩⲟⲣⲁ[ⲧⲟⲥ]
ⲛϥⲕⲁ ⲛⲉⲛⲛⲟⲃⲉ’ ⲛⲁⲛ’ ⲉⲃ[ⲟⲗ·]
ⲁⲛⲉⲓ ⲉⲡⲉⲕⲙⲁⲣⲧⲩⲣⲓⲟⲛ’ ⲱ
ⲡⲉⲛⲧⲁϥⲡⲁⲣⲁⲇⲓⲇⲟⲩ ⲙ-
ⲡⲉϥⲥⲱⲙⲁ’ ⲉⲡⲙⲟⲩ ⲉⲧⲃⲉ-
ⲓ̅ⲥ̅ ⲡⲱⲛϩ̄ ⲛ̄ⲟⲩⲟⲛ’ ⲛⲓⲙ’ ⲡⲁ-
ⲣⲁⲕⲁⲗⲉⲓ ⲙ̄ⲡⲉⲭ̅ⲥ̅ ⲡⲣ̄ⲣⲟ’ ⲛ̄-
ⲛⲁⲓⲱⲛ’ ⲛϥⲭⲁⲣⲓⲍⲉ’ ⲛⲁⲛ’
ⲙ̄ⲡⲕⲱ’ ⲉⲃⲟⲗ’ ⲛ̄ⲛⲉⲛⲛⲟⲃⲉ’
Ϯⲡⲁⲣⲁⲕⲁⲗⲉï ⲇⲉ ⲙ̄ⲙⲱⲧ̣ⲛ̣̄
ⲱ̄ ⲛⲁⲙⲉⲣⲁⲧⲉ’ ⲙⲁⲣⲛ̄ⲥⲟ-

[a] ⲟⲛ quite uncertain.

[1] The sense involved by my reading here is scarcely acceptable.

ⲉⲩⲉ' ⲙ̄[ⲡⲙ]ⲁⲣ[ⲧⲩⲣ]ⲟⲥ [ⲉⲧⲟⲩ-]
ⲁⲁⲃ' ⲡⲁⲓ ⲉⲧⲛ̄ⲣ̄ϣⲁ' ⲛⲁϥ
ⲙ̄ⲡⲟⲟⲩ ⲙ̣ⲁⲣⲛ̄ⲥⲱⲟⲩϩ
Ϣ̄ ⲛⲁⲙ[ⲉⲣⲁ]ⲧⲉ ⲉⲡⲉϊⲛⲟϭ
margin

ⲡ̣ⲥ̣ ⲙ̄ⲡϩⲁⲅⲓⲟ[ⲥ ⲙ̄ⲙⲁ]ⲣ̣[ⲧⲩ̣-]
[ⲣⲟⲥ] ⲙ̄ⲡⲉⲭ̄ⲥ̄ ⲁⲡⲁ ⲙⲟⲩϊ ⲛ̣ϥ̣-
ⲣ̄ϩⲙ̄ⲙⲉ ⲙ̄ⲙⲟⲛ' ϩⲙ̄ⲡⲉⲓⲡⲉ-
ⲗⲁⲅⲟⲥ' ⲉⲧⲙ̣[ⲉϩ] ⲛ̣̄ϣⲧⲟⲣⲧ[ⲣ]
ⲉⲧⲉⲡⲉⲓⲕⲟⲥ[ⲙⲟⲥⲡⲉ] ⲁⲩ[ⲱ]
margin

(Fol. 4. *Recto.*) that we celebrate [to-day], little he is in [age (ἡλικία)], but (ἀλλά) great in the true wisdom (σοφία, ἀληθινός). And (δέ) they said[1] also (?), 'Many a time did the spirit (πν.) of the Lord catch him up to the celestial (places ἐπουράνιον) of light, because of his purity; and he was given the baptism (φώτισμα) of heaven, because of the great power (δύναμις) that went with him at all times.' Then (εἶτα) furthermore, I will not keep silence regarding the commemoration of the saintly martyr (μαρ.), him that we celebrate to-day. Let us gather, O my beloved, to this great [and honou]red

(*Verso.*) festival], and may the noble champion (ἀθλητής, γενναῖος) entreat (παρακαλεῖν) the invisible (ἀόρατος) God that He forgive us our sins. We are come unto thy shrine (μαρτύριον), O thou that didst give thy body (σῶμα) over (παραδιδόναι) unto death for the sake of Jesus, the life of every one; entreat thou (παρακ.) the Christ, the king of the ages (αἰών[2]), that He grant (χαρίζειν) us the forgiveness of our sins. But (δέ) I beseech (παρακ.) you, O my beloved, let us pray the holy (ἅγ.) martyr (μαρ.) of Christ, Apa Moui, that he guide us in this sea (πέλαγος) that is full of trouble, namely the world (κόσ.) and . . . . .

No. 20.

From an unidentified Martyrdom. *Recto* shows Christ appearing to several martyrs, in prison or under torture together; *verso*, a single martyr, healed after torture.

→ *Recto.*

[. . . . .]ⲡ̣ⲱⲕ
[. . . . .]ⲧⲛ ⲛ̄
margin

margin
↑ *Verso.*

ⲛⲧ̣[ⲉⲩⲛⲟⲩ]
ⲁϥⲧ̣[ⲱⲟⲩⲛ]

[1] *I.e.* the saints, or = 'it was said'.

[2] *Cf.* 1 Tim. i. 17.

[ⲧⲱ]ⲧ̣ⲛ̄ ϫⲣⲟ ⲙ̄-
[ⲙ]ⲱⲧⲛ̄ ⲱ̄ ⲛ̄-
ϣⲟⲉⲓϫ ⲛ̄ϫⲱ-
ⲱⲣⲉ ⲛⲉⲛ-
[ⲧ]ⲁ̣ⲩϩⲩⲡⲟⲙⲓ-
ⲛⲉ ⲛ̄ⲙ̄ⲙⲁï
ϩⲛ̄ⲛⲁⲡⲓⲣⲁⲥ-
ⲙⲟⲥ · ⲉⲃⲟⲗ ϫⲉ-
ⲙ̄ⲛ̄ⲛ̄ⲥⲁⲕⲉ-
ⲕⲟⲩï ⲧⲉⲧⲛⲁ-
ⲟⲩⲱⲙ ⲛ̄ⲧⲉ-
ⲧⲛ̄ⲥⲱ ⲛ̄ⲙ̄-
ⲙⲁï ϩⲓϫⲛ̄[ⲧ]-
ⲧⲣⲁⲡⲉ[ⲍⲁ ⲛ-]
ⲧⲁⲙⲛ̄[ⲧⲉⲣⲟ]
ⲁⲩⲱ ⲛ̄[
margin

margin

margin

ϩⲣⲁⲓ ⲉϥⲟ[ⲩ-]
ⲟϫ ⲧⲏⲣϥ̄ ⲉ-
ⲙ̄ⲛ̄ⲗⲁⲁⲩ ⲙ̄-
ⲡⲱⲗ̄ϩ̄ ϩⲓⲱ-
ⲱϥ ⲉⲣⲉⲛⲉϥ-
ⲙⲉⲣⲟⲩⲟⲟϭⲉ
ⲟⲩⲟϫ · ⲙ̄ⲛ̄-
ⲛⲉϥⲟⲃϩⲉ ⲁϥ-
† ⲉⲟⲟⲩ ⲙ̄ⲡ-
ⲛⲟⲩⲧⲉ · ⲉϥ-
ϫⲱ ⲙ̄ⲙⲟⲥ ϫⲉ-
[ⲁϥⲟ]ⲩⲱ̣ⲛ̄ϩ̄ ⲉ-
[ⲃⲟⲗ ⲉϫ]ⲱⲛ ⲛ̄-
[ϭⲓ ⲡⲟ]ⲩⲟⲉⲓⲛ
margin

Recto. . . . . 'you (?). Hail to you, O mighty champions, that have endured (*ὑπομένειν*) with me in my trials (*πειρασμός*)! For after yet a little (while) ye shall eat and drink with me at the table (*τρά.*) of my kingdom.'[1] And . . . . .

Verso. . . . Forth[with] he a[rose] all whole, with no wound upon him, his cheeks being whole and his teeth.[2] And he gave glory to God, saying,[3] 'The light [of Thy countenance] hath been displayed upon us' . . . . .

[1] Luke xxii. 30.

[2] This might recall the martyrdom of Philotheus (*v.* Wüstenfeld, *Synax.* 242, 21 ff.), but the script here does not appear to be that of Nos. 16 or 17.

[3] Ps. iv. 6.

No. 21.

From an unidentified Martyrdom, as it would appear from fol. 2.

Fol. 1. → *Recto.*

	ⲉⲙ̣[
	ⲡⲛⲟⲩ[ⲧⲉ
	ϭⲱⲛ̄ⲧ [
	ⲉ̄ϥϥⲟⲧⲟⲩ ⲉⲃ̄[ⲟⲗ]
] ⲙ̣ⲙⲟ-	ⲁⲕⲃⲱⲕ ⲟⲩ̣[ⲛ]
ⲟⲩ ⲙⲡⲟⲩⲣⲱ-	ⲁⲕϣⲱⲡⲉ
ϣⲉ ⲉⲣⲟⲕ	ϩⲛ̄ⲛⲉⲓⲣⲱ-
ⲁⲗⲗⲁ ⲁⲕⲃⲱⲕ	ⲙⲉ ⲛ̄ϭⲛⲁϣ[ⲧ]
ⲟⲛ ⲉⲛⲟⲩ . [	ϣⲁⲛⲧⲉⲛ[
ⲭⲛⲏ̣ . ⲙ̄	?

margin

↑ *Verso.*

]ⲡ̣ⲉⲓ	
]ϭⲱϣⲧ̄	. ϥϫ̣[
] ϩⲓⲣⲁⲧⲕ̄	ⲉϥⲉ[
[ⲧⲉ]ⲛⲟⲩϭⲉ ⲉⲓⲥ	ⲧⲙⲛ[
[ⲡ]ϫⲟⲉⲓⲥ ⲁϥ-	ϫⲉⲟⲩ[ⲟⲓ] ⲛⲁⲕ̣
[ⲧ]ⲛⲛⲟⲟⲩⲕ	ⲡϫⲁϫⲉ ⲙ̄-
ϣⲁⲣⲟⲓ̈ · ⲁ-	ⲡⲛⲟⲩⲧⲉ
[ⲛ]ⲁⲩϭⲉ̣ ⲧⲉⲛⲟⲩ	ⲙ̣ⲛ̄ⲧⲡⲉ ⲙⲛ̄-
[ϯⲛ]ⲟⲉ̣ⲓ̈ ⲡⲉⲧⲛ-	ⲡⲕⲁϩ ⲉ̣ⲕⲛⲁ-
?	ⲣ̣ⲟⲩ ⲉ̣[. .]ϣⲁⲛ-

margin

Fol. 1. *Recto.* . . . 'them. They sufficed thee not, but (ἀλλά) thou didst go also to' . . . . .[1] . . . 'God . . . wrath . . .; blotting[2] them out. Thou didst go, then (? οὖν), and wast in these men and didst grow strong, until' . . . . .

Verso. . . . 'behold . . . toward thee.[3] So now, lo, the Lord hath sent thee unto me. See then, now, [I ?] know (? νοεῖν) your' . . . . .
. . . 'he shall . . . ., woe unto thee, enemy of God and heaven and earth! What wilt thou do when' . . . . .

Fol. 2. ↑ *Recto.*

ϣⲁⲛ̣[ⲧⲱ]ⲙ ⲉ-
ⲣⲟ̣ⲟⲩ ⲥⲉⲛⲁⲛⲟ-
ⲉⲓⲛ ⲛ̄ϭⲓ ⲛ̄ⲥⲛ̄-

→ *Verso.*

	Ⲛⲧⲉ̣ⲣⲟ̣ⲩⲉⲓ ⲇⲉ
	ⲉⲡⲉϣⲧⲉⲕⲟ
]ⲩⲧ̣	ⲁⲩⲧⲱϩⲙ̄ ⲉ-

[1] This may be a place or personal name, beginning with ⲛⲟⲩ-, less probably with plur. art. ⲛ-; or a word such as σύντεχνος.

[2] Reading ⲉϥϥⲟⲧⲟⲩ.

[3] ϩⲓⲣⲁⲧ- is rare. In Josh. ii. 5 = ὀπίσω ('follow after'), similarly in Budge *Homilies*, p. 16 ('towards'), and Pap. Bruce 239.

ⲧⲉ ⲙ̄ⲡⲉϣⲧⲉ-		]ⲏ ⲛ̄ⲙ̄-	ⲡⲣⲟ ⲁϥⲟⲩⲱ̄
ⲕⲟ ⲙ̄ⲛ̄ⲛ̄ⲥⲛ̄-	ⲟ̣[	]ⲛ	ⲛ̄ⲧⲉⲩⲛⲟⲩ
ⲧⲉ ⲙ̄ⲡⲕⲁϩ· ⲉ-	ⲛ[	]ⲛ̣̄ⲙ̣̄	7Ⲡⲙⲏⲏϣⲉ ⲇⲉ
ⲛ̣ⲉⲛⲧⲁⲩ(*sic*)ⲉⲛⲧⲁⲩ-	ⲛ[	]ⲛ	ⲛ̄ⲣⲱⲙⲉ ⲉⲧ-
ⲛ̄ⲧ[ⲟⲩ] ⲉ[ⲃ]ⲟⲗ ⲛ̄-	ⲡⲁ[	?	ⲣⲟⲉⲓⲥ ⲁⲩⲣ̄ⲑⲉ
ⲥⲉϣ[ⲁⲁ]ⲧ̣ⲕ̄[a]· ⲟⲩ̈	ϩⲙ̣[	]ⲉ̣ϥ-	ⲛ̄ⲛⲉⲧⲙⲟⲟⲩⲧ
ⲡⲉⲧⲕⲙⲉⲉⲩⲉ	ϫ̣[	ϫⲧ̣	ⲛⲧⲉⲣⲉϥⲉ̣ⲓ̣
ⲉⲣⲟϥ·	ⲉ[		ⲇⲉ ⲉϩⲟⲩⲛ ⲛ̄-[c]
7Ⲗϥⲟⲩⲱϣⲃ̄ ⲛ̄[b]	?		margin
margin			

[a] My copy gives as alternative ⲙ[. .]ⲡⲕ, so ? ϣⲟⲡⲕ or ϣⲟϫⲡⲕ (*cf.* Ps. cxxxviii. 10), or ⲙⲟⲟⲩⲧⲕ. [b] ⲛϭⲓ. [c] ⲛϭⲓ.

Fol. 2. *Recto.* . . . 'if [they ? he ?] shut (the door) upon them, shall the foundations of the prison and the foundations of the earth tremble at the things they have (*or* that have been) brought forth, and require (? them) of thee[1]? What thinkest thou ?' . . . . . answered . . . . .

Verso. . . . And (δέ) when they had come to the prison, they knocked at the door and straightway it opened. But (δέ) the multitude of men that kept watch were as if dead. And (δέ) when . . . had come in . . . . .

No. 22.

From the beginning of a Martyrdom. Diocletian's gods are enumerated and a part of the edict is to be read, whereby he ordered their worship.[2] Some 20 goddesses were named in the space of this fragment; may we conclude that the complete list gave 35, since in the passages usually parallel to this the 70 deities are divided equally into male and female ?[3] I know of no other Coptic martyrdom showing a like list of names. If we assume the text to be a translation, there is no need to seek for egyptianized forms of the divinities.

[1] This sentence is not necessarily interrogative, but the following question makes it likely. An alternative reading allows 'and they slay thee', which would show that the person addressed is not the devil, as fol. 1 *vo.* might suggest.

[2] Similar edicts: *CSCO.*, vol. 42, 89, 157, 200.

[3] *Cf. op. cit.* 200; Hyvernat *Actes*, 78, 202.

→ p. ⲅ̅.

margin

ⲧⲁ]ⲣ̣ⲑⲉⲙⲓⲥ
ⲧ]ⲃⲉⲣⲥⲉⲫⲱ-
[ⲛⲏ]ⲁⲭⲏ, ⲧⲥⲩⲗⲏ-
[ⲛⲏ]ⲕ̣ⲏ · ⲧⲑⲉⲗⲗⲁⲥ
] ⲧⲕⲁⲗⲗⲓⲟⲡⲏ
]· ⲧⲉⲣⲩⲛⲓⲥ ·
]ⲁ̣ⲧⲏ · ⲧⲡⲟⲛ-
]ⲛⲱ · ⲧⲛⲏⲙⲉ-[a]
[ⲥⲓⲥ]. ⲛ̣ · ⲧϩⲩⲣⲁ
]ⲓ̣ⲥ· ⲧⲇⲩⲣⲁⲛⲟ̣ⲥ[b]
ⲛ]ⲁ̣ⲓ̈ⲛⲉ ⲛ̄ⲣⲁⲛ
ⲛⲟⲩ]ⲧⲉ ⲛ̄ⲥϩⲓⲙⲉ
ⲇⲓⲟⲕⲗⲏⲧ]ⲓ̣ⲁⲛⲟⲥ ⲇⲉ ⲡ-
[ⲣⲣⲟ]ⲡ̣ ⲉⲃⲟⲗ ⲛ̄[
]ϩⲓⲣ̄ⲙ̣̄[
]ⲁ̣ⲧ[

margin

↑ p. ⲇ̅.

margin

ⲡⲣⲉⲥⲃ[ⲩⲧⲉⲣⲟⲥ · ⲉⲓⲧⲉ ⲇⲓⲁ-]
ⲕⲟⲛⲟⲥ · ⲉⲓ[ⲧⲉ ⲁⲛⲁⲅ̅ⲛⲱⲥ-]
ⲧⲏⲥ · ⲉⲓⲧⲉ [ⲣⲙ̄ϩⲉ · ⲉⲓⲧⲉ]
ϩ̄ⲙ̄ϩⲁⲗ · ⲉⲓ[ⲧⲉ
ⲑⲩⲥⲓⲁⲍⲉ .[ⲛⲟⲩ-]
ⲧⲉ ⲁⲩⲱ ⲡ[ⲉⲧⲛⲁϫⲟⲟⲥ]
ϫⲉⲁⲛ̄ⲅ̄ⲟⲩⲭ[ⲣⲏⲥⲧⲓⲁⲛⲟⲥ]
ⲉⲩⲉⲇⲏⲙⲉⲩ[ⲉ ⲙ̄ⲡⲉϥ-]
ⲙⲟⲩ ϩ̄ⲛ̄ⲧⲥ̣[ⲏϥⲉ · ⲛⲧⲱⲧⲛ]
ⲇⲉ ⲧⲏⲣⲧ̄ⲛ̄ [ⲛⲁⲍⲓⲱⲙⲁ-]
ⲧ̣ⲓⲕⲟⲥ ⲙ̄ⲡ[
ⲥϩⲁⲓ̈ ⲉⲣⲏⲥ[
ⲧⲏⲣⲟⲩ ⲕⲁ[ⲧⲁ ⲙⲁ
. . .] ϫⲉⲕⲁ[ⲥ
. . . .]ⲛⲁϣ[
]ϫⲉ[

margin

[a] ⲉ altered from (or to ?) ⲏ.

[b] Or -ⲁⲥ.

(p. 3.) . . ., Artemis, ..., Persephone, . . . achê, Selene, . . . kê,[1] Thellas,[2] . . . . ., Calliope, ..., Erinys, . . . atê,[3], Pon . . ., . . . nô, Nemesis, ... n,[4] Hera, . . .,[5] Dyranos,[6] . . . . . These are the names [of . . . god]desses . . . And (δέ) [Diocle]tian the [king . . . . .

(p. 4.) '. . . whether] presbyter (πρεσ.) or (εἴτε) deacon (διάκονος) or (εἴτε) reader (ἀναγ.) or (εἴτε) freeman [or (εἴτε)] slave or (? εἴτε) . . . . . sacrifice (θυσιάζειν) . . . . . god(s ?). And whoso [shall say], I am a Ch[ristian (χρ.),

[1] k uncertain. Nike, Ananke?

[2] Assuming ⲧ the article. But perhaps misspelt (for ⲑⲉⲗ-), so 'Hellas'. The name may have continued into next line.

[3] a uncertain. Hekate (even Aphrodite) too short for space, which may have held two names.

[4] n uncertain.

[5] Themis ? (or in l. 1, for Artemis).

[6] Or Dyranas. After this probably another name.

his] death shall be adjudged ($\delta\eta\mu\varepsilon\acute{\upsilon}\varepsilon\iota\nu$[1]) with the s[word]. But ($\delta\acute{\varepsilon}$) do ye all, [offici]als (*ἀξιωματικός*) of . . . . ., write[2] to the south, [to] all . . . in turn (*κατα-*) . . . . ., so that . . . . .'

No. 23.

Perhaps from a Martyrdom. The sequence of *recto* and *verso* are doubtful.

→ *Recto.*

margin

[. .] ⲁ[ⲩⲱ] ⲡⲁⲛⲟⲩ-
ⲧⲉ ⲉⲕⲉ̄ϫⲓ ⲙⲟⲉⲓⲧ
ϩⲏⲧ ϩⲓⲛⲉ̈[ϩ]ⲓⲟⲟⲩⲉ
ⲧⲏⲣ̈ⲟⲩ ⲉϯⲛ̄ⲁⲃ̄ⲱⲕ
ⲛϩⲏⲧⲟⲩ̄ ϫⲉⲛ[. .]
ϣⲁ̣ ⲙⲡⲟⲗⲩⲙⲟⲥ
ⲉⲧϩⲏⲡ ϩⲙⲡϫⲁ-
ϫⲉ ⲉϩⲟ̄ⲩⲛ ⲉⲓ̄ⲧⲉ ϩ[ⲓ]
[. .]ⲁ̣ⲗ. . . [(*sic*)
[. . .]ⲡ̣ ϣⲁⲡⲁ[
[. . ⲁ]ⲩ̣ⲱ ⲡ̣[

↑ *Verso.*

]ⲧ̣ⲉϥ ⲉϣϩ̣ⲱ̣ⲱ̣ⲙ̣[
]ⲧ ⲟⲩ̈ⲛ[a] ϩⲁⲣⲟϥ ⲁϥⲛ-
ⲕ[ⲟⲧ]ⲕ ⲁϥⲱ[ⲃ̄]ϣ
ǂ ⲁⲩⲱ ⲛⲧⲉⲩⲛⲟⲩ
ⲉⲓⲥ ⲡϣⲏⲣ̈ⲉ ⲛⲧⲙ̣[ⲛⲧ-]
ⲁⲅⲁ̄ⲑⲟⲥ ⲁϥⲧⲱ-
ⲟⲩ̈ⲛ ⲁϥ[ⲁ]ⲗⲉ ⲉϫⲛ-
ⲟⲩ̈ⲕⲗⲟⲟⲗⲉ [ⲛⲟⲩⲟ-]
[ⲉⲓ]ⲛ ⲙⲛⲙ[
[. ⲁ]ⲣ̄ⲭ̄ⲁⲅⲅ[ⲉⲗⲟⲥ]
[. . .]ⲡ̣ⲉⲛ[

margin

[a] Perhaps ⲧⲱ]ⲟⲩⲛ.

Recto. . . . '[and] my God, do Thou guide me upon all the ways wherein I shall go; for (?) . . . . . hidden war (*πόλεμος*) with the enemy within,[3] or (*εἴτε*)' . . . . .

Verso. . . . bear (?) it (? him), and he lay down and slept. And straightway, behold, the Son of Goodness (*-ἀγαθός*[4]) arose and mounted upon a cloud [? of ligh]t . . . . . archangel[s ?] . . . . .

[1] Or ?'be publicly executed'; *cf.* δήμιος.

[2] Or ['this] rescript'.

[3] The text, as I have read it, scarcely allows of this. After ⲉⲓⲧⲉ, ϩⲓⲃ̄ⲟⲗ seems impossible.

[4] *Cf.* Rossi ii. IV. 65, 'Son of Compassion,' as epithet of Christ.

No. 24.

Life of (or Encomium on) Pachomius. There is little to guide us as to the sequence either of leaves or pages here, if indeed all nine fragments belong to one MS. The order I have adopted is merely tentative. Pachomius' name occurs only in foll. 7 and 9, but 4, 5, and 6 may, with much probability, be claimed for the same subject. As to the remainder it is impossible to feel any certainty; they might be from parenetic introductions to or digressions from known incidents of the history. Certain incidents (foll. *6 ro.*, *9 vo.*) are only conceivable as part of this Life if we assume a widely different or much amplified recension to be at the base of our text.[1] It must however be confessed that the reading of scarcely a phrase but is open to question.

Fol. I. ↑ *Recto.*

margin

[. . .]ⲧⲓⲙⲉ	ⲣⲟ ⲛⲁ̣ⲓ̣ⲧ[c].[
[. . .]ⲛ̅ⲣ̅ⲣⲟ ⲛⲁ-	ⲉⲧⲟⲩⲁⲁⲃ ⲡ̣[ⲣⲟ-]
[ⲧⲁ]ⲁⲥ[a] ⲛⲁⲩ ϣⲁⲛ-	ⲧⲣⲉⲡⲉ ⲙ̅ⲙ̣[ⲟ-]
[.]ⲁ̣ⲧ̅ⲥ̅ⲟ ⲛⲉⲩϯ	ⲟⲩ· ⲙ̅ⲡⲉⲓ̣[
[ⲙⲉ][b] ⲉⲧⲙ̅ⲙ̅ ⲉⲃ̣ⲗⲁⲛ-	ⲛ̅ϩⲁϩ ⲛ̅ⲥ̣[ⲟⲡ
[ⲧ]ⲉⲓ ⲙ̣̅ⲙⲟⲟⲩ	ⲉⲧ[ⲥ-]
[ϩ]ⲙ̣̅ⲗⲁⲁⲩ ϫⲉ̣ⲛ̅-	ⲃ̅ⲱ̅ [
ⲛ̣ⲉⲡⲣ̅ⲣⲟ̅ ϭⲱ-	ⲉⲧ[
ϣ̅ⲧ̅ ⲉⲣⲟⲟⲩ· ⲟⲩ-	ⲛ̅ϩ[
[Ⲧ]ⲉϊⲙⲓⲛⲉ ⲅⲁⲣ-	ⲡ̣[
ⲡⲉ ⲡⲃⲓⲟⲥ ⲛ̅-	
ⲛ̣ⲉⲧⲟⲩⲁⲁⲃ̣.[	
[. . .]ⲛⲁ̣ⲅⲁ[	

→ *Verso.*

margin

[ⲡⲉⲧ]ⲥ̣ⲟ̣ⲟ̣ⲩⲛⲛ̣̅ϥ̅[d] ⲁⲩ-	ⲛ̅ⲧⲟϣ [
[ⲧⲟ]ⲣⲡ̅ϥ̅ ϣⲁ-	{ Ⲧⲉϥⲡⲁ[ⲧⲣⲓⲥ]
[ⲧ]ⲙⲉϩϣⲟⲙⲧⲉ	ⲇⲉ ⲛ̅ⲁⲗⲏ[ⲑⲓ-] }
[ⲙ̅]ⲡⲉ· ⲁⲩⲉⲓⲥ	ⲛⲏ· ⲟⲩⲥⲩ[ⲙⲡⲟ-]
[. .]ⲛ̅ⲧⲉⲭⲁⲣⲓⲥ	ⲗⲓⲧⲏⲥ ⲡ[ⲉ ⲛ̅-]
[ⲙ̅ⲡⲛⲟⲩ]ⲧⲉ ⲛ̅-	ϊⲉⲣⲟⲥⲟⲗⲩⲙ[ⲓ-]
]ⲛⲉ	ⲧⲏⲥ ⲛ̅ⲧⲉ
]ϩⲉⲛ-	ⲧⲙⲉϩⲥⲁϣ[ϥⲉ]
ⲡⲣ]ⲟⲥ ⲑⲉ	ⲙ̅ⲡⲉ· ⲧⲉⲕ[ⲕⲗⲏ-]
]ϭⲙ̅-	ⲥⲓⲁ ⲛⲁⲙⲉ ⲛ̅[ⲛ̅-]
	ϣⲣ̅ⲡ̅ⲙ̅ⲙⲓⲥ[ⲉ]
	[ⲉ]ⲧϩ̅ⲛ̅ⲙ̣̅ⲡ̣[ⲏⲩⲉ]
	[.]ⲁϥϣ[

[a] Or ⲕⲁⲁⲥ. [b] Apparently not space for [ⲙⲉ]. In 4 perhaps [ⲧ]ϥⲧⲥⲟ. [c] Perhaps ⲣⲉ for ⲣⲟ. [d] This cannot be correct: either ⲡⲉⲧⲥⲟⲟⲩⲛ ⲉⲁⲩ- (*v.* Bible text) or ⲡⲉⲧ-ⲥⲟⲩⲱⲛϥ ⲁⲩ-.

[1] That it is already far removed from the primary recensions of the Life may be gathered from the mere citation of the Psalms by P., before his conversion (fol. 8).

Fol. 1. *Recto.* . . . village (?) . . . . . the king shall grant (?) them, that he would spare their villages and not injure (βλάπτειν) them in aught, lest the king should behold them. For (γάρ) such is the life (βίος) of the saints . . . . [the] king shall (?) . . . saints (?) exhort (προτρέπειν) them to . . . oftentimes . . . . . instruction . . .

Verso. . . . God it is] knoweth. He was caught up to the third heaven.[1] Give . . . the grace (χάρις) of God . . . . according as (πρός) . . . . nome. But (δέ) his true fatherland (πατρίς, ἀληθινός) (was that) he was a fellow citizen (συμπολίτης), one of Jerusalem (ἱεροσολυμίτης) of the seventh heaven, the true church (ἐκκλ.) of the first-born that are in heaven[2] . . .

Fol. 2. ↑ *Recto.*	→ *Verso.*
ⲙ̅ⲡⲣ̣[	]ϥ̅
ⲱ ⲡ[ⲇⲓⲁⲃⲟ-]	]ⲙ̣ⲡⲉϥ̣-
ⲗⲟⲥ ⲛ̅ⲧ̅ϫ[ⲟⲟⲥ]	] . . ⲉⲛⲛⲁ-
ϫⲉⲁⲛ̅ⲧ̅ⲟⲩ[ⲥⲟⲟ-]	[ⲛ]ⲟ̣ⲩϫⲉ ⲙⲡⲙⲩͦ
ⲛⲉ ⲛ̅ϯⲙ[[a]	[ⲛ̅ⲥ]ⲁ̣ⲛⲃⲟⲗ ⲙ̅-
ⲁⲛ ⲙ̅ⲡⲉ[	[ⲙⲟ]ⲛ ϫⲉⲛ̣ⲁ-[c]
ⲙ̅ⲡⲁϫⲟ̣[ⲉⲓⲥ	] . ⲛϩ̣ⲟ̣ ⲉ̣ⲣⲟ̣ϥ
ⲉⲓⲟ̣ⲧ̣[[b]	]ⲉ̣ ⲉⲙ̣ⲁⲩ
ⲧ[	]ⲛ̅
	]ϩ

[a] ⲙ[ⲉⲓⲛⲉ] is tempting, but a verb is equally probable. [b] Perhaps ⲥ for ⲟ. [c] Perhaps ⲡⲁ- for ⲛⲁ-.

Fol. 2. *Recto.*[3] Do not . . . . ., O Devil (διάβ. ?)[4], saying, I am not a thief (?) of this (sort) . . . . . my Lord (?) . . .

Verso. . . . we (?) will cast death forth from us, for . . . .

[1] 2 Cor. xii. 2. The words do not coincide with Ciasca's text. *Cf.* the similar words used in Am. 543.

[2] *Cf.* Heb. xii. 23. Such phrases, as to heavenly citizenship, are used by martyrs under trial, *e.g.* Hyvernat *Actes*, 197.

[3] Scarcely a word can be read here with certainty.

[4] If not διάβολος, perhaps σύμβουλος? Ἄγγελος seems still less suitable.

Fol. 3. ↑ *Recto.*[a]	→ *Verso.*
margin	margin
[ⲡⲛⲟ]ⲩⲧⲉ ϯ ⲛⲟ-	ⲙⲡϫⲁ[ϫⲉ
[ⲙⲟⲥ] ⲙ̣ⲡⲉϥ-[b]	ⲛⲁⲉⲓⲣ̣[
]ⲛⲧⲁϥ-	ⲡⲉϥⲧ[
]ϩⲉⲛ-	ⲥ̣ⲓ̣ⲛ[
ⲛ̄]ⲛⲟⲩⲃ	ⲙ. [
ⲁ]ⲗⲗⲁ	ⲛⲧ[
ϫ]ⲟⲓ̈ⲥ̣	ⲧⲕ[

[a] I am not sure that this fragment does not rather belong to No. 21. [b] Perhaps ⲁⲡⲉϥ-.

Fol. 3. *Recto.* . . . God gives laws (*νόμος*) to (?) his . . . . which he had . . . . golden . . . But (*ἀλλά*) . . . Lord (?) . . .

Verso. . . . the enemy . . . will (*fut.*) . . . his . . .

Fol. 4. ↑ *Recto.*

]ⲣ̣ⲟⲕ
[ⲧⲁϩⲉ]ⲗⲡⲓⲥ
[ϫⲓⲛⲉⲓϫⲓ] ⲉⲕⲓⲃⲉ
[ⲛ̄ⲧⲛⲧⲁ]ⲙⲁⲁⲩ
[ⲁⲓⲛⲟϫⲧ] ⲉⲣⲟⲕ
[ϫⲓⲛⲉⲓϩ]ⲛ̄ⲧⲟⲟⲧⲉ

ⲣⲟⲥ ϭⲛ̄ ⲗ[ⲁⲁⲩ]
ⲙ̄ⲙⲁ ϩⲣⲁⲓ̈ [ⲛ̄ϩⲏ-]
ⲧϥ̄ · ⲡⲉⲓ̈ⲡ̣[ⲉ-]
Ⲧⲟⲩⲁⲁⲃ ⲇ[ⲉ]
ⲛⲉϥⲡⲣⲟⲕⲟ-
ⲡⲧⲉ ϩ̄ⲛ̄ⲟⲩⲗⲓ-
ⲕⲓⲁ · ⲛⲉⲩⲛ̄
Ⲟⲩⲣ̄ⲡⲉ ⲇⲉ ⲙ̄-
ⲡⲣ[ⲏⲥ] ⲙ̣̄ⲡϯ-
ⲙⲉ ⲛ̄ⲟⲩⲕⲟⲩⲓ̈
ⲧⲁⲭⲁ ⲉϣⲁⲩ-
ⲧ̄ⲛ̄ⲛⲟⲟⲩ ⲛ̄-
[ⲛ̄]ⲕⲟⲩⲓ̈ ⲛ̄ϣⲏ-
[ⲣⲉ ⲉ]ⲧⲣⲉ̣ⲩⲣ̄ϩⲱⲃ
[ⲛ̄ϩ]ⲏⲧ̄ϥ̄ ϩⲱⲥ

→ *Verso.*

[. . .]. ϩⲙ̄ⲡⲙⲟ-
[ⲟⲩ]. ⲛⲁⲓ̈ ⲉⲧⲉ-
[ϣ]ⲁⲩⲙⲟⲩⲧⲉ ⲉ-
[ⲣ]ⲟⲟⲩ ϫⲉⲛ̄ⲧⲁⲓ̈-
ⲣⲉ · ϩⲁϩ̄ⲧ̄ⲙ̄ⲙ̄-
ⲡⲟⲛⲏⲇⲏⲥ ⲇⲉ ⲛ̄-
ⲧⲁⲩⲥⲙⲓⲛⲉ ⲛ̄-
ⲛ̄ϫⲱⲱⲙⲉ ⲛ̄-
ⲛ̄ϩⲉⲗⲗⲏⲛ ⲉ-
ϣⲁⲩⲙⲟⲩⲧⲉ ⲉ-
ⲣⲟⲟⲩ ϫⲉⲛ̄ϣ[ⲏ-]
ⲣⲉ ⲙ̄ⲡⲟⲥⲓ̣[ⲇⲱⲛ]
ϩⲙ̄ⲡⲉϩⲟⲟ̣[ⲩ
ⲟⲩⲛ̄ⲛ̄ⲧ̣[
ⲙ̣̄ⲡ[

Ⲗⲩⲱ̣[
ⲛⲁ[
ⲛ̄ⲟ]
ⲧⲁ[
Ⲡⲉ[

Fol. 4. *Recto* (*cf.* AS. § 2). . . . Thou[1] art my hope (ἐλπίς) since I took the breast of my mother: I cast myself upon Thee since I was in the womb . . . . . [not] find any place therein.[2] But (δέ) this saint advanced (προκόπτειν) in age (ἡλικία). And (δέ) there was a temple, a little to the south of the village. Now (τάχα[3]) they would send boys to work therein, as (ὡς) . . .

Verso. . . . in the water, which are called 'sprites?'[4], but (δέ) by the authors (ποιητής) that have composed the books of the Greeks (ἕλλην) they are called 'the children of Poseidon'.[5] On the day therefore (οὖν) when . . .

Fol. 5. ↑ *Recto.*		→ *Verso.*[a]	
margin			⳨ ⲁ̅
ϩⲓⲧ̅ⲛ̅ⲛⲉϥⲉⲓ̂ⲟⲧⲉ	ⲧⲉ ⲛ[	ⲛ̄]ⲧⲉⲣⲟⲩ-	ⲛ̄ⲛⲟⲩⲧⲉ ϩⲟ̅ⲧ̅ⲡ̅
ⲉⲃⲟⲗ ϫⲉϩⲉⲛ-	ⲛ̄ⲧⲉ[	]ⲛϭⲓ ⲛ-	ⲁⲛ ⲙ̅ⲡ̅ⲛ̅ⲛⲉⲩϣⲏ-
ⲥⲡⲟⲩⲇⲁⲓ̂ⲟⲥⲛⲉ	ⲉⲡⲣ̣̄[ⲡⲉ	[ⲧⲁⲗⲁⲓ]ⲡ̣ⲱⲣⲟⲥ	ⲣⲉ· ⲟⲩⲁⲧϭⲟⲙ ⲅⲁⲣ-
ϩ̅ⲛ̅ⲧ̅ⲙ̅ⲛ̅ⲧ̅-		]ⲩ	ⲡⲉ ⲉⲧⲣⲉⲛ̄ⲗⲏⲥ-
ϩⲉⲗⲗⲏⲛ· ⲙ̅-			ⲧⲏⲥ ϥⲓ ⲡ̅ⲙ̅ⲙ̅ⲁⲩ
ⲡⲟⲩⲉⲓ̂ⲙⲉ ⲇⲉ ⲉ-			ⲙ̄ⲡϩ̅ⲏ̅ⲃ̅ⲥ̅ ⲉⲧ-
ⲧⲙⲉⲣⲓⲥ ⲛ̄ⲓ̈ⲁ-			ⲙⲟⲩϩ ⲉⲡⲙⲁ ⲉ-
ⲕⲱⲃ ϫⲉⲛⲟⲩ-			ⲧⲟⲩⲛⲁϫⲓⲟⲩⲉ
ⲧⲉⲓ̈ⲙⲓⲛⲉ̣ ⲁ̣ⲛ[ⲡⲉ]		]ⲉϥ	ⲛ̄ϩⲏⲧ̅ϥ̅· ⲁⲗⲗⲁ
ϫⲉⲡⲉⲛ[			ϣⲁⲩⲃⲱⲕ ϩ̅ⲛ̅-
[. . .]ⲧ̅ⲡ̣̅[			[ⲟⲩⲕ]ⲁⲕⲉ ϫⲉⲛ̄-
[. .]ⲙ̣ · ⲁϥ̣[			[ⲛⲉⲩ]ⲧⲁϩⲟⲟⲩ
			]ⲓ̣ϩⲉ[
			]ⲧϭⲟⲙ̣[

[a] The ⳨ above line 1 in different ink. Quires thus indicated in Rossi, i. II. 10, 36; ii. IV. 96. The ⲁ̅ indicates the last leaf of first quire.

[1] Ps. xxi. 9, 10. Perhaps ⲛ]ⲧⲟⲕ[ⲡⲉ, though no MS. of the Psalm reads thus.

[2] Or 'in him'.

[3] Τάχα with some such meaning in F. Robinson *Ap. Gosp.* 182, *PSBA.* xxv. 273 (= Syr. γάρ alone, Nau p. 76); *Miss.* iv. 671, 678, 715; Crum *Copt. Ostr.* no. 290.

[4] Taking ⲛⲧⲁⲓⲣⲉ for an incorrect plur. of ⲛⲟⲩⲧⲉ (*v.* Erman *ÄZ.* xxxiii. 47, Griffith *ib.* xxxviii. 88). This is supported by the 'name' ⲉⲛⲧⲁⲓⲣ, *Pistis* 376. But ⲧⲁⲓⲣⲉ may be a descriptive name, with ⲛ- of plur.

[5] *Cf.* Amélineau's note, Am. 340 and his reference to *Mém. Inst. Eg.* ii. 407.

Fol. 5. *Recto* (*cf.* AS. § 2). by his parents; for they were zealous (σπουδαῖος) in paganism (-ἕλλην) and (δέ) they knew not the portion (μερίς) of Jacob, that it is not of this sort.[1] For our . . .[2] . . . . to the temple (?) [3] . . .

Verso. when the wretched (ταλαίπωρος *pl.*) . . . . . had . . .
. . . the gods were[4] not content with their children. For (γάρ) it is impossible that thieves (λῃστής) should take with them the lamp that lighteth the place where they would thieve; rather (ἀλλά) they go in darkness, lest they be caught . . . . . authority . . .

Fol. 6. → *Recto.*[a]		↑ *Verso.*	
ⲃ̄			margin
Ⲉⲧⲓ ⲇⲉ ⲟⲩⲛ ⲉⲩ-	ⲛ̄ⲧⲡⲟ̣[ⲗⲓⲥ	ⲕⲁ]ⲕⲉ ⲙ̄ⲡⲉ-	ⲡⲛⲟⲩⲧⲉ ⲉϥ-
ϩⲙ̄ⲡⲏⲓ̈ ⲛ̄ϭⲓ	ⲉ[	]ⲡ̣ⲉϩⲟⲟⲩ ⲧⲏ-	ϣⲓⲛⲉ ⲛ̄ⲥⲁ-
ⲛⲉⲧⲟⲩⲁⲁⲃ· ⲁϥ-	ⲁ[	[ⲣ̄ϥ̄]ⲩ	ⲡⲟⲩϫⲁⲓ̈ ⲛ̄ⲣⲱ-
ϣⲱⲡⲉ ⲛ̄ϭⲓ ⲡϣⲏ-	?[	]ⲟ̣	ⲙⲉ ⲛⲓⲙ· ϩⲙ̄-
ⲣⲉ ⲛ̄ⲧⲥⲱⲛⲉ ⲙ̄-	ⲧ[	]?	Ⲡⲉϩⲟⲟⲩ ⲇⲉ ⲟⲩⲛ
ⲡⲉⲩⲉⲓ̂ⲱⲧ· ⲁⲩ-	[	]?	ⲛ̄ⲧⲁϥⲣ̄ⲣ̄ⲣⲟ̄· *sic*
ⲧⲱⲟⲩⲛ ⲁⲩⲃⲱⲕ		]ⲩ	ⲛ̄ϭⲓ ⲡⲁⲩⲅⲟⲩⲥ-
ⲉϩⲟⲩⲛ ϩⲱⲥ ⲉⲩ-			ⲧⲟⲥ ⲛ̄ⲣⲉϥϫⲣⲟ̄
ⲛⲁϭⲙ̄ ⲡⲉϥ[ϣⲓ-]			[ⲕ]ⲱⲥⲧⲁⲛⲧⲓ-
ⲛⲉ[· ⲁ]ⲩⲱ ϩ[ⲙ̄ⲡ-]			[ⲛⲟ]ⲥ· ϩⲓⲧⲛ̄ⲟⲩⲟⲓ̈-
[ⲧⲣⲉ			[ⲕⲟⲛⲟⲙⲓⲁ ⲛ̄ⲧⲉ]
			[ⲡⲛⲟⲩⲧⲉ

[a] The first of quire 2.

Fol. 6. *Recto.* While yet therefore (ἔτι δὲ οὖν) the saints were in the house, their father's sister's son fell sick. And they arose and went in, as if (ὡς) they would visit him. And as they (?) . . .
the city (? πόλις) . . .

[1] Jer. x. 16.

[2] 'Our father Pahôm' possible but improbable.

[3] Refers ? to temple whither his parents took the child.

[4] Tense uncertain.

Verso (*cf.* AS. § 2). dark (?) all (?) the day . . .
God, seeking the salvation of every man. And so (*δὲ οὖν*) on the day when the victorious[1] Augustus (*αὔγουστος*), Constantine, became king, by [God's] providence (*οἰκονομία*) . . .[2]

Fol. 7. → *Recto.*

margin

ⲡⲉⲡⲣⲟⲥⲧⲁⲅ̄-
ⲙⲁ ϫⲉ ⲛ̄ⲧⲉⲣⲟⲩ-
ⲛ̄ⲧϥ ⲉⲣⲏⲥ ϩⲛ̄-
ⲕⲏⲙⲉ · ⲁⲩϯ
ⲡⲉⲩⲟⲓ̈ ⲉⲡⲙⲁ-
ⲣⲏⲥ ⲛ̄ⲕⲏⲙⲉ ·
Ⲁⲩⲱ ⲛ̄ⲧⲉⲣⲟⲩϭⲱ-
ⲡⲉ ⲛ̄ϩⲁϩ ⲕⲁⲧⲁ
ⲙⲁ · ⲁⲩϭⲱⲡⲉ
ϩⲱⲱϥ ⲙ̄ⲡⲁ-
ϩⲱⲙ ϩⲓⲧⲛ̄ⲛ̣̄-[a]
ⲛⲟϭ ⲙ̄ⲡ[
[.]ⲉ · ⲉⲧⲃ̣[

ⲉⲩϭⲱϣ[ⲧ ϩⲏ-]
ⲧϥ ⲙ̄ⲡⲣ̄[ⲣⲟ ·]
Ⲉⲧⲓ ⲟⲩⲛ[
ⲡⲉ ⲱ̣[
ⲁ[
ⲡ[
ⲡ[
ϫ[
ϫ[

↑ *Verso.*

margin (*page no. here ?*)

]ⲙⲉⲛⲧⲁⲥ̣-
]ⲟⲩⲁϩⲱⲙ (*sic*)
ϯ] ⲡⲉϥⲟⲩⲟⲓ̈
]ⲕⲟⲩⲓ̈ ϩⲛ̄ⲛ̄-
ⲑⲉ]ⲃ̣ⲁⲓ̈ⲥ[b] ⲙ̄-
]ⲉ̣ⲉ
ⲛ̄]ⲧ̣ⲉⲣⲉϥ-
]ⲁ
]ⲁϥ

ϩⲏ ⲉⲃⲟⲗ ϫⲉ-
ⲟⲩⲥⲕⲉⲟⲥ ⲛⲁⲓ̈
ⲛ̄ⲥⲱⲧⲡ̄ⲡⲉ
Ⲛ̄ⲧⲟⲕ ϫⲉ ⲡⲁ-
ϩⲱⲙ ⲡⲟⲗⲉ-
ⲙⲉⲓ̈ ⲙ̄ⲛ̄ⲛ̄-
ϫⲁϫⲉ ⲉⲑⲏⲡ
ⲉⲧⲉⲛ̄ⲃⲁⲣⲃⲁ-
ⲣⲟⲥⲛⲉ ⲛ̄ⲇⲁⲓ̈-
ⲙⲱⲛⲟ[c] ⲛ̄ⲧⲁⲕ-
ϭ[ⲟ]ⲧⲡⲟⲩ ϩⲓⲧⲙ̄-
[ⲡⲉ]ⲥ⳨ⲟⲥ · ⲛ̄ⲧ̄-

[a] Perhaps ⲡⲛⲟϭ. But ⲡ- with ⲙⲏⲏϣⲉ (*cf.* Bo.) is unlikely. [b] Perhaps ⲣ for ⲃ. [c] ⲟ erased.

Fol. 7. *Recto* (*cf.* AS. § 3). And (*δέ*) when they had brought the order (*πρόσταγμα*) southward in Egypt, they betook them to the southern part of Egypt. And after they laid hold on many in various (*κατά*) places, they laid hold also on Pahôm, because of the great (*pl.*) number (?) that[3] . . . . which waited for the king. Thus while (*ἔτι οὖν*) . . .

Verso. . . . which had . . . . . an eagle[4] . . . went . . . . . little in the (*pl.*) . . . . .[5] . . . . . after it (he ?) had . . .

[1] *Cf.* ὁ τὰ πάντα νικῶν (Brit. Mus. Gk. Cat. ii. 328, iii. 253; P. Amh. no. cxl &c.). Νικηφόρος = ⲣⲉϥϫⲣⲟ appears to be applied only to martyrs (*v.* Crum-Steindorff, *Kopt. Rechtsurk.* i, Index).

[2] *Cf.* Am. 342.

[3] *Cf.* Bo. 5 *infra.*

[4] 'Eagle' (*ahôm*) possibly in reference to Pahôm, whose name is compounded with that word.

[5] 'Thebais' just possible.

. . . before (him ? it ?) ; for he is unto me a chosen vessel (*σκεῦος*).[1] But (*δέ*) thou,[2] Pahôm, fight (*πολεμεῖν*) with the hidden foes, which are the barbarous demons (*βάρβαρος, δαίμων*), whom thou hast overcome by the cross (*σταυρός*) ; and do thou . . .

Fol. 8. ↑ *Recto.*

margin

[.]ⲁ̣ⲡⲥⲁϩ ⲡⲁⲩ-	ϩⲓⲥⲛⲟϥ [. . ⲙ̄-]
[ⲗ]ⲟⲥ ⲡⲗⲁⲥ ⲙ̄-	ⲡⲉⲡⲙ[ⲁⲕⲁ-]
ⲡⲉⲥϯⲛⲟⲩϥⲉ	ⲣⲓⲟⲥ ⲣ̄[
ϫⲉϩ̄ⲙ̄ⲡⲧⲣⲉϥ-	ⲉⲟⲩⲁϩ̄ϥ̄ [ⲛ̄ⲥⲱ-]
ⲣ̣̄ϩⲛⲁϥ ⲛ̄ϭⲓ	ⲟⲩ ⲛ̄ⲥ̣[
ⲡⲛⲟⲩⲧⲉ ⲡⲁϊ	ⲛⲉ ⲛ̄ⲛ[
Ⲛ̄ⲧⲁϥ ⲡⲟⲣϫ̄ⲧ̄	ⲧⲉ· [
ⲉⲃⲟⲗ ϫⲓⲛⲉϊϩ̄ⲛ̄-	Ⲅⲁⲣ ⲙ[
ϩⲏⲧ̄ⲥ̄ ⲛ̄ⲧⲁⲙⲁ-	ⲧⲟϥ[
ⲁⲩ· ⲉⲟⲩⲉⲛ̄ϩ̄ ⲡⲉϥ-	ϫⲉ[
ϣⲏⲣⲉ ⲉⲃⲟⲗ ⲛ̄-	ϩ[
ⲛ̄ϩⲉⲑⲛⲟⲥ· [ϩⲛ-]	
[ⲧ]ⲉⲩⲛ̣ⲟⲩ ⲙ̣̄[ⲡⲓ-]	
[ⲟⲩⲁϩⲧ ⲉⲥⲁⲣⲝ][a]	

→ *Verso.*

margin

[. . . .]ⲛⲁⲕⲗⲏ-	ⲏ̣ ? ? [
[ⲣⲟⲛ]ⲟⲙⲉϊ ⲛ̄-	ⲕⲣⲓⲥⲓⲥ ⲁⲩ[ⲍⲁ-]
[ⲧⲙ]ⲛ̄ⲧ̄ⲉⲣⲟ ⲙ̄-	ⲛⲉ ϩⲣⲁϊ ⲛ̄ϩⲏ-
[ⲡ]ⲛⲟⲩⲧⲉ· ϩⲉⲛ-	ⲧ̄ϥ̄ ⲛ̄ⲑⲉ ⲛ̄ⲟⲩ-
[ⲥⲁⲣⲝ] ⲅ̣ⲁⲣ ϩⲓⲥ-	ϣⲏⲛ ⲉⲩⲧⲥⲟ
[ⲛⲟϥⲛⲉ] ⲧⲏⲣⲟⲩ	ⲙ̄ⲙⲟϥ ϩ̄ⲛ̄ϯ-
]ⲡⲁⲡⲟⲥ-	ⲱⲧⲉ ⲛ̄ⲧⲡⲉ·
ⲧⲟⲗⲟⲥ[b] ⲉ]ⲧⲟⲩⲁⲁⲃ	Ⲁϥⲙⲉⲕⲙⲟⲩⲕ̄ϥ̄
[. . .ⲧⲁ]ⲙⲟⲛ[c]	ϩⲣⲁϊ ⲛ̄ϩⲏⲧ̄ϥ̄
[ϫⲉⲣⲱⲙ]ⲉ ⲛⲓⲙ	ⲛ̄ⲧⲉϊϩⲉ ⲉϥ-
]ⲉϥ-	ⲧⲁⲩⲟ̄ ⲛ̄ⲧⲉⲥⲙⲏ
]ⲛ̣̄ⲥⲁ-	ⲉⲧⲟⲩⲁⲁⲃ ϫⲉ-
	ⲙ̣ⲁⲧⲥⲁⲃⲟϊ ⲧⲁ-
	[ⲣ̄]ⲡⲉⲕⲟⲩⲱϣ

[a] Hence we see that a full column had 14 or 15 (*cf.* fol. 4) lines. [b] Perhaps capital ⲧ. [c] Perhaps [ⲧⲁⲙⲟ ⲙ]ⲙⲟⲛ.

Fol. 8. *Recto.* . . . according to (?) the teacher, Paul, the tongue of perfume[3]: 'When it pleased God, who set me apart since I was in my mother's womb, to reveal His Son unto the heathen (*ἔθνος*) ; immediately I [followed not flesh] and blood,' . . . . . the blessed one (*μακάριος*) did not . . . to follow after them . . . . For (*γάρ*) . . .

Verso. . . . shall inherit (*κληρονομεῖν*) the kingdom of God.'[4] For (*γάρ*) they are all flesh (*σάρξ*) and blood ; [For ?] the holy apostle (*ἀπ.*) [hath]

[1] Acts ix. 15.

[2] Perhaps a development of the Spirit's words, Bo. 8.

[3] Gal. i. 15, 16 (*om.* 'and called me through His grace').

[4] *Cf.* 1 Cor. xv. 50.

told us: 'Every man (?) . . . . discernment ([? δια]κρισις) increase[1] (? αὐξάνειν) in him, even as a tree that is watered with the dew of heaven.' Thus did he meditate within himself, pronouncing the holy words (*lit.* voice): 'Teach me and I will do Thy will[2] . . .'

Fol. 9. ↑ *Recto.*

margin

[. . . .] ⲙⲁⲣⲉ-
Ⲡⲓ̣ⲱⲧⲁ ϩⲱⲱϥ
ⲕⲁⲧⲁⲣⲅⲉⲓ̈ ⲛ̄-
ⲧⲁⲓ̈ ϩⲙ̄ⲡⲧⲣⲉⲕ-
ⲧⲥⲁⲃⲉ ⲛ̄ⲣⲱⲙⲉ
ⲉⲣⲟⲥ · ⲙ̄ⲡⲉⲥ-
Ⲡⲟⲧ ⲉϣⲁⲣⲉⲡⲉ-
ⲭⲁⲗⲓⲛⲟⲥ ⲁⲙⲁϩ-
ⲧⲉ ⲉϫⲙ̄ⲡⲉϩ-
ⲧⲟ ϩⲛ̄ⲧⲉϥϭⲟⲙ ·
Ϫⲉⲕⲁⲥ ⲛ̄ⲛⲉⲛⲱ-
ⲥ̄ⲕ ϩⲙ̄ⲡϣ[ⲁϫⲉ]
ⲁϥⲟⲩⲱϩ ϩ̣[ⲛ
?

ⲁϥ ⲛ̄ⲣⲣⲟ [ϩⲙ̄-]
Ⲡⲛⲁⲩ ⲛ̄ⲧ̣[ⲁⲩ-]
ϫⲡⲟϥ ⲟⲩ[ⲛ̄ⲟⲩⲣ-]
ⲡⲉ ⲛⲧⲁϥ[ϣⲣ̄-]
ϣⲱⲣ̄ϥ̣ [
Ⲥ[
ⲡ[
ⲉ[
ⲛ̄[

→ *Verso.*

margin

[ⲡⲙⲁ]ⲕⲁⲣⲓⲟⲥ ⲁ-
[ⲡⲁ] ⲡⲁϩⲱⲙ ⲟ̄
[ⲟⲩ]ⲱϩ ϩⲛ̄ⲟⲩⲣ̄-
[ⲡⲉ] ⲉϥⲧⲁⲙⲟ ⲙ̄-
[ⲙⲟ]ϥ ϫⲉϩⲉⲛ-
[. .]ⲕ̣ⲁⲛⲛⲉ ⲛ̄ϩⲉ-
[ⲑⲛⲓⲕⲟⲥ] ⲙ̣ⲁ
ⲉⲃ]ⲟⲗ ϩⲛ̄-
ϩⲉⲑ]ⲛⲟⲥ
]ⲧ̣ⲁ-
ⲡⲉ]ⲭ̄ⲥ̄

ⲕⲁ ⲛ[ⲛ-]
ⲥⲱⲟⲩ · ⲁⲩⲟⲩ-
ⲱϩ ϩⲙ̄ⲡⲙⲁ ⲉ-
ⲧⲙ̄ⲙⲁⲩ ⲉⲧⲃⲏ-
ⲏⲧϥ̄ · ⲙ̄ⲡ-
Ⲛⲧⲁⲗϭⲟ[a] ⲛ̄-
ⲧⲁⲡⲛⲟⲩⲧⲉ
ⲭⲁⲣⲓⲍⲉ ⲙ̄ⲙⲟ-
ⲟⲩ ⲉⲃⲟⲗ ϩⲓⲧⲟⲟ-
ⲧϥ̄ ⲉⲧⲓ ⲉϥⲟ̄ ⲛ̄-
ϩⲉⲑⲛⲓⲕⲟⲥ
[Ⲛ̄]ⲧⲉⲣⲉϥⲱⲥ̄ⲕ
[ⲟⲩ]ⲛ ϩⲙ̄ⲡ†ⲙⲉ
ⲟ]ⲩ̣ⲁ

[a] ⲛ- corrected from ⲡ-.

Fol. 9. *Recto* (*cf.* AS. § 3). . . . May the . . . . .[3] too bring this to nought (καταργεῖν), whilst thou teachest it unto men, like as the bridle (χαλινός) controlleth the horse by its power. That we may not delay in the story (*lit.* word), he dwelt in . . . . made him (?) king. At the time when he was born, there was a temple[4] that he had destroyed . . .

Verso. . . . the blessed (μακ.) Apa Pahôm also (?)[5] dwell in a temple,[6]

[1] Tense uncertain.

[2] Ps. cxlii. 10.

[3] 'the Spirit' perhaps possible.

[4] All quite uncertain as to number and person of pronouns.

[5] The form *Pahômo* does not occur in this text; otherwise ⲟⲛ 'also' must be omitted. Tense of verb uncertain.

[6] Presumably the ruined Serapis temple. The name by which this seems elsewhere to be designated, ⲡⲙⲁ ⲙⲡⲉⲥⲧⲉⲣⲡⲟⲥⲉⲓⲛ (*Miss.* 535), is, I think, merely a deformed reproduction of ⲡⲙⲁ ⲙⲡⲥⲉⲣⲁⲡⲉⲓⲟⲛ (*cf.* Bo. 8).

telling him that it was heathen (*pl.* ? ἐθνικός) . . . . . pagans (? ἔθνος) . . . . Christ . . . . left behind them . . . . . and they dwelt in that place on account of him (? it) and of the healings that God granted (χαρίζειν) by his (? its) means,[1] while yet (ἔτι) he was pagan (ἐθνικός). So (οὖν) when he had continued in the village . . .

No. 25 (called, in Appendix and elsewhere, SaX).

The history of Pachomius and Theodore. That this MS. did not form part of No. 24 is evident from the following considerations: (1) the divergent spelling of the name Pachomius, (2) the absence of the paragraph-mark such as used by no. 24, (3) the abnormal forms here of certain letters, *e.g.* ϩ,[2] (4) the usually greater number of letters in a line in the present MS., (5) finally, the entire dissimilarity between the texts of no. 24 and of Am., a version based, as will be shown, strictly upon the present text.

A column of our text is 23 cm. high, and has 26–28 lines. Of the 32 foll. here preserved, in greater or less completeness, only three still show pagination (foll. 2, 4, 5). Were it not therefore for the uninterrupted text of Am., it might have been impossible to assign any plausible sequence to the fragments, which I found dispersed throughout the whole collection of papyri. As it is, however, a few of them fortunately show the junctures, upon one and the same leaf, of two paragraphs of AS. (foll. 9 *vo.*–10 *ro.*, 11 *ro.*, 12 *ro.*, 13 *ro.*, 18 *vo.*, 24 *vo.*, 25 *vo.*, 26 *vo.*); and it is thence evident that, not only is the new text verbally identical with Am., but that in arrangement of paragraphs they likewise agree. This should suffice to justify the assignment of the remaining paragraphs to positions relatively such as they hold in Am. The latter offers no parallels to the text of foll. 1, 2, 7, 29, 32. The absence (scarcely fortuitous) of quire-numbers prevents us from using the relative sequence of *horizontal* and *vertical* fibres as a further guide to the sequence of the leaves. Leaves, the continuity of whose text allows of no doubt as to their order,[3] show the simple sequence *hv, vh, hv, vh.*

The practical identity of the two texts SaX and Am. can scarcely be doubted by any one who will compare the parallel passages (observing at the same time the alterations to the French translation which I have given in the notes). The text of Am. is, in no instance, materially longer than that of the corresponding Sa. passage; whereas the latter shows, often enough, phrases, nay whole paragraphs, lacking from the parallel Arabic. These are proof enough that, as would be expected, the younger is abridged from the older text.

[1] *Sc.* the temple's?

[2] Palaeographical features do not otherwise afford very cogent arguments here (*cf.* facsimiles).

[3] *E.g.* foll. 8–14, 16–22.

The chief interest of this new addition to the Coptic recensions is genealogical: we now see clearly the source whence Am. was derived. It has been long recognized that Am. neither translates immediately any of the Sa. versions hitherto known [1] nor Bo. which is derived from certain of these. Am. neither follows them (except intermittently) in paragraph sequence nor in details of phraseology or vocabulary. With our present text, on the contrary, it agrees in both these particulars; as to the last, with often surprising closeness. The new text is of course too fragmentary to allow of our assuming that it alone was the immediate source translated by Am.[2] Prof. Ladeuze has called attention to portions of the latter which appear to be derived from Bo.,[3] *i. e.* ultimately from one of the other Sa. versions.

Fol. I. → *Recto.*[a]

	]ⲙ̣ · ⲁϥ-
	]ϥ̄ ⲛ̄ⲟⲩ
	ⲕⲟⲩϊ ⲛ̄ⲧⲙⲏⲧⲉ
	ⲛ̄ⲛⲉϥⲙⲁⲑⲏⲧⲏⲥ
. . . .]. ⲁ̣ⲁⲩ	ⲉϥϫⲱ ⲙ̄ⲙⲟⲥ ϫⲉ-
. . . .]ⲉϊⲙⲓ-	ⲡⲉⲧⲛⲁϣⲱⲡ' ⲉ-
. . . . . .] ϥⲛⲁⲩ	ⲣⲟϥ' ⲛ̄ⲟⲩϣⲏⲣⲉ ϣⲏⲙ
ⲉⲡϫⲟ]ⲉⲓⲥ ⲙ̄ⲡⲧⲏ-	ⲛ̄ⲧⲉϊϩⲉ ⲉϩⲣⲁϊ ⲉϫⲙ̄-
ⲣ̄ϥ̄] ⲡϣⲏⲣⲉ ⲙ̄ ⳽	ⲡⲁⲣⲁⲛ. ⲉϥϣⲱⲡ'
ⲡⲛ]ⲟⲩⲧⲉ ⲉⲁϥⲣ̄ⲥⲁ-	ⲙ̄ⲙⲟϊ ⲉⲣⲟϥ · ⲉⲧⲃⲉ-
ⲣ]ⲝ̄ ⲉⲧⲃⲉⲡⲉⲛⲟⲩ-	ϩⲉⲛⲕⲉⲕⲟⲩϊ ⲇⲉ ⲉ-
ϫⲁϊ · ⲙⲁⲗⲓⲥⲧⲁ ⲇⲉ	ⲁⲩϫⲡⲟ' ⲛⲁⲩ ⲛ̄ⲟⲩ-
ⲟ]ⲛ ⲉⲛⲥⲱⲧⲙ̄ ⲉⲣⲟϥ	ⲡⲣⲟϩⲁⲓⲣⲉⲥⲓⲥ ⲉⲥ-
ϩ]ⲙ̄ⲡⲉⲩⲁⲅⲅⲉⲗⲓⲟⲛ	ϩⲟⲟⲩ, ϩ̄ⲛ̄ⲧⲉⲩⲙⲛ̄ⲧ-
ϫⲉ]ⲙ̄ⲡⲣ̄ⲕⲱⲗⲩⲉ ⲛ̄-	

margin

↑ *Verso.*

ⲥ̣ⲧⲉ̣ⲣ̣[. . . . .]	
ϫⲱ ⲙ̄ⲙⲟⲥ ϫⲉ-	
ⲡⲉⲧⲥⲡⲁⲧⲁⲗⲁ'	
ϫⲓⲛⲧⲉϥⲙⲛ̄ⲧ-	ⲧⲟ̣[
ⲕⲟⲩϊ ⲛⲁⲣ̄ϩⲙ̄ϩⲁⲗ ·	ⲉⲧⲉ̣[
ⲧⲉⲛⲟⲩϭⲉ ⲛⲉⲥⲛⲏⲩ,	ⲁⲁⲥ · [
ϣⲏⲣⲉ ϣⲏⲙ' ⲛⲓⲙ	ⲉⲛϣⲁⲁ̣[
ⲙ̄ⲛⲛⲉⲛⲧⲁⲩⲣ̄-	ⲛ̄ϩⲁϩ ⲛ̄ⲥⲟⲡ [ⲙⲁ-]
ⲛⲟϭ ⲉⲣⲟⲟⲩ ϩ̄ⲛ̄ⲑⲏ-	ⲣ̄ⲛ̄ⲧⲁⲙⲟⲟⲩ [ϫⲉ-]
ⲗⲓⲕⲓⲁ, ⲉⲛⲧⲁⲡϫⲟ-	ⲡⲛⲟⲩⲧⲉⲡⲉ ⲉⲛ̣-
ⲉⲓⲥ ⲉⲓⲛⲉ ⲙ̄ⲙⲟⲟⲩ	ⲧⲁϥⲧⲁⲙⲓⲟⲟⲩ
ⲉϩⲟⲩⲛ ϣⲁⲣⲟⲛ, ⲉ-	ⲁⲩⲱ ⲉⲧⲃⲉⲧⲡ̣[ⲉ]
ⲡⲉϫⲡⲟ' ⲛ̄ⲕⲉⲥⲟⲡ.	ⲟⲛ ⲙ̄ⲡⲛ̄ⲕⲁϩ' ⲙ̣[ⲛ̄-]
ⲙⲁⲣⲛ̄ⲥⲡⲟⲩⲇⲁⲍⲉ	ⲡⲣⲏ' ⲙ̄ⲡⲟⲟϩ [

margin

[a] The position of this fol. is hypothetical. It is assumed to precede that placed next (pp. 63, 64).

[1] Nor the lost Sa. represented by Av. *V.* Appendix.

[2] I assume, from our foll. 1, 2, that the Palladian version of the Rule (Am. 366–369) did not figure in SaX. But not all MSS. of Am. include it (*v.* Appendix).

[3] Ladeuze, *Étude &c.*, 53 ff.

Fol. 1. (The proper positions of this and the next 2 foll. are uncertain.)

Recto. . . . he saw (? seeth) the Lord of all, the Son of God, having become flesh (σάρξ) for our salvation. But (δέ) above all (μάλιστα) too we hear Him in the Gospel (εὐ.) saying,[1] 'Forbid (κωλύειν) not . . . . .

. . . He . . . a little one in the midst of His disciples (μαθ.), saying,[2] 'Whoso shall receive a young child such as this in my name receiveth me.' But (δέ) as for the young that have gotten for themselves an evil resolve (προαίρεσις), in their[3] . . . . .

Verso. . . . saying,[4] 'Whoso liveth wantonly (σπαταλᾶν) from his youth shall be a servant.' Now therefore, brethren,[5] every young child and such as are greater than they in age (ἡλικία), whom the Lord hath brought in unto us for the second birth, let us be zealous (σπουδάζειν) . . . . .

. . . we . . . . . many times, let us tell them how that God it was did create them. And concerning the heaven also and the earth and the sun and the moon . . . . .

Fol. 2.	↑ p. ⲝ̅ⲅ̅	→ p. ⲝ̅ⲇ̅	
	margin	margin	
]ⲉ̣ⲥⲱ	ϯⲥⲃⲱ̅ ⲛⲁⲩ ⲛ̄ⲟⲩ[ⲟ-]	ⲙ̅ⲛ̅ⲡⲉϥⲟⲩⲱϣ' ⲉ-	ⲡ[
]ⲩⲉ ⲛ̄-	ⲉⲓϣ ⲛⲓⲙ' ⲉⲧⲣⲉ[ⲩ-]	[ⲃ]ⲟⲗ ϩ̅ⲙ̅ⲡⲉϥⲛⲟⲙⲟⲥ·	ⲉⲩ[
]ϥ̣ⲧⲁ-	ⲥⲙⲟⲩ ⲉⲡⲉⲛⲧⲁϥ-	ⲙ̅ⲛ̅ⲛ̄ⲕⲱⲧ' ⲉⲛⲧⲁ-	ⲉⲃⲟ̣[
ⲉ]ⲩϣⲁ̅	ⲧⲁⲙⲓⲉ ⲛⲁϊ ⲧⲏⲣ[ⲟⲩ]	ⲉⲓⲧⲁⲁⲩ ⲛⲏⲧ̅ⲛ̅ ⲉ-	ⲙⲧ̣[
] ⲡⲣⲟⲥ	ⲁϫ̅ⲛ̅ⲱϫ̅ⲛ̅· ⲉⲓⲧⲉ	ⲃⲟⲗ' ⲛ̄ϩⲏⲧ̅ϥ̅ ϫⲉ-	ⲉⲧ[
ⲟⲩⲟ]ⲉ̈ⲓϣ	ϩ̅ⲛ̅ⲧⲉⲩⲧⲁⲡⲣⲟ	ⲕⲁⲥ ⲉⲛ(ⲩ *sic*)ⲛⲁⲙⲉⲣⲉ	ⲟⲟⲩ[
]ⲓ̣ ⲙⲟ̅[a]	ⲉⲓⲧⲉ ϩ̅ⲙ̅ⲡⲉⲩϩⲏⲧ	ⲡϫⲟⲉⲓⲥ ⲡⲉⲛⲛⲟⲩ-	ϫⲉ[
]ⲫⲏⲧ'	ⲉⲩϫⲱ' ⲙ̅ⲙⲟⲥ ϫⲉ-	ⲧⲉ ⲉⲃⲟⲗ ϩ̅ⲙ̅ⲡⲉⲩ(*sic*)ϩⲏⲧ'	ⲡⲛ[
ⲟ]ⲩϥ	ⲕⲥⲙⲁⲙⲁⲁⲧ' ⲡϫⲟ-	ⲧⲏⲣ̅ϥ̅ ⲙ̅ⲛ̅ⲧⲉⲩ-	ⲧⲁϥ̣[
]ⲁⲙ̣	ⲉⲓⲥ ϫⲉⲕⲁⲥ ϩⲱⲟⲩ	ⲯⲩⲭⲏ ⲧⲏⲣ̅ⲥ̅ ⲙ̅ⲛ̅-	ⲱⲛ[
]̅.	ⲉⲩⲉϣⲱⲡⲉ ⲛ̄ϣⲏ-	ⲛⲉⲩⲙⲉⲉⲩⲉ ⲧⲏⲣⲟⲩ	ⲁⲩ[

[a] Line over ⲙ not certain.

[1] ? Matt. xix. 14.

[2] Matt. xviii. 5.

[3] An abstract, ? 'youth'.

[4] Prov. xxix. 21. So Ciasca; LXX κατασπαταλᾷ.

[5] I assume that this and the next fragment are from instructions given by Pachomius, corresponding perhaps to Am. 372 ff. Evidence for the independent existence of the Pachomian Rule is given by the book catalogue, *Rec.* xi. 133, no 31 (the βίος there figures as no. 34).

]ⲉ̣ⲑ̣ⲉ̣	ⲣⲉ ⲛ̄ⲇⲁⲩⲉⲓⲇ' ⲡⲁⲓ̈	ⲙ̄ⲛ̄ⲧⲉⲩϭⲟⲙ ⲧⲏ-	ⲉⲧ[
]ⲛ̣ϩⲁϩ,	ⲉⲧϫⲱ ⲙ̄ⲙⲟⲥ ϫⲉ[ϯ-]	ⲣ̄ⲥ̄ · ⲁⲩⲱ ⲉⲧⲣⲉⲩⲙⲉ-	ⲟⲩⲧ̣[
]ⲟ̣ⲛ	ⲛⲁⲥⲙⲟⲩ ⲉⲡϫⲟⲉⲓ[ⲥ]	ⲣⲉ ⲡⲉⲧϩⲓⲧⲟⲩⲱⲟⲩ	ⲉ̣ⲣⲉ[
ⲉ]ⲧⲃⲉ-	ⲛ̄ⲟⲩⲟⲉⲓϣ' ⲛⲓⲙ' ⲛ̄-	ⲛ̄ⲧⲉⲩϩⲉ · ⲉⲧⲣⲉⲩ-	ⲁⲩ̣[
]ⲛ̣	ⲟⲩⲟⲉⲓϣ' ⲛⲓⲙ' ⲉⲣⲉ-	ⲉⲓⲙⲉ ϩⲛ̄ⲟⲩⲱⲣϫ̄	ⲟ̣ . [
]ⲧ	ⲡⲉϥⲥⲙⲟⲩ ϩⲛ̄ⲣⲱⲓ̈ ·	ⲉⲛⲉⲛⲧⲁⲩⲥϩⲁⲓ̈ⲥⲟⲩ	ⲉϣ̣[
]ⲕ̣ⲉ	ⲙⲛ̄ⲛ̄ⲥⲱⲥ ⲇⲉ ⲟⲛ ⲉ-	ϩⲙ̄ⲡⲉⲡⲛ̄ⲁ̄ ⲉⲧⲟⲩ-	ⲥ̣[
]	ϯ ⲛⲁⲩ ⲛ̄ϩⲉⲛⲯⲁⲗ-	ⲁⲁⲃ · ϫⲉⲕⲁⲥ ⲉⲩ-	[
	ⲙⲟⲥ ⲛ̄ⲁⲡⲟⲥⲧⲏ-	ϣⲁⲛϩⲁⲣⲉϩ' ⲉⲡⲉⲩ-	
	ⲑⲟⲩⲥ · ⲁⲩⲱ ⲟⲛ ⲉⲧ-	ⲥⲱⲙⲁ' ⲉϥⲟⲩⲁⲁⲃ	
	[ⲣⲉⲩ]ϫⲓ̈ ⲉⲃⲟⲗ ϩⲛ̄ⲛⲕⲉ-	ϫⲓⲛⲧⲉⲩⲙ[ⲛ̄ⲧ-]	
	[ϫⲱ]ⲱⲙⲉ ⲛ̄ⲧⲉⲅⲣⲁ-	ⲕⲟⲩⲓ̈, ⲥⲉⲛⲁϣ[ⲱ-]	
	[ⲫⲏ] ⲉⲧⲟⲩⲁⲁⲃ · ⲁⲩⲱ	ⲡⲉ ⲛ̄ⲣ̄ⲡⲉ' ⲙ̄[ⲡϫⲟ-]	
	[ⲙⲛ̄]ⲛ̄ⲥⲱⲥ ⲉⲧⲥⲁⲃⲟ̣	ⲉⲓⲥ ⲁⲩⲱ ⲛ̄ϥⲟ̣[ⲩⲱϩ]	
	[ⲛ̄ⲛ]ⲕⲟⲩⲓ [	[ϩ]ⲣⲁⲓ̈ ⲛ̄ϩ]ⲏ̣ⲧⲟ̣[ⲩ	

Fol. 2. P. 63. . . . 'Teach them at all times that they bless Him that created all these things, without ceasing, whether (εἴτε) with their mouths, or (εἴτε) with their heart, saying, Blessed art thou, Lord, that they also may become children of David, who saith,[1] I will bless the Lord at all times; at all times His blessing is in my mouth. And (δέ) afterwards too, (see) that (thou) give unto them Psalms (to learn) by heart[2] (*ἀπὸ στηθοῦς*); and moreover, that they get (by heart) from the other books of holy scripture (*γραφή*). And afterwards, (see) that (thou) teach the young . . . . .

P. 64. . . . and His will, from out His law (*νόμος*), and the rules that I have given you therefrom, that they[3] shall love the Lord our God with all their heart and all their soul (*ψυ.*) and all their thoughts and all their strength; and that they should love their neighbour as themselves; that they may know of a surety the things that have been written of the Holy Spirit (*πν.*), so that, if they keep their body (*σῶ.*) pure from their youth, they shall become temples of the Lord and He shall [dwell with]in [them . . . . .

[1] Ps. xxxiii. 1.

[2] *Cf.* Ladeuze, 291 *inf.*; Butler, *Laus. Hist.* ii, note 58; Crum, *Ostr.* no. 29, note 5.

[3] Corrected from 'that we'. *Cf.* Luke x. 27.

Fol. 3. ↑ *Recto* (?).

[ⲟⲩⲱ]ϣ [ⲁⲛ ⲛⲧⲉⲣⲉϥⲁⲛ-]
[ⲁⲅⲕ]ⲁⲍⲉ ⲇⲉ ⲙ̅ⲙⲟϥ̣
[ⲟⲛ] ⲉϫⲓⲧⲟⲩ · ⲡⲉ[ϫ]ⲁϥ ⲛ̣ⲁϥ̣
[ϫⲉⲛ̄]ⲛⲟ' · ⲁⲩⲱ ⲡⲉϫⲁϥ ⲉ-
[ϩⲟⲩ]ⲛ ⲉϩⲣⲁϥ' ϫⲉⲟⲩ'ⲡⲉ
[ⲡⲉⲓ̈]ϣⲁϫⲉ ⲛⲧⲁⲕ-
[ϫⲟⲟ]ϥ' ϫⲉⲛ̄ⲛⲟ. ⲉⲁⲕϯ
[ⲙⲁ] ⲛ̄ϩⲏⲧⲕ ⲛ̄ⲟⲩⲇⲁⲓ-
[ⲙⲟⲛⲓ]ⲟ̣ⲛ ⲙ̅ⲙ̅ⲛ̅ⲧⲁⲧ-
[ⲥⲱⲧ]ⲙ̣̅ · ⲕⲁⲛ ⲉϣϫⲉ ⲛ̄ⲅ-
[ⲟⲩⲱϣ ⲁ]ⲛ ⲉϫⲓⲧⲟⲩ. ⲁ-
[ϫⲓⲥ ϫⲉⲛ̄ϯ]ⲟⲩⲱϣ ⲁⲛ
[ⲧⲉⲛⲟⲩ ⲙ]ⲟ̣ⲛⲟⲛ ϫⲓⲧⲟⲩ
[ⲛⲅⲕⲁⲁⲩ ⲉϩ]ⲣⲁⲓ̈ · ⲙⲟ-
[ⲛⲟⲛ

margin

→ *Verso* (?).

[. .]ⲁⲛ̣ ⲛϥⲧ̣ⲱ̣ϣ[a] ⲙ̣[
ⲙⲟ̣ [ⲙ̅]ⲡ̄ⲗⲁⲁⲩ ⲙ̅ⲙ̣̅[ⲛ̄ⲧ-]
ⲁⲧⲥⲱⲧⲙ̅ ⲙ̅ⲛ̄ⲛ̄-
ⲥⲱⲥ · ⲁⲩⲱ ⲁⲥϣⲱ-
ⲡⲉ ⲁ̣ⲥϣⲱⲡⲉ (*sic*) ϩⲓ[ⲛ-]
ⲡⲉϩⲟⲟⲩ ⲉⲧⲙ̅ⲙⲁ̣[ⲩ]
ⲉϥϣⲁⲛⲛⲁⲩ ⲉⲡ-
ⲉⲧⲙ̅ⲙⲁⲩ ⲉ̣ϥⲙ̣[ⲟⲟ-]
ϣⲉ ϩ̅ⲛ̅ⲑⲉⲛⲉⲉ[ⲧⲉ]
ϣⲁϥϣⲓⲡⲉ [ⲛϥⲕⲁ]
ϫⲱϥ ⲉⲡⲉ̣[ⲥⲏⲧ ⲛⲉ-]
ⲣⲉⲛⲉϥⲃⲁ̣[ⲗ' ϯ ⲣ̅ⲙ̅[b]-]
ⲉⲓⲏ · ⲛ̣ . [
ⲉⲩⲙⲏ̣ . [
ⲧⲁϥϫ[

margin

[a] Perhaps ⲥⲱϣ (ⲥⲱϣⲙ).

[b] Perhaps more in gap; ⲟⲛ or ⲇⲉ?

Fol. 3. *Recto* (*v.* Am. 396). . . . I] wish [not.'] But (*δέ*) [after that he had] constrained (*ἀναγκάζειν*) him [again] to take of them, he said unto him, 'I will not.' And he said unto him,[1] 'What is [this] word that thou hast [said], I will not, having given [place] in thyself to a demon (*δαιμόνιον*) of disobedience[2]? If so be (*κἄν*) thou [wishest] not to take of them, say, [I] wish not [now][3]; but (*μόνον*) take them [and lay? them] down. But (*μόνον*) . . .

Verso.[4] . . . and he determined (?)[5] . . . . . no disobedience thereafter. And it befell from that day, if he saw that (brother) walking in the monastery, he would be ashamed and bend down his head, his eyes shedding tears . . .

[1] ⲉϩⲟⲩⲛ ⲉϩⲣⲁϥ, of earnest or angry talk, *e.g.* Num. ix. 7, Josh. ix. 12, Brit. Mus. no. 342 ϥ̅ⲉ̅, Rossi *Nuov. Cod.* 89, Budge *Homil.* 127.

[2] So Am., not 'pécher'.

[3] Am. should be 'And if it be that thou wishest not to take (thereof), say, I wish (for it) not now, and take and use (? eat) a little; then lay it down'.

[4] This is not in Am.

[5] Perhaps 'despised'.

Fol. 4. ↑ p. ⲣ̄ⲓ̄ⲁ̄[a]

margin

ϣⲉ[b] ⲁⲛ ϩ̄ⲙ̄ⲡⲉⲩ-
ⲡⲣⲁⲝⲉⲓⲥ ⲙ̄ⲡⲛ̄ⲕⲱ-
ⲣ̄ϣ̄ ⲛ̄ⲧⲉⲩⲧⲁⲡⲣⲟ'
ⲧ̄ⲡⲟⲩⲟⲛ̄ϩ̄ ⲉⲃⲟⲗ' ϫⲉ-
ⲙ̄ⲡⲙ̄ⲙⲉⲣⲓⲧⲟⲩ
ⲕⲁ̣ⲧⲁ̣ ⲑⲉ ⲉⲧ̣ⲥ̣ⲏϩ·
ϫⲉ[ⲡⲉ]ⲧⲛⲏ[ⲩ ϣⲁⲣ-]
[ⲟⲓ ⲉⲛϥ]ⲙ[ⲟ]ⲥⲧ[ⲉ ⲁⲛ]
[ⲙ̄ⲙⲟ]ⲟⲩ . . ⲥ̣ⲛⲉⲥ̣
[. . .]ⲉⲡⲁⲣⲁⲛ ⲙ̄-
[ⲙⲟⲟⲩ . .]ⲛ̣ⲉⲣⲙⲁ̣

ⲙ̄ⲡϫⲟⲉⲓⲥ· ⲁⲩⲱ
ⲉϥⲁⲩⲝⲁⲛⲉ ϩ̄ⲙ̄ⲡⲉ-
ⲥⲃⲟⲟⲩⲉ' ⲉⲧϥ̄ⲥⲱⲧⲙ̄
ⲉⲣⲟⲟⲩ ϩⲓⲧⲟⲟⲧϥ̄
ⲙ̄ⲡⲉⲛⲉⲓⲱⲧ' ⲡⲁ-
ϩⲱⲙ' [sic] ⲉϥⲙ̣ⲟⲟϣⲉ' ⲕⲁ-
ⲧⲁ ⲡⲉϥⲉⲓⲛⲉ ⲁⲩⲱ
ⲕⲁⲧⲁ̣ ⲧⲉϥϩ̣ⲉ·
ⲛⲉⲥⲛⲏⲩ ⲇⲉ ⲛⲧⲉ-
ⲣⲉⲩⲛⲁⲩ ϫⲉϥ̣ϯ . . ⲧ̣[c]

[a] Sir H. Thompson has discovered a fragment with part of this text in the binding of Br. Mus. Or. 7024 (4), and this allows me to fill some lacunae.

[b] ⲙⲟⲟ]ϣⲉ.

[c] Not ⲟⲩⲱ. Perhaps ⲉⲑⲏ.

→ p. ⲣ̄ⲓ̄ⲃ̄

margin

ϣⲗⲏⲗ' ⲡ̄ⲙ̄ⲙⲁⲩ,ⲡⲉ
ⲛ̄ⲧⲉⲓ̈ϩⲉ ϩⲛ̄ϩⲉⲛⲣⲙ̄-
ⲉⲓⲟⲟⲩⲉ ϣⲁⲛⲧϥ̄ϯ
ⲙ̄ⲧⲟⲛ ⲛⲁⲩ ⲛ̄ϭⲓ
ⲡϫⲟⲉⲓⲥ ⲉⲃⲟⲗ' ϩⲓ-
ⲧⲟⲟⲧϥ̄· ⲁⲩⲱ ⲁⲥ-
Ϣⲱⲡⲉ ⲛ̄ⲧⲉⲣⲉϥ-
ⲉⲓ' ⲉϩⲟⲩⲛ, ⲉⲛⲉⲥⲛⲏⲩ
ⲛ̄ⲧⲁⲣⲭⲏ ϩⲛ̄ⲧⲉϥ-
ⲙⲛ̄ⲧⲕⲟⲩⲓ̈ ⲁϥϯ
ⲡⲉϥⲟⲩⲟⲉⲓ' ⲉⲡⲉⲛ-
[ⲉⲓⲱⲧ

ⲛⲁⲩ ⲉⲡⲉⲛⲧⲁϥⲧⲁ-
ⲙⲟⲓ̈, ⲟⲩⲡⲉ ⲡϩⲏⲩ
ϫⲉⲁⲩϫⲡⲟⲓ̈ ⲉⲡⲉⲉⲓ- [sic]
ⲕⲟⲥⲙⲟⲥ· ⲛⲉⲛⲁ-
ⲛⲟⲩⲥ ⲅⲁⲣ ⲛⲁⲓ̈ ⲉⲛⲉ-
ⲙ̄ⲡⲟⲩϫⲡⲟⲓ̈· ⲡⲉ-
ϫⲁϥ ⲛⲁ[ϥ] ϫⲉⲁϫⲓⲥ
ⲉⲣⲟⲓ̈ ϫⲉⲉⲛⲟⲩⲉϣ
ⲛⲁⲩ ⲉⲣⲟϥ' ϩ[ⲙ̄ⲡⲉⲓ-]
ⲙ̣[ⲁ . .]ⲉ̣[
. . ⲛ[

Fol. 4. P. 111 (*v.* Am. 402[1]). . . . walk not in their deeds (πρᾶξις) and the entreaties of their mouths, we show that we love them not, as (κατά) it is written,[2] 'Whoso cometh unto me and hateth them not . . . . . my name . . .

. . . the Lord,[3] and (he) growing (αὐξάνειν) in the instructions that he heard from our father Pahômius,[4] walking after (κατά) his likeness and according to (κατά) his manner. And (δέ) the brethren, when they saw that he . . .

P. 112. . . . he would] pray[5] with them thus, with tears, until the Lord gave them rest by his means. And[6] it befell that when he came in to the brethren, at the beginning (ἀρχή[7]), in his boyhood, he betook him to our [father Pahômius . . .

. . . see Him that created me, what profit is there that I have been begotten into this world (κόσμος)? For (γάρ) it would have been good for me if I had not been begotten.' He said unto him, 'Tell me, dost thou desire to see Him in this world (*lit.* place) . . .

Fol. 5. → p. ⲣ̄ⲓ̄ⲅ̄

margin

ⲛⲏ̣ⲣⲟⲛ ⲛ̄ⲑⲉ ⲉⲧ-
ⲥⲏϩ' ϩ̄ⲙ̄ⲡⲉⲩⲁⲅ'ⲅⲉ-
ⲗⲓⲟⲛ ϫⲉⲛⲁⲓ̈ⲁⲧⲟⲩ
ⲛ̄ⲛⲉⲧⲟⲩⲁⲁⲃ' ϩ̄ⲙ̄-
ⲡⲉⲩϩⲏⲧ' · ϫⲉⲛ̄ⲧⲟ-
ⲟⲩ ⲛⲉⲧⲛⲁⲛⲁⲩ, ⲉ-
ⲡⲛⲟⲩⲧⲉ · ⲉϣⲱ-
ⲡⲉϭⲉ ⲉⲣϣⲁⲛⲟⲩⲙⲉ-
ⲉⲩⲉ ⲛ̄ϫⲱ[ϩ]ⲙ̄ ⲁⲗⲉ'
ⲉϩⲣⲁⲓ̈ ⲉϫ̄ⲙ̄ⲡⲉⲕϩⲏⲧ' .
[+ⲏ ⲟⲩⲙⲟ]ⲥⲧⲉ ⲉϩⲟⲩⲛ
[ⲉⲡⲉⲕⲥⲟⲛ] +ⲏ̣ ⲟⲩ-
]ⲛ̣ +ⲏ ⲟⲩⲫ'-
[ⲑⲟⲛⲟⲥ] . ⲱ̣ⲣ̣ⲁ̣

ϭ̄ⲙ̄ϭⲟⲙ' ⲉⲣⲟⲕ . ⲕⲁⲣ-
ⲡⲟⲥ ⲛⲓⲙ' ⲉⲧⲥⲏϩ
ϩ̄ⲛ̄ⲛⲉⲅⲣⲁⲫⲏ ⲙⲉ-
ⲗⲉⲧⲁ ⲙ̄ⲙⲟⲟⲩ ϩ̄ⲙ̄-
ⲡⲉⲕϩⲏⲧ' ⲁϫ̄ⲛ̄ⲱ̄-
ϫ̄ⲛ̄ · ⲉⲕⲧⲱϣ' ⲙ̄ⲙ\ⲟ/ⲕ
ⲙ̄ⲙⲓⲛ ⲙ̄ⲙⲟⲕ' ⲉⲙⲟ-
ⲟϣⲉ ⲛ̄ϩⲏⲧⲟⲩ · ⲛ̄-
ⲑⲉ ⲉⲧⲥⲏϩ ϩ̄ⲛ̄+ⲏⲥⲁ-
ⲓ̈ⲁⲥ ϫⲉⲧⲉⲧⲛ̄ⲯⲩ-
ⲭⲏ' ⲛⲁⲙⲉⲗⲉⲧⲁ' ⲛ̄-
ⲑⲟⲧⲉ ⲙ̄ⲡϫⲟⲉⲓⲥ
ⲁⲩⲱ ⲛⲁⲓ̈ ⲧⲏⲣⲟⲩ
[ⲛⲁ]ⲱ̣ϫⲛ ⲛ̄ϩⲏⲧ̄ⲕ̄

[1] The sequence does not continue as in Am. *Cf.* Bo. 49, 50. [2] *Cf.* Lu. xiv. 26. [3] *V.* Am. 406.

[4] Here and once again written Pahôm. Elsewhere in this MS. Pahôme, *i.e.* Pahomius, as Makare = Macarius, Ammône = Ammonius &c. The form Pahôme in *Miss.* iv. 607 (*sic*), Hall *Copt. and Gk. Texts* p. 143. *Cf.* ⲡⲁϩⲱⲙ, Br. Mus. no. 1252.

[5] *V.* Am. 407. [6] *V.* Am. 402.

[7] *Cf.* ἀρχή in Br. Mus. Cat. p. 97 *a*, p. 168 *a*.

↑ p. ⲣ̄ⲓ̄ⲁ̄

margin

ⲁⲏⲥⲓⲥ[a] ⲅⲁⲣ ⲁⲡϫⲟ-
ⲉⲓⲥ ⲕⲁⲁⲥ ϩⲙ̄ⲡⲣⲱ-
ⲙⲉ ⲙ̄ⲡ̄ⲛ̄ⲡⲁⲩⲧⲉⲍⲟⲩ-
ⲥⲓⲟⲛ · ⲙ̄ⲛ̄ⲧⲁⲓⲁ-
ⲕⲣⲓⲥⲓⲥ · ⲙ̄ⲛ̄ⲧⲁⲓⲥ-
ⲑⲏⲥⲓⲥ · ⲙ̄ⲛ̄ⲧⲙ̄ⲛ̄ⲧ-
ⲥⲁⲃⲉ · ⲛ̄ⲑⲉ ⲅⲁⲣ ⲛ̄-
ⲙ̄ⲙⲉⲗⲟⲥ ⲙ̄ⲡⲥⲱ-
ⲙⲁ ⲉⲧⲟⲩⲟⲛ̄ϩ ⲉⲃⲟⲗ’
ⲉϣⲁϥⲣ̄ϩⲱⲃ’ ⲛ̄ϩⲏ-
ⲧⲟⲩ ⲛ̄ϭⲓ ⲡⲣⲱⲙⲉ̣
ⲛⲟⲩⲁ ⲛⲟⲩⲁ ⲕⲁⲧⲁ
ⲧⲉϥⲭ̣ⲣⲓ̣ⲁ̣ ?

ⲛⲓ ⲉⲩⲛ̄ⲧⲁⲥ ⲙ̄ⲙⲁⲩ
ⲙ̄ⲡⲉⲥⲣⲟ’ ⲉⲧⲉⲡϩⲏⲧ’-
ⲡⲉ · ⲁⲩⲱ ⲛ̄ⲑⲉ ⲟⲛ ⲙ̄-
ⲡⲣⲟ’ ⲉⲩⲛ̄ⲧϥ ϣ[ⲟ]ⲙ̄ⲧ
ⲙ̄ⲙⲁⲩ ϩⲓⲕⲗ̄ⲗⲉ · ϩⲓ-
ⲙⲟⲭⲗⲟⲥ ϩⲓⲉⲡⲱ’ ϩⲓ-
ⲱⲣϫ̄ ⲛⲓⲙ. ⲧⲁї-
ⲧⲉ ⲑⲉ ⲙ̄ⲡⲁⲩⲧⲉⲍ-
ⲟⲩⲥⲓⲟ[ⲛ] ⲙ̄ⲛ̄ⲧⲥⲩ-
ⲛⲉⲓⲁⲏⲥⲓⲥ · ⲙ̄ⲛ̄-
ⲧⲁⲓⲥⲑⲏⲥ[ⲓⲥ ⲙ̄ⲛ̄-]
ⲧⲁⲓⲁⲕ̣[ⲣⲓⲥⲓⲥ ⲙ̄ⲛ̄-]
ⲧⲙⲛ̄ⲧ[ⲥⲁⲃⲉ
ⲉ̣ⲧ̣[

[a] ⲥⲩⲛⲉⲓⲁⲏⲥⲓⲥ.

Fol. 5. P. 113 (*v.* Am. 402, *cf.* Bo. 50). . . . wicked (? πονηρόν[1]), as it is written in the Gospel (εὐαγγ.),[2] 'Blessed are the pure in heart, for they it is shall see God.' If then an impure thought rise up in thy heart, [or] hatred toward [thy brother], or ἤ) . . . . . or (ἤ) envy (φθόνος) . . .

. . . have power over thee,[3] every fruit (καρπός) that is written in the scriptures (γραφή), meditate (μελετᾶν) them in thy heart without ceasing, resolving of thyself to walk therein, as it is written in Esaias,[4] 'Thine heart shall meditate (μελ.) the fear of the Lord'; and all these things shall cease from thee . . .

[1] A slight change would allow of reading 'all'.

[2] Matt. v. 8.

[3] Text hence as Am., not Bo. The former should read (402 *ult.*) 'And if thou wouldest that all the thoughts should diminish in thee and not have power over thee, so meditate in thy heart, without ceasing, always, the good fruit written in the scriptures. And do thou be of steadfast mind and sure in all steadfastness, that thou be careful to walk therein, to the extent of thy power; and thus shall the evil thoughts decrease in thee, little by little, and shall grow weak, like the spider'. (The last word due to confusion in meanings of ϩⲁⲗⲗⲟⲩⲥ.)

[4] xxxiii. 18.

P. 114. ... For[1] (γάρ) the Lord hath placed the conscience (συνείδησις) in man, and free-will (αὐτεξούσιον) and judgement (διάκρισις) and understanding (αἴσθησις) and knowledge. For (γάρ) even as the members (μέλος) of the body (σῶμα) that are visible, wherewith man worketh, each according to (κατά) his need ...

... a] house that hath its door, which is the heart. And further, like as the door hath key and bolt and chain (μοχλός) and .....[2] and every surety, even thus it is with free-will (αὐτ.) and conscience (συν.) and judgement (διακ.) and wisdom ...

Fol. 6. ↑ *Recto.*

[ⲉ]ϣⲱ[ⲡ]ⲉ ⲙⲉⲛ ⲉⲣ̣ⲉ̣-
ⲡ̣ⲣ̣ⲱ̣ⲙⲉ ⲟ' ⲛ̄ⲁⲧ-
ⲥⲟⲟⲩⲛ ⲙ̄ⲡⲛⲟⲙ^{ⲟ}ⲥ
ϣⲁⲥⲧⲟⲃⲥ̄ϥ̄ ϫⲉⲙ̄-
ⲡⲉϊϩⲱⲃ' ⲛⲁⲛⲟⲩϥ
ⲁⲛ · ϩⲟⲉⲓⲛⲉ ⲙⲉⲛ
ϣⲁⲥⲣ̄ⲙ̄ⲛ̄ⲧⲣⲉ ⲛⲁⲩ
ⲕⲁⲧⲁ ⲡⲥⲟⲟⲩⲛ ⲙ̄-
ⲡϩⲏⲧ' · ϫⲉⲕⲛⲁⲣ̄-
ⲛⲟⲃⲉ ⲉⲡϫⲟⲉⲓⲥ ⲉⲕ-
ϣⲁⲛⲉⲓⲣⲉ ⲙ̄ⲡⲁϊ ·
ϩⲉⲛⲕⲟⲟⲩⲉ ⲇⲉ ⲟⲛ
ϣⲁⲥⲣ̄ⲙ̄ⲛ̄ⲧⲣⲉ ⲛⲁⲩ
ϫⲉⲉⲩϣⲁⲛⲧⲁϩⲟⲕ'
ⲕⲛⲁⲕⲓⲛⲇⲩⲛⲉⲩⲉ ·
+ⲏ ⲛ̄ⲧⲟϥ ⲥⲉⲛⲁⲙⲟ-[a]

ⲛⲛⲟⲙⲟⲥ]
ⲉⲧⲥⲏϩ ⲉ[
ⲙ̣ⲛⲛ̄ⲥⲁⲛⲧ[ⲱⲃⲥ̄]
ⲛⲧⲉⲛ̣ⲉ̣ⲓ̣ⲛ̣ⲉ . . .[b]
ⲉⲧⲥ̄ⲧ̄ⲱ̄ⲃ̄ⲥ̄ ⲙ̣̄ⲙ̣[ⲟϥ]
ⲛ̄ϩⲏⲧϥ̄ ϣⲁϥⲧⲁ-
ⲕⲉ' ⲧⲉϥⲥⲩⲛⲉⲓⲇⲏ-
ⲥⲓⲥ ⲙ̄ⲙⲓⲛ ⲙ̄ⲙ[ⲟϥ]
ⲛ̄ϥⲣⲟⲕϩ̄ⲥ̄ ϩⲱ̣[ⲥ]
ⲉⲧⲙ̄ⲧⲣⲉⲥⲧⲟⲃ̣[ⲥ̄ϥ̄]
ϫⲓⲛⲡⲉϊⲛⲁⲩ · [ⲛ̄-]
ⲑⲉ ⲉⲧⲥⲏϩ ⲉⲧⲃⲉ̣[ⲛ̄-]
ⲕⲟⲟⲩⲉ ⲛ̄ⲧⲉϊⲙⲓ[ⲛⲉ]
ϫⲉⲉⲣⲉⲧⲉⲩⲥⲩⲛ[ⲉⲓ-]
ⲇⲏⲥⲓⲥ ⲣⲟⲕ̄ϩ̄ ⲉ[ⲣⲟⲟⲩ]

[a] Perhaps ⲙⲟ[ⲟⲩⲧⲕ.

[b] Perhaps ⲛⲧⲉⲓⲙⲓⲛⲉ ⲛⲁⲓ.

[1] Am. should be, 'For the Lord hath set conscience in all men, and free-will and judgement and perception (حس) and knowledge. For conscience pricketh a man by reason of evil and saith to him, That which thou hast done is evil &c.'

[2] ⲉⲡⲱ, *v. Aeg. Z.* xxxvi. 147. Rylands no. 252 shows that it is attached to the door; perhaps the lock.

→ *Verso.*

]ⲛϣⲁϫⲉ ⲇⲉ
[. . .]ⲓ̣ϭⲉ̣ ⲡⲁⲩⲗⲟⲥ
ⲉⲧⲃⲉⲛⲁϊ ⲛ̄ⲧⲉϊ-
ⲙⲓⲛⲉ ⲉⲧⲣⲉⲩⲉⲓ’ ⲉ-
ϩⲟⲩⲛ, ⲉⲩⲙⲉⲧⲁⲛⲟⲓⲁ
ⲉⲃⲟⲗ’ ϫⲉⲙ̄ⲡⲟⲩⲥⲟⲩ-
[ⲙ̄]ⲡ̣ⲛⲟⲙⲟⲥ · ϣⲁϥ-
[ⲥ]ⲏ̣ϩ̣ ⲛ̄ⲧⲉϊϩⲉ ϫⲉ-
ⲉⲣⲉⲡⲉⲛϩⲏⲧ’ ϭⲉϣ-
[ϭ]ⲱϣ ⲉⲃⲟⲗ’ ϩ̄ⲛ̄ⲥⲩ-
ⲛⲉⲓⲇⲏⲥⲓⲥ ⲛⲓⲙ’
[ⲙ̄]ⲡⲟⲛⲏⲣⲟⲛ, ⲁⲩⲱ
[ⲉⲣⲉ̇]ⲡⲉⲛⲥⲱⲙⲁ
[ϫⲟ]ⲛ̄ⲙ̄ ϩ̄ⲛ̄ⲟⲩⲙⲟⲟ̣[ⲩ]

[ⲟ̇ⲩ]ⲛ̣ⲧⲟⲩ ⲛⲟⲙⲟⲥ [ϩⲓ-]
ⲧ̄ⲛ̄ⲧⲉⲩⲥⲩⲛⲉⲓ[ⲇⲏ-]
ⲥⲓⲥ · ϥⲧⲁⲙⲟ’ ⲙ̄-
ⲙⲟⲛ ⲛ̄ⲧⲉϊϩⲉ’ ⲛ̄ϭⲓ
ⲡⲕⲏⲣⲩⲝ’ ⲙ̄ⲡⲉⲩ-
ⲁⲅⲅⲉⲗⲓⲟⲛ ϫⲉϩⲟ-
ⲧⲁⲛ ⲅⲁⲣ ⲛ̄ϩⲉⲑⲛⲟⲥ
ⲉⲧⲉⲙ̄ⲙ̄ⲛ̄ⲧⲟⲩ-
ⲛⲟⲙⲟⲥ ⲫⲩⲥⲉⲓ ⲥⲉ-
ⲉⲓⲣⲉ ⲛ̄ⲛⲁⲡⲛⲟⲙⲥͦ
ⲛⲁϊ ⲉⲙ̄ⲙ̄ⲛ̄ⲧⲟⲩ-
ⲛⲟⲙⲟⲥ ⲥⲉϣⲟⲟⲡ’
ⲛⲁⲩ ⲛ̄ⲛⲟⲙⲟⲥ ⲙⲁⲩ-
ⲁⲁⲩ · ⲛⲁⲓ ⲉⲩⲧⲥⲁ-
ⲃⲟ’ ⲙ̄ⲙⲟⲕ’ ⲉⲡϩⲱⲃ
ⲙ̄ⲡⲛⲟⲙⲟⲥ ⲉϥⲥⲏϩ
ϩ̄ⲙ̄ⲡⲉⲩϩⲏⲧ’, ⲉⲣⲉ-
ⲧ[ⲉⲩⲥⲩⲛⲉⲓⲇⲏⲥⲓⲥ]

Fol. 6. *Recto* (*v.* Am. 403). Now (*μέν*) if the man be ignorant of the law (*νόμος*), it (*sc.* conscience) prompteth him, (saying), This thing is not good. Some indeed (*μέν*), it testifieth to them according to (*κατά*) the knowledge of the heart, (saying), Thou wilt sin against the Lord if thou do this ; while (*δέ*) others again, to them it testifieth, If thou be discovered, thou shalt be in danger (*κινδυνεύειν*), or (*ἤ*) indeed, they will [? slay thee . . . . .

. . . laws (*νόμος*)] that are written . . . after the prompting (?) of this sort (?) wherewith it hath prompted him, he will destroy his own conscience (*συν.*) and sear it, so that (*ὡς*) it shall not thenceforth prompt him, as it is written concerning others of this sort,[1] ‘ Their conscience being seared for [them ’]

Verso (not in Am.). . . . but (*δέ*) the words . . . Paul concerning such as these, that they should come in unto repentance (*μετάνοια*), because they

[1] 1 Tim. iv. 2.

have not known the law (*νόμος*). It is written thus,[1] 'Our hearts being sprinkled from all evil conscience (*συν. πονηρός*) and our body (*σῶμα*) washed with [pure] water .....

... they [have] a law (*νόμος*) through their conscience (*συν.*). Thus doth the herald (*κῆρυξ*) of the Gospel (*εὐαγ.*) tell us,[2] 'For when (*ὅταν γάρ*) the Gentiles (*ἔθνος*), that have not law (*νόμος*), by nature (*φύσει*) do the (things) of the law, these, having not law, are a law unto themselves. These teach thee (*sic*) the work of the law written in their heart, their [conscience .....

Fol. 7. → *Recto.*

margin

]ⲙ̣ⲟⲕ ⲟ̣ⲩϩⲓⲏ
ⲛ̣ϩⲟⲟ̣. ⲁ̣[..]ⲩⲣⲱ
ⲙ̣ⲃ̣ⲉ̣ⲛ[.].[..]ⲁⲩ ⲁⲛ
ⲛ̣ϭⲓ̣ⲩ..[ⲙ̅ⲛ̅]ⲛ̅ⲥⲁ-
ⲛⲁï [ⲟⲛ] ⲛ̣[ⲧⲉ]ⲣⲉϥⲁⲓ-
ⲥⲑⲁⲛⲉ ⲛ̣̅ⲛ̣ⲉ[ϩ]ⲙⲟⲧ'
ⲉⲧⲉⲣⲉⲡϫⲟⲉⲓⲥ ⲉⲓⲣⲉ
ⲙ̅ⲙⲟⲟⲩ ⲛ̅ⲙⲙⲁϥ ⲛ̅-
ⲑⲉ ⲉⲧⲉⲣⲉⲇⲁⲩⲉⲓⲇ'
ϫⲱ ⲙ̅ⲙⲟⲥ ϫⲉⲉ̈ⲓⲛⲁ-
ϯ ⲟⲩ' ⲛ̅ϣ̅ⲃ̅ⲃⲓⲱ̅ ⲙ̅-
ⲡϫⲟⲉⲓⲥ ⲉⲡⲙⲁ ⲛ̅ⲛⲉ̅-
ⲧⲁϥⲁⲁⲩ ⲛⲁï ⲧⲏ-
ⲣⲟⲩ· ⲁⲩⲱ ⲛ̅ⲑⲉ ⲟⲛ
ⲉⲧϥⲇⲓⲁⲕⲣⲓⲛⲉ ⲙ̅ⲛ-
ⲧⲉϥⲯⲩⲭⲏ ⲙ̅ⲙⲓⲛ
ⲙ̅ⲙⲟϥ ϩ̅ⲛⲟⲩⲁⲓⲥⲑⲏ-
ⲥⲓⲥ ⲉϥϫⲱ ⲙ̅ⲙⲟⲥ ϫⲉ-
ⲧⲁⲯⲩⲭⲏ ⲥⲙⲟⲩ ⲉ-
ⲡϫⲟⲉⲓⲥ· ⲁⲩⲱ ⲛⲉⲧⲙ̅-

ⲛⲉ̅ ⲉⲃⲟⲗ' ⲛ̅ⲛⲟⲩⲁ[ⲛⲟ-]
ⲙⲓⲁ ⲧⲏⲣⲟⲩ. ⲡⲉ[ⲧ-]
ⲧⲁⲗϭⲟ' ⲛ̅ⲛⲟⲩϣ[ⲱ-]
ⲛⲉ ⲧⲏⲣⲟⲩ. ⲡⲉ[ⲧ-]
ⲥⲱⲧⲉ ⲙ̅ⲡⲟⲩ[ⲱⲛ̅ϩ̅]
ⲉⲃⲟⲗ' ϩⲙ̅ⲡⲧⲁⲕ[ⲟ]
ⲡⲉⲧϯ ⲛ̅ⲟⲩⲕⲗ[ⲟⲙ]
ⲉϫⲱ̅ ⲛ̅ⲛⲁ' ϩⲓⲙ[ⲡ̅ⲧ-]
ϣⲁⲛϩⲧⲏϥ· [ⲡⲉⲧ-]
ⲧⲥⲓⲟ' ⲙ̅ⲡⲟⲩⲟⲩ[ⲱϣ]
ⲛ̅ⲁⲅⲁⲑⲟⲛ· ϫⲉ[ⲕⲁⲥ]
ⲇⲉ ⲉⲛⲉⲉⲓⲙ̣ⲉ̣ ϫ[ⲉⲙ-]
ⲙⲉⲗⲟⲥ ⲛ̅ⲧⲉ̣[ⲯⲩⲭⲏ-]
ⲛⲉ ⲛⲉⲛⲧⲁⲛϣ[ⲣ̅ⲡ̅-]
ϫⲟⲟⲩ ⲕⲁⲧⲁ ⲡϣⲁϫ[ⲉ]
ⲛ̅ⲇⲁⲩⲉⲓⲇ' ϩⲙ̅ⲡⲧⲣ[ⲉϥ-]
ⲡⲣⲟⲧⲣⲉⲡⲉ ⲛⲧ̣ⲉ̣[ϥ-]
ⲯⲩⲭⲏ ⲉⲥⲙⲟⲩ ⲉⲡϫ[ⲟ-]
ⲉⲓⲥ ⲉ̣ϥⲡ̣ⲣⲟⲧⲣⲉ̣ⲡ̣[ⲉ]
ⲟⲛ ⲛ̅ⲛⲉⲥⲕⲉⲙⲉⲗⲟⲥ

[1] Heb. x. 22.

[2] Rom. ii. 14.

ⲡⲁⲥⲁⲛϩⲟⲩⲛ ⲧⲏ-
[ⲣ]ⲟⲩ ⲥⲙⲟⲩ ⲉⲡⲉϥ-
[ⲣⲁⲛ’ ⲉ]ⲧⲟⲩⲁⲁⲃ· ⲧⲁ-
[ⲯⲩⲭ]ⲏ ⲥⲙⲟⲩ ⲉⲡϫⲟ-
[ⲉⲓⲥ ⲁⲩⲱ ⲙ̅]ⲡⲣ̅ⲣ̅ⲡⲱ-
[ⲃϣ ⲛ̅ⲛⲉϥⲧⲱ]ⲱⲃⲉ
[ⲧⲏⲣⲟⲩ· ⲡⲉⲧⲕⲱ̅]

ⲉⲧⲟ̣̅ ⲛ̅ⲟ̣ⲩⲁ̣’ ⲛ̅ⲟⲩⲱ̣ⲧ̣
ⲛⲙ̣ⲙ̣ⲁⲥ̣ . ⲛ̣ . ⲩⲛ̣ ?
ⲛⲉⲛ̣ ⲉ̣ϥϫⲱ ⲙ̣ⲙ̣ⲟⲥ
ⲉⲧⲃⲏ̣ⲧ̣ⲟ̣ⲩ ϫⲉ̣[ⲛⲉ-]
ⲧ̅ⲙ̅ⲡ̣ⲁ̣ⲥ̣ⲁⲛϩⲟⲩⲛ
ⲧ[ⲏⲣⲟⲩ ⲥⲙⲟⲩ ⲉⲡⲉϥ-]
ⲣⲁⲛ’ ⲉⲧⲟⲩⲁⲁⲃ· [ⲟⲩ]
ⲙ̣ⲟ̣ⲛ̣ⲟ̣ⲛϭⲉ ϫⲉⲉⲣ[ⲉ-]

margin

↑ *Verso.*

margin

ⲧ̣ⲁⲓⲥⲑⲏⲥⲓⲥ ϣⲟⲟⲡ
ϫⲉⲉⲣⲉⲡⲣⲱⲙⲉ ⲙ̅ⲡⲓ̣-
ⲥ̣ⲧⲟⲥ ⲁⲓⲥⲑⲁⲛⲉ ⲛ̅-
[ϩⲏ]ⲧⲥ̅ ⲛ̅ⲧⲉⲭⲁⲣⲓⲥ
[ⲙ̅]ⲡϫⲟⲉⲓⲥ ⲁ̣[ⲗⲗ]ⲁ̣ ⲉ̣-
[ⲧⲣ]ⲉϥⲁⲓⲥⲑⲁⲛⲉ ⲟ̣ⲛ̣
[ⲛ̅]ⲙ̣ⲡⲉⲧⲛⲁⲛⲟⲩϥ̣
[. .[a]]ⲉ̣ⲧⲟⲩ̣[ⲉⲓ]ⲣⲉ ⲙ̅ⲙⲟ-
[ⲟⲩ] . ϫ̣[b] [ϩ]ⲓ̣ⲧⲛ̅ⲛ̅-
[. . . . .] ⲙ̣ⲡⲛⲟⲩⲧⲉ·
[ⲉϥϭⲛ̅]ⲁ̣ⲣⲓⲕⲉ ⲅⲁⲣ
[ⲉ]ϩⲟⲉⲓⲛⲉ ⲉⲙⲡⲟⲩ-
ⲁⲓⲥⲑⲁⲛⲉ ⲛ̅ⲛⲉϩ-
ⲙⲟⲧ’ ⲧⲏⲣⲟⲩ ⲉⲛ-
ⲧⲁϥⲁⲁⲩ ⲛ̅ⲙ̅ⲙⲁⲩ
ⲛ̅ϭⲓ ⲡⲉⲛⲧⲁϥⲥⲁ-
ⲛⲟⲩϣⲟⲩ ⲉϥϫⲱ̅ ⲙ̅-
ⲙⲟⲥ ϫⲉⲁⲛⲟⲕ ⲅⲁⲣ

ϩⲏⲧ ⲧⲙ̅ⲛ̅ⲧ̅[ⲥⲁ-]
ⲃⲉ ⲇⲉ ⲕⲁⲧⲁ ⲡⲛⲟ̣ⲩ̣ⲧ̣ⲉ̣
ⲉⲧⲣ[ⲉ]ⲡⲣⲱⲙⲉ ⲥⲟⲩ̅-
ⲛ̅ ⲡ[ⲉⲧ]ⲣ̅ⲁⲛⲁϥ’ ⲧⲏ-
ⲣϥ̅ ⲙ̅[ⲡ]ϫⲟ[ⲉⲓ]ⲥ ⲙ̅ⲛ̅-
ⲡⲉϥ[ⲟⲩ]ⲱϣ ⲏ̣ ⲛ̅-
ⲧⲟϥ ⲛ̅ϥ̅ⲥⲟⲩⲛ̅ ⲡⲉ-
ⲧⲟⲩⲛⲁϭⲟⲗⲡ̅ϥ̅ ⲛⲁϥ
ⲉⲃⲟⲗ’ ϩⲓⲧⲟⲟⲧϥ̅ ⲛ̅-
ⲑⲉ ⲉⲧⲥⲏϩ ϫⲉϩⲱⲃ
ⲛⲓⲙ’ ⲉⲧⲉⲧⲛ̅ⲙⲉⲉ-
ⲩⲉ ⲉⲣⲟⲟⲩ ⲛ̅ⲕⲉⲥ̣-
ⲙⲟⲧ, ⲡⲁⲓ̈ ⲡⲛⲟⲩⲧⲉ
ⲛⲁϭⲟⲗⲡ̅ϥ̅ ⲛⲏⲧⲛ̅
ⲉⲃⲟⲗ’· ⲕⲁⲓ ⲅⲁⲣ’ ⲇⲁ-
ⲛⲓⲏⲗ ⲛ̅ⲧⲉⲣⲉϥ-
ϭⲱⲗⲡ̅ ⲉⲣⲟϥ ⲛ̅ⲧⲣⲁ-
ⲥⲟⲩ ⲙ̅ⲡⲡⲉⲥⲕⲉ-

[a] ? ⲡⲁⲓ.   [b] ? ⲉⲃⲟⲗ.

ⲛ̣ⲉϣϣⲉⲡⲉ[a] ⲉⲧⲣⲉⲩ-
ⲥⲩⲛϩⲓⲥⲧⲁ ⲙ̅ⲙⲟⲓ̈
ϩⲓⲧⲟⲧⲧⲏⲩⲧⲛ̅ ·
ⲁⲩⲱ ⲙ̅ⲛ̅ⲛ̅ⲥⲁⲧⲁⲓ-
ⲥⲑⲏⲥⲓⲥ ϣⲁⲥⲟⲩⲱ-
ⲛ̅ϩ ⲉⲃⲟⲗ' ⲛ̅ϭⲓ ⲧⲉϥ-
ⲙⲛ̅ⲧⲥⲁⲃⲉ ⲙ̅ⲛ̅-
[ⲧ]ⲉϥⲙⲛⲧ[ⲣ̅ⲙ̅ⲙ]ⲛ̣̅-

ⲃⲱⲗ' ⲛ̅ⲧⲉ̣ⲩϣⲏ ⲛ̅-
ϭⲓ̣ ⲡϫⲟⲉⲓⲥ . ⲁϥ-
ⲥⲙⲟⲩ ⲉⲣⲟϥ' ⲉϥϫⲱ
ⲙ̅ⲙⲟⲥ ϫⲉⲡⲉⲧϯ
ⲛ̅ⲧⲥⲟⲫⲓⲁ ⲛ̣̅ⲛ̣̅[ⲥⲟ-]
ⲫⲟⲥ · ⲁⲩⲱ ⲧ[ⲙⲛ̅ⲧ-]
ⲥⲁ[ⲃⲉ
.̅[

margin

[a] *Cf.* Woide, Balestri (less correct).

Fol. 7. (*The right position of this fol. is uncertain.*)

Recto. . . . a . . . road . . . . . not . . . . . Thereafter [again?], after he hath recognized (αἰσθανέσθαι) the mercies that the Lord doeth with him, even as David saith,[1] 'What shall I give in exchange unto the Lord, in place of all the (things) that He hath done unto me?' And like too as he doth argue (διακρίνειν) with his own soul (ψυ.), in understanding (αἴσθησις), saying,[2] 'My soul, bless the Lord, and all (things) that are within me, bless His holy name. My soul, bless the Lord, and forget not all His requitals. Who

forgiveth thee all thy iniquities (ἀνομ.), who healeth all thy diseases, who redeemeth thy life from destruction, who setteth a crown upon thee of mercy and compassion, who satisfieth thy desire with good-things (ἀγαθός).' And (δέ) so that[3] we may know (?) that it is the members (μέλος) of the [soul (ψυ.)] whereof we have already spoken,[4] according to (κατά) the words of David, when he doth exhort (προτρέπειν) his soul (ψυ.) to bless the Lord, exhorting (πρ.) besides its members (μέλ.) also, that are one with it . . . , . ., saying of them, 'All (things) that are within me, [bless His] holy name.' For not only (οὐ μόνον) (is it so) that

Verso. the understanding (αἰσ.) doth exist in order that the believing (πιστός) man may recognize (αἰσθανέσθαι) thereby the grace (χάρις) of the Lord, but (ἀλλά) that he may also recognize (αἰσ.) the benefits that are done him by God's . . . . . For (γάρ) some He blameth, in that they have not recognized (αἰσ.) all the graces that He who nourished them hath done

[1] Ps. cxv. 3.

[2] Ps. cii. 1–5.

[3] The uncertainty of the conjunction renders the logic of the sentence obscure.

[4] *V.* Am. 403 *infra*. If that were the passage here referred to, the position given to this leaf would be justified.

with them saying,[1] 'For (γάρ) I ought to have been commended (συνίστασθαι) of you.' And after the understanding (αἰσ.), his knowledge is displayed and his wisdom.

But (δέ) knowledge according to (κατά) God (is) that man should know all that is pleasing to the Lord and His will, or (ἤ) else that he know that which shall be revealed unto him by Him, as it is written,[2] 'Every thing whereof ye shall think otherwise, this shall God reveal unto you.' For (καὶ γάρ) Daniel, after that the Lord had revealed unto him the dream and also its interpretation, at night, blessed Him saying,[3] 'He that giveth wisdom (σοφία) unto the wise (σοφός) and knowledge . . . . .

Fol. 8. → *Recto.*

margin

ⲧⲁʼ[a] ⲉⲣⲟⲥ ϫⲉⲁⲩⲧⲁⲙⲟⲓ̈	ϩⲟⲟⲩ ⲉϥⲛⲁⲃⲱⲕ ⲉ[ⲩ-]
[ϫ]ⲉ̣ⲥⲣⲓⲙⲉ ⲁⲩⲱ ⲥⲙⲟ-	ⲙⲁ̄ ⲛ̄ⲃⲟⲗʼ ⲛ̄ⲧⲥⲟⲟⲩϩ[ⲥ̄]
ⲕϩ ⲛ̄ϩⲏⲧ. ⲙⲏⲡⲟ-	ⲉⲣ̄ϩⲱⲃʼ ⲙ̄ⲡⲛⲉⲥⲛⲏ[ⲩ]
ⲧⲉ ⲛ̄ⲡ̄ⲥⲱⲧⲙ̄ ⲛ̄ⲧ̣̄-	ⲁⲩ̣ϫ̣ⲓ̣ⲧ̣̄ⲥ̄ ⲉϩ̣ⲣⲁⲓ̈ . . .
ϭⲏ̣ⲡ ϩ̄ⲛ̣̄[ⲡⲉ]ⲕϩⲏⲧ·[b]	ⲉⲩϫⲉⲛⲉⲡⲱⲣ ⲉ̣ⲥ-
ⲁⲛⲟ[ⲕ ⲇⲉ] ⲡⲁⲓ̈ⲡⲉ	. ⲉ . . ⲧ̣[e] [ⲧⲁ-]
ⲡⲁ[ⲟⲩⲛⲟ]ϥ̣ [ⲉⲕ]ϣⲁⲛ-	ⲃ̄ⲛ̄ⲛ̄ⲏⲥⲉ ⲉⲩϫ̣[ⲱ ⲙ̄-]
ϣⲱ̣[ⲡⲉ] ⲉⲕ̣[ⲧⲁ]ϫⲣⲏⲩ	ⲙⲟⲥ ⲛ̣ⲁ̣ⲥ̣ ϫ[ⲉⲉⲓⲥ ϩⲏ-]
[ⲉϫⲛ̄ⲛⲉ]ⲛⲧ[ⲟⲗ]ⲏ̣ ⲧⲏ-	ⲛⲧ[ⲉ] ⲛ̄ⲧⲟ[ϥ]
[ⲣⲟⲩ ⲙ̄]ⲡⲱⲛϩ· ⲁⲩⲱ	ⲛ[
[. .[c] ⲡⲉ]ⲡⲓⲥⲕⲟⲡⲟⲥ	
[. .·. . .[d] ⲥ]ϩⲁⲓ̈ ϣⲁⲣⲟ[ⲛ]	

[a] ⲁⲡⲁⲛ]ⲧⲁ. [b] Perhaps ϭⲟⲧϩ ⲛⲡⲉⲕϩⲏⲧ. [c] Apparently not ⲟⲛ. [d] Scarcely space for ⲡⲉⲛⲧⲁϥ. [e] Adjective or participle referring to ϫⲉⲛⲉⲡⲱⲣ.

↑ *Verso.*

margin

ⲙ̄ⲡⲉⲟⲩⲟⲉⲓϣʼ· ⲛ̄ⲑⲉ	ⲧⲉⲛⲟϭⲉ (*sic*) ϯⲛⲁⲧⲁ-
ⲧ̣ⲁⲣ[a] ⲉⲧⲙ̄ⲙⲟⲟϣⲉ ⲙ̄-	ⲙⲱⲧⲛ̄ ϩ̣ⲙ̄ⲡⲁⲓ̈ ⲉ-

[a] [ⲛ]ⲧⲁⲣⲉ-, which I at first read, is difficult to deal with.

[1] 2 Cor. xii. 11. [2] Phil. iii. 15. [3] Dan. ii. 21.

[ⲙ]ⲟⲥ ϩⲛ̄ⲟⲩⲙⲛ̄ⲧⲁⲅⲣⲓ-
[ⲟ]ⲥ ϣⲁⲡⲟⲟⲩ. ⲛ̄ⲛⲉⲛ-
[ⲣ̄]ϩⲟⲩⲟ ⲁⲛ, ⲡⲁⲣⲁ ⲛⲉⲧ-
[ⲥⲏϩ ⲛⲁ]ⲛ̣, ϩⲛ̄ⲛⲉ̣-
[ⲅⲣⲁ]ⲫⲏ· ⲛ̄ⲧⲉⲣⲟⲩ-
[. . . .] ⲡⲥⲱⲧⲏⲣ' ⲉ-
[. . . . .]ⲥⲙ̄ⲛ̄

ⲕⲉⲁⲛⲁⲥⲧⲣⲟⲫ[ⲏ]
ⲧⲁϊ ⲉⲧⲛ̄ⲛⲁⲁⲁⲥ, ⲉ-
ⲧ̣ⲣⲉⲛ̣[.]ϣ[.]ⲉⲓ' ⲛ̄ⲟ̣ⲩ-
ⲕⲟⲩϊ ⲙⲛ̣̄[ⲛⲣ]ⲱⲙⲉ
ⲉⲧϩ[ⲓⲃⲟⲗ'· ⲛ̄]ⲑⲉ ⲉ-
ⲧⲉⲣ[ⲉⲡ]ⲁ̣ⲩ[ⲗⲟⲥ ϫ]ⲱ'
ⲙ̄ⲙ[ⲟⲥ] ϫ̣ⲉⲉ[
ϣⲱⲡ' ⲙ̄ⲡ[
ⲛ̄ⲛⲁϩⲣⲛ̄[

Fol. 8. *Recto* (*v.* Am. 405). . . . mee]t (ἀπαντᾶν) her; for I have been told she weepeth and is distressed; lest (μήποτε) thou shouldest hear and be pricked (?) in thy heart. As for (δέ) me, my joy it is if so be thou art firmly established in all the commandments (ἐντολή) of life. And . . . the bishop (ἐπ.) that (?) did write unto us . . . . .

(*v.* Am. 406) . . . on a] day (that) he should go to a place without the monastery (*lit.* congregation), to work[1] with the brethren. They took her up . . . to a roof, which . . . . . Tabennêse, saying unto her, 'Lo, he [is there . . . . .

Verso (*v.* Am. 406). . . . in time past. For (γάρ) like as[2] we walk in savagery (-ἄγριος[3]) until to-day, let us not do more than (παρά) the things written for us (?) in the Scriptures. After that they had . . . the Saviour (σωτήρ) . . . . .

. . . So now I will tell you herein another (manner of) converse (ἀναστροφή) that we will do, (namely,) . . . go (?) a little with[4] the men that are without, as Paul (?) saith, ...

[1] Ac. 33, 12 (= G ⲣ̄ⲗ̄ⲁ̄ b) reads 'they arranged a work outside, with the brethren, that they would do; and they informed her thereof at Tabennêse and said unto her, 'Lo, he is there with the brethren, working &c.' (Unless واطلعوها عليه refers to bringing her up on to the roof.)

[2] *I.e.* ? seeing that.

[3] ⲙⲛ̄ⲧⲁⲅⲣⲓⲟⲥ, *e.g.* Steindorff, *Gram.*[2] 55*, *CSCO.* vol. 42 (Sinuth.), 113.

[4] *Cf.* συγκαταβαίνειν.

Fol. 9. ↑ *Recto.* margin

[ⲙ̄ⲡⲉϥⲙⲁⲑⲏ]ⲧⲏⲥ
[ⲉⲃⲱⲕ ⲛ̄ϥⲧ]ⲱⲙ̄ⲥ̄ ⲙ̄-
[ⲡⲉϥⲉⲓⲱⲧ]· ⲁϥ-
[ⲟⲩⲱϣⲃ ⲛ̄ϭⲓ] ⲡⲉⲧⲙ̄-
[ⲙⲁⲩ ⲉ]ϥϫ[ⲱ] ⲙ̄ⲙⲟⲥ
[ϫⲉⲙ̄]ⲡⲉϥ[ⲕ]ⲁⲁϥ [ⲁ]ⲛ̣
[ϫⲉ]ⲛ̄ϥⲃⲱⲕ [ⲛ̄ϥ-]
[ⲧⲙ̄ⲕⲟ]ⲧϥ ⲛ̄ⲧⲟ̣ϥ
[ⲁⲉ ⲡ]ⲉϫⲁϥ ⲛⲁϥ ϫⲉ-
[ϣⲁⲥ]ϣⲱⲡⲉ ⲛ̄ⲧⲉ-
[ⲟⲩⲁ] ⲙ̄ⲡⲟⲟⲩ ⲃⲱⲕ'
[ϣⲁ]ⲛⲉϥⲣⲱⲙⲉ ⲕⲁ-
[ⲧⲁ ⲥ]ⲁⲣⲝ ⲉⲙ[ⲡ]ϥ̣̄ⲡⲁ-
[ⲣⲁⲃ]ⲁ ⲛ̄ⲧⲉ[ⲛⲧ]ⲟⲗⲏ
[ⲙ̄ⲡ]ⲉⲩⲁⲅⲅⲉⲗⲓ[ⲟ]ⲛ·
[ⲡⲉ]ϫⲁϥ ⲛⲁϥ [ϫⲉⲉ]ϣ-
[ϫⲉϥ]ⲛ̣ⲁϭⲙ̄ⲡⲉⲩϣ[ⲓ-]
[ⲛⲉ] ⲙ̣ⲙⲁⲧⲉⲡ̣ⲉ ⲛ-
[ⲟⲩ]ⲛ̣ⲟⲃⲉ ⲁⲛ̣ⲡⲉ· ⲁⲩ-
[ⲱ ⲡⲉ]ϫ̣ⲁϥ ⲛⲁϥ ϩⲛ̄-
[ⲟⲩ]. . . ⲩⲥ. ⲧ̣ⲁ[a] ϫ̣ⲉ-
[ⲧⲁⲓ̈]ⲧ̣ⲉ̣ ⲧⲡⲓⲥⲧⲓⲥ
[ⲛ̄ⲛⲣ]ⲱⲙⲉ ⲛ̄ⲧⲁⲃⲛ̄-
[ⲛⲏⲥ]ⲉ ⲉⲩϫⲱ ⲙ̄ⲙⲟⲥ
[ϫⲉⲛ̄ⲟ]ⲩⲛⲟⲃⲉ ⲁⲛⲡⲉ
[. . . . .]ⲥ̣̄[b] ⲛ̄ⲛⲉⲛⲧⲟ̣-
[ⲗⲏ ⲙ̄ⲡ]ⲉⲩⲁⲅⲅⲉⲗ-
[ⲓⲟⲛ· ⲕⲁⲓ] ⲅⲁⲣ̣ ⲁⲛⲟⲕ

ⲉⲙⲡⲁϯⲉⲓ' ⲉⲡ[ⲉⲓ̈ⲙⲁ']
ⲛⲉⲓ̈ⲁⲅⲱⲛⲓⲍⲉ [ⲕⲁ-]
ⲧⲁ ⲧⲁⲙⲛ̄ⲧⲕⲟⲩⲉ[ⲓ̈]
ϩⲙ̄ⲡ[ⲉ]ⲧⲟⲩⲟⲛϩ̣̄ ⲉⲣⲟ[ⲓ]
ϫⲉ[ⲡⲁⲓ̈ⲡⲉ] ⲛⲟⲩⲱ̣ϣ
ⲙ̄ⲡϫ̣[ⲟⲉⲓⲥ ⲁ]ⲩⲱ ⲛ̄-
ⲧⲉⲣⲓ̣[ⲥⲱⲧ]ⲙ ϫⲉⲧⲉ-
ⲧⲙ̄ⲙ[ⲟ]ⲟ̣ϣⲉ ϩⲛ̄ⲟⲩ-
ⲙⲛ̄ⲧⲧⲉⲗⲉⲓⲟⲥ ⲕⲁ-
ⲧⲁ ⲛ̄ⲉⲛⲧⲟⲗⲏ ⲙ̄ⲡⲉⲩ-
ⲁⲅⲅⲉⲗⲓⲟⲛ ⲁⲓ̈ⲉⲓ' ⲉ-
ⲡⲉⲓ̈ⲙⲁ'· ⲧⲉⲛⲟⲩϭⲉ
ⲛϯⲛⲁϭⲱ̣ ⲁⲛ ⲁⲗ-
ⲗⲁ ϯ̣ⲛⲁⲃ̣[ⲱⲕ] ⲟⲛ ⲉ-
ⲡⲙⲁ ⲉⲛ̣[ⲧ]ⲁ̣ⲓⲉⲓ' ⲛ̄-
ϩⲏⲧϥ̄· ⲁ[ϥϥ]ⲓ̣ ϩⲣⲁϥ[c]
ⲉⲃⲟⲗ' ⲁϥⲣⲓⲙⲉ ⲉϥⲙ[ⲟ-]
ⲕϩ̄ ⲛ̄ϩⲏⲧ ⲉϫⲱϥ ⲛ̄-
[ϭⲓ ⲑ]ⲉⲟⲇⲱⲣⲟⲥ· ⲛ̄-
ⲧ̣[ⲉⲩ]ⲛⲟⲩϭⲉ̣ ⲡⲉⲧⲙ̄-
ⲙ[ⲁⲩ ⲁ]ϥⲃⲱⲕ' ⲉ̣. .-[d]
ⲡⲉ̣[ⲛ]ⲉⲓⲱⲧ ⲡⲁϩⲱ-
ⲙⲉ' ⲉ̣ϥϫⲱ' ⲙ̄ⲙⲟ̣ⲥ̣ [ϫⲉ-]
ⲁⲙⲟⲩ ⲧⲛ̄ⲥ̄ⲗⲥ̄ⲗ ⲡ̣ⲉ̣[ⲓ-]
ⲕ̣ⲟ̣ⲩⲓ̈ ⲛ̄ⲥⲟⲛ· ?[e]
ⲧ̣ⲉ ⲛ̄ϥⲥⲕⲁⲛⲇ[ⲁⲗⲓ-]
[ⲍⲉ·] ⲁϥϫⲱ ⲉⲣⲟϥ [ⲉ-]
ⲡϣⲁϫⲉ ⲉⲛⲧⲁ̣ϥϫⲟ-

margin

[a] Probably ⲡⲁⲛⲟⲩⲣⲅⲓⲁ (AS. *πανούργως*). [b] ⲡⲁⲣⲁⲃⲁ seems impossible. [c] Am. 408, 5 ادار وجهه, through confusion of meanings of ϩⲣⲁϥ. [d] ⲉⲧⲁⲙⲉ, if there were space enough. [e] Probably ⲙⲏⲡⲟⲧⲉ.

→ *Verso.* margin

[ⲟϥ] ϫⲉⲁⲓ̈ⲥⲕⲁⲛⲇⲁⲗⲓ-
[ⲍⲉ] ⲛ̄ϩⲏⲧϥ̄ · ⲁⲩⲱ
ⲛⲧⲉ[ⲣ]ⲉϥⲉⲓⲙⲉ ⲉⲧ-
ⲡⲁⲛⲟⲩⲣ[ⲅⲓ]ⲁ ⲉⲛⲧⲁϥ-
ⲁⲁⲥ ϩ̄[ⲛ̄ⲧⲙ̄ⲛ̄]ⲧⲣ̄ⲙ̄-
ⲛ̄ϩⲏⲧ [ⲙ̄ⲡⲉ]ⲡ̄ⲛ̄ⲁ̄
ⲡⲉϫⲁϥ [ⲇⲉ[a] ⲛⲁ]ϥ' ϫⲉⲛ̄ⲅ̣̄-
ⲥⲟⲟⲩⲛ' ⲁ[ⲛ] ϫⲉⲟⲩⲧⲱ-
ϭⲉ ⲛ̄ⲃ̄ⲣ̄ⲣⲉⲡⲉ, ⲛ̄ⲛⲉⲕ-
ⲙ̄ⲡϣⲁ' ⲁⲛ ⲛ̄ϣⲁ-
ϫⲉ ⲡ̄ⲙ̄ⲙⲁϥ ⲛ̄ⲧⲉⲓ̈-
ϩⲉ · ϩⲟⲙⲱⲥ ⲙⲟⲩⲧⲉ
ⲉⲣⲟϥ [ⲛ̄]ⲧ̣ⲁⲡⲓⲑⲉ ⲙ̄-
ⲙⲟϥ [ⲛ̄]ⲧⲉⲣⲉϥⲙⲟⲩ-
ⲧⲉ [ⲉⲣⲟ]ϥ' ⲡⲉϫⲁϥ
ⲛⲁϥ' [ϩ]ⲱ̣ⲥ ⲉϥⲡⲓⲑⲉ
ⲙ̄ⲙⲟϥ ϫⲉⲙ̄ⲡⲣ̄ⲙ̄-
ⲕⲁϩ ⲛ̄ϩⲏⲧ ϩ̄ⲙ̄ⲡ̄ⲡ̣̄-
ⲧⲁⲕⲥⲟⲧⲙⲉϥ' [ϩⲓⲧⲙ̄-]
[ⲡⲥⲟⲛ] ⲛ̄ⲧⲁϥ[ϣⲁ]ϫⲉ
ⲡ̄ⲙ̄ⲙⲁⲕ ⲉ[. . .] ⲉⲉⲓ̣'
ⲡ̄ⲙ̄ⲙⲁⲕ ϩⲱ̣[ⲥ] ⲧⲱ-
ϭⲉ ⲛ̄ⲃ̄ⲣ̄ⲣⲉ · ⲉⲡⲉⲓ ⲛ̄-
ⲧⲁⲓ̈ ⲁⲛⲧⲉ ⲧⲉϥⲡⲓ-
ⲥⲧⲓⲥ · ⲛ̄ⲧⲟϥ ⲇⲉ ⲑⲉ-
ⲟⲇⲱⲣⲟⲥ ⲁϥⲟⲩⲱϣ̄ⲃ̄
ⲉ̣ϥϫⲱ ⲙ̣ⲙⲟ̣ⲥ̣ ϫⲉⲛ̄ⲅ̄-
ⲛⲁϣⲡⲓⲑⲉ ⲙ̄ⲙⲟⲓ

ⲁ̣ⲛ ⲓ̣[
ⲡⲉⲓϣ[ⲁ̣ϫⲉ
[.]ⲙⲛ̣[. ϫⲉⲛⲧⲁⲓ ⲁⲛ-]
ⲧ̣ⲉ ⲧⲉϥ[ⲡⲓⲥⲧⲓⲥ ⲉⲓ-]
ⲙⲏⲧⲓ̄ ⲛ̣ⲧ[ⲟϥ ⲉϥⲛⲁ-]
[ϩⲟ]ⲙⲟⲗⲟ[ⲅ]ⲉⲓ' [ⲛ̄ⲧⲉϥ-]
[ⲧⲁ]ⲡⲣⲟ ⲙ̄ⲙⲉ[ⲓⲛ ⲙ̄-]
[ⲙ]ⲟϥ ϫⲉⲡⲉ̣[ⲧⲛⲁⲃⲱⲕ]
ⲉϭ̄ⲙ̄ⲡϣⲓⲛⲉ̣ [ⲛ̄ⲛⲉϥ-]
ⲣⲱⲙⲉ ⲟⲩⲡⲁ[ⲣⲁⲃⲁ-]
ⲧⲏⲥⲡⲉ̣ ⲛ̄ⲛ̄[ⲉⲛⲧⲟ-]
ⲗⲏ ⲙ̄ⲡⲉⲩⲁⲅ[ⲅⲉⲗⲓ-]
ⲟⲛ[· ⲉ]ϣⲱⲡⲉ [ⲉⲓ-]
ϣ[ⲁⲛ]ⲥⲱⲧⲙ̄ [ⲉⲣⲟϥ]
ⲉϥ[ϩ]ⲟⲙⲟⲗⲟⲅⲉ[ⲓ']
ⲡ̣[. .].[b] ⲧⲟⲧⲉ ϯ[ⲛⲁⲉⲓ-]
[ⲙ]ⲉ̣ ϫⲉⲛ̄ⲧⲁⲓ̈ ⲁ̣[ⲛⲧⲉ]
ⲑⲉ ⲉⲧϥ̄ⲡⲓⲥⲧ[ⲉⲩⲉ]
[ⲙ̄ⲙ]ⲟ̣ⲥ̣ · ⲛⲧⲉ̣[ⲣⲉϥ-]
ⲉ̣ⲓ̣ⲙ̣ⲉ ⲇⲉ ⲛϭⲓ ⲡ̣[ⲉⲧⲙ̄-]
ⲙⲁ̣ⲩ [ϫ]ⲉ̣ⲛ̄ϥ̄ⲡ[ⲉⲓ-]
ⲑⲉ ⲁⲛ ⲛ̄ϭⲓ ⲡϣ[ⲏⲣⲉ]
ϣⲏ̣ⲙ̣ ⲭⲱⲣⲓ̣[ⲥ ϩⲟⲙⲟ-]
ⲗⲟ̣ⲅ̣ⲓⲁ ⲁϥϩⲟ̣[ⲙⲟⲗⲟ-]
ⲅ̣ⲉ̣ⲓ ϫⲉⲡⲣ[ⲱⲙⲉ ⲉⲧ-]
ⲛⲁⲉ̣ⲓ̣ⲣⲉ ⲙ̄[ⲡⲁⲓ[c]
ⲉⲃⲟⲗ ⲛ̄ⲛ̄[ⲉⲛⲧⲟⲗⲏ]
ⲙ̄ⲡϫⲟⲉⲓ̣[ⲥ

margin

[a] ⲇⲉ seems superfluous. [b] Perhaps -ⲅⲉⲓ ⲛ]ⲧⲉ[ⲓϩ]ⲉ. Am. هكذا. [c] Scarcely space for ⲛⲁⲃⲱⲗ] or ⲉϥⲃⲱⲗ]. Am. يخالف.

Fol. 9. *Recto* (*v.* Am. 407). . . . suffer His] disciple (μαθ.) [to go and] bury [his father?'] That (brother) answered, saying, 'He suffered him not, [lest] he should go [and not] return.' [But (δέ)] he said unto him, ['If it] befall that one to-day go [to] his kinsfolk according to the flesh (κατά, σάρξ), he hath not (surely) transgressed (παραβαίνειν) the command (ἐντολή) of the Gospel (εὐ.)?' He said unto him, 'If he shall but visit them, it is not a sin.' He said unto him with guile (? πανουργία [1]), 'This is the faith (πίστις) of the men of Tabennêse, that say, It is not a sin to transgress (?) the commandments (ἐντ.) of the Gospel (εὐ.). For (καὶ γάρ) I, ere I came hither, did strive (ἀγωνίζειν), so far as (κατά) my youth (permitted), in what was evident unto me that it was the Lord's will. And when I had heard that ye do walk in perfection (-τέλειος), according to the commandments of the Gospel (κατά, ἐντ. εὐ.), I came hither. Now therefore I will not remain, but (ἀλλά) will go again unto my place whence I came.' And Theodore lifted up his voice and wept, being grieved for him. Straightway then that (brother) went to [tell?] our father Pahômius, saying, 'Come, that we comfort this young brother, lest (? μήποτε) he be offended (σκανδαλίζειν).' He told him the word that he had said

Verso (*v.* Am. 408, 409). (saying,) 'I am offended (σκαν.) thereat.' And when he knew the guile (παν.) that he had wrought, by the wisdom of the Spirit (πνεῦμα), he said (+δέ?) unto him, 'Knowest thou not that he is a neophyte? It was not meet for thee to speak so to him. Howbeit (ὅμως [2]) call him and I will persuade (πείθειν) him.' When he had called him, he said unto him, as if (ὡς) persuading him, 'Be not grieved at that thou hast heard [? from the brother] that spake with thee . . . . . go with thee, as a neophyte. For (ἐπεί) this is not his belief (πίστις).' But (δέ) as for Theodore, he answered saying, 'Thou wilt not be able to persuade (πείθειν) me,

[3] O, my father with] this word [that thou sayest, that this is not] his [belief (πίσ.), ex]cept (εἰμήτι) he shall himself declare (ὁμολογεῖν) with his own mouth that he that shall go to visit his kinsfolk is a transgressor (παραβάτης) of the commandments of the Gospel (ἐντ. εὐαγ.). If [I] hear [him] declare (ὁμ.) thus (?), then (τότε) shall I know that not thus doth he believe (πιστεύειν).' And (δέ) when that (brother) knew (?) that the youth would not be persuaded without a declaration (πείθειν, χωρίς, ὁμολογία), he declared (ὁμ.), saying that the man that shall do [this un]doeth (?) the commandments (ἐντ.)?] of the Lord . . . . .

[1] Am. should be 'said to him in deceit'.

[2] Accented in the text: a rare occurrence.

[3] Gaps filled from Am., although I cannot satisfactorily complete the Coptic text.

Fol. 10. → *Recto.*

[ϣ]ⲱⲡⲉ[a] ⲇⲉ ⲟ[ⲛ ⲛ̄ⲧⲉ-]
ⲣ̣ⲉ[ϥ]ϩ̣ⲉ' ⲉⲕⲉⲥⲟⲛ [ⲛ̄]ϭⲓ
ⲑⲉⲟⲇⲱⲣⲟⲥ ⲉⲣ[ⲉⲡⲉ]ϥ-
ϩⲏⲧ' ⲗⲩⲡⲉⲓ ⲉ̣[ⲃⲟ]ⲗ'
ϫⲉⲁϥϫⲡⲓⲟ̣[ϥ ⲛ̄ϭ]ⲓ'
ⲡⲉⲛⲉⲓⲱⲧ [ⲡⲁϩ]ⲱ̣-
ⲙⲉ ϩ̄ⲛ̄ⲟⲩϩ[ⲱ]ⲃ ⲉ-
ⲡⲟⲩϫⲁï ⲛ̄ⲧ[ⲉϥⲯ]ⲩ-
ⲭⲏ· ϩⲱⲥ̣ⲧⲉ ⲉ̣[ⲧⲣⲉ-]
ⲡⲉϥϩⲏⲧ' ⲣⲓⲕⲉ ⲉⲃⲟ̣[ⲗ]
[ⲉ]ⲧⲣⲉϥⲡⲱⲣ̄ϫ ⲉⲧ̣[ⲕⲟⲓ-]
[ⲛⲱⲛⲓⲁ[b]

]ⲧ̣ⲁ
ⲙⲉⲉ]ⲩ̣ⲉ[c] ϫⲉⲧⲁï
[ⲟⲛⲧ]ⲉ ⲑⲉ ⲉϯⲙⲟⲕϩ̄
[ⲛ̄ϩⲏⲧ] ϫⲉⲡⲉïⲣⲱ-
[ⲙⲉ ⲛ̄ϣ]ⲙ̄ⲙⲟ ⲉⲓ
]ⲟ̣ⲡ' ⲛ̄ⲧⲟϥ
ⲟⲩ]ⲱ̣ϣ' ⲉⲧⲣⲉϥ-
]ϫⲓ ϩⲙⲟⲧ
]ⲛ̄ϣⲁ-
[ϫⲉ]ⲙ̣ⲟⲥ

[ⲇⲉ] ⲙⲁⲣ[ⲛ̄ϭ]ⲱ [ⲟⲩⲛ ⲙ̄ⲡⲉ-]
ⲥⲛⲁⲩ ϩⲓⲟⲩⲥⲟⲡ [ⲛ̄-]
ⲧ̄ⲡ̄ⲥⲗ̄ⲥⲗ̄ ⲛⲉⲛⲉⲣ[ⲏⲩ]
ϣⲁⲛⲧ̄ⲛ̄ⲛ̣ⲁ̣ⲩ ⲉ̣[. . ⲙⲉ-]
ϣⲁⲕ ϥ̄ⲛⲁ[ⲗⲟ
ⲙⲙⲟⲥ̣ ⲉ̣ϫ[ⲡⲓⲟⲛ· ⲉ-]
ϣⲱⲡ̣ⲉ̣ [ⲇⲉ ⲉⲛϣⲁⲛ-]
ⲉⲓⲙ̣ⲉ̣ ϫⲉⲛ̣[ϥ̄ⲛ]ⲁⲗ̣ⲟ
ⲁⲛ ⲧ̄ⲛ̄ⲛⲁⲃⲱⲕ
ⲛ̄ⲧ̄ⲛ̄ⲁⲛⲁⲭⲱⲣⲉⲓ'
[ⲛⲁⲛ] ⲉⲕⲉⲙⲁ' ⲛ̄ⲧⲉ-
[. . . .] . ⲧ . . . . . .
[. . . . . .]ⲧ̣ . . . ⲉ . . .
ⲧ̣ⲉ̣[. . . . .] . ⲉ̣ⲉ ⲛⲧⲟϥ
ϣⲁϫ̣[ⲉ
ϩⲏⲧ[
ⲡ[
ⲥⲱ[ϩⲩ-]
ⲡⲟⲙ[ⲓⲛⲉ
ⲛ . . [
ⲧ̄ⲙ̄ⲁ̣[
ⲉϥⲛ̣̄[

[a] ⲁⲥϣⲱⲡⲉ. [b] Or ⲧⲥⲟⲟⲩϩⲥ. Size of following gap uncertain, as the two fragments do not join. [c] Perhaps ⲉⲧ]ⲃⲉϫⲉ.

↑ *Verso.*

]ⲉ ⲉⲙ[.]
]ⲁ[a] ⲁ̣[ⲛ] ⲙ̄ⲡⲡⲉⲛⲉⲓ-
[ⲱ]ⲧ ⲡⲁϩⲱⲙⲉ ϩ̄ⲛ-
[ⲟⲩ]ⲟⲩⲱⲛ̄ϩ ⲉⲃⲟⲗ·
[ϩ̄ⲛ̄ⲧ]ⲡⲁϣⲉ ⲇⲉ ⲛ̄-
[ⲧⲉⲩϣⲏ] ⲛ̄ϩⲁϩ ⲛ̄-
[ⲥⲟⲡ ⲛ]ⲉϣⲁϥⲃⲱⲕ’
ⲛ̄ϥⲁⲡⲁⲛⲧⲁ’ ⲉⲣⲟϥ
ⲛ̄ϩⲁϩ’ ⲛ̄ⲥⲟⲡ ⲛϥ-
ϫⲱ̄ ⲉⲣⲟϥ’ ⲙ̄ⲡ[ⲉⲙ-]
ⲕⲁϩ’ ⲛ̄ϩⲏⲧ [ⲙ̄ⲡⲥⲟⲛ ⲉ-]
ⲧⲙ̄ⲙ̄ⲁⲩ [ⲁⲩⲱ
ⲉ̣ϥⲁ . ⲧ̣̄[

[ⲡⲉⲧ]ⲟ̣ⲩⲏϩ ⲛ[ϩⲏⲧ̄ⲕ̄]
[ⲟⲩ]ⲛϣϭⲟⲙ’ ⲙ̄[ⲙⲟϥ]
ⲉ̣[ⲧ]ⲟⲩϫⲟⲛ ⲁ̣ⲩⲱ
ⲙ̣̄ⲙ̄ⲡⲗⲁⲁⲩ ⲛ̄ⲁⲧ-
ϭ[ⲟⲙ] ⲛ̄ⲛⲁϩⲣⲁϥ·
ⲁ̣[ⲩⲱ] ⲁⲥϣⲱⲡⲉ
ⲙ[ⲛ̄ⲛ̄]ⲥⲁⲡⲉⲃⲟⲧ’
[ⲛ̄ϩ]ⲟ̣ⲟⲩ ⲡⲉϫⲁϥ
[ⲛ̄]ϭⲓ ⲑⲉⲟⲇⲱⲣⲟⲥ ⲉ-
ϩⲟⲩⲛ ϩ̄ⲛ̄ⲡⲥⲟⲛ ⲉ-
ⲧ̄ⲙ̄ⲙ̄ⲁⲩ’ ϫⲉⲙⲁⲣ̄[ⲛ̄-]

ⲛ . [ ] ⲉϥ-
[ϫⲱ ⲙ̄ⲙⲟⲥ ϫ]ⲉ̣ⲃⲟⲛ-
[ⲑⲉⲓ ⲉⲣⲟⲛ ⲱ ⲡⲉ]ⲛⲉⲓ-
[ⲱⲧ]ⲁ̣ . ⲛ
ⲉⲧⲉⲡ]ⲁⲥⲟⲛ-
[ⲡⲉ ⲛ̄ⲧⲉⲛⲁϩⲙⲉ]ⲛ̣ ⲛ̄ⲧⲟ-
[ⲟⲧϥ ⲙ̄ⲡⲇⲓ]ⲁ̣ⲃⲟ-
[ⲗⲟⲥ ⲡⲁⲓ ⲉⲧⲉ]ⲗ̣[ϩ]ⲏ̣ⲙ’
[ⲉⲧⲱⲣⲡ ⲛⲛⲉ]ⲛ̣ⲯⲩ-

ⲛⲙ̣[ⲛ̄ⲧⲛ-]
ϣⲁϫⲉ ⲛⲙ̣[ⲙⲁϥ ⲁⲩⲱ]
ⲉϣⲱⲡⲉ ⲁⲩ̣[
ϣⲁⲛϣ[ⲱⲡⲉ . . . ⲛ̄ⲙ-]
ⲙⲁⲛ ⲉϥ[
ⲧ̄ⲛ̄ⲛⲁ . [ⲉⲕⲉ-]
ⲙⲁ’ ⲛ̄ⲧ[ⲛ̄ⲡⲟⲣϫ̄ⲛ ⲉⲃⲟⲗ]
ⲉⲣⲟϥ· [ⲉϣⲱⲡⲉ ⲇⲉ]
ⲉϥϣ[ⲁⲛ
ϩ̄ⲛ̄ⲗ̣[

margin

[a] Should be ⲁⲡⲁⲛⲧ]ⲁ.

Fol. 10. *Recto* (*v.* Am. 409). . . . And ($\delta\acute{\epsilon}$) [it] befell again, when Theodore found another brother grieved ($\lambda\upsilon\pi\epsilon\hat{\iota}\nu$) at heart because that our father Pahômius had reproved him in a matter for the salvation of his soul ($\psi\upsilon.$), so that ($\check{\omega}\sigma\tau\epsilon$) his heart was inclined that he should separate from the [community . . . . 'thought (?), for even so is it also that I am sad at heart. For this stranger . . . he . . . wish that he . . . find grace . . . . .

. . . let us two stay therefore ($o\hat{\upsilon}\nu$) together and console one another, until we see . . . perhaps he will [cease] . . . reproving [us. But ($\delta\acute{\epsilon}$)] if we shall know that will not cease, we will go and betake us ($\dot{\alpha}\nu\alpha\chi\omega\rho\epsilon\hat{\iota}\nu$) elsewhere . . . . .

Verso (*v.* Am. 410). . . . not with our father Pahômius openly. But ($\delta\acute{\epsilon}$) in the middle of the night, many a time, he would go and meet ($\dot{\alpha}\pi\alpha\nu\tau\hat{\alpha}\nu$) him, many a time (*sic*), and tell him of the grief of that [brother] . . . . [saying,] 'Help ($\beta o\eta\theta\epsilon\hat{\iota}\nu$) [us, O] our father, ... [who is] my brother,[1] [and? save] us from the devil ($\delta\iota\acute{\alpha}\beta.$), that roareth [to devour?] our souls ($\psi\upsilon.$) . . . . .

. . . [that] dwelleth in [thee] hath power to save us. And there is no impossibility with Him.'[2] And it befell, after the month of days, that Theodore spake to that brother, saying, 'Let us . . . . [and we] speak with [him. And] if . . . . . with us, he . . . . ., we will [go else]where and [separate ourselves from] him. [But ($\delta\acute{\epsilon}$) if] he should . . . . . with . . . . .

Fol. 11. ↑ *Recto.*

ⲙⲛⲧⲥⲩⲛ]ⲉ̣ⲧⲟⲥ
[ⲙ̅ⲡ̅ⲟ]ⲩⲛⲟϭ ⲙ̅ⲙⲛ̅[ⲧ-]
[ⲁⲅⲁ]ⲑ̣ⲟⲥ . ϩⲱⲥⲧⲉ
[ⲉⲧ]ⲣⲉⲡⲉⲩϩⲏⲧ' ⲙ̅-
[ⲧ]ⲟⲛ ⲉⲙⲁⲧⲉ ⲙⲡ̣ⲉ-   ⲉ[
[ⲥⲛ]ⲁⲩ · ⲁⲩⲱ ⲧⲁϊ̣-   ⲣ̣ⲁ̣[ⲕⲟ-]
[ⲧⲉ ⲑ]ⲉ ⲉⲛⲧⲁϥⲧⲟⲩ-   ⲧϥ ϣⲁⲣ[ⲟⲛ[a]
[ϫⲟϥ] ⲛ̅ϭⲓ ⲑⲉⲟⲇⲱ-   ⲁⲩⲱ ⲁⲥϣ[ⲱⲡⲉ ⲛ̅-]

[a] *Cf. Miss.* 546, 6. But perhaps here ⲛ]ⲧϥ. In gap ⲉⲡⲉⲓⲙⲁ (Am. الى هاهنا) or ⲛⲕⲉⲥⲟⲡ (*v. verso*).

[1] Am. should be, 'Help us, O our father, me and this one that is my brother, that thou seize us from out the hand of the devil, who would devour our souls. For we are small and feeble in the faith.'

[2] Am. *sic*.

[ⲣⲟⲥ ϩ]ⲛ̣ⲟⲩⲡⲁⲛⲟⲩⲣ-
[ⲅⲓⲁ ⲉⲛ]ⲁⲛⲟⲩⲥ·
[Ⲟⲩⲁ ⲟ]ⲛ ϩⲛ̄ⲛⲉⲥ-
[ⲛⲏ]ⲩ̣ ⲉⲩϣⲏⲣⲉ ϣⲏⲙ'-
[ⲡⲉ ⲉ]ⲁ̣ϥⲉⲛⲱⲭⲗⲉⲓ'
[ⲙ̄ⲡⲉ]ⲛⲉⲓⲱⲧ' ⲡⲁ-
[ϩⲱⲙ] ⲉ̣ϥⲟⲩⲉϣ
[ⲃⲱⲕ ⲉ]ϭⲙ̄ ⲡϣⲓⲛⲉ
[ⲛ̄ⲛⲉϥⲉⲓ]ⲟⲧⲉ· ⲛ̄ⲧⲉ-
[ⲣϥⲉⲓⲙ]ⲉ̣ ⲇⲉ ϫⲉⲉϥ-

ⲧⲉⲣⲟⲩⲃⲱ̣[ⲕ ⲉϩⲟⲩⲛ]
ⲉⲡⲉϥⲏⲓ̈ [ⲁⲩ
ⲧⲁ̣ⲓ̣ ⲉⲣⲟϥ̣ [ⲛ̄ϭⲓ
? ⲙ̄ⲛ̄ⲛ̄-]
ⲥⲱⲥ̣
ϩⲛ̄ⲟ[ⲩ
ϫⲉ[ⲉⲩⲛⲁⲟⲩⲱⲙ
ⲁⲩ[ⲱ
?

margin (?)

→ *Verso.*

]ⲙ̣ⲁⲩ[a]
] ?
] ? ⲛⲧⲟϥ
[ⲇⲉ ⲛ̄ⲧ]ⲉⲣⲉϥⲥⲱⲧⲙ̄
[ⲉⲛⲉϥϣ]ⲁϫⲉ ⲁϥⲣ-
[ⲡⲙⲉⲉ]ⲩⲉ ⲛⲑⲉ ⲉⲛ-
[ⲧⲁϥϣ]ⲁϫⲉ ⲛ̄ⲙ̄-
[ⲙⲁϥ ⲛ̄ϭⲓ] ⲡⲉⲛⲉⲓ-
[ⲱⲧ' ⲡⲁϩⲱ]ⲙⲉ ⲉϥ-
[ϫⲱ ⲙ̄ⲙⲟⲥ ϫ]ⲉⲁⲣⲓ̈
[ⲁⲡⲁⲧⲟⲟⲧⲕ] ⲛ̄ⲙ̄-
[ⲙⲁϥ ⲉⲧⲣⲉⲕⲉⲓⲛ]ⲉ ⲙ̄-
[ⲙⲟϥ ⲛ̄ⲕⲉ]ⲥⲟⲡ·
?

ⲡⲁϩⲱⲙⲉ [ⲁϥⲣ̄ⲟⲩ-]
ⲛⲟϭ ⲛ̄ⲟⲩⲟ[ⲉⲓϣ ⲉϥ-]
ⲧⲱⲃϩ ⲙ̄ⲡϫ[ⲟⲉⲓⲥ]
ⲉϥϫⲱ ⲙ̄ⲙⲟⲥ [ϫⲉ-]
ⲕⲱ̄ ⲛⲁⲓ ⲉⲃⲟⲗ' ϫ[ⲉ-]
ϯϣⲟⲃⲉ ⲁⲛ ⲉⲩ[ⲣⲱ-]
ⲙⲉ ⲉⲁϥⲡⲟⲣ[ⲛⲉⲩⲉ]
ϩⲙ̄ⲡⲉⲛⲧ[ⲁⲓⲁⲁϥ·]
ϫⲉⲁⲓⲡⲁⲣⲁ[ⲃⲁ ⲛ̄ⲛ-]
ⲛⲟⲙⲟⲥ ⲉⲛ̣[ⲧⲁⲕⲧⲁ-]
ⲁⲩ ⲉⲧⲟⲟⲧϥ̣ [ⲙ̄-]
ⲡⲉⲕϩⲙ̄ϩⲁⲗ [·]
ⲁϥⲥⲱⲧⲙ̄ [ⲅⲁⲣ ⲉ-]
ⲡⲉⲛⲉⲓⲱⲧ [ⲡⲁ-]
ϩⲱⲙⲉ ⲛ̄ⲟⲩ[ϩⲟⲟⲩ]
ⲉϥϫⲱ ⲙ̣ⲙ̣[ⲟⲥ ϫⲉ-]
ϫⲓⲛⲡⲉ[ϩⲟⲟⲩ ⲛ̄ⲧⲁⲓ-]
ⲣ̄ⲙⲟⲛⲁⲭ[ⲟⲥ ⲛ̄ϩⲏⲧϥ ⲙ̄-]

[a] Perhaps ⲛⲙ̄ⲙ]ⲙⲁⲓ.

Fol. 11. *Recto* (*v.* Am. 410). . . . prudence (-συνετός) [and] great goodness (-ἀγαθός), so that (ὥστε) the heart of both of them was greatly quieted. And thus it was that Theodore saved him, by a kindly (*lit.* good) guile (πανουργία). One also of the brethren, that was a youth, importuned (ἐνωχλεῖν) our father Pahôm,[1] wishing to go and visit his parents. But (δέ) when he knew that he . . . . .

. . . return him unto [us hither ? [2]]. And it befell, after that they had gone [in] unto his house, [his people] . . . him. [And] afterwards . . . . . in a . . ., that [they might eat]. And . . . . .

Verso (*v.* Am. 411). . . . But (δέ) he, when he had heard these words, remembered the manner in which our father Pahômius had spoken with him,[3] saying, ' Do thy utmost to bring him (hither) again . . . . .

. . . Pahômius, spent a great while beseeching the Lord, saying, ' Forgive me; for I am not different from a man that hath fornicated (πορνεύειν), in that which I have done. For I have transgressed (παραβαίνειν) the laws (νόμ.) which Thou didst commit unto Thy servant.' For (γάρ) he had heard our father Pahômius, on a day, saying, ' Since the [day whereon I] became a monk (μον.),

Fol. 12. → *Recto.*

margin

ⲡⲉⲗⲁⲁⲩ ⲛ̄ⲣⲱⲙⲉ
ⲛ̄ⲕⲟⲥⲙⲓⲕⲟⲥ ⲛⲁⲩ
ⲉⲣⲟï ⲉïⲟⲩⲱⲙ' ⲏ ⲉï-
ⲥⲉ' ⲙⲟⲟⲩ · ϫⲉⲕⲁⲥ
ⲉⲣⲉⲡϫⲟⲉⲓⲥ ϫⲓ ⲉⲟⲟⲩ
ⲟⲛ ϩ̅ⲙ̅ⲡ̅ⲁ̅ï · ⲛ̄-
[Ⲧ]ⲟϥ' ⲇⲉ ⲡⲉⲛⲉⲓⲱⲧ'
ⲡⲁϩⲱⲙⲉ' ⲛⲉⲣⲉ-
ⲡϫⲟⲉⲓⲥ ϣⲟⲟⲡ'
ⲛ̅ⲙ̅ⲙⲁϥ ϩ̅ⲛ̅ϩⲱⲃ

ⲟⲩϩ̅ⲗ̅ⲗ̅[ⲟ' ϩ̅ⲛ̅ⲛⲉ-]
ⲥⲛⲏⲩ ⲉⲙⲡⲁ̣[ⲧⲉⲑⲟ]
ⲧⲉ ⲙ̄ⲡϫⲟⲉⲓⲥ [ϣⲱ-]
ⲡⲉ ⲛ̄ϩⲏⲧ̅ϥ̅ · ⲛ̣ⲉ̣-
ⲙ̄ⲡⲁⲧ̅ϥ̅ⲱ'ⲥ̅ⲕ̅ⲡ̣ⲉ̣
ϫⲓⲛⲧⲁϥⲉⲓ' ⲉϩⲟⲩ[ⲛ]
ⲉⲛⲉⲥⲛⲏⲩ · ⲁⲩ[ⲱ]
ⲡⲁï ⲛ̄ⲧⲉⲣⲉϥⲥⲱ̣-
ⲧ̅ⲙ̅ ϫⲉⲁⲛⲉⲥⲛⲏ[ⲩ]
ⲃⲱⲕ' ⲉⲡⲉⲥⲏⲧ

[1] So ? for usual 'Pahôme'. There is not space for second ⲉ in the text.

[2] Am. should be, 'until thou bring him (back) hither.'

[3] Am. should be, 'Make with him all efforts until thou bring him unto me again. And he stretched forth his hand and did eat with him a little; then he withdrew his hand. And Theodore, by reason of this thing that he had done, in stretching forth his hand to eat, so as to bring back the youth unto our father P., spent &c.'

ⲛⲓⲙ' ⲉϥⲉⲓⲣⲉ ⲙ̅ⲙⲟ-
[ⲟ]ⲩ· ⲉϥϯ ⲉⲟⲟⲩ ⲛⲁϥ
[ⲁ]ⲩⲱ ⲉϥⲟⲩⲱⲛ̅ϩ
[ⲙ̅]ⲙⲟϥ' ⲉⲃⲟⲗ' ⲛ̅ⲛⲉ-
[ⲥ]ⲛⲏⲩ ⲧⲏⲣⲟⲩ ϫⲉ-
[ⲟⲩ]ⲁ̂ⲡⲉ ϩⲙ̅ⲡⲉϥ-
[ϩⲙ̅ϩ]ⲁⲗ'·
[Ⲁⲥϣ]ⲱⲡⲉ ⲇⲉ ⲛⲟⲩ-
[ϩⲟⲟⲩ] ⲉⲧⲣⲉⲩⲣ̅ⲭⲣⲓⲁ
[ⲛ̅ⲕ]ⲁⲑⲁⲣⲓⲍ[ⲉ ⲙ̅-]
[ⲡϣ]ⲏⲓ̈ ⲛ̅ⲑ[ⲉⲛ]ⲉⲉⲧ[ⲉ]
[ⲁϥ]ⲙⲟⲩⲧⲉ ⲉϩⲟⲉⲓ-
[ⲛⲉ ⲛ̅]ⲛⲉⲥⲛⲏⲩ ⲉⲧ-
[ϭⲙ̅ϭ]ⲟ̣ⲙ' ⲁϥⲃⲱⲕ
[ⲉⲡⲉⲥ]ⲏⲧ' ⲉⲣⲟϥ

ⲉⲡϣⲏⲓ̈ ⲁϥⲕⲣ̅[ⲙ̅-]
ⲣ̅ⲙ ⲉϥϫⲱ' ⲙ̅ⲙⲟⲥ
ϫⲉⲡⲉⲓ̈ⲣⲱⲙⲉ ⲟⲩ-
ⲁⲧⲛⲁ'ⲡⲉ ⲉϥⲙⲟ-
ⲕ̣ϩ̣ ⲛ̅ⲡϣⲏⲣ[ⲉ ⲛ̅-]
ⲛ̅ⲣⲱⲙⲉ· ϩⲱ[ⲥⲧⲉ]
ⲉⲧⲣⲉϥϫⲟ̣ⲟ̣ⲩ ⲉ̣-[a]
ⲡⲉⲥⲏⲧ' ⲉ[ⲡϣⲏⲓ̈]
ⲙ̅ⲡⲉⲓⲙ̣[ⲁⲩ·]
ⲁⲥϣⲱⲡ[ⲉ[b] ⲛ̅ⲧⲉⲩ-]
ϣⲏ ⲉⲧ[ⲙ̅ⲙⲁⲩ ⲁϥ-]
ⲛⲁⲩ ⲉ[ⲩϩⲟⲣⲁⲙⲁ ⲛ̅-]
ϭⲓ ⲡ[ϩⲗ̅ⲗⲟ' ⲉⲧⲙ̅ⲙⲁⲩ]
ⲉⲁϥ̣[

[a] Probably more here: ϫⲟⲟⲩⲥⲉ ⲉ-?

[b] Or ⲁⲥϣⲱⲡⲉ ⲇⲉ.

↑ *Verso.*

margin

ⲟⲩⲁⲅⲅ]ⲉⲗⲟⲥ ⲛ̅-
[ⲧⲉ] ⲡϫⲟⲉⲓⲥ ⲛ̅ⲧⲉⲩ-
[ⲙⲛ]ⲧⲉ ⲉϥⲱϣ' ⲉⲃ⸌ⲟ⸍ⲗ
[ⲉ]ϩⲟⲩⲛ ⲉϩⲣⲁⲩ, ⲉϥ-
ϫⲱ ⲙ̅ⲙⲟⲥ ϫⲉϫⲓ
ⲡ̅ⲛ̅ⲁ̅ ⲉϥⲟⲩⲁⲁⲃ ⲛ[ⲏ-]
ⲧ̣ⲛ̅· ⲛ̅ⲛⲉⲧⲛ̅ⲣ̅-
ϩⲱⲃ' ⲅⲁⲣ ⲁⲛ, ⲛ̅ⲣⲱ-
ⲙⲉ· ⲁⲗⲗⲁ ⲉⲧⲉⲧⲛ̅-
ⲣ̅ϩⲱⲃ' ⲛ̅ⲛ̅ϩⲙ̅ϩⲁⲗ

ϫⲉⲉⲣⲉⲡϫⲟⲉⲓⲥ ϥ[ⲓ]
ⲉⲃⲟⲗ ⲙ̅ⲙⲟⲓ̈ ⲙ̅ⲡⲉ-
ⲡ̅ⲛ̅ⲁ̅ ⲙ̅ⲙⲛ̅ⲧⲁⲧ-
ⲛⲁϩⲧⲉ ϫⲉⲁⲓ̈ⲕⲁⲧ[ⲁ-]
ⲗⲁⲗⲉⲓ' ⲙ̅ⲡⲣⲱⲙⲉ
ⲙ̅ⲡⲛⲟⲩⲧⲉ· ⲁⲩⲱ
ⲙ̅ⲡⲓⲡⲓⲥⲧⲉⲩⲉ ϫ[ⲉ-]
ϩⲱⲃ' ⲛⲓⲙ ⲉϥⲉⲓⲣⲉ [ⲙ̅-]
ⲙⲟⲟⲩ. ⲉϥⲉⲓⲣⲉ ⲙ̅ⲙ[ⲟ-]
ⲟⲩ ϩⲛ̅ⲟⲩⲥⲟⲟⲩⲧⲛ̅ [·]

ⲙ̄ⲡⲛⲟⲩⲧⲉ· ⲁϥ-
ⲛⲁⲩ ⲇⲉ ⲉⲣⲟϥ ϩⲱ-
ⲱϥ’ ⲉϥϭⲱϣ̄ⲧ ⲉ-
ϩⲣⲁï ⲉⲣⲟϥ’ ⲉϥϫⲱ
[ⲙ̄]ⲙⲟⲥ ϫⲉⲡⲣⲉϥ-
[ⲕ̄ⲣ̄]ⲙ̄ⲣ̄ⲙ̄ ⲛ̄ϩⲗⲗⲟ’ ⲁⲩ̣[ⲱ]
[ⲛ̄]ⲁⲡⲓⲥⲧⲟⲥ. ϫⲓ
[ⲡ̄ⲛ̄ⲁ̄] ⲛⲁⲕ ⲙ̄ⲙ̄ⲛ̄ⲧ-
[ⲁⲧⲛⲁ]ϩ̣ⲧⲉ ⲁⲩⲱ
[ⲁⲥϣⲱ]ⲡ̣ⲉ ⲙ̄ⲡⲛⲁⲩ̣
[ⲛ̄ϣⲟⲣ̄ⲡ̄] ⲉⲣⲉⲛⲉⲥ-
[ⲛⲏⲩ ⲛ̄ϩⲟⲩ]ⲛ ⲛ̄ⲧⲥⲩ-
[ⲛⲁⲝⲓⲥ ⲉⲩϣⲗ]ⲏⲗ·[a] ⲁϥ-
[ⲉⲓ ⲉⲧⲉⲩⲙⲏ]ⲧ̣ⲉ ⲁϥ-
[ⲱϣ ⲉⲃⲟⲗ. . . .].

Ⲉⲣⲉⲛⲉⲥⲛⲏⲩ ⲇⲉ ⲛ[ⲁ-]
ⲃⲱⲕ’ ⲉⲩⲙⲁ’ ⲉⲱϩ̄[ⲥ̄]
ⲛ̄ⲟⲩϣⲏⲙ’ ⲛ̄ⲕⲁ[ⲙ’]
ⲁⲩⲱ ⲉⲣⲉⲡⲉⲛⲉⲓⲱ[ⲧ]
ⲡⲁϩⲱⲙⲉ̇ ⲛ̄ⲙ̄ⲙ̄[ⲁⲩ]
ⲛⲉⲁϥⲧⲱϣ’ ⲇ[ⲉ ⲛ̄-]
ⲑⲉⲟⲇⲱⲣⲟⲥ ⲉⲧ[ⲃⲉ-]
ⲟⲩϩⲱⲃ’ ϩ̄ⲛ̄[
ⲛ̄ϥ̄ⲧ̄ⲙ̄ⲃⲱⲕ̣ [ⲙ̄ⲡ̄ⲛⲉⲥ-]
[ⲛ]ⲏ̣ⲩ· ⲛ̄ⲧⲉⲣ[ⲉⲩⲉⲓ]
ⲇⲉ ⲉⲃⲟⲗ ⲛ̄ⲙ̄ⲙ̣̄[ⲁϥ ⲛ̄-]
ϭⲓ ⲛⲉⲥⲛⲏⲩ [ⲉⲩⲑ-]
ⲡⲟ̄ ⲙ̄ⲙⲟϥ’ ⲉⲣ̣[ⲉ-]
ⲑⲉⲟⲇⲱⲣⲟⲥ ⲛ̣[ⲙ-]
ⲙⲁⲩ ϩⲱⲱ[ϥ . .]

[a] Perhaps ⲉϣⲗⲏⲗ, as space is short.

Fol. 12. *Recto* (*v.* Am. 411). no worldling (-*κοσμικός*) hath beheld me eating or (*ἤ*) drinking water,[1] that herein also the Lord might be glorified.' But (*δέ*) as for our father Pahômius, the Lord was with him in everything he did, glorifying him (Pahômius) and displaying him unto all the brethren for one of His servants.

It befell now (*δέ*) on a day that they had need (*χρεία*) to cleanse (*καθαρίζειν*) the well of the monastery, and he called certain of the brethren that were strong and went down to it . . . . .

. . . an old man among the brethren, in whom the fear of the Lord was not yet; it was not yet long since he had come in among the brethren. And he, when he heard that the brethren had gone down to the well, murmured saying, 'This man is pitiless, distressing the sons of men,[2] in that (*ὥστε*) he sendeth them down unto the well at this time.' It befell, on that night, that that old man beheld a dream (*ὅραμα*) . . . . .

[1] Am. differs slightly.

[2] Am. should be '. . . sons of men'. And as he beheld the brethren working, he beheld an angel of the Lord in their midst, and he crying into their faces (*v.* note on fol. 3), 'Receive ye &c.' Then he beheld him looking up to him, saying to him &c.

Verso (*v.* Am. 412). an] angel (ἄγγ.) of the Lord in their midst, crying out at them, saying, 'Receive unto yourselves a holy spirit (πν.); for (γάρ) ye labour not for man, but (ἀλλά) ye labour for the servant of God.' And (δέ) he beheld him (the angel) likewise, looking up at him, saying, 'Murmuring and faithless (ἄπιστος) old man, receive for thyself a spirit (πν.) of unbelief.' And it befell at morning, the brethren being within the meeting-place (σύναξις[1]), praying, he [came into their] midst and [cried out . . . . .

. . . that the Lord take from me the spirit (πν.) of faithlessness, for I did slander (καταλαλεῖν) the man of God and believed (πιστεύειν) not that everything he doeth, he doth it in uprightness.'

And (δέ) the brethren being about to go to a place, to reap a few reeds, and our father Pahômius being with them, but (δέ) having appointed Theodore concerning a (certain) matter in . . ., and he (Th.) went not [with the] brethren; but (δέ) when the brethren had [gone] forth with [him], speeding him, Theodore being with them also, ...

Fol. 13. ↑ *Recto.*

margin

[. . ⲛ̄ⲑ]ⲉⲟⲇⲱⲣⲟⲥ ϫⲉ-
[ⲁⲗⲉ ⲉ]ⲡϫⲟⲓ̈ ⲧⲁⲭⲩ·
[ⲁⲩⲱ] ⲛ̄ⲧⲟϥ’ ⲛ̄ⲧⲉⲩ-
[ⲛⲟ]ⲩ ⲙ̄ⲡ̄ϥ̄ⲇⲓⲁⲕⲣⲓ-
[ⲛⲉ ⲛ̄ⲗ]ⲁⲁⲩ ⲁϥⲁⲗⲉ’ ⲉ-
[ⲡϫⲟ]ⲓ̈ ⲙ̄ⲡ̄ϥ̄ϥⲓ̈ ⲡⲉϥ-
[ⲡⲣ]ⲏϣ’ ⲛ̄ⲙ̄ⲙ̄ⲁϥ’
[ⲟⲩ]ⲧⲉ ⲡⲉϥϫⲱⲱⲙⲉ
[ⲉ]ⲧ̄ϥ̄ϫⲓ ⲁⲡⲟⲥⲧⲏ̄-
[ⲑⲟ]ⲩⲥ ⲛ̄ϩⲏⲧ̄ϥ̄· ⲁⲩ-
[ⲱ] ⲛ̄ⲧⲉⲩⲛⲟⲩ ⲁϥ-
[ⲥⲙ]ⲟⲩ ϩ̄ⲙ̄ⲡⲉϥϩⲏⲧ’
[ⲉϥϫ]ⲱ ⲙ̄ⲙⲟϥ ϫⲉⲕ̄-
[ⲥⲙⲁ]ⲙⲁⲁⲧ’ ⲡϫⲟⲉⲓⲥ

Ⲉϥⲡⲱⲛ̄ϯ ⲇⲉ ⲛ̄ϭⲓ ⲡⲉ[ⲛ-]
ⲉⲓⲱⲧ’ ⲡⲁϩⲱⲙⲉ’ ⲁⲩ-
ⲱ’ ⲛⲉⲥⲛⲏⲩ ⲛ̄ⲙ̄ⲙ̄ⲁϥ·
ⲁϥϭⲱϣ̄ⲧ̄ ϩ̄ⲛ̄ⲛⲉϥ-
ⲃⲁⲗ’ ⲁϥⲛⲁⲩ ⲉⲩϭⲱ̄ⲗ̄ⲡ̄
ⲉⲃⲟⲗ’ ⲉϥⲟ ⲛ̄ϩⲟⲧⲉ· ⲁϥ-
ⲛⲁⲩ ϯⲁⲣ’ ⲁⲩⲱ ⲉⲓⲥ ϩⲏ-
ⲏⲧⲉ ϩⲟⲉⲓⲛⲉ ⲙⲉⲛ
ϩ̄ⲛ̄ⲛⲉⲥⲛⲏⲩ ϩ̄ⲛ̄ⲣ[ⲱ-]
ⲟⲩ ⲛ̄ϩⲉⲛⲑⲏⲣⲓⲟⲛ
ϩⲉⲛⲕⲟⲟⲩⲉ ⲇⲉ ϩ̄ⲛ̄ⲣ[ⲱ-]
ⲟⲩ ⲛϩⲉⲛⲙ̄ⲥⲟⲟϩ·
ⲁⲩⲱ ϩⲟⲉⲓⲛⲉ ⲉⲩϩ̄ⲛ̄-
ⲧⲙⲏⲧⲉ ⲛ̄ⲟⲩⲕⲱ[ϩⲧ]

[1] Σύναξις as the *place* of service in AS. §§ 56 (= *Miss.* 553, *Mus. Guim.* 105), 88, 92; *Miss.* 559 (= *Mus. Guim.* 283 ἐκκλησία), 823; *Mus. Guim.* 92 (= *ib.* 318 and our present text), 132, 171. So far as I can ascertain, not thus used outside the Pachomian texts.

[ϫⲉⲁⲕ]ⲁⲁⲧ' ⲙ̄ⲙ̄ⲡϣⲁ'
ϩⲱ' ⲛ̄ⲣ̣ϣⲏⲣⲉ ⲛ̄ⲁⲃ-
ⲣⲁϩⲁⲙ' ϩ̄ⲙ̄ⲡϩⲱⲃ
ⲉⲛⲧⲁϥⲁⲡⲁⲛⲧ[ⲁ]
ⲉⲣⲟï ⲧⲉⲛⲟⲩ ⲛ̄ⲑⲉ ⲉⲛ-
ⲧⲁϥⲉⲓ' ⲉⲃⲟⲗ' ϩ̄ⲙ̄ⲡⲉϥ-
ⲕⲁϩ' ⲉⲛ̄ϥⲥⲟⲟⲩⲛ ⲁⲛ
ϫⲉⲉϥⲛⲁ̄ ⲉⲧⲱⲛ·
[Ⲁⲩⲱ ⲁⲥ]ϣⲱⲡⲉ ⲛ̄ⲧⲉ-
[ⲣⲟⲩ . .]ⲁ̣[a] ⲙ̄ⲡⲱⲛⲅ̄
[. . . . . . .]ϫ̣ⲟϥ'[b] ⲉ-

ϩⲉⲛⲕⲟⲟⲩⲉ ⲉ[ⲩ]ϩⲁⲡ̣[ⲉ-]
[ⲥⲏ]ⲧ ⲛ̄ⲟⲩϣ̣[ⲱⲙⲉ]
[ⲉⲩⲟ]ⲩⲱϣ ⲉⲉ[ⲓ ⲉϩⲣⲁï]
ⲉⲙⲡⲟⲩⲉϣϭⲙ̄[ϭⲟⲙ]
ⲁⲩⲱ ⲛ̄ⲧⲟⲟⲩ ⲧⲏ̣[ⲣⲟⲩ]
sic ⲉⲃⲟⲗ
ⲛⲉⲩⲁϣⲕⲁⲕ ⲉⲩϣ[ⲟ-]
ⲟⲡ' ϩ̄ⲛ̄ⲛⲉïⲑⲗⲓⲯ[ⲓⲥ]
ⲉⲩϫⲱ ⲙ̄ⲙⲟⲥ ϫⲉ[ⲃⲟ-]
ⲏⲑⲉⲓ̈ ⲉⲣⲟⲛ· ⲛ̄[ⲧⲉ-]
ⲣⲉϥⲛⲁⲩ ⲇⲉ ⲉ[ⲣⲟⲟⲩ]
ⲧ[

[a] Apparently not ⲗ]ⲟ nor ⲟⲩ]ⲱ ; ⲕ]ⲁⲙ grammatically difficult. [b] Perhaps ϫⲟï.

→ *Verso.*

margin

ⲉⲃⲟⲗ'[a] ⲛ̄ⲧⲉⲧⲛ̄ⲱ̂ ⲛ̄-
ⲕⲁⲙ' ⲉⲧϩⲓϫⲱϥ' ⲛ̄-
ⲧⲙ̄ⲛⲧⲉ' ⲛ̄ⲧⲉϩⲓⲏ[·]
ⲁϥⲁϩ'ⲉ ⲣⲁⲧϥ̄ ⲛ̄ⲧⲉⲩ-
ⲛⲟⲩ ⲁϥⲡ̄ⲣ̄ϣ̄ ⲛⲉϥ-
ϭⲓϫ' ⲉⲃⲟⲗ' ⲁϥⲁϣ ⳨
ⲕⲁⲕ' ⲉⲃⲟⲗ' ϩ̄ⲛ̄ⲟⲩⲛⲟϭ
ⲛ̄ⲥⲙⲏ ⲁϥϣⲗⲏⲗ'
ⲉϥⲉⲡⲓⲕⲁⲗⲉⲓ' ⲙ̄-
ⲡⲛⲟⲩⲧⲉ ⲉⲧⲃⲏⲏ-
ⲧⲟⲩ ⲉⲧⲣⲉⲟⲩⲃⲟⲏ-
ⲑⲉⲓⲁ ϣⲱⲡⲉ ⲛⲁⲩ
ⲉⲃⲟⲗ ϩⲓⲧⲟⲟⲧϥ̄·

ⲧⲁϥⲛⲁⲩ ⲉ[ⲣⲟϥ ϫⲉ-]
ⲉϥⲛⲁϣⲱ[ⲡⲉ ⲛ̄-]
ⲛⲉⲥⲛⲏⲩ ⲙ[ⲛ̄ⲛ̄-]
ⲥⲁⲧⲣⲉϥⲛ̄ⲕ[ⲟⲧⲕ̄·]
ⲛ̄ⲧⲉⲣⲟⲩⲥⲟ[ⲃⲧⲉ ⲇⲉ]
ⲛ̄ⲛⲉⲥⲛⲏⲩ, [ⲉⲧⲣⲉⲩ-]
ⲟⲩⲱⲙ' ⲉⲣⲟⲩϩ[ⲉ·]
ⲁⲩⲱ ⲛ̄ⲧⲟϥ ⲙ̄[ⲡϥ̄-]
ⲟⲩⲱⲙ· ⲑⲉⲟⲇⲱ[ⲣⲟⲥ]
ⲇⲉ ⲡⲉⲙ̄ⲡϥⲉⲓ[ⲙⲉ-]
ⲡⲉ ⲉⲡⲉⲛⲧⲁϥ[ϣⲱ-]
ⲡⲉ· ⲡⲉⲁϥϫⲟ̣[ⲟⲩϥ]
ⲅⲁⲣ' ⲙ̄ⲡⲟⲩⲁ'[ϩ̄ⲙ̄ⲡⲉ-]

[a] ⲁϥⲛⲟⲩϫⲉ] ⲉⲃⲟⲗ : *v.* below.

ⲁⲩⲱ ⲁⲥϣⲱⲡⲉ ⲉⲣ-
[ϣⲁⲛ]ⲡⲟⲩⲁ ⲡ[ⲟⲩ]ⲁ
[ⲛ̄ⲛⲉⲥ]ⲛⲏⲩ ⲉⲓ’ [ⲉϫⲱϥ][a]
[ⲉϥⲟⲧ]ⲡ̄ · ⲛⲉϣⲁⲩ-
[ⲛⲟⲩ]ϫⲉ ⲉⲃⲟⲗ’ ϩⲱⲟ̣ⲩ
[ⲛ̄ⲛ]ⲉⲩⲉⲧⲡⲱ’ ⲛ̄-
[ⲥ]ⲉϣⲗⲏⲗ’· ⲁⲩⲱ ⲁϥ-
[ϭ]ⲱ ⲉϥⲙⲏⲛ ⲉⲃⲟⲗ’
[ⲛ̄]ⲧⲉϊϩⲉ ⲉϥϣⲗⲏⲗ’
[ϣⲁⲛ]ⲧⲉⲣⲟⲩϩⲉ ϣⲱ-
[ⲡⲉ . . . .]ϥ[b]

ⲥⲛⲏⲩ ⲛ̄ⲟⲩ[ϩⲱⲃ ·[c]]
ⲁⲩⲱ ⲛ̄ⲧⲉⲣⲉϥⲉⲓ̈
ⲙ̄ⲛ̄ⲛ̄ⲥⲱⲥ’ ⲁⲩϫⲱ̄
ⲉⲣⲟϥ ⲛ̄ⲑⲉ ⲧⲏⲣ̄ⲥ̄
ⲉⲛⲧⲁⲥϣⲱⲡⲉ ·
ⲁⲩⲱ ⲟⲛ ⲁⲩⲧⲁⲙⲟϥ
ϫⲉⲙ̄ⲡ̄ϥⲟⲩⲱⲙ’ ⲉ-
ⲃⲟⲗ’ ϫⲉϥⲙⲟⲕ̄ϩ̄ ⲛ̄-
ϩⲏⲧ’ ⲉϫⲙ̄ⲛ̄ϭⲱⲗ̄ⲡ̄
ⲉⲃⲟⲗ’ ⲉⲛⲧ[ⲁϥⲛⲁⲩ]
ⲉⲣⲟϥ · ⲛ̄[ⲧⲟϥ ⲇⲉ]

[a] The last of these letters was tailed.

[b] [ⲡⲉ· ϩⲙⲛⲧⲣⲉ]ϥ or [ⲡⲉ ⲁⲩⲱ ⲉⲧⲓ ⲉ]ϥ.

[c] Am. Ac. شغل.

Fol. 13. *Recto* (*v.* Am. 412, 413). . . . unto] Theodore, 'Go aboard the boat quickly (*ταχύ*).' And as for him, he doubted (*διακρίνειν*) not at all[1] and went aboard the boat and took not his coverlet with him, neither (*οὐδέ*)[2] his book wherein he learnt by heart (*ἀπὸ στήθους*). And forthwith he blessed in his heart, saying, 'Blessed art Thou, Lord, for that Thou hast made me also worthy to be a child of Abraham, in the matter that hath happened (*ἀπαντᾶν*) unto me now, even as he came forth from his country, knowing not whither he went.'[3] [And] it befell, after that [they had ceased ?] to load . . . . . the] boat (?) . . . . .

Now (*δέ*) as our father Pahômius was loading (the boat) and the brethren with him, he looked with his eyes and beheld a terrible revelation. For (*γάρ*) he beheld and lo, certain of the brethren were in the jaws of wild beasts (*θηρ.*); others again (*δέ*) in the jaws of crocodiles; and some were in the midst of a fire, others at the bottom of a cliff, desiring to come up, (yet) not being able. And they all were crying out, being in these tribulations (*θλῖψις*), and saying, 'Help (*βοηθεῖν*) us.' And (*δέ*) when he had seen them (?) . . . . .

[1] Am., asked concerning naught, neither refused, but &c.

[2] his—neither *om.* Am.

[3] Am. *add.* 'even so Thy servant' (*sic*, 413, 1).

Verso (*v.* Am. 413, 414). . . . he cast] down the load of reeds that was upon him, midway in the road,[1] and stood still forthwith[2] and spread forth his hands and cried out with a loud voice and prayed, beseeching (ἐπικαλεῖν) God[3] concerning them, that help (βοήθεια) might be unto them from Him. And[4] it befell, as each one [of the] brethren came up [to him?] laden (?), they also cast down their loads and prayed. And he stayed, continuing thus to pray, until evening fell. [And while yet (?)] he [prayed . . . . .

. . . the revelation that] he had seen, that it should befall the brethren after he had fallen asleep. But (δέ) after they had made ready for the brethren that they should eat, at even, and as for him (*sc.* Pahômius) he ate not. But (δέ) Theodore had not known of what had befallen, for (γάρ) he had sent [him] with one [from among the] brethren for (?) an [affair?]. And when he afterwards came (back), they told him all the fashion of its happening; and furthermore they informed him that he (*sc.* P.) had not eaten because he was sad at heart concerning the revelation that [he had beheld.[5] But (δέ)] he (?) . . . . .

Fol. 14. → *Recto.*

]ⲙ ⲛ[
[ⲉϣⲁⲩ]ⲟⲩⲟⲙϥ̄ ⲛ̄ϭⲓ
ⲛⲉⲥⲛⲏⲩ, ⲁϥϫⲟ-
[ⲟ]ⲩ ϣⲁⲣⲟϥ ⲛ̄ⲟⲩ-
ⲥⲟⲛ ⲉϥϫⲱ ⲙ̄ⲙⲟⲥ
ϫⲉⲑⲉⲟⲇⲱⲣⲟⲥ ⲙⲟⲩ-
ⲧⲉ ⲉⲣⲟⲕ· ⲁⲩⲱ ⲛ̄-
ⲧⲟϥ ⲛ̄ⲧⲉⲩⲛⲟⲩ ⲛ̄-
ⲧⲉⲣⲉϥⲥⲱⲧⲙ̄ ⲁϥ-
ⲧⲱⲟⲩⲛ ⲁϥⲉⲓ' ϣⲁ-

[
ⲉ̣[ⲙ̄-]
ⲡⲉⲑⲉⲟⲇⲱⲣ[ⲟⲥ ⲟⲩ-]
ⲱⲙ' ϩⲱⲱϥ ⲙ̄ⲡ[ⲟⲟⲩ·]
ⲡⲉϫⲁϥ ⲛⲁϥ ϫ[ⲉⲁ-]
ⲗⲱⲧⲛ̄ ϩⲁⲣⲟϥ [ⲙ̄-]
ⲡⲣ̄ⲧⲣⲉϥⲟⲩⲱⲙ
ⲁⲗⲗⲁ ⲕⲁⲁϥ' ⲙⲁⲣ[ϥ̄-]
ⲣⲓⲙⲉ· ⲁⲩⲱ ⲛ̄ⲧ[ⲟϥ]
ⲛ̄ⲧⲉⲩⲛⲟⲩ ⲁϥϩ[ⲙⲟ-]

[1] Am. *sic.*

[2] Am. *sic.*

[3] Am. *sic.*

[4] Am. should be, 'And each one of the brethren was bearing his load. And when they saw him cast down his load, each one of them cast down his load also, and stood and prayed. And he stayed continuing thus until the time of evening. And as he prayed, he was informed as to the vision, that it should befall the brethren after his death.'

[5] Am. *sic*, in all this sentence.

ⲣⲟϥ· ⲁϥⲁⲣⲭⲉⲓ, ⲛ̄-
ϣⲁϫⲉ ⲛ̄ⲙ̄ⲙⲁϥ
ϩ̄ⲛ̄ϩⲉⲛϣⲁϫⲉ ⲛ̄-
ⲙ̄ⲕⲁϩ’ ⲛ̄ϩⲏⲧ’ ϩⲱⲥ
ⲉϥϭ̄ⲙ̄ⲁ[ⲣⲓⲕ]ⲉ̣’ ⲉⲣⲟϥ·
ⲁ̣ⲩ̣ⲱ ⲁ̣[ⲡⲉϥϩ]ⲏⲧ’
[ⲙ̄]ⲕ̣ⲁϩ ⲁ̣ϥ̣ⲣ̣ⲓ̣ⲙ̣ⲉ ⲛ̄-
[ϭⲓ] ⲑⲉⲟⲇⲱⲣⲟⲥ [ⲁ]ϥ-
[ⲉⲓ̈ ⲉ]ⲃⲟⲗ’ ϩⲓⲧⲟⲟ[ⲧ]ϥ’
[ⲡⲉ]ϫⲁϥ ⲛⲁϥ ϫⲉ[ⲙ]ⲟ-
[ⲟϣ]ⲉ ϩⲱⲱⲕ’ ⲛ̄ⲧ̄ⲣⲓ-
[ⲙⲉ ⲉ]ϩ̣[ⲟⲩⲛ] ⲉⲡϫⲟⲉⲓⲥ
[ⲛ̄ⲑⲉ] ⲉ̣ⲛⲧⲁⲓ̈ⲣⲓⲙⲉ
[ϩⲱ ⲟ]ⲛ̣ ⲁϥⲟⲩⲱ-
[ϣ̄ⲃ̄ ⲇ]ⲉ ⲛ̄ϭⲓ ⲟⲩⲁ ϩ̄ⲛ̄-
[ⲛⲉⲧ]ⲥⲱⲧ̄ⲙ̄ ⲉⲣⲟϥ

ⲟⲥ ⲁϥⲟⲩⲱⲙ’ ϩ̄ⲛ̄[ⲟⲩ-]
ⲙ̄ⲧⲟⲛ ⲛ̄ϩⲏⲧ·
ⲁⲩⲱ ⲁⲥϣⲱⲡⲉ ⲉ[ϥ-]
ϩⲙⲟⲟⲥ ⲛ̄ⲥⲁⲟⲩⲥⲁ [ⲛ̄-]
ϭⲓ ⲑⲉⲟⲇⲱⲣⲟⲥ ⲙⲁⲩ̣-
ⲁⲁϥ’ ⲉϥⲙⲟⲕ̄ϩ̄ ⲛ̄ϩⲏ̣[ⲧ]
ⲁⲩⲉⲓⲙⲉ ⲛ̄ϭ[ⲓ ⲥ]ⲟⲛ
ⲥⲛⲁⲩ ϫⲉϥⲗⲩⲡⲉ[ⲓ’]
ⲁⲩϯ ⲡⲉⲩⲟⲓ̈ ⲉⲣⲟ[ϥ]
ⲡⲉϫⲁⲩ ⲛⲁϥ ϫⲉⲁ-
ϫⲓ ⲟⲩϣⲁϫⲉ ⲉⲣⲟⲛ̣
ⲛ̄ⲧⲟϥ ⲇⲉ ⲡⲉϫⲁϥ
ⲛⲁⲩ ϫⲉⲧⲉⲛⲟⲩ ⲣⲱ̣’
ⲁⲛⲟⲕ’ ⲉⲧ̄ⲣ̄ⲭⲣⲓⲁ ⲛ̣-
ϫⲓ ⲥⲟⲗⲥ̄ⲗ̄ ϩⲓⲧ̄[ⲛ̄-]
ⲟⲩⲁ· ⲡⲉϫⲁⲩ ⲛ[ⲁϥ]
ϫⲉϣⲁⲥϣⲱⲡⲉ

margin

↑ *Verso.*

ⲡ]ⲉ̣ⲕ-
[ⲙⲕⲁϩ] ⲛϩⲏⲧ̣, ⲁⲩⲱ
[ⲁ]ⲛⲟⲛ ⲧ̄ⲛ̄ⲛⲁⲥ̄ⲗ̄ⲥⲱ-
[ⲗ]ⲕ· ⲛ̄ⲧⲟϥ ⲇⲉ ⲡⲉ-
[ϫ]ⲁϥ ⲛⲁⲩ ϫⲉ ⲛ̄ⲧⲱ-
ⲧ̄ⲛ̄ ⲛ̄ⲧⲉⲧⲛⲁϣ-
ϭ̄ⲙ̄ϭⲟⲙ’ ⲁⲛ ⲛ̄ⲥ̄ⲗ̄ⲥⲱ-
ⲗ̄ⲧ̄ ⲙ̄ⲡⲉⲥⲛⲁⲩ· ⲉⲓ-
ⲙⲏⲧⲓ̈ ⲛ̄ⲧⲉⲟⲩⲁ’
ⲛ̄ⲟⲩⲱⲧ ⲥ̄ⲗ̄ⲥⲱ̄ⲗ̄ⲧ̄

[ⲡ]ⲉ̣ ⲛ̄ϩⲓⲇ̣ⲓ̣[ⲱⲧⲏⲥ]
ⲛ̄ϥ̄ⲥⲟⲟⲩⲛ ⲁⲛ [ⲛ̄ⲗⲁⲁⲩ]
ⲛ̄ⲧⲟϥ ⲇⲉ ⲁϥⲁⲅ[ⲁⲛⲁ-]
ⲕⲧⲉⲓ, ⲡⲉϫⲁϥ ϫⲉⲡ[ⲉⲛ-]
ⲉⲓⲱⲧ’ ⲡⲁϩⲱⲙⲉ ⲛ[ϥ̄-]
ⲥⲟⲟⲩⲛ ⲁⲛ ⲛ̄ⲗⲁⲁⲩ, [ⲁ-]
ⲣⲏⲩ ⲟⲛ, ⲕⲛⲁϫⲟⲟⲥ̣ [ⲉ-]
ⲧⲃⲉⲛⲁⲡⲟⲥⲧⲟⲗⲟ[ⲥ]
ϫⲉⲛ̄ⲥⲉⲥⲟⲟⲩⲛ ⲁⲛ [ⲛ-]
ⲗⲁⲁⲩ· ⲉⲃⲟⲗ’ ϫⲉϥⲥⲏ[ϩ]

ⲡϣⲁϫⲉ ⲇⲉ ⲉⲛⲧⲁϥ-
ϫⲟⲟϥ' ⲛ̄ⲛⲉϥⲥⲟⲟⲩⲛ[a]
ⲁⲛ ϫⲉⲟⲩ'ⲡⲉ · ⲉⲧⲓ̈ ⲇⲉ
ⲉϥϣⲁϫⲉ ⲛ̄ⲙ̄ⲙⲁⲩ
ⲁϥϭⲱϣ̄ⲧ ⲁⲩⲱ ⲉⲓⲥ
ϩⲏ[ⲏ]ⲧⲉ ⲉⲓⲥ ⲡⲉⲥⲙⲟⲧ'
ⲛ̄ⲟⲩⲣⲱⲙⲉ ⲁϥϩⲙⲟ-
[ⲟ]ⲥ̣ ⲉ̣ϩⲣⲁⲓ̈ ⲉϫⲙ̄ⲡⲉϥ-
ⲡⲁⲧ' ⲁϥⲁⲣⲭⲉⲓ̈ ⲛ̄-
ϣⲁϫⲉ ⲛ̄ⲙ̄ⲙⲁϥ' ⲉϥ-
ⲟ̣ ⲛ̄ⲑⲉ ⲛ̄ⲛⲉⲧⲥⲟϣ̄ϥ[b]
ⲙ̄ⲡⲉⲛⲉⲓⲱⲧ' ⲡⲁ-
ϩⲱⲙⲉ ⲉϥⲡⲉⲓⲣⲁⲍⲉ
ⲙ̄ⲙⲟϥ' ⲉϥϫⲱ ⲙ̄ⲙⲟ̄ⲥ
[ϫⲉ]ⲛⲓⲙ'ⲡⲉ ⲡⲁϩⲱⲙⲉ ·
[ⲙⲏ] ⲛ̄ⲟⲩⲣⲱⲙⲉ ⲁⲛ-

ⲉⲧⲃ̄ⲏⲏⲧⲟⲩ ϫⲉϩⲉⲛ-
ϩⲓⲇⲓⲱⲧⲏⲥⲛⲉ ⲛ̄ⲥⲉ-
ⲥⲟⲟⲩⲛ ⲁⲛ ⲛ̄ⲥϩⲁⲓ̈ ·
ⲛ̄ⲧⲟϥ ⲅⲁⲣ ϥⲃ̄ⲱⲗ'
ⲉⲣⲟⲛ ⲛ̣̄ⲙ̄ⲙⲩⲥⲧⲏ-
ⲣⲓ[ⲟⲛ ⲛ̄ⲛⲉ]ⲅⲣⲁⲫⲏ
ⲁⲩⲱ [ϥⲧⲁⲙⲟ[c] ⲙ̄-]
ⲙ̣[ⲟ]ⲛ̣ ⲉ̣ϩⲉⲛⲥϩⲁ[ⲓ ⲉⲩ-]
ⲟ̣[ⲩⲁⲁ]ⲃ' ⲛ̄ⲑⲉ ⲉⲧⲥ̣[ⲏϩ]
ⲟ̣[ⲩ ⲙ]ⲟ̣ⲛⲟⲛ ⲇⲉ ϩ̣[ⲱ]
[. .]ϥⲥⲟⲟⲩⲛ ⲉϩ[ⲟⲩⲉ-]
ⲣⲟⲕ · ⲁⲩⲱ ⲙ̄ⲛ̄[ⲛ̄ⲥⲁ-]
ⲧⲣⲉϥϫⲱ ⲛ̣̄[ⲛⲁⲓ ⲁ-]
ⲡⲉⲧϣⲁϫⲉ [ⲛ̄ⲙ̄ⲙⲁϥ]
† ⲑⲉ ⲛⲁϥ ⲉⲧ[ⲣⲉϥⲥⲟⲩ-]
ⲱⲛϥ ϫⲉⲟⲩⲁⲅ[ⲅⲉⲗⲟⲥ-]
ⲡⲉ ⲛ̄ⲧⲉ ⲡϫ̣[ⲟⲉⲓⲥ

margin

[a] So my copy; should be ⲛⲛⲉⲩ-. [b] So copy; read ⲥⲱϣϥ. [c] Following Am., يعلمنا.

Fol. 14. *Recto* (*v.* Am. 414). . . . which] the brethren [use ?] to eat ; and he sent to him a brother, saying, 'Theodore doth call thee.' And as for him, forthwith[1] when he heard, he arose and came unto him, and began (ἄρχειν) to speak with him in words of sadness, as if (ὡς)[2] finding fault with him. And Theodore's heart was grieved and he wept and went forth from him. He (*sc.* P.) said unto him,[3] 'Do thou too go and weep unto the Lord, [even as] I [myself] also have wept.' But (δέ) one of [them that] heard him answered[4] . . . . .

. . . neither hath[5] Theodore eaten to-day.' He said unto him, 'Leave ye him; let him not eat, but (rather) (ἀλλά) let him weep.' And he (*sc.* P.)

[1] Am. *sic.* [2] Am. *sic.*

[3] Am., 'because he had said unto him.'

[4] Am., 'And one of the brethren heard him while he spake unto him, and he said &c.'

[5] Am., 'Theodore also hath eaten naught to-day.' And he said, 'And what have ye (to do) with him (misunderstood for ⲁϩⲣⲱⲧⲛ ⲛⲙ-ⲙⲁϥ)? Let him &c.'

forthwith sat down and did eat with his mind at rest.[1] And it befell, as Theodore[2] sat apart alone, sad at heart, two brethren knew that he was grieved (λυπεῖν) and they betook themselves unto him and said unto him, 'Speak a word unto us.' But (δέ) he said unto them, 'Now[3] indeed I it is have need (χρεία) to get comfort from one.' They said unto him, 'It may happen . . . . .

Verso (*v.* Am. 414, 415). . . . thy [sadness] of heart and we will comfort thee.' But (δέ) he said unto them, 'Not ye it is will together be able to console me, except (εἰ μήτι) one alone console me.' But (δέ) the word that he spake, they knew not what (it meant). And (δέ) whilst yet (ἔτι) he spake with them, he looked and lo, the semblance of a man did sit at his feet[4] and began to speak with him, being like to them that revile our father Pahômius, tempting (πειράζειν) him and saying, 'Who is Pahômius? [Is he (μή)] not an ignorant (ἰδιώτης) man, knowing nothing?' But (δέ) he (*sc.* Theodore) was indignant (ἀγανακτεῖν) (and) said, 'Our father Pahômius knoweth (then) nothing? Perchance too thou wilt say concerning the apostles (ἀπ.) that they know nothing, for that it is written[5] concerning them that they were ignorant men (ἰδ.), knowing not how to write.[6] For (γάρ) he solveth for us the mysteries (μυστήριον) of the Scriptures (γρ.) and [teacheth] us holy writings, as it is written.[7] But not only (οὐ μόνον δέ) . . .,[8] he knoweth more than thee.' And after that he had said this, he that spake with him gave him means that he should know him for an angel (ἄγ.) of the Lord.

Fol. 15. ↑ *Recto.*

[. . . . . . .]ⲓ̣ϣⲓ		
[. . . . ϩ]ⲱⲃ̄ ⲛⲓⲙ' ⲛ̄-	ⲛⲁ[	ⲛ-]
[. . . .]ⲁ[.]ⲉ̣ϥ ⲁⲩ-	ⲧⲁϥ[	
[ⲣⲱⲙ]ⲉ ϫⲉ ⲟⲛ ⲉⲓ' ϣⲁ-	ϥⲥⲟⲩ[ⲧⲱⲛ	
[ⲣⲟ]ϥ ⲛ̄ⲟⲩⲟⲩⲟⲉⲓϣ'	ⲁⲩⲱ̣ [	
ⲉϥⲟⲩⲱϣ' ⲉⲣ̄ⲙⲟⲛⲁ-	ⲟⲩⲕⲟ̣[	

[1] Am., 'in great grief of heart.' But read ودع for وجع.

[2] Am. *sic.*

[3] Am. should be, 'I have need that ye two comfort me.' And they said unto him, 'It is indeed possible that the fathers be comforted even by their children &c.'

[4] Am. (Ac. 51, G ⲣ̄ⲗ̄ⲏ̄ b) 'before him'.

[5] Acts iv. 13.

[6] Am. *sic.*

[7] *Cf.* Luke xxiv. 32.

[8] Am. should be, 'and not this only, but he is &c.'

ⲭⲟⲥ · ⲁⲩ[ⲱ] ⲛ̄ⲧⲉⲣⲉϥ'-
ⲁⲡⲁⲛ[ⲧⲁ] ⲉⲣⲟϥ' ⲁϥ-
ϣⲁϫⲉ ⲛ̄ⲙ̄ⲙⲁϥ ⲁϥ-
ϩⲉ ⲉⲣⲟϥ [ⲉ]ϥ̣ⲥⲟⲩⲧⲱ̄
ⲛ̄ⲛⲁϩⲣ[ⲁ]ϥ ⲉⲡϩⲱⲃ
[. . .][a] ⲁ̣ⲩⲱ̣ ⲁϥϩⲱⲛ
[ⲉ]ⲧ̣ⲟⲟⲧϥ ⲙ̄ⲡⲥⲟⲛ
ⲉ̣ⲧ̣ϩⲁⲧ̣ⲙ̣̄ⲡ̣[ⲣ]ⲟ' ⲛ̄ⲑⲉ-
ⲛⲉⲉⲧⲏ ⲉⲧⲣⲉϥⲉⲓ-
ⲛⲉ ⲙ̄ⲙⲟϥ ⲉϩⲟⲩⲛ
ⲛ̄ⲛⲉⲥⲛⲏⲩ · ⲛ̄ⲧⲉ-
[ⲣⲉϥ]ⲙ̣ⲟⲟϣⲉ ϫⲉ ⲉⲑⲏ
[ⲛⲟⲩⲕ]ⲟⲩ[ⲓ] ϩⲱⲥ ⲉϥ-
[ⲛⲁⲃⲱⲕ ⲉϩⲟ]ⲩⲛ ⲉⲧ-[b]

ϩⲃⲏⲩ[ⲉ ⲙⲉ-]
ⲉⲩⲉ ϩ̄ⲙ̄[
ⲉⲓ ⲉ̣ⲃⲟⲗ [
ϩⲛ̄ⲧⲉⲩ[ⲛⲟⲩ ⲉⲧⲙ̄-]
ⲙ̣ⲁⲩ · ⲛ̄[
[
ⲙ̣ⲛ̣ⲛⲉⲡⲉⲧ̣[
ⲙ̄ⲡⲥⲟⲛ ⲉⲛ̣[ⲧⲁϥ-]
ϫⲟⲟⲥ ⲛⲁϥ ⲉ[ϫⲓ-]
ⲧϥ̄ ⲉⲉⲓⲛⲉ [ⲙ̄ⲙⲟϥ]
ⲉϩⲟⲩⲛ ⲉⲧ[
ϫⲉⲙⲁ[
ⲣⲱⲙ̣[ⲉ
ⲛ̄[

[a] I do not think there is a line missing between this and last; *cf. verso.* [b] ⲧⲥⲟⲟⲩϩⲥ or ⲧⲙⲏⲧⲉ. So too in col. 2.

→ *Verso.*

]ⲛ̣ⲥⲁ
ⲉⲃ]ⲟⲗ ⲛ̄-
[ⲧⲉⲩⲛⲟⲩ] ⲡⲉϫⲁϥ
[ⲛⲁϥ ϫⲉⲃⲱⲕ] ⲛ̄ⲡ̄-
[ⲙⲟⲩⲧⲉ ⲉⲛⲓ]ⲙ' ⲛ̄-
[ⲥⲟⲛ ϩⲓⲛⲓ]ⲙ· ⲁⲩⲱ
[ⲛ̄ⲧⲉⲣⲟⲩⲉⲓ] · ⲡⲉ-
[ϫⲁϥ ⲛⲁⲩ] ϩⲱⲟⲩ ϫⲉ-
[ⲛ̄ⲧⲁⲓ]ϫⲟⲟⲥ ⲛⲏⲧⲛ̄
[ϫⲉⲟⲩ'·] ⲡ̣ⲉϫⲁⲩ ⲛⲁϥ

ⲗ̣ⲉ[ⲡⲉ-]
ϫⲁϥ ⲛⲁ̣[ϥ ϫⲉⲉⲧⲃⲉ-]
ⲧⲁⲫⲟⲣⲙⲏ [ⲙ̄ⲡⲛⲟ-]
ⲃⲉ ⲉⲛⲧⲁϊⲁ[ⲁϥ ϩⲛ̄-]
ⲟⲩⲙⲛ̄ⲧⲁⲧⲥⲟ[ⲟⲩⲛ ⲱ[a]]
ⲑⲉⲟⲇⲱⲣⲉ. ⲥⲡⲟⲩⲇⲁ-
ⲍⲉ ⲉⲧⲣⲉⲕϣⲱⲡⲉ
ⲛ̄ⲧ̣[ⲟ]ⲕ ϩⲛⲟⲩⲙⲛ̄ⲧ-
ⲁⲧⲛⲟⲃⲉ ⲛ̄ⲟⲩⲟⲉⲓϣ
ⲛⲓⲙ'· ⲛ̄ⲑ̣ⲉ ⲉⲛⲧⲁϊ-
ⲉⲡ̣ⲓ̣ⲧⲓⲙ̣ⲁ ⲛⲁⲕ' ⲉ-

[a] Scarcely space for ⲱ, though it seems needed.

[ϫⲉⲛ]ⲧⲁⲕϫⲟⲟⲥ ϫⲉ
[ⲃⲱⲕ] ⲛ̄ⲧⲉⲧⲛ̄ⲁ-
[ⲛⲁⲭ]ⲱⲣⲉⲓ ⲛⲏⲧⲛ̄·
[Ⲛⲧ]ⲟϥ ⲇⲉ ⲛ̄ⲧⲉ-
[ⲣⲉϥⲥⲱ]ⲧⲙ̄ ⲁϥⲁ[ϣ]
[ⲁϩⲟⲙ]· ⲡⲉϫⲁϥ ϫⲉ-
. . .]ⲥⲧ[a] ⲉⲛⲉⲉⲓ-
[ϣⲁϫⲉ ⲛ̄ⲙ̄]ⲙⲏⲧⲛ̄
[ⲁⲓⲛⲁⲩ ⲉⲩⲡ]ⲛ̄ⲁ ⲛ̄-
ⲉ]ϥ-

[ⲡ]ϫⲓⲛϫ[ⲏ] ϩⲛ̄[ⲟ]ⲩ-[b]
[
ϣⲱ-]
ⲡⲉ ⲇⲉ ⲛ̄ⲟⲩⲥ[ⲟⲛ ⲉⲕ-]
ⲙⲟⲩⲧⲉ ⲉⲩⲣⲱ[ⲙⲉ]
ⲁⲩⲱ ⲛ̄ⲧⲟϥ ⲛ̄ϥ-
ⲡⲱⲧ ⲛⲁϥ ⲛ̄ⲧⲉⲩ-
ⲛⲟⲩ ⲙ̄ⲡⲣⲛⲟⲩϭⲥ
ⲉⲣⲟϥ· ⲁⲗⲗⲁ ⲁϫ[ⲓⲥ]
ⲛ̄ⲧⲟϥ [ϩ]ⲙ̄ⲡ[ⲉⲕϩⲏⲧ]
ϫⲉⲛⲁⲛ[ⲧⲱⲥ ⲙ̄ⲡϥⲉⲓ-]
ⲙⲉ ⲉⲩ[c]

a Am. حين كنت اكلمكم, Ac. 53 حين كلامى. b Whether two or three lines lost is uncertain.
c Or ϯ]ⲙⲉⲉⲩⲉ ϫ[ⲉ. But this hardly fills the space.

Fol. 15. *Recto* (*cf.* Am. 416). . . . everything that . . . . .[1] But (δέ) a man also came unto him, once on a time, desiring to become a monk (*μον.*). And after that he had met (ἀπαντᾶν) him, he talked with him and found him fitted (*lit.* upright) before him (*i.e.* in his opinion) for the matter . . . . . And he bade the brother that was at the gate of the monastery, that he should bring him in unto the brethren. But (δέ) when he had gone forward a little, as if (ὡς) he [would go in] unto the [congregation [2]
. . . in that hour . . . . . the brother to whom [he] had said to [take] him and bring [him] in unto the . . ., saying,[3] . . . . . man (?) . . . . .

Verso (*v.* Am. 418). . . . went] forth at [once?]. He said [unto him, 'Go (?)] and [call] such a [brother and] such an one.' And [when they were come,] he [said unto them] likewise, [' What] said [I] unto you?' They said unto him, 'Thou didst say, [' Go] and depart (ἀναχωρεῖν).'[4] But (δέ) he, when he heard, sighed. He said, ' . . . I [spake with] you, [I beheld a] spirit (*πν.*) of . . . . .
. . . and said unto him, 'Because of the occasion (ἀφορμή) of sin that I (*sic*)[5] have given (*lit.* done), in ignorance, [O ?] Theodore, strive (σπουδά-

1 Apparently not as in Am.'s context. What follows (§ 46) differs also considerably from Am.
2 Or 'midst'.
3 An imperative followed here.
4 Am. *sic.*
5 Am., 'By reason of this sin which I have done.'

ζειν) for thy part to be alway without sin, as I admonished (ἐπιτιμᾶν) thee freely, with[1] . . . . . But (δέ) if perchance on a time thou call a man and he forthwith hasten away, be not wroth with him, but (ἀλλά) rather say in thy heart, 'Surely (πάντως) he hath not understood . . . . .

Fol. 16. → *Recto.*

] ?
ⲧⲥⲩⲛⲧⲉ]ⲗⲉⲓ̈ⲁ
[a]ⲙ̄ⲡⲁⲓ]ⲱ̣ⲛ ⲉⲩ-
]ⲧⲟⲩ ⲁⲛ
[ⲉⲃ]ⲟⲗ ϩⲛ̄ⲛⲉⲩⲥⲱ-
ⲱ̣ϥ̣ ⲉⲛⲧⲁⲩ. . ⲁ̣ⲥ̣ⲉ̣
[. .] ⲙⲙⲟⲟⲩ ⲛ̄ϩⲏⲧⲟⲩ
[. . . .]ⲙ̄ⲡ[

] ⲛⲧⲉⲣⲉϥ-
[ⲛⲁⲩ] ⲛϭⲓ ⲡⲉⲛⲉⲓ-
ⲱⲧ ⲡⲁϩⲱⲙⲉ ⲉⲩ-
ⲡ̄ⲛ̄ⲁ̄ ⲙ̄ⲡⲟⲣⲛⲓⲁ
ⲁⲩⲱ ⲛ̄ⲥⲱⲱϥ' ⲉϥ-
ⲡⲁⲣⲁⲅⲉ ϩⲛ̄ⲛⲉⲥⲛⲏⲩ,
ⲉⲩⲣ̄ϩⲱⲃ' ϩⲛ̄ⲟⲩⲙⲁ·
ⲁϥⲥⲱⲟⲩϩ' ⲙ̄ⲙⲟⲟⲩ
ⲉⲛⲉⲩⲉⲣⲏⲩ ⲉⲣⲟⲩϩⲉ
ⲕⲁⲧⲁ ⲧⲉⲩⲥⲩⲛⲏ-
ⲑⲉⲓⲁ· ⲡⲉϫⲁϥ ⲛⲁⲩ·
ϫⲉⲁⲣⲓ ⲡⲙⲉⲉⲩⲉ ⲙ̄-
ⲡϣⲁϫⲉ ⲉⲧⲥⲏϩ ϫⲉ-
ⲧⲡⲓⲥⲧⲓⲥ ⲟⲩⲉⲃⲟⲗ

[a] Perhaps here ⲅⲁⲣ, ⲟⲩⲛ or some such word.

↑ *Verso.*

ⲛ[
ⲉⲛⲧⲁⲩϣ[ⲱⲡⲉ[a] ⲛ-]
ϩⲏⲧⲟⲩ ⲥⲉϣ[ⲱⲡⲉ]
ⲟⲛ ⲧⲉⲛⲟⲩ ⲁⲩⲱ ⲥⲉ-
ⲙⲟⲟϣⲉ ϩⲙ̄ⲡⲕⲟⲥ-
ⲙⲟⲥ· ϯⲥⲟⲟⲩⲛ' ⲙⲉ̄
ϫⲉⲛϥ̣ ?

[a] Or ϣ[ⲓⲛⲉ], and in next line.

[1] Am. should be, 'As I reprimanded thee freely, with reproof, do thou also, if thou call a man &c.'

ϩⲛ̄ⲧ ?
? ?
ⲥⲉⲛⲁϯ ⲙⲁ ⲁⲛ' ⲛ-
ϩⲏⲧⲟⲩ ⲛ̄ⲟⲩϫⲁⲓ-
ⲙⲱⲛ ⲛ̄ⲧⲉⲓ̈ⲙⲓⲛⲉ
ϩⲛ̄ⲗⲁⲁⲩ ⲛ̄ϩⲱⲃ·
ⲁⲗⲗⲁ ⲟⲩⲁⲅⲁⲑⲟⲛ
ⲛⲁ̣ⲩⲡ̣ⲉ ⲉⲧⲣⲉ̣ⲩϥⲓ̣'

ⲟⲩϫⲡ̣ⲁ̣ⲛ . ⲁϫⲓ̣
ϩⲛ̄ⲛϣⲁϫⲉ ⲉ[ⲛⲧ]ⲁ̣ϥ-[a]
ϫⲟⲟⲩ ⲛⲏⲧⲛ̄· ⲁⲗ-
ⲗⲁ ϫⲱⲕ ⲉⲃⲟⲗ' ⲛ̣̄-

[a] Or]ⲁⲓ.

Fol. 16. *Recto* (*v.* Am. 424). . . . the end (*συντέλεια*) [. . . of the] age (? *αἰών*), they not . . .[1] them from out their pollutions wherein they . . . themselves . . . . .

. . . When our father Pahômius saw a spirit (*πν.*) of fornication (*πορνεία*) and pollution passing (*παράγειν*) among the brethren, while they worked in a (certain) place, he gathered them together at evening, according to (*κατά*) their custom (*συνήθεια*). He said unto them, 'Remember the word that is written,[2] that Belief (*πίσ.*) is of [hearing . . . . .

Verso (*v.* Am. 424). . . . wherein they have been, they are therein[3] now also and do walk in the world (*κόσ.*). Now (*μέν*) I know that . . . . . will not give place in themselves unto a demon (*δαίμων*) such as this, in anything. But (*ἀλλά*) it (were) good (*ἀγαθός*) for them that they bear . . . . .
. . . by the words that he (?)[4] spake unto you. But (*ἀλλά*) fulfil . . . . .

Fol. 17. ↑ *Recto.*

ⲧ[
ⲡⲉ[a] ϣⲁⲉⲛ̣[ⲉϩ
ⲡϫⲟ̣ⲉⲓⲥ . [ⲉⲃⲟⲗ]
ϫⲉⲁⲩⲧⲟ[ϣⲟⲩ ϩⲙ̄-]
ⲡⲉⲩϩⲏⲧ [ⲙ̄ⲙⲓⲛ ⲙ̄-]
ⲙⲟⲟⲩ ⲉⲩϩ̣[b]

[a] Perhaps ϣⲱ]ⲡⲉ. [b] Apparently not ⲉⲩϫ[ⲟⲟⲥ or ϫ[ⲱ ⲙⲙⲟⲥ.

[1] Fut. indic. or part. pres.

[2] Rom. x. 17 (probably; *ed.* Wessely, *Stud.* xii. 157).

[3] Or 'have been ashamed, they are ashamed now also'.

[4] Or 'that I'.

ϫⲉⲡⲉⲩⲟ[ⲉⲓϣ ⲧⲏⲣ̄ϥ]
ⲉ̣ⲧ̣ⲙ̣. . [ⲛ̄-]
ϩⲏⲧ̣[ϥ] ϩⲓϫⲙ̄ⲡⲕⲁϩ
ⲛ̄ⲧ̣ⲛⲛⲁ̣ⲣⲁⲕⲧ̄ⲛ
ⲁⲛ ⲉⲃⲟⲗ ⲙ̄ⲡⲉⲕⲟⲩ-
ⲱϣ' ⲕ̣ⲁ̣[ⲛ] ⲉⲕ[ϣ]ⲁ̣ⲛ-
ⲕⲁⲁⲛ ϣⲁⲧⲥⲩⲛⲧⲉ-
ⲗⲉⲓⲁ ⲙ̄ⲡⲁⲓⲱⲛ·
ⲛⲁϊ ⲇⲉ [ⲛ̄]ⲧⲉϊⲙⲓ-
ⲛⲉ ⲕⲁ[ⲛ ⲟ]ⲩⲣⲟⲙⲡⲉ
ⲛ̄ⲟⲩⲱⲧ [ⲧ]ⲉⲧⲟⲩ-
ⲛⲁⲁⲁⲥ ⲉⲩ[ϩⲩ]ⲡⲟⲙⲓ-
ⲛⲉ ⲉⲡϫⲟⲉ[ⲓⲥ] ⲏ (+) ⲙⲏ-
ⲧⲉ ⲛ̄ⲣⲟⲙⲡⲉ· ⲏ (sic) ϩⲟⲩⲟ
ⲉⲛⲁϊ ⲉⲩⲡⲟⲗⲓⲧⲉⲩⲉ
ⲕⲁⲧⲁ ⲡⲧⲱϣ ⲛ̄ϩⲏⲧ'

? [
ϣⲁ̣[
ⲡⲣ̣[
ϫⲓ̣ⲛ̣[
ⲁ̣. ⲃⲉⲗ̣[
⁊ⲙ̣̄ⲡ̄ⲛ̣̄[ⲥ [a]
ⲕⲁ ⲧⲟⲟⲧ[ⲟⲩ
ϩⲙ̄ⲡⲧ[ⲣⲉ
ϩⲏⲧ' ϩⲙ̄ⲡ̣ⲟⲩⲉⲕ̣[ϩⲩ-]
ⲡⲟⲙⲓⲛ[ⲉ] ⲧⲏⲣⲟ[ⲩ ⲛ̄-]
ⲧⲁⲩⲁⲁⲩ̣ [b] [ⲉ]ⲧ̣ⲣⲁ̣ⲛⲁ[ϥ]
ⲙ̄ⲡϫⲟⲉ[ⲓⲥ] ⲁⲩⲱ ⲉⲩ[ϯ]
ⲟⲩⲃⲉ'ⲡ[ⲇ]ⲓⲁⲃⲟⲗⲟⲥ
ϩⲱⲥⲧ[ⲉ .]. ⲓ̣ⲛⲉ[

margin

⁊ⲙ̄ⲡ̄ⲛ̄[

[a] Paragraph-mark very doubtful. Can the similar mark and words in smaller script, below the text, have reference to this? [b] One is tempted to read ϩⲙⲡⲟⲩⲉ ⲛ[ⲁⲓ ⲛ]ⲧⲉⲓⲙⲓⲛ[ⲉ] ⲧⲏⲣⲥ (or -ⲟ[ⲩ]) [ⲉⲛ]ⲧⲁⲩⲁⲁⲥ [ⲉ]ⲩⲣⲁⲛⲁ[ϥ].

→ *Verso.*

]ⲃ̄

ⲛ]ⲁϣⲱⲡⲉ
[ϣⲁⲉⲛⲉ]ϩ' ϩⲛ̄ⲧⲙ̄ⲛ̄-
[ⲧⲉⲣⲟ ⲉ]ⲛ̣ⲧⲁⲩⲥⲃ̄-
[ⲧⲱⲧ̄ϥ] ⲛⲁⲩ ϫⲓⲛ-
[ⲧⲕⲁⲧⲁ]ⲃⲟⲗⲏ ⲙ̄-
[ⲡⲕⲟⲥ]ⲙⲟⲥ ⲉⲃⲟⲗ
[ϫⲉⲁⲩϣ]ⲱⲡⲉ ⲉⲩ-

]ⲱ̣ⲡⲉ̣
ⲉ]ⲧⲃⲉ-
]ⲛ̣ⲛⲣⲱ-
[ⲙⲉ]ⲡⲇⲓⲁⲃⲟ-
[ⲗⲟⲥ] ? ϣⲟ̣
]ⲉ̣ⲟⲩⲟ.
]ⲃ̣ . . . ⲩ̣ⲱ
ⲉⲛ]ⲧⲁϥⲣ̄ⲁⲛⲁϥ
]ϩ̣ . ⲥ̣ ⲁϥϣ̣ⲱ̣-
ⲡ̣ⲉ ⲛⲁⲧⲛⲟⲃⲉ ⲙ̄-
[ⲡ]ⲉϥⲙ̄ⲧⲟ ⲉⲃⲟⲗ · ⲧ̄ⲛ̄-
ϩ̣ⲏ̣ⲩ ⲉⲓ̣ⲉ̣ⲣⲓ̣ⲭⲱ
ⲙ̣̄ⲛ̄ⲥⲟ[ⲇ]ⲟⲙⲁ' ⲙ̄ⲛ̄-
. ⲁ . ⲉ̣ⲣ̣[.]ⲉⲗⲁⲙⲁ̣ .[a]
[ⲙ]ⲛⲥⲉⲃ[ⲟⲓ]ⲙ' ⲉⲁⲩ-
]ⲩⲕⲱ

ⲛϩ̣ⲟ̣ⲧ' ⲙ̄ⲡϫⲟⲉⲓⲥ
ⲕⲁⲧⲁ ⲧⲇⲓⲁ̣ⲑⲏⲕⲏ
ⲉⲛⲧⲁⲩⲥ̄ⲙ̄ⲛ̄ⲧ̄ⲥ̄
ⲛ̄ⲙ̄ⲙⲁϥ · ⲧⲁї ⲟⲛ-
ⲧⲉ ϭⲉ ⲛ̄ⲛ̄ⲣⲉϥⲣⲛⲟ̣-
ⲃⲉ ⲉⲛⲧⲁⲩⲧⲟϣⲟⲩ
ⲉ̣ⲣⲛⲟ̣[ⲃⲉ] ⲙ̄ⲛ̄ⲛⲉⲧ-
ⲙⲏⲛ [ⲉⲃⲟ]ⲗ' ϩ̄ⲙ̄-
ⲡⲥⲱ[ⲱ]ϥ ⲉⲛⲧⲁⲩ-
ⲣ̄ϫⲟ[ⲉⲓⲥ] ⲉⲣⲟⲟⲩ ⲛ̄ϩ[ⲏ-]
ⲧⲟⲩ [ϩⲓ]ⲧ̄ⲙ̄ⲡⲇⲓⲁ-
ⲃⲟⲗⲟⲥ ⲙ̄ⲛ̄ⲛⲉϥⲇⲁ[ⲓ-]
ⲙⲱⲛ ⲛⲁї ⲉⲛⲧⲁ[ⲩ-]
ϣⲱⲡⲉ ⲛⲁϥ ⲛ-
ϣⲏⲣⲉ · ⲛ̄ⲑⲉ ⲉⲧ-
ⲥⲏϩ ϩ̄ⲙ̄ⲡⲉⲩⲁⲅ-

margin

[a] One is tempted to read ⲉⲗⲁⲙ or ⲁⲇⲁⲙⲁ, preceded by ⲥⲉⲗⲗⲁⲥⲁⲣ or ⲅⲟⲙⲟⲣⲣⲁ. Jericho elsewhere always ϩⲓⲉⲣⲓⲭⲱ.

Fol. 17. *Recto* (*v.* Am. 425). . . . unto everlasting . . . the Lord,[1] because they have decided in their own heart, being . . ., that ['All] the time [where]in we . . . upon the earth, we will not decline from Thy will, even (κἄν) shouldest Thou suffer us until the end (συντέλεια) of the age (αἰών).' Those of this sort, whether (κἄν) it be a single year that they shall pass, waiting for (ὑπομένειν) the Lord, or (ἤ) ten years, or (ἤ) more than these, living (πολιτεύειν) according to (κατά) the decision of heart [2] [which . . . .[3] afterwards (?) . . . desist . . . while . . . .[4] all their perseverance (? ὑπομένειν) that they have done,[4] pleasing the Lord and resisting the devil (δι.), so that (ὥστε) . . . . .

[1] Am. should be, 'And those shall be like unto the Lord; they have decided in themselves saying, in presence of the Lord, with a good conscience and sure, If Thou leave us on the earth unto the end, we will not decline from Thy will; but all our time for which Thou shalt leave us on the earth, we will continue in Thy will, even shouldest Thou leave us unto the end of the age.'

[2] Am. *sic.*

[3] This passage not in Am.

[4] Slight alterations would give, 'afar off, all such-like things that they have done'; but grammatically the changes are hardly admissible.

Verso (*v.* Am. 425, 426). ...[1] the devil (*διάβ.*) .... that pleased him ... he was (?) sinless before Him ..... Jericho and Sodom and ... and (?) Elam (?) and Seboim,[2] that did .....

... shall be for ever in the kingdom that hath been prepared for them since the foundation (*κατ.*) of the world (*κόσ.*); because that they have been faithful unto the Lord, according unto the covenant (*κατά, διαθ.*) which they did establish with Him. And[3] this likewise is the fashion of the sinners that have decided to sin[4] and those that remain in pollution, whereby the devil (*διάβ.*) and his demons (*δαίμ.*) have lordship over them; unto whom they are become children; as it is written in the Gospel (*εὐ.*).....

Fol. 18. ↑ *Recto.*

ⲧ̄ϥ̣ϫⲛ̣ⲟⲩ̣[a] ⲡⲉⲧⲉϣ̣-
ϣⲉ ⲉ̣ϫⲛⲟⲩϥ ⲁⲩⲱ ⲙ̣-
ⲡ̣ⲟⲩϫ̣ⲟⲟⲩϥ · ϫⲉⲕⲁⲥ
ⲛ̄ⲛⲉⲡϫⲁϫⲉ ϯ ϩⲏⲩ
ⲛ̄ϩⲏⲧ,ⲧⲏⲩⲧⲛ̄ ⲉ- (*sic*)
ⲡ̣ⲧⲏⲣ̄ϥ̄ ⲕⲁⲧⲁ ⲑⲉ
[ⲉ]ⲧⲥⲏϩ’ · ⲛ̄ⲧⲉⲣⲟⲩ-
ⲥⲱⲧⲙ ⲇⲉ ⲉⲛⲁ̣ⲓ̣̈ ⲛ̄ϭⲓ
[ϩⲟⲉⲓⲛⲉ ⲛ̄ϩ́ⲏⲧⲟⲩ]
ⲉϩⲉⲛⲁⲛⲁⲭⲱⲣⲓⲧⲏⲥ-
ⲛ̣ⲉ ⲛ̄ϣⲟ̣ⲣⲡ ⲉⲙⲡⲁ-
ⲧⲟⲩⲉⲓ’ ⲉ̣ⲧⲕⲟⲓⲛⲱⲛⲓⲁ
ⲁⲩⲗⲩⲡⲉⲓ’ ⲉⲙⲁⲧⲉ ϩ̄ⲙ̄-

→ *Verso.*

[ⲡⲕⲟⲥ]ⲙ̣ⲟ̣ⲥ̣ · ⲁⲗⲗ[ⲁ]
ⲁ̣ⲛⲟⲛ ⲙ̄ⲛ̄ⲛ̄ⲥⲁⲡⲥⲟ-
ⲟⲩⲛ ⲙ̄ⲡⲛⲟⲩⲧⲉ, ⲛ̄-
ⲛⲉⲥϣⲱⲡⲉ ⲉⲧⲣⲉⲛ̣-
ⲉⲓ’ ⲉϩⲣⲁ̈ⲓ ⲉⲛⲉⲓ̈ϫⲱ-
ϩ̄ⲙ̄ ⲛ̄ⲧⲉⲓ̈ⲙⲓⲛⲉ ·
ⲁⲩⲱ ⲁⲩⲣ̄ⲧⲉⲩϣ̣[ⲏ]
ⲧⲏⲣ̄ⲥ̄ ⲉⲧ̄ⲙ̄ⲙ̄ⲁⲩ [ⲉⲩ-]
ⲙⲟⲕ̄ϩ̄ ⲛ̄ϩⲏⲧ ⲁⲩⲱ
ⲉⲩⲕⲣ̄ⲙ̄ⲣ̄ⲙ̄ ⲉⲧⲃⲉⲛ-
ϣⲁϫⲉ ⲉⲛⲧⲁⲩⲥⲟⲧ-
ⲙⲟⲩ · ⲛ̄ⲧⲉⲣⲟⲩⲧⲱ-
ⲟⲩⲛ ⲇⲉ ⲉϩⲧⲟⲟⲩⲉ ⲉ-

[a] Or ⲧⲙϫⲛⲟⲩ.

[1] This passage not in Am.

[2] *Cf.* Gen. xiv. 1, 2. It is difficult to complete the names satisfactorily.

[3] Am., 'Even thus also the sinners that have decided to sin and that remain in pollutions which do rule over them by means of the devil and his demons; these (it is) that are become children unto him, and they shall be children also unto him in punishment for ever.'

[4] 'Those (for whom) it hath been decided that they should sin' is grammatically possible.

ⲡⲉⲩϩⲏⲧ' ⲉⲩϫⲱ ⲙ̄ⲙ̄-'
ⲙⲟⲥ ϫⲉϩⲉⲛⲟⲩ'ⲛⲉ ⲛⲉï-
ϣⲁϫⲉ ⲛ̄ⲧⲉïⲙⲓⲛⲉ·
]ⲉ̣ⲣⲏⲥ ·[a] ⲉϥⲉⲁⲁⲛ ⲛ̄ⲁⲅⲣⲓⲟⲥ ⲉ-
]ϣⲁ ⲛⲉⲛⲉⲣⲏⲩ· ⲙⲏ ⲟⲩⲛ̄-
]ϫ̣ⲛ̄ ⲗⲁⲁⲩ, ⲛ̄ⲥϩⲓⲙⲉ ⲛ̄ϩⲏ-
]ϣⲱ- ⲧⲛ̄· ⲙⲏ ⲁⲛⲟⲛ ⲧⲏⲣⲛ̄
]ⲡ̣ⲉ ⲛⲉⲛϣⲟⲟⲡ' ⲁⲛ', ⲕⲁⲧⲁ
margin

ⲣⲉⲛⲉⲥⲛⲏⲩ ⲛⲁⲃⲱⲕ
ⲉⲣϩⲱⲃ' ⲉⲙⲡⲟⲩⲃⲱⲕ
ⲡ̄ⲙ̄ⲙⲁⲩ· ⲉⲁⲩⲁⲅⲁ-
ⲛⲁⲕⲧⲉⲓ̄ⲡⲉ' ⲉϫⲛ̄-
ⲡⲉⲛⲧⲁⲩⲥⲟⲧⲙⲟⲩ· ⲛ[
ⲙ̄ⲡⲛⲁⲩ ⲇⲉ ⲛ̄ϫⲡ- ⲡ[
ϥⲧⲟ' ⲉⲓⲥ ϩⲉⲛⲙⲟⲛⲁ- ϣ[
ⲭⲟⲥ ⲁⲩⲉⲓ' ⲉⲁⲡⲁⲛⲧⲁ ⲙ[
ⲉⲡⲉⲛⲉⲓⲱⲧ' ⲡⲁ- ⲓ̣[
ⲥⲡ̣[
margin

[a] Perhaps ⲥ]ⲉⲣⲏⲥ.

Fol. 18. *Recto* (*v.* Am. 427). . . . while they ?] are awake[1] . . . . . not (?) to ask that which it is meet to ask and he hath not been sent,[2] lest the enemy have profit of you at all, as it is written.[3] But (δέ) when certain of them heard these (words), that were aforetime anchorites (*ἀναχ.*) ere they had come to the community (*κοινωνία*), they were much grieved (*λυπεῖν*) in their heart, saying,[4] 'What are words such as these? He would make us ill-disposed (*ἄγριος*) one to another. Is there (*μή*) any woman among us? Are (*μή*) not we all according to (*κατά*) . . . . .

Verso (*v.* Am. 427). . . . the wor]ld (? *κόσ.*). But (*ἀλλά*), after the knowledge of God, let it not be that we descend to pollutions such as these.' And they passed all that night sad at heart and murmuring because of the words that they had heard. But (*δέ*) when they arose in the morning, when the brethren were about to go forth to work, they went not with them, being indignant (*ἀγανακτεῖν*) at that which they had heard. And (*δέ*) at the fourth hour,[5] lo, there came monks (*μον.*) to meet with (*ἀπαντᾶν*) our father Pahômius . . . . .

[1] Difficult to accommodate this to Am. Relates perhaps to the precepts as to sleeping.

[2] *I.e.* unless he hath been sent = Am. 'without a mission.'

[3] Ps. lxxxviii. 22.

[4] Am. should be, saying one to another, 'What is this word? He hath made us odious and estranged one from another.'

[5] Am. *om.*

Fol. 19. → *Recto.*

ⲧ]ⲙ̣ⲛ̄ⲧ̣ⲙⲁⲓ̈-
[ϣⲙ̄ⲙⲟ ϫⲉ[a]] ⲙ̄ⲡⲣ̄ⲣ̄-
[ⲡⲉⲥⲱ]ⲃϣ· ϩⲓⲧⲛ̣̄-
[ⲧⲁⲓ ⲅⲁ]ⲣ ⲁ̣ϩⲟ̣ⲉ̣ⲓ̣ⲛ̣ⲉ̣[b]
[ϣⲡ] ϩⲉⲛⲁⲅⲅⲉⲗⲟⲥ
ⲉⲣⲟ̣ⲟ̣ⲩ ⲉⲛⲥⲉⲥⲟⲟⲩⲛ
ⲁⲛ· ⲡⲉⲓ̈ⲣⲱⲙⲉ
ⲅⲁⲣ ⲉ̣ϯ[ⲛ]ⲁⲩ ⲉⲣⲟϥ
ⲟⲩⲥ̣ⲙⲟ̣[ⲧ] ⲛ̄ⲁⲅⲅⲉ-
ⲗⲟⲥ ⲡⲉⲧⲙ̄ⲙⲟϥ·
ⲁϥⲟⲩⲱϣⲃ̄ ϫⲉ ⲛ̄ϭⲓ
ⲑⲉⲟⲇⲱⲣⲟⲥ ⲡⲉϫⲁϥ

ⲥϩ[ⲁⲓ . . . .[c] ⲛ̄ⲧⲉⲓ-]
ϩⲉ [ⲉϥϫⲱ ⲙ̄ⲙⲟⲥ]
ϫⲉⲡ̣[
ⲧ̄ⲛ̄ⲛ[ⲟⲟⲩϥ
ⲉ̣ⲧⲉⲡ̣[
ⲡⲉ ⲛ[
ⲛ̄ϭⲟⲟⲩ[ⲛⲉ ⲡⲉⲓⲱⲧ-]
ⲡⲉ ⲉ̣ⲩⲥⲟ̣[ⲟⲩϩ̄ⲥ̄ ϩⲁϩ-]
ⲧⲏⲛ ⲁⲩ̣[ⲱ ⲟⲩⲡⲣⲉ-]
[ⲥ]ⲃ̣ⲩⲧⲉⲣ̣[ⲟⲥ
? [

margin

[a] ϫⲉ inserted in order adequately to fill the gap.

[b] Here (and in line 6) scarce a letter can be read, but what remains guarantees the citation.

[c] ⲥϩ[ⲁⲓⲥⲟⲩ ('letters') or ⲥϩ[ⲁⲓ ⲙ̄ⲙⲟⲥ ('epistle').

→ *Verso.*

]ⲱ
ⲕⲛ]ⲁ̣ϯ
]ϩ̣ⲏⲧϥ̄·
]. ⲡⲉ,
]ϩⲓⲧⲙ̄-
[ⲡⲛⲟⲩⲧⲉ]· ⲉϣⲱ-
[ⲡⲉ ⲙⲉⲛ ⲉⲕ]ϣⲁⲛϯ
[ⲙⲉⲧⲁⲛⲟⲓ]ⲁ ⲛⲁϥ
[ⲧ̄ⲛ̄ⲛⲁϯ ϩⲱ]ⲱⲛ· ⲉⲕ-
[ϣⲁⲛⲛⲟ]ϫϥ̄ ϫⲉ ⲉⲃⲟⲗ.
]ⲉ̣ ⲛⲟⲩϫⲉ̣

ⲧⲉ̣ϥⲙⲛ[ⲧ̄ⲡⲣⲉⲥⲃⲩ-]
ⲧⲉⲣⲟⲥ· ⲛ̄ⲥ̣[ⲉⲛⲟϫϥ̄]
ⲉⲃⲟⲗ ϩ̄ⲛ̄ⲧ[ⲥⲟⲟⲩϩ̄ⲥ̄]
ⲉⲧϥ̄ⲛ̄ϩⲏ[ⲧ̄ⲥ̄· ⲙⲁ-]
ⲣⲉϥⲃⲱⲕ' ⲉⲕⲉⲙⲁ
ⲛ̄ϥ̄ⲁⲛⲁⲭⲱⲣⲉⲓ' ⲛ̄ϥ̄-
ⲉⲓⲣⲉ ⲛ̄ⲟⲩⲣ[ⲟ]ⲙⲡⲉ
ϩ̄ⲙ̄ⲡⲙ̄[ⲁ ⲉ]ⲧ̄ⲙ̄ⲙⲁⲩ.
ⲛ̄ⲧⲉⲧⲙ̄ⲗⲁⲁⲩ
ϣⲗⲏⲗ' ⲛ̄ⲙ̄ⲙⲁϥ.
ⲟⲩⲧⲉ ⲟⲩⲱⲙ· ⲁⲩⲱ

margin

Fol. 19. *Recto* (*v.* Am. 428). . . . But (? δέ) love unto strangers neglect not; for (γάρ) thereby have some received unto themselves angels (ἄγ.) and knew it not.[1] For (γάρ) this man that I see, an angel's form is his.'[2] But (δέ) Theodore answered and said, ...

. . . had] written [it ?] thus, [saying,] . . . . . [that I] send [thee] . . . . of sackcloth is [the father] of a con[gregation under] us and (?) [a pres]-byter (πρεσβ.) . . . . .

Verso (*v.* Am. 429). . . . the judgement that thou] shalt (?) give . . . . . from [God[3]]. Now (μέν) if thou wilt grant repentance (μετάν.) unto him, [we] also will [grant (it)]; but (δέ) if thou cast him forth, ... cast [him forth . . . . .

. . . his presbytership (-πρεσβ.) and (let them) cast him forth from the [congregation] where[in] he is. [Let] him go unto another place and live apart (ἀναχωρεῖν) and pass a year there, and let none pray with him, neither (οὐδέ) eat. And . . . . .

Fol. 20. ↑ *Recto.*

]ⲧ
] ?
]. ⲛⲁϥ · ⲁⲛ[ⲉ-]
[ⲥⲛ]ⲏⲩ ⲁⲙⲁϩⲧⲉ ⲙ̄-

[. . .]ⲩ[a] ⲛ[ⲧⲉϣⲧⲏⲛ ⲛ̄-]
[ⲧ]ⲙ[ⲛ]ⲧⲙⲟ[ⲛⲁⲭⲟⲥ]
ⲉⲧϩⲓⲱⲱϥ [ⲁⲩⲱ]
ⲁϥϯ ϩⲓⲱⲱ[ϥ ⲛⲟⲩ-]
ϣⲧⲏⲛ ⲛ̄ⲕⲟⲥ[ⲙⲓ-]
ⲕⲟⲛ ⲁϥⲕⲁⲁϥ ⲉⲃ[ⲟⲗ]
ⲉⲧⲣⲉϥⲃⲱⲕ' ⲁϥ-
ⲟⲩⲉϩⲥⲁϩⲛⲉ ⲇⲉ ⲟⲛ
ⲉⲛ̄ ϩⲉⲛϭⲉⲣⲟⲟⲃ' ⲁϥ-
ϩⲓⲟⲩⲉ̄ ⲉⲡⲕⲟⲩϊ ⲉⲧ[ⲙ̄ⲙ̄-]
ⲙⲁⲩ · ⲙ̄ⲡⲛ̄ⲥⲱⲥ

margin

[a] Perhaps ⲕⲁϩⲏ]ⲩ or ⲙⲙⲁ]ⲩ.

[1] Heb. xiii. 2. [2] Stern, *Gr.* § 298 (4). [3] Am., 'from Him.'

↑ *Verso.*

[. . . .]ⲇⲉ ⲙ̄[ⲙⲟϥ
[ⲉⲧⲙ̄]ⲧⲣⲉϥⲙⲟⲟϣ[ⲉ]
[ⲙⲛ̄ⲣ]ⲱⲙⲉ ⲉⲛ̄ϥ-
[ⲛ]ⲁϯ ϩⲏⲩ, ⲁⲛ ⲛ̄ⲙ-
[ⲙ]ⲁϥ· ⲉϣⲱⲡⲉ ⲇⲉ
[ⲉ]ϥϣⲁⲛⲧⲙ̄ⲥⲱ-
[ⲧ]ⲙ̄ ⲛ̄ⲥⲱⲧⲛ̄ ⲁⲗⲗⲁ
ⲛ̄ϥϣⲱⲡⲉ ϩⲛ̄ⲟⲩ-
ⲙⲛ̄ⲧⲁⲧⲥⲃⲱ,
ⲛⲟⲩϫⲉ ⲙ̄ⲙⲟϥ' ⲉ-[a]

[ⲱ] ⲡ̣ⲉ̣ⲛⲉⲓ̣[ⲱⲧ ⲛ̄ⲧⲟⲕ]
ⲉⲧϣⲓⲛⲉ ⲛ[ⲥⲁⲛⲉⲛ-]
ⲯⲩⲭⲏ ⲉⲧⲟⲩϫ̣[ⲱⲟⲩ]
~ ~ ~ ~ ~ ~

margin

[a] ⲉ[ⲃⲟⲗ.

Fol. 20. *Recto* (*v.* Am. 429, 430). . . . him. The brethren laid hold[1] on him . . . . .

. . . [the robe of] monkhood (-*μον.*) that was upon him [and] he put upon him [a] worldling's (*κοσμικός*) garment and let him go that he should depart.[2] And (*δέ*) he bade moreover bring staves and he beat that young(er) one. Thereafter . . . . .

Verso (*v.* Am. 430). . . . but (*δέ*) [counsel] him that he walk not [with a] man of whom he getteth not profit. But (*δέ*) if he shall not hearken unto you, but (*ἀλλά*) remain unteachable, cast him [forth . . . . .

. . . [O] our fath[er,[3] thou it is] dost seek after [our] souls, to save [them.]

Here an ornament, indicating the end of a section.

[1] Am., 'hindered.' [2] Am., *add.* to the world (*sic*). [3] Am. *om.*

Fol. 21. → *Recto.*

ⲉϣⲁⲣⲉ ⲡⲉ]ⲛ-
[ⲉⲓ]ⲱ̣ⲧ̣ ⲡⲁϩⲱ[ⲙⲉ]
[ⲁϩⲉⲣ]ⲁ̣ⲧϥ ⲛ̄ϩⲏⲧϥ
[ⲁⲩⲱ] ⲡⲉⲛⲉⲓⲱⲧ' ⲡⲁ-
[ϩⲱ]ⲙⲉ ϩⲱⲱϥ' ⲛⲉϥ-
[ⲁϩ]ⲉⲣⲁⲧϥ̄ ϩⲱⲥ ⲉⲟⲩⲁ'

[ⲛ]ⲟⲩⲟⲉ̣ⲓ̣[ϣ ⲛⲓⲙ ⲁϥ-]
ⲁⲣⲭⲉⲓ̈ ⲛ̄[[a]
ⲛ̄ⲕⲁⲑⲏⲕⲉⲓ ⲛ̄[ⲛⲉ-]
ⲥⲛⲏⲩ· ⲡⲁⲓ̈ⲡⲉ [ⲡϣⲟ-]
ⲣ̄ⲡ ⲛ̄ϩⲣⲏⲧⲟⲛ ⲉ[ⲛ-]
ⲧⲁϥϫⲟⲟϥ' ⲉⲃⲟⲗ' ϩⲛ̄-
ⲛⲉⲅⲣⲁⲫⲏ ϫⲉⲙⲟⲩ-
ⲧⲉ ⲉⲛⲉϩⲓⲟⲙⲉ ⲛ̄ⲣⲉϥ-
ⲧⲟⲉⲓⲧ' ⲙⲁⲣⲟⲩⲉⲓ'·
ϫⲟⲟⲩ ⲛ̄ⲥⲁⲛ̄[ⲥ]ⲁⲃⲏ
ⲙⲁⲣⲟⲩⲟⲩⲱⲛ, ⲛ̄ⲣⲱⲟ[ⲩ]

margin

[a] Perhaps ⲡ[ⲧⲉⲩⲛⲟⲩ].

↑ *Verso.*

]ⲛⲧ[
] ⲁⲩⲱ ⲛ̄ⲁϣ
[ⲛ̄ϩⲉ ⲛ̄]ⲧ̣ⲱⲧⲛ̄ ⲁⲧⲉ-
[ⲧⲛ̄]ϣⲱⲡⲉ ϩⲛⲟⲩ-
[ⲙ̄]ⲛⲧϫⲁⲥⲓϩⲏⲧ .·
ⲉⲁⲧⲉⲧⲛ̄ⲕⲉⲧ'ⲧⲏⲩ-
ⲧⲛ̄ ⲉⲛⲁϩⲟⲩ ⲉⲧⲙ̄-
ⲥⲱⲧⲙ̄ ⲉⲛϣⲁϫⲉ ⲙ̄-
ⲡⲛⲟⲩⲧⲉ· ⲏ̄ ⲙⲉ-
ϣⲁⲕ' ⲙ̄ⲡⲉⲧⲛ̄ⲥⲱⲧⲙ
ⲉⲧⲃⲉⲡϫⲟⲉⲓⲥ ⲛ̄ⲑⲉ

ⲡ̣ⲉ ⲧⲉⲛⲟ̣ⲩ [†ϫⲱ]
ⲙ̄ⲙⲟⲥ ⲛⲏⲧ[ⲛ ϫⲉ-]
ⲡⲉⲓ̈ⲛⲟⲃⲉ ⲉⲛⲧ[ⲁⲧⲉ-]
ⲧⲛ̄ⲁⲁϥ' ⲛ̄ⲥⲉⲕ[ⲁⲁϥ]

margin

Fol. 21. *Recto* (*v.* Am. 431). . . . wherein our father Pahômius was [wont to] stand, while our father Pahômius stood as if (ὡς) (he were) one . . . . .

. . . [at all] times, [he] began (ἄρχειν) [? forthwith] to instruct (κατηχεῖν[1]) the brethren. This is the first word (ῥητόν) that he spake from the scriptures (γρ.),[2] 'Call the mourning women; let them come. Send for the wise women; let them open [their] mouths . . . . .

Verso (*v.* Am. 431, 432). . . . And [how] is it ye have been in pride of heart, having turned you back, not to hear the word of God? Or (ἤ) perchance ye have not heard concerning the Lord, how . . . . .

. . . Now [I say] unto you, this sin that ye [have] done, [it] shall not be forgiven.

Fol. 22. ↑ *Recto.*

[ⲛⲁⲩ] ⲉ̣ⲣⲟϥ' ⲙ̣[ⲙⲓⲛ ⲙ̄-]
ⲙⲟϥ ⲉϥⲃⲏⲕ ⲉϩⲟ[ⲩⲛ]
[ⲉ]ⲡⲉϥⲥⲱⲙⲁ· ϩⲁϩ
[ⲇ]ⲉ ⲟⲛ ϩ̄ⲛ̄ⲛ̄ⲛⲟϭ ⲉⲧ-
ⲡⲟⲗⲓⲧⲉⲩⲉ ϩ̄ⲛ̄ⲛⲉ-
ⲥⲛⲏⲩ. ⲉⲃⲟⲗ' ⲙ̄ⲡ̄ⲧ̄ⲃ̄-
ⲃⲟ [ⲙ̄]ⲡⲉⲩϩⲏⲧ' ⲙ̄ⲛ̄-
[ⲡⲉⲩ]ⲥⲱⲙⲁ· ⲛⲉⲩ-
[ⲛⲁⲩ] ⲉϩⲁϩ ⲛ̄ϭⲱ̄ⲗ̄ⲡ̄
[ⲉⲃⲟⲗ] ϩⲓϩⲟⲣⲁⲙⲁ·

margin

margin

→ *Verso.*

margin

[. . . .]ϩ ⲛⲥ̣ⲉ̣[. . .]
[. . . .]ⲉⲡⲉⲓ̈ϩⲱⲃ̣
ⲛ̄ⲁⲡⲓⲥⲧⲟⲛ ⲛ̄ⲛⲁ-
ϩⲣⲁϥ' ⲉⲧⲣⲉϥϣ̣[ⲱ-]
ⲡⲉ ⲛⲉϥⲛ̄ⲧⲟⲟ[ⲧ̄ϥ̄]
ⲙⲉⲛ, ϩⲱⲥ ⲣⲱⲙⲉ ⲛ-
ⲧⲉ ⲡⲛⲟⲩⲧⲉ. ⲁⲗⲗ[ⲁ]
ϩ̄ⲙ̄ⲡⲉⲓ̈ϩⲱⲃ' [.]ⲉ.[
ⲧⲥ̣. . . . . [
ⲉⲣⲟϥ· ⲁⲥϣⲱ[ⲡⲉ]
ⲇⲉ ⲛ̄ⲧⲉⲣⲟⲩ[

margin

Fol. 22. *Recto* (*v.* Am. 432). . . . [saw?] it[3] [him]self, entering into his body (σῶμα). And (δέ) many also of the elders (*lit.* great-ones) that lived religiously (πολιτεύειν) among the brethren, by reason of the purity [of] their heart and [their] body (σῶ.), beheld many revelations and visions (ὅραμα) . . . . .

[1] That this is the true equivalent of the persistent Coptic form ⲕⲁⲑⲏⲅⲉⲓ is clear from *e.g.* Luke i. 4, Acts xviii. 25, 1 Cor. xiv. 19.

[2] Jer. ix. 17.

[3] The pronoun being masculine, must refer to πνεῦμα, not to ψυχή.

Verso (*v.* Am. 433?). . . . this faithless (ἄπιστος) act (*lit.* thing) before him, that it should befall. He was indeed (μέν) with him (*or* me *or* them) as a man of God; yet (ἀλλά) in this matter . . . . . him. And (δέ) it befell, after they had . . . .

Fol. 23. → *Recto* (?).

ⲉ-]
ϣⲱⲡ̣[ⲉ ⲉϥϣⲁⲛ-]
ϫⲟⲟⲥ̣ ⲛ[ⲁⲓ ϫⲉ-]
ⲱ̣ⲛ̣ϩ̣·[
]ⲱⲡⲉ ϫⲉϯⲛⲁ[ⲱⲛϩ ⲉϥ-]
]ⲧ̣ⲕⲁ ϣⲁⲛϫⲟⲟ[ⲥ ϫⲉ
margin

↑ *Verso* (?).

] ⲉϥⲉⲓⲣⲉ
[ⲙ̄ⲡⲙⲉⲉⲩⲉ] ⲙⲡϣⲁϫⲉ ⲡⲉ[
[ⲉⲧⲥⲏϩ ϩ̄ⲙ̄]ⲡⲉⲩⲁⲅ- ⲛⲁⲩ [
[ⲅⲉⲗⲓⲟⲛ] ϫⲉⲙⲉⲣⲉⲛⲉ- ⲉⲃⲟⲗ [
margin

Fol. 23. *Recto* (?) (*v.* Am. 433?). . . . 'If so be [he should] say unto me, Live, ...[1] that I shall [live. But (δέ)] if he should say . . . . .

Verso (?). . . . remem[bering] the word [that is written in] the Gos[pel],[2] 'Love . . . . .

Fol. 24. ↑ *Recto.*

ⲁⲥϩⲉ [ⲉϫⲙ̄ⲡⲕⲁϩ]
ⲁⲩⲱ ⲉⲁ[ⲩϫⲟⲟⲥ ⲛⲁϥ]
ϩ̄ⲙ̄ⲡϩⲟⲣ[ⲁⲙⲁ ϫⲉ-]
]ⲓ̣ ϯ ϩⲧⲏⲕ' ⲉⲡ[ⲉⲓϣⲁ-]
]ϥ̄ .· ϫⲉ ϫⲉϥⲛⲁϫⲱ̣[ⲕ']
]ⲱ̣ ⲉⲃⲟⲗ' ⲉϫⲱⲕ' ⲙ̄ⲛ-
ⲛ̄ⲥⲁⲟⲩⲟⲩⲟⲉⲓϣ·
ⲁⲩⲱ ⲛ̄ⲧⲟϥ ⲙ̄ⲛ-
ⲛ̄[ⲥ]ⲱⲥ ⲁⲩⲧⲁⲙⲟϥ
[ⲉⲃⲟⲗ ϩⲓⲧⲙ̄ⲡ]ⲉⲡ̄ⲛ̄ⲁ̄

[1] Perhaps 'I know', 'I believe', though Am. has nothing.

[2] There is, I think, only one phrase in the Gospels beginning with ⲙⲉⲣⲉ ⲛⲉ-, *viz.* Matt. v. 44 = Luke vi. 27 ('Love thine enemies').

[. . ϩⲟⲣ]ⲁⲙⲁ ⲁϥⲣ-
[ⲡⲙ]ⲉⲉⲩⲉ ⲙ̄ⲡⲉⲛ-
[ⲧⲁ]ϥⲛⲁⲩ ⲉⲣⲟϥ ϩⲙ̄-
ⲡϩⲟⲣⲁⲙⲁ' ϩⲓⲧⲙ̄-
ⲡϫⲟⲉⲓⲥ ⲙ̄ⲡⲉϩⲟⲟⲩ
ⲉⲛⲉⲩⲕⲁⲑⲏⲕⲉⲓ ⲙ̄-
ⲙⲟϥ ⲛ̄ϩⲏⲧϥ ⲉⲣ̄-
ⲭⲣⲓⲥⲧⲉⲓⲁⲛⲟⲥ ⲛ̄-
ⲑⲉ ⲉⲛⲧⲁϥⲛⲁⲩ
[ϩ]ⲙ̄ⲡϭⲱⲗ̄ⲡ ⲉⲃⲟⲗ'
[ⲉ]ⲧⲙ̄ⲙⲁⲩ ⲉϯⲱ-
[ⲧ]ⲉ ⲛ̄ⲧⲡⲉ' ⲉⲛⲧⲁⲥ-
ⲉⲓ' ⲉϩⲣⲁï ⲉϫⲱϥ·
[ⲙ]ⲛ̄ⲛ̄ⲥⲱⲥ ⲉⲁⲥⲥⲱ-
[ⲟⲩ]ϩ ⲁⲥⲣ̄ⲟⲩⲧⲁϭ ⲛ̄-

[ϫⲉⲡ]ⲉⲓⲧ̣[ⲁϭ ⲛ̄ⲉⲃⲓⲱ]
[ⲉ]ⲛⲧⲁ[ϥⲥⲱⲟⲩϩ] ⲉ-
ϩⲟⲩⲛ ϩⲛ̣̄[ⲧⲉⲕϭⲓϫ]
ⲁϥϩⲉ'[a] ⲉϫⲙ̄ⲡ̣[ⲕⲁϩ ⲛⲁⲓ-]
ⲛⲉ ⲛⲉⲭⲁⲣ[ⲓⲥⲙⲁ]
ⲧⲏⲣⲟⲩ ⲉⲧⲛ̣̄[[b]
ϣⲱⲡⲉ ⲛⲁⲕ [ϩⲓⲧⲙ̄-]
ⲡϫⲟⲉⲓⲥ· ⲁⲩⲱ [ⲟⲛ]
ⲥⲉⲛⲁϣⲱⲡⲉ ϩⲱ-
ⲟⲩ ⲛ̄ⲛⲉⲕⲥⲛⲏⲩ
ⲉⲧⲉⲛⲁïⲡⲉ ⲡⲕ[ⲁϩ]
ⲉⲩϣⲁⲛϣⲱⲡⲉ
ϩⲙ̄ⲡⲉϫⲡⲟ' ⲛ̄ⲕ[ⲉ-]
ⲥⲟⲡ' ⲉϥⲧⲃ̄ⲃⲏⲩ
ⲉⲃⲟⲗ' ϩⲙ̄ⲙⲛ̄ⲧϫ̣[ⲁ-]

margin

[a] ⲁϥ- must refer to ⲧⲁϭ, ⲁⲥ- in line 1 to ⲉⲓⲱⲧⲉ.
[b] ⲉⲛⲧ[ⲁⲩ] is inevitable here. Am. (G ⲣ̄ⲙⲏ) التى صاروا لك.

→ *Verso.*

]ⲉ̣ⲓ̣·
ⲡ]ⲁ̣ⲙⲉ̣' ⲛⲉ[ⲧ-][a]
[ⲧⲃ̄ⲃⲟ ⲙ̄]ⲡⲉⲩϩⲏⲧ'
[ⲉⲙⲁ]ⲧⲉ[b] ⲉⲃⲟⲗ' ϩⲙ̄ⲙⲉ-
[ⲉⲩⲉ] ⲛⲓⲙ' ⲙ̄ⲡⲟⲛⲏ-
ⲣⲟⲛ· ⲉⲩⲇⲓⲁⲕⲣⲓⲛⲉ
ⲛ̄ⲧⲙⲛ̄ⲧⲉ ⲙ̄ⲡⲡⲉ-
ⲧⲛⲁⲛⲟⲩϥ' ⲙⲛ̄ⲡ̄-
ⲡⲉⲑⲟⲟⲩ· [ⲁⲩⲱ ⲁ]ⲥ-
Ϣⲱⲡ[ⲉ ⲛⲉⲣⲉⲟⲩ-]
ϣⲏ̣[ⲣⲉ ϣⲏ]ⲙ̣ ϣ[ⲱ-]

[a] Or ⲡⲉⲧⲛⲁⲧⲃ̄ⲃⲟ or ⲡⲉⲧⲧⲃ̄ⲃⲏⲩ ϩⲙ̄-.
[b] Doubtful; equivalent to من هذه باسره.

ⲛⲉ̣[ ]ⲩ· [
]ⲛⲉⲥⲱϥ'
[ϩⲙ̄ⲡⲉϥⲉ]ⲓⲛⲉ ⲛ̄ⲧⲟ̣ϥ
] ⲛ̄ⲧⲉⲣⲟⲩⲛ̄-
[ⲧϥ] ⲉ̣ⲡⲙⲁ ⲉϣⲁⲩ-
[ⲟⲩ]ⲱⲙ' ⲛ̄ϩⲏⲧϥ̄ ⲛ̄-
[ϭⲓ] ⲛⲉⲥⲛⲏⲩ ⲉⲧ-
ϣⲱⲛⲉ ⲉⲧⲙ̄ⲙⲟϥ·
ⲁ̣ⲡⲥⲟⲛ ⲉⲧⲙ̄ⲙⲁⲩ
ⲉⲧⲇⲓⲁⲕⲟⲛⲉⲓ̄ ⲉⲛⲉ-
ⲥⲛⲏⲩ, ⲉⲟⲩⲁⲥⲕⲏⲧⲏⲥ
ⲉⲙⲁⲧⲉⲡⲉ ⲛ̄ⲣⲉϥ-
ⲣϩⲟⲧⲉ ⲉⲡⲉϥⲣⲁⲛ-
ⲡⲉ ⳨ⲧⲟⲩⲉ' ⲉⲩⲣⲉϥ-

ⲛ̄ⲧⲙⲛ̄ⲧ[ⲉ ⲙ̄ⲡⲡⲉ-]
ⲧⲛⲁⲛⲟⲩϥ [ⲙⲛ̄-]
ⲡ̄ⲡⲉⲑⲟⲟⲩ· [ⲡⲉ-]
ⲧⲙ̄ⲙⲁⲩ ⲇⲉ ⲛ̄ⲧ[ⲉ-]
ⲣⲉϥⲛ̣ⲁⲩ ⲉⲡⲟⲩ-
ⲣⲟⲧ' ⲙ̄ⲡⲉϥϩⲏⲧ
ⲉⲧⲣⲉϥⲇⲓⲁⲕⲣⲓⲛⲉ (*sic*)
ⲙ̄ⲡϣⲏⲣⲉ ϣⲏⲙ'
ⲕⲁⲗⲱⲥ· ⲁⲩⲱ ⲉϥ-
ⲥⲟⲃⲧⲉ ⲛⲁϥ ⲛⲉϥ[ⲁ-]
ϣⲁϩⲟⲙ'ⲡⲉ ϩⲣⲁ̈ⲓ [ⲛ̄-]
ϩⲏⲧϥ̄ ⲁⲩⲱ ⲉϥ[ⲇⲓⲁ-]
ⲕⲣⲓⲛⲉ ⲉϥϫⲱ ⲙ̄-
ⲙⲟⲥ ϫⲉⲡϫⲟⲉⲓⲥ
ⲟ̣ⲩ'ⲡⲉ ⲡⲉ̈ⲓⲟⲩⲣⲟ[ⲧ]

margin

Fol. 24. *Recto* (*v.* Am. 434, 435). . . . vision[1] (ὅραμα), and he remembered that which he had beheld in the vision (ὅρ.) from the Lord, on the day whereon he was being instructed (κατηχεῖν) towards becoming a Christian (χρ.); how he had beheld in that revelation the dew of heaven descending upon him, (how) afterwards it had collected and had become a cake of [honey . . . . .

. . . and it fell [upon the ground] and it had been [said to him] in the vision (ὅρ.), 'Give heed unto this word, for it shall be fulfilled upon thee after a time.' And as for him, he was informed [by the] Spirit (πν.) that 'this [cake of honey] that did [collect] in [thy hand] and fall upon the [ground, these (*sic*)] are all the gifts (χάρισμα) that came to thee [from] the Lord. And they shall come also unto thy brethren, that is, the earth.[2] When they shall have become born again, being cleansed from [all] pride [of heart] . . . . .

[1] Am. should be 'visions from the Lord, he remembered the revelation of the vision that he (? they) had seen at first, on the day whereon he had been instructed (وعظوه) that he should become a Christian (مسيحي); how he had beheld that the dew of heaven descended upon him and thereafter became in his hand a cake of honey and fell upon the ground; and (how) it was said unto him in the vision &c.'

[2] So G ⲣⲙ̄ⲙ̄ⲏ, omitting Am.'s على (435, 1).

Verso (*v.* Am. 435). . . . of[1] a truth that [purify] their hearts gre[atly (?)] from every evil (πον.) thought, discerning (διακρίνειν) between good and evil. And it befell [that a] youth [was] sick . . . . . comely [in his] appearance (?). [And] he, when they had brought [him] to the place wherein the sick brethren used to eat, to feed him, that brother[2] that served (διακονεῖν) the brethren and was very ascetic (ἀσκητής) and (God-) fearing, whose name was Titoue, being a . . . . .

. . . discerned] between good [and] evil. But (δέ) that one, when he saw the gladness of his heart that he should serve (διακονεῖν) the youth well (καλῶς) and prepare (food) for him, would sigh[3] within himself and doubt (διακρίνειν), saying, 'Lord, what is this gladness . . . . .

Fol. 25. → *Recto.*

[ⲁⲩⲱ ⲁϥ]ⲙ̣ⲟⲩⲧⲉ ⲉ-
[ⲕⲉⲟⲩ]ⲁ ϩⲛ̄ⲛⲉⲥⲛⲏⲩ
[ⲁϥ]ϫⲟⲟⲩϥ ⲛ̄ⲙ̄ⲙⲁϥ·
[ⲁⲥ]ϣⲱⲡⲉ ⲛ̄ⲧⲉⲣⲟⲩ-
ⲣ̄ⲡⲁϣⲉ (sic) ⲛ̄ⲧⲉϩⲓⲏ
ⲙ̄ⲙⲟⲟϣⲉ ⲁϥ[ϭ]ⲱ-
ϣⲧ ⲁⲩ[ⲱ] ⲉⲓ[ⲥ ⲟⲩ]ϩⲣ̄-
ϣⲓⲣⲉ ⲁϥⲉⲓ' ⲉ[ⲃⲟⲗ'] ϩⲛ̄-
ϩⲉⲛϣⲟⲛⲧⲉ ⲕⲁⲧⲁ
ⲑⲉ ⲉⲛⲧⲁϥϣⲁϫⲉ ⲛ̄ⲙ̄-
ⲙⲁϥ ⲛ̄ϭⲓ ⲡⲉⲛⲉⲓⲱⲧ
ⲡⲁϩⲱⲙ· ⲛ̄ⲧⲉ-
ⲣⲉϥⲛⲁⲩ ⲇⲉ ⲉⲣⲟϥ' ⲁϥ-
ⲧⲁⲙⲉ' ⲡ̄ⲥⲟⲛ ⲉⲧⲙⲟ-
ⲟϣⲉ ⲛ̄ⲙ̄ⲙⲁϥ ⲉⲑⲉ
ⲉⲛⲧⲁϥϫⲱⲕ ⲉⲃⲟⲗ'

ⲙ̄ⲛ̄-]
ⲛ̄ⲥⲱⲥ ⲁϥⲕ̣[ⲧⲟϥ' ⲁϥ-]
ⲃⲱⲕ· ⲁⲥϣ[ⲱⲡⲉ]
ⲇⲉ ⲙ̄ⲛ̄ⲛ̄ⲥⲁⲛⲁⲓ [ⲉϥ-]
ϣⲗⲏⲗ' ⲛ̄ϭⲓ ⲡⲉⲛⲉⲓ-
ⲱⲧ ⲡⲁϩⲱⲙ ⲉⲓⲥ
ⲟⲩⲁⲅⲅⲉⲗⲟⲥ ⲛ̄ⲧⲉ
ⲡϫⲟ[ⲉⲓⲥ] ⲁϥⲟⲩⲱⲛ[ϩ̄]
ⲛⲁϥ [ⲉ]ⲃⲟⲗ ⲡⲉϫⲁϥ
ⲛⲁϥ· ϫ[ⲉⲟⲩ' ⲡⲉⲧⲕ̄-]
ⲛⲁⲉⲣⲏ[ⲧ ⲙ̄ⲙⲟϥ ⲉ-]
ⲧⲁⲁϥ' ⲙ̣ⲙ̄[ⲛ̄ⲧⲛⲁ']
ⲉⲣϣⲁⲛⲡ[ϫⲟⲉⲓⲥ]
ⲕⲱⲗⲩⲉ' ⲛ̄[ⲧⲟⲣⲅⲏ]
ϩⲙ̄ⲡⲧⲣⲉϥ[ϣⲱϣⲧ]
ⲛ̄ⲛ̄ⲃⲁⲣⲃⲁⲣ[ⲟⲥ· ⲛ̄-]

[1] Am. should be, 'And thus they of a truth shall become pure in their hearts from all this and from every evil thought.'

[2] Am. should be, 'And the brother that served the sick brethren, his name was Didûye, and he was pious and discerned (the nature of) his thoughts aright. And when he saw &c.'

[3] Am. should be, 'He sighed to himself alone and set about doubting within himself, saying, 'O Lord, what is this gladness &c.'

ⲛ̄ϭⲓ ⲡϣⲁϫⲉ ⲉⲛ >
ⲧⲁϥϫⲟⲟϥ· ⲁⲩⲱ ⲟⲛ
ⲁϥⲧⲁⲙⲟϥ ϫⲉⲁϥ-
ϩⲱⲛ ⲉⲧⲟⲟⲧϥ̄ ⲉϥϫⲱ
ⲙ̄ⲙⲟⲥ ϫⲉⲙ̄ⲡⲣ̄ⲣ̄ϩⲟ-
[ⲧ]ⲉ· ϥⲛⲁϣϭⲙ̄ϭⲟⲙ
[ⲅ]ⲁⲣ ⲁⲛ ⲛ̄ⲣ̄ⲗⲁⲁⲩ ⲙ̄-
[ⲡ]ⲉⲑⲟⲟⲩ ⲛⲏⲧⲛ̄·

ⲧⲟϥ ⲇⲉ ⲡⲉϫⲁϥ ϫⲉ-
ϯⲛⲁϫⲟⲟⲩ ⲉⲧⲉⲕⲕⲗⲏ-
ⲥⲓⲁ ⲛ̄ⲧⲡⲟⲗⲓⲥ ⲉⲛ-
ⲧⲁⲩϣⲟⲗⲥ̄ ⲛ̄ϭⲓ ⲛ̄-
ⲃⲁⲣⲃⲁⲣⲟⲥ ⲛ̄ⲟⲩⲁⲡⲥ̄
ⲛ̄ϣⲉ ⲛ̄ⲥⲟⲩⲟ ⲙ̄ⲛ̄-
ϩⲉⲛϫⲱⲱⲙⲉ ⲙ̄ⲛ̄-
ϩⲉⲛⲕⲉⲉⲓⲇⲟⲥ ⲉⲩⲣ̄ⲭ̣

margin

↑ *Verso.*

[ⲡⲟⲩ]ⲱ ⲉⲛⲉⲥⲛⲏⲩ
[ⲙ̄]ⲡⲉⲛⲧⲁϥⲛⲁⲩ
[ⲉⲣ]ⲟϥ ⲉϥⲛⲁϣⲱⲡⲉ̣
ϩⲁⲑⲏ ⲉⲙⲡⲁⲧϥ̄-
ϣⲱⲡⲉ· ⲁⲩⲱ ⲛ̄-
ⲧⲉⲓ̈ϩⲉ ⲁⲩ[ϭⲟ]ⲧⲡ̄
ⲛ̄ϭⲓ ⲛ̄ⲃ[ⲁⲣⲃ]ⲁⲣⲟⲥ
ⲙ̄ⲡⲉϥⲣⲁⲥⲧⲉ ⲁⲩⲱ
[ⲁ]ⲩⲕ[ⲧⲱⲟ]ⲩ ⲉⲡⲁϩⲟⲩ
[ⲕⲁⲧⲁ ⲑ]ⲉ ⲉⲛⲧⲁⲩ-
[ϫⲟⲟⲥ[a]] ⲛ̣̄ⲙ̄ⲙⲁϥ:
[ϩⲟⲥⲟⲛ] ⲇⲉ ⲉⲩϫⲣⲁ-
[ⲉⲓⲧ ⲛ̄]ϭⲓ ⲛ̄ⲃⲁⲣⲃⲁ-
[ⲣⲟⲥ] ⲁⲩϩⲉ ⲉⲩⲙⲟⲛⲁ-
ⲭⲟⲥ ⲉϥⲁⲛⲁⲭⲱⲣⲉⲓ
ⲛ̄ⲟⲩⲙⲁ ⲁⲩⲁⲓⲭⲙⲁ-

ⲛ̄-]
ϣⲟⲣⲡ̣ .[. . . ⲧⲥⲟ]
ⲛⲁⲛ· ⲛ̄ⲥ̣[b ⲙ̄-]
ⲡ̄ϥⲟⲩⲱϣ· ⲛ̄[ⲧⲉ-]
ⲣⲟⲩⲛⲁⲩ ⲇⲉ ϫⲉ̣[ⲙ̄-]
ⲡ̄ϥⲥⲱⲧⲙ̄ ⲛ̄ⲥ[ⲱ-]
ⲟⲩ [ⲁⲩ]ϥⲓ̈ ⲛ̄ⲟⲩⲙⲁ-
ⲕⲟ[ⲧ ⲉ]ⲩϫⲱ ⲙ̄ⲙⲟⲥ
ⲛⲁ[ϥ ϫ]ⲉⲟⲩⲱⲧⲛ̄
ⲉⲃⲟ[ⲗ] ⲉϣⲱⲡⲉ ⲙ̄-
ⲙⲟⲛ ⲧⲛ̄ⲛⲁⲕⲟⲛ-
ⲥⲕ̄· ⲁⲩⲱ ⲛ̄ⲧⲉⲣⲉϥ-
ⲣ̄ϩⲟⲧⲉ ϫⲉⲛ̄ⲛⲉⲩ-
ⲕⲱⲛⲥ̄ ⲙ̄ⲙⲟϥ. ⲁϥ-
ⲟⲩⲱⲧⲛ̄ ⲉⲃⲟⲗ·
ⲁⲩⲱ ⲙ̄ⲛ̄ⲛ̄ⲥⲱⲥ ⲁϥ-
ⲧⲥⲟⲟⲩ ϣⲁⲛⲧⲟⲩ-

[a] Or [ϣⲁϫⲉ], *cf. recto*, l. 10.

[b] These lines may be ⲛ̄]ϣⲟⲣⲡ ⲙ[ⲛ̄ⲛ̄ⲥⲱⲥ ⲧⲥⲟ] ⲛⲁⲛ· ⲛ̄ⲧ[ⲟϥ ⲇⲉ ⲙ], or ⲛ̄]ϣⲟⲣⲡ ⲙ̄[ⲡⲁⲧⲕ̄ⲧⲥⲟ].

ⲗⲱⲧⲓⲍⲉ ⲙ̄ⲙⲟϥ·
ⲁⲩⲱ ⲁⲥϣⲱⲡⲉ ⲛ̄ⲟⲩ-
ⲥⲟⲡ' ⲛ̄ⲧⲉⲣⲟⲩⲉⲓ' ϫⲉ-
ⲉⲩⲛⲁⲥⲱ' ⲛ̄ⲟⲩⲏⲣⲡ̄
ⲡⲉϫⲁⲩ ⲉϩⲟⲩⲛ ⲉϩⲣⲁϥ
ϫⲉⲙⲟⲣⲕ̄ ⲛ̄ⲧⲟⲩⲱ-
ⲧϩ̄ ⲉⲣⲟⲛ· ⲁⲩⲱ ⲛ̄ⲧⲉ-

ϯϩⲉ' ⲁⲩⲱ̄ⲃϣ̄ ⲁϥ-
ⲡⲱⲧ' ⲛ̄ϭⲓ ⲡ̄ⲙⲟ-
ⲛⲁⲭⲟⲥ· ⲁⲩⲱ ⲙ̄ⲛ̄-
ⲛ̄ⲥⲁⲛⲁï ⲁⲡⲉⲩϩⲏⲧ[a]
ⲟⲩⲱϣϥ̄ ϩⲱⲥⲧ[ⲉ ⲉ-]
ⲧⲙ̄ⲧⲣⲉϥⲉϣϭⲙ̄-
ϭⲟⲙ' ⲉⲡⲱⲣϣ̄ ⲉⲃ̣[ⲟⲗ]

margin

[a] So my copy; but ⲁⲡⲉϥ- is required.

Fol. 25. *Recto* (*v.* Am. 438). . . . [And? he] called another of the brethren and sent him with him. It befell, when they had done half of the journey (*lit.* road of walking), he looked and lo,[1] a youth came forth from some thorn-bushes, even as our father Pahômius had said unto him. But (δέ) when he beheld him, he told the brother that walked with him how the word that he (*sc.* P.) had spoken was fulfilled. And moreover he told him that he had bidden him, saying, Be not afraid, for (γάρ) he shall not be able to do you[2] any ill . . . . .

. . . After]wards he turned about and departed. And (δέ) it befell thereafter, as our father Pahômius prayed, lo, an angel (ἄγ.) of the Lord appeared unto him and said unto him, '[What[3]] wilt [thou] vow [to] give in [charity], if so be the [Lord] hinder (κωλύειν) [the wrath (ὀργή)], in that He [impede] the barbarians (βάρβ.)?' And (δέ) he said, 'I will send unto the church (ἐκκ.) of the city (πόλις) which the barbarians (βάρβ.) have laid waste many (*lit.* an amount of) hundred(weight)[4] of corn, with books and other things (εἶδος) [whereof] they have ne[ed (χρεία) . . . . .

Verso (*v.* Am. 439). . . . related to the brethren what he had seen that should befall ere it had befallen.[5] And thus were the barbarians (βάρβ.) conquered on the morrow and were driven back, even (κατά) as it had been said unto him.[6] And while yet (ὅσον δέ) the barbarians (βάρβ.) were

[1] Am. should be, 'they looked and lo (اذا), a youth came forth from the bushes.' (The word, two lines above, translated *cilice*, is not مسح but مسحاة 'spade'.)

[2] Am. *om.* you.

[3] Am. (Ac. 73 *infra*), 'What wilt thou vow (تنذر) to give as charity, if the Lord should calm (هدأ) the (*sic*) wrath &c.'

[4] Am., 'an hundred artabae.'

[5] Am. *sic.*

[6] Am., 'as the angel had said unto him.'

victorious, they found a monk living apart (*μον.*, *ἀναχωρεῖν*) in a (certain) place and they took him captive (*αἰχμαλωτίζειν*).[1] And it befell on a time, when they came and would drink wine, they said unto him, 'Gird thyself[2] and pour (wine) for us.' And when . . . . .

. . . ere [thou give] us [to drink.'[3] But (*δέ*)] he (?) would not.[4] And (*δέ*) when they saw that he hearkened not unto them, they took a spear,[5] saying unto him, 'Pour forth[6]; if not, we will slay thee.' And when he was afraid lest they should slay him, he poured forth. And afterwards he gave them to drink until they were drunken and slept; and the monk (*μον.*) fled.[7] And thereafter his heart was broken, so that (*ὥστε*) he was not able to stretch forth . . . . .

Fol. 26. ↑ *Recto.*

[ⲛⲁϣ] ⲛϩ[ⲉ ϯⲛⲁⲥⲟⲡ̅ⲥ̅]
[ⲙ̅ⲡ]ⲉⲛⲧⲁⲓⲁⲣⲛ̣[ⲁ’ ⲙ̅-]
ⲙⲟϥ· ϥ[ⲥ]ⲏϩ’ ⲅⲁⲣ ϫⲉ-
[ⲡ]ⲉⲧⲛⲁⲁⲣⲛⲁ’ ⲙ̅-
[ⲙ]ⲟï ϯⲛⲁⲁⲣⲛⲁ’ ⲙ̅-
ⲙⲟϥ· ⲁϥⲙⲉⲕⲙⲟⲩ-
ⲕ̅ϥ̅ ⲇⲉ ⲟⲛ ϩⲣⲁï ⲛ̅ϩⲏ-
ⲧ̅ϥ̅ ⲉϥϫⲱ ⲙ̅ⲙⲟⲥ ϫⲉ-
ⲁïⲥⲱⲧ̅ⲙ̅ ϫⲉⲟ̅ⲩ̅ⲛ̅ ⲟ̣[ⲩ-]
ⲣⲱⲙⲉ ⲛ̅ⲧⲉ ⲡ[ⲛⲟⲩ-]
ⲧⲉ ⲟ’ ⲛ̅ⲉⲓⲱⲧ’ [ⲛ̅ⲧⲕⲟⲓ-]
ⲛⲱⲛⲓⲁ ⲛⲧ[ⲁ]ⲃⲛ-
ⲛⲏⲥⲉ ϫⲉⲡⲁ[ϩ]ⲱⲙⲉ
ϯⲛⲁⲧⲱⲟⲩⲛ ⲛ̅ⲧⲁ-
ⲃⲱⲕ’ ϣⲁⲣⲟ̅ϥ̅ ⲛ̅ⲧⲁ-

ⲙ̅ⲙⲁ[ⲩ ϣⲁⲛϯⲁ-]
ⲡⲁⲛ[ⲧⲁ ⲉⲣⲟⲕ ⲛ̅ϣⲟ-]

[1] Am. 439, 2 (G ⲣ̅ⲡ̅), read سبوه 'captured him'.

[2] Am., 'thy middle.'

[3] Or 'and afterwards give us to drink'. Am. should be, 'Sacrifice unto our gods ere thou give us to drink.'

[4] Am., 'and he did not.'

[5] Lemm, *KKS.* xlv, p. 403, accepts Peyron's ⲙⲁⲕⲱⲧ = *τάφρος* (Mic. v. 6); but that the usual meaning is there the correct one is shown by Aquila's *λόγχη*.

[6] Am., 'Raise an offering unto our gods.'

[7] Am., 'arose and fled.'

ⲧⲁⲙⲟϥ' ⲉⲑⲉ' ⲧⲏⲣ̅ⲥ̅
ⲉⲛⲧⲁϊⲁⲁⲥ· ⲉϣⲱ-
ⲡⲉ ⲙⲉⲛ, ⲉϥϣⲁⲛ-
ϯ ⲙⲉⲧⲁⲛⲟⲓⲁ ⲛⲁϊ,
ϯⲡⲓⲥⲧⲉⲩⲉ ϫⲉⲡϫⲟ-
ⲉⲓⲥ ⲛⲁϯ ⲛⲁϊ· ⲉϣⲱ-
ⲡⲉ ⲇⲉ ⲟⲛ ⲉϥϣⲁⲛ-
ϫⲟⲟⲥ ϫⲉⲙ̅ⲛ̅ⲧ̅ⲕ̅ⲙⲉ[a]

ⲣ̅ⲡ̅ ⲛ[ⲅ̅ⲧⲥⲁⲃⲟⲓ ⲉ-]
ⲡⲱⲣ̅ϫ̅ [ⲙ̅ⲡϩⲱⲃ·]
ⲡⲉϫⲁ[ϥ ⲛⲁϥ ϫⲉⲱ']
ⲡⲧⲁⲗ[ⲁⲓⲡⲱⲣⲟⲥ]
ⲙ̅ⲛ̅ⲛ̅[ⲥⲁⲧⲣⲉⲡⲁⲅ-]
ⲅⲉⲗⲟⲥ ⲙ̅ⲡϫ[ⲟⲉⲓⲥ]
ⲁϩ'ⲉ ⲣⲁⲧ̅ϥ̅ ϩⲓϫ̣[ⲱⲕ]
ⲉⲣⲉⲡⲉⲕⲗⲟⲙ' [ϩⲛ̅-]

margin

[a] ⲙⲉⲧⲁⲛⲟⲓⲁ.

→ *Verso.*

[ϩⲱⲛ[a] ⲉⲧⲟⲟ]ⲧ̅ϥ̅ ⲉⲧ-
[ⲣⲉϥⲛⲏⲥⲧⲉ]ⲩⲉ̣ ⲙ̅-
[ⲙⲏⲛⲉ ⲁⲩ]ⲱ ⲉⲧⲙ-
[ⲟⲩⲉⲙ ⲗⲁⲁ]ⲩ ⲛ̅ⲛ̅ⲕⲁ'
[ⲉϥⲡⲟⲥⲉ ⲭⲱ]ⲣⲓⲥ ⲁ-

[. . . . ⲁⲩⲱ] ⲁⲛ̣[ⲟⲕ]
[ϩ]ⲱ̣ ⲛⲙⲙ̣ⲁⲩ [ϩⲙ̅-]
ⲡⲛ̣ⲁⲩ ⲉ[ⲧ]ⲉⲣⲉⲡ[ϫⲁ-]
ϫⲉ ⲛⲁⲕⲁⲧⲏⲅ[ⲟ-]
ⲣⲉⲓ ⲙ̅ⲙⲟⲕ·
Ⲁⲩⲱ ⲁⲥϣⲱⲡⲉ ⲛ-
ⲧⲁⲣⲭⲏ ⲛ̅ⲧⲉⲣⲉϥ-
ⲧⲱϣ ⲛ̅ⲑⲉⲟⲇⲱ-
ⲣⲟⲥ ⲉⲧⲣⲉϥϣⲱⲡⲉ
[ⲡⲉⲓ]ⲱⲧ' ⲉⲧⲥⲟⲟⲩ-
[ϩ̅ⲥ̅ ⲛ̅]ⲧⲁ[ⲃ]ⲛⲛⲏⲥⲉ
[ⲁⲩⲱ] ⲛⲧⲟϥ ⲑⲉⲟ̄-
ⲇⲱⲣⲟⲥ ⲉϥⲥⲟⲟⲩⲛ
ϫⲉϣⲁϥϣⲁϫⲉ
ⲛ̅ϭⲓ ⲡⲉⲛⲉⲓⲱⲧ
ⲡⲁϩⲱⲙⲉ ⲙ̅ⲙⲏ-
ⲛⲉ ⲉⲛⲉⲥⲛⲏⲩ, ϩⲙ̅-
ⲡϣⲁϫⲉ ⲙ̅ⲡⲛⲟⲩ-

[a] Completion of first three lines uncertain, as Am. differs somewhat.

[ⲛⲁⲅⲕⲏ ⲛ̄ϣ]ⲱⲛⲉ·
[. . .] . ⲣ̣ⲁⲥ̣ⲓ̣ⲥ[a] ⲛⲁϥ
[ϫⲉ]ⲕϣⲁⲛⲉⲓⲣⲉ ⲕⲁ-
[ⲧⲁ ⲧ]ⲉϊϩⲉ· ⲛⲉⲧⲟⲩ-
[ⲁⲁⲃ] ⲛⲁϣⲱⲡⲉ ⲛ̄-
•

ⲧⲉ· ⲛⲉϣⲁϥⲥⲡⲟⲩ-
ⲇⲁⲍⲉ ⲇⲉⲡⲉ ⲙⲛ-
ⲛ̄ⲥⲁⲧⲣⲉϥⲟⲩⲱ’ ⲉϥ-
ⲉⲓⲣⲉ ⲙ̄ⲡⲉϥϩⲱⲃ’
ⲛⲉϥⲧⲁⲗⲉ̄ ⲧⲙⲏ[b]

margin

[a] Probably [ⲁⲩⲱ] ⲁϥϫⲟⲟⲥ (Am. وقال). [b] Perhaps followed by ⲅⲁⲣⲡⲉ (Am. لأنه كان).

Fol. 26. *Recto* (*v.* Am. 439, 440). How [shall I entreat] Him that I have denied (*ἀρνᾶσθαι*)? For (*γάρ*) it is written,[1] Whosoever shall deny (*ἀρ.*) me, him will I deny (*ἀρ.*).' And (*δέ*) then he thought within himself, saying, 'I have heard that there is a man of God (that) is father of the community (*κοινωνία*) of Tabennêse, namely Pahômius. I will arise and[2] go to him and will tell him of all that I have done. If so be (+*μέν*) that he give me repentance (*μετ.*), I believe (*πιστεύειν*) that the Lord shall give (it) me. But (*δέ*) if so be that he say, There is not for thee repentance (*μετ.*) . . . . .

. . . there [is not repentance for me until I] meet with (*ἀπαντᾶν*) [thee[3]] first and thou [show me] the certainty [of the matter.'] He said [unto him, 'O] wretch[ed one (*ταλαίπωρος*)], after [that the an]gel (*ἄγ.*)[4] of the Lord had stood by [thee], the crown being [in . . . . .

Verso (*v.* Am. 440). . . . [bade] him to [fast (? *νηστεύειν*) daily[5]] and not to [eat aught] of things [cooked], save by (*χωρίς*) necessity (*ἀνάγκη*) of sickness. And he said unto him,[6] 'If thou act in this wise, the saints shall be . . . . .

. . . And] I likewise with them, [in] the hour when the enemy shall accuse[7] (*κατηγορεῖν*) thee.'

And it befell, at the beginning (*ἀρχή*), when he had set Theodore to be father for the congregation of Tabennêse, and Theodore for his part, knowing how our father Pahômius was wont to speak daily unto the brethren the word of God, would be diligent (*σπουδάζειν* + *δέ*), after that he had ceased to do his work, [for] he wove[8] mats, ...

[1] Matt. x. 33.

[2] Am. *sic.*

[3] Am., 'until I meet with thy paternity.'

[4] Am. *sic.*

[5] Am., 'to fast until evening daily,' for which there seems not space in the Coptic.

[6] Uncertain according to my copy.

[7] So Am., not 'rejoice'.

[8] For this use of ⲧⲁⲗⲟ, *v. Mus. Guim.* 327. 14, with Amélineau's note. Other instances: Lev. xix. 19, Isa. iii. 23, Zoega 375.

Fol. 27. → *Recto.*

]ⲗⲉ ⲉ̣.
]ⲃ̣. ⲛ̄ⲑ̣ⲉ̣
[ⲛⲟⲩⲣⲱⲙⲉ] ⲉϥϩⲟ̣ϫ-
[ϩⲉϫ ⲙ̄ⲙⲟϥ] ⲟⲩⲧⲱϥ'
[ⲙ̄ⲡϫⲟ ⲥ̄ⲛ̣̄ⲧ]ⲉ[a] ⲁⲩⲱ
[ⲛ̄ⲧⲉⲣϥⲑ]ⲗⲓⲃⲉ ⲉ-
[ⲃⲟⲗ ϩⲛ̄]ⲧⲁⲡⲉⲓ̈ⲗⲏ
[ⲙ̄ⲡⲙⲁ ⲉ]ⲧ̣ⲙ̄ⲙⲁⲩ.
[ⲁϥⲉⲓ ⲉ]ϩⲣⲁⲓ̈ ⲁϥ-
[ⲡⲱⲧ ⲛⲁϥ ⲉ]ⲃⲟⲗ'[b]
[ϩⲛ̄ ?

ϣⲗⲏⲗ · ⲁϥϭ̣ⲱ̣ϣ̣ⲧ̣
ⲁϥⲛⲁⲩ · ⲁⲩⲱ ⲉⲓⲥ ϩⲏ-
ⲛⲧⲉ ⲧϫⲟ' ⲉⲧⲥⲁⲉⲓ̈-
ⲃ̣̄ⲧ ⲁⲥϣⲱⲡⲉ ⲛ̄ⲑⲉ̣
ⲛ̄ⲟⲩⲛⲟⲩⲃ' ⲧⲏⲣ̄ⲥ̄ ·
ⲁ̣ⲩ̣ⲱ ⲡⲉⲥⲙⲟⲧ' ⲉⲛ-
ⲧⲁⲡϫⲟⲉⲓⲥ ⲟⲩⲱⲛ̄ϩ̄
ⲛⲁϥ ⲉⲃⲟⲗ ⲙ̄ⲡⲛⲁⲩ
ⲉⲧⲙ̄ⲙⲁⲩ ⲡⲁⲓ̈ⲡⲉ
ⲉⲓⲥ ⲡⲉⲥⲙⲟⲧ' ⲛ̄ⲟⲩ-
ⲛⲟϭ ⲛ̄ϩⲟ' ⲛ̄ⲑⲉ ⲛ̄ⲟⲩ-
ⲧⲣⲁⲡⲉⲍⲁ' ⲉϥⲟⲩⲟ-
ⲛ̄ϩ̄ ⲉⲃⲟⲗ' ϩⲓⲧϫⲟ ⲛ̄-
ⲛⲟⲩⲃ' ⲁⲩⲱ ⲉϥϩⲓ-
ϫⲛ̄ⲧⲉϥⲁⲡⲉ ⲛ̄ϭⲓ
ⲟⲩⲕⲗⲟⲙ' ⲉⲙⲙ̄ⲛ̄ϣⲓ
ϣⲟⲟⲡ' ⲙ̄ⲡⲉϥⲉⲟⲟⲩ ·
ⲁⲩⲱ ⲛⲉⲩϩⲓϫ̄ⲙ̄ⲡⲉ-
ⲕⲗⲟⲙ' ⲉϥⲕⲱⲧⲉ[c] ⲛ̄-
ϭⲓ ϩⲉⲛⲉⲓ̣ⲛⲉ[d] ⲙ̄ⲙⲉ̣
ⲉⲛⲁϣⲉ' ⲥⲟⲩⲛ̄ⲧ[ⲟⲩ]
? ?

[a] Does ⲟⲩⲧⲱϥ allow of the construction thus given it by the following words? For the construction here, *cf.* Bo. 105. [b] Or ⲥⲁ]ⲃⲟⲗ [ⲛ. [c] ϥ has been altered, probably to ⲩ. [d] ⲓ erased, leaving ⲉⲛⲉ.

↑ *Verso.*

[ⲕⲁⲓⲟⲥⲩ]ⲛⲏ̣ ·[a] ϯⲣ̣[ⲏ-]
ⲛⲏ · ⲡ̣ⲉ̣ⲑⲃ̄ⲃ̄ⲓⲟ' ⲛ̄-
ϩⲏⲧ · ⲧⲙ̄ⲛ̄ⲧϩⲁ-

[a] ⲧⲇⲓ[ⲕⲁⲓⲟⲥⲩ]ⲛⲏ = Am. البر.

ⲣ̄ϣϩⲏⲧ · ⲧⲙ̄ⲛ̄ⲧ-
ⲭⲣⲏⲥⲧⲟⲥ · ⲧⲙ̄ⲛ̄ⲧ-
ⲣ̄ⲙ̄ⲣⲁϣ' · ⲧⲉⲅⲕⲣⲁ-
ⲧⲉⲓ'ⲁ · ⲡⲣⲁϣⲉ ϩ̄ⲛ̄-
ⲑⲉⲗⲡⲓⲥ · ⲧⲁⲅⲁⲡⲏ ·
ⲛⲉⲩϣⲟⲟⲡ' ⲇⲉ ⲙ̄ⲡⲉϥ-
ⲙ̄ⲧⲟ' ⲉⲃⲟⲗ' ⲛ̄ϭⲓ ⲛⲟϭ
ⲥⲛⲁⲩ ⲛ̄ⲁⲣⲭⲁⲅⲅⲉ-
ⲗⲟⲥ ⲉⲩⲧⲁⲉⲓⲏⲩ ⲉ-
ⲙⲁⲧⲉ ⲉⲛⲥⲉⲕⲱ̣ ⲇⲉ
ⲁⲛ ⲉⲩϭⲱϣ̄ⲧ̄ ⲉⲡⲉ̣ⲓ̣-
ⲛⲉ ⲙ̄ⲡϫⲟⲉⲓⲥ ⲉⲛ-
ⲧⲁϥⲟⲩⲱⲛ̄ϩ̄ ⲉⲃⲟⲗ ·
ⲡⲉⲛⲉⲓⲱⲧ' ⲡⲁϩⲱ-
ⲙⲉ ⲇⲉ ⲛⲉϥϣⲗⲏⲗ'ⲡⲉ
ⲉϥⲧⲱⲃ̄ϩ̄ ⲙ̄ⲡϫⲟ̈ⲓ̈ⲥ
ⲉϥϫⲱ ⲙ̄ⲙⲟⲥ ϫⲉⲙⲁ-
[ⲣ]ⲉⲧⲉⲕϩⲟⲧⲉ ⲧⲏⲣ̄ⲥ̄

ⲉϥϩ̣̣[
?
ϫ̣ · ϩ̣[
ⲙⲁⲣⲉ̣[ⲧⲉⲕϩⲟⲧⲉ[a]
ϫⲛ̣ⲁ̣[ⲣ̄ϩⲟⲧⲉ]
ϩⲏⲧ[ⲕ ⲉϥ-]
ϣⲗⲏⲗ [ⲁⲩⲱ ⲉϥⲧⲱ-]
ⲃ̄ϩ̄ ⲉⲧ[ⲃⲉⲡⲁⲓ ⲉⲓⲥ]
ϩⲏⲏⲧ[ⲉ
ⲧ[
ⲙ[

margin

[a] Perhaps ⲉⲓ ⲉ]ϫⲱⲛ[.

Fol. 27. *Recto* (*v.* Am. 443). . . . even as (?)[1] [a man] that is straitened between [two walls], and [since (*lit.* when) he] was oppressed (θλίβειν) by reason of the danger (? ἀπειλή) of that place, he [went?] down and [fled?] forth [from . . .

. . . whilst he] prayed. He looked and beheld and lo, the wall upon the eastern side became all as it were of gold. And the form wherein the Lord did then reveal Himself[2] was this: lo, the form[3] of a great face in the likeness of a table (τράπ.), appearing upon the golden wall, and upon its head a crown of immeasurable glory. And there were[4] upon the crown precious stones round about, of great price . . . . .

[1] This whole sentence is uncertain. I have failed to reconstruct a text corresponding with Am.

[2] Am. *sic.*

[3] So G ⲣ̄ⲡ̄ⲁ̄ b مثال for مثل.

[4] Am., 'around the crown divers colours, like to jewels of great price.'

Verso (*v.* Am. 443, 444). . . . righteous]ness (δικαιοσύνη), peace (εἰρήνη), humbleness of heart, longsuffering, kindness (-χρηστός), meekness, temperance (ἐγκράτεια), joy in (*sic*) hope (ἐλπίς), love.[1] And (δέ) there were in his presence two great archangels (ἀρχάγ.), honourable exceedingly, and (δέ) they ceased not to look upon the likeness of the Lord that had been revealed. But (δέ) our father Pahômius prayed, beseeching the Lord and saying, 'Let all Thy fear . . . . .

. . . let [Thy fear (?) . . . . . fear] Thee (?) . . . while he] prayed [and] beseeched concerning [this,] lo,[2] . . . . .

Fol. 28. ↑ *Recto.*

[ⲣⲏ ⲉ]ϥϣ̣[ⲁ ⲉϫⲙ̄ⲡⲕⲁϩ]
[ⲡⲉϥ]ⲉⲓⲛⲉ ⲇⲉ ⲉ̣[ϥ-]
[ⲟⲩⲉ]ⲧⲟⲩⲱⲧʼ ⲉⲙ[ⲁ-]
[ⲧⲉ ⲉ]ⲙⲁⲧⲉ· ⲁⲥϣⲱ-
[ⲡⲉ] ⲛ̄ⲧⲉⲣⲉⲥⲧⲁϩⲟϥʼ
[ⲛ̄ϭⲓ] ⲑⲟⲧⲉ ⲁϥϩⲉʼ ⲉ-
[ⲡⲉ]ⲥ̣ⲏⲧʼ ⲁⲩⲱ ⲁϥϭⲱ̄
[ⲉϥ]ϥⲱϭⲉ ϩⲓϫⲙ̄ⲡⲕⲁϩ
[ⲛ̄ⲑ]ⲉ̣ ⲛ̣ⲟⲩⲧⲃ̄ⲧ ⲉϥ-
[ⲟⲛ̄ϩ] ⲉϥϥⲱϭⲉ ϩⲓ-
[ϫⲙ̄]ⲡ̣ⲕⲁϩ· ⲉⲁⲥϫⲱ-
[ⲧⲉ[a] ⲛ̄]ⲛⲉϥⲙⲉⲗⲟⲥ
[ⲙⲛ̄]ⲛⲉϥϩⲁⲣⲙⲟⲥʼ
[ⲙⲛ̄]ⲛ̣ⲉϥⲁⲗⲧⲕⲁⲥ
[ⲁⲩⲱ ⲡ]ⲉϥⲥⲱⲙⲁ ⲧⲏ-
[ⲣϥ̄ ⲁⲩ]ⲱ ⲧⲉϥⲯⲩⲭⲏ·
[ⲛ̄ⲧⲉⲣ]ⲉϥⲙ̄ⲕⲁϩ ⲇⲉ

ⲕ̣[
ϥⲓ̈ ⲁ[ⲛ ϩⲁⲑⲟⲧⲉ ⲧⲏ-]
ⲣ̄ⲥ̄ ⲙ̄ⲡϫ̣[ⲟⲉⲓⲥ ⲛ̄ⲧⲉ-]
ⲣⲉϥⲑⲗⲓⲃ[ⲉ . . . .][b]
ⲁϥⲁϣⲕ[ⲁⲕ ⲉⲃⲟⲗ ⲛ̄-]
ϩⲁϩ ⲛ̣[ⲥ]ⲟⲡ̣ [ϫⲉⲡϫⲟ-]
ⲉⲓⲥ. ⲛⲁ ⲛⲁⲓ̈· [[c]
ⲛ̄ⲧⲉⲩⲛⲟⲩ ⲁ[ⲥⲙⲟⲟ-]
ϣⲉ ⲕⲟⲩⲓ̈ ⲕⲟⲩⲓ̈ [ⲛ̄ϭⲓ]
ⲧⲁⲕⲧⲓⲛʼ ⲛ̄ⲑ[ⲟⲧⲉ]
ⲁⲥⲕⲟⲧ̄ⲥ̄ ⲉⲡⲉⲥ̣[ⲙⲁʼ·]
ⲙ̄ⲛ̄ⲛ̄ⲥⲱⲥ ⲇⲉ ⲟ[ⲛ ⲁϥ-]
ⲙⲟⲟϣⲉ ⲛ̄ϭⲓ ⲡ̄[ⲉⲓⲛⲉ]
ⲙ̄ⲡⲛⲁʼ ⲕⲟⲩⲓ̈ ⲕ[ⲟⲩⲓ̈]

[a] Bo. p. 107 has ϭⲱ[. [b] ⲧⲟⲧⲉ seems unlikely. [c] Probably nothing here.

[1] *Cf.* Gal. v. 22 (also Budge, *Hom.* 67, Leyden *MSS.* 335). The enumeration corresponds exactly to Am., البر to المحبة, and differs from Bo. 106 (= Av. 46 b). For 'joy in hope', *cf.* ? Rom. xii. 12. Lemm *KKS.* 432 ff. has discussed similar lists.

[2] Am. should be, 'And while he prayed and beseeched on account of this, lo &c.'

[ⲉⲙⲙⲁ]ⲧⲉ ϩⲱⲥⲧⲉ ⲉⲧ-
[ⲣⲉϥ]ⲕ̣ⲁ ⲧⲟⲟⲧϥ̅ ⲉ-
[ⲃⲟ]ⲗ̣ ⲉⲡⲙⲟⲩ· ⲁⲩϭⲱ-
[ϣ]ⲧ̣ ⲛ̅ⲥⲱϥ ϩ̅ⲛ̅ⲟⲩ-
[ⲙⲉ]ⲣ̣ⲟⲥ ⲙ̅ⲡⲉⲩϩⲟ ⲛ̅ϭⲓ

ϣⲁⲛⲧϥ̅ⲡⲱ[ϩ' ϣⲁⲣⲟϥ]
ⲁⲩⲱ ⲡⲉϥⲉⲓⲛⲉ [ⲡⲉϥ-]
ⲟ' ⲛ̅ⲑⲉ ⲙ̅ⲡⲛⲉϩ' ⲉϥ[ⲕⲓ-]
ⲱⲟⲩ ⲉⲙⲁⲧⲉ· ⲛ̅ⲧ[ⲉ-]
ⲣⲉϥⲉⲓ' ⲇⲉ ⲉϫⲱϥ' ⲛ̅-[a]

margin

[a] ? ⲛⲧⲉⲩⲛⲟⲩ.

↑ *Verso.*

[. . . . . . .] ⲛⲧⲉï-
[ϩⲉ . . . . ⲧⲟ]ⲟⲧϥ̅
[. . . . ⲡ]ⲉïⲥⲙⲟⲧ'
[ⲉⲛ]ⲧⲁϥⲧⲥⲁⲃⲟϥ'
[ⲉⲣⲟϥ] ⲛϭⲓ ⲡϫⲟⲉⲓⲥ
[ϫⲉⲕ]ⲁⲣⲡ[ⲟⲥ ⲛ]ⲓⲙ' ⲙ̅-
[ⲡⲉ]ⲡ̅ⲛ̅ⲁ̅ ⲉⲧϩ̅ⲛ̅ⲣⲱ-
[ⲙⲉ] ⲛⲓⲙ'. ⲉⲩⲛⲏⲩ
[ⲉⲃⲟ]ⲗ ϩⲓⲧⲟⲟⲧϥ̅ ⲉ-
[ϫⲱ]ⲟⲩ· ⲕⲁⲧⲁ ⲡϣⲁ-
[ϫⲉ] ⲉⲛⲧⲁïⲁⲕⲱⲃⲟⲥ
[ϫⲟ]ⲟϥ· ϫⲉϯ ⲛⲓⲙ'
[ⲉⲧ]ⲛⲁⲛⲟⲩϥ' ⲁⲩⲱ
[ⲇ]ⲱⲣⲟⲛ ⲛⲓⲙ' ⲉⲧ-
[ϫ]ⲏⲕ' ⲉⲃⲟⲗ ⲟⲩⲉⲃⲟⲗ'
ϩ̅ⲛ̅ⲧⲡⲉ'ⲡⲉ ⲉϥⲛⲏⲩ
ⲉⲡⲉⲥⲏⲧ' ϩⲓⲧⲙ̅-
ⲡⲉⲓⲱⲧ' ⲛ̅ⲛ̅ⲟⲩⲟ-
[ⲉ]ⲓⲛ· ⲉⲁϥⲉⲓⲙⲉ ⲟⲛ

[. . . . .]ⲛ̣ⲧ[
[. . .] ϩⲁⲧⲉⲧ[ⲏⲩ-]
[ⲧ]ⲛ. ⲁⲗⲗⲁ ϯⲡ̅ⲙ̣̅[ⲙⲏ-]
ⲧ̅ⲛ̅ ϩ̅ⲙ̅ⲡⲉⲡ̅ⲛ̅ⲁ̣̅ [ϩ̅ⲙ̅-]
ⲡⲧⲩⲡⲟⲥ ⲙ̅ⲡ[ⲣⲏ]
ⲉⲧϣⲁ' ⲉϫ̅ⲙ̅ⲡ̣[ⲕⲁϩ']
ⲧⲏⲣϥ̅ ⲁⲩⲱ ⲉⲣ[ⲉⲛ-]
ⲣⲱⲙⲉ ⲉⲧϩ̅ⲛ̅ⲭ̣[ⲱⲣⲁ]
ⲛⲓⲙ' ⲙⲟⲟϣⲉ ϩ[ⲙ̅-]
ⲡⲉϥⲟⲩⲟⲉⲓⲛ· [ⲧⲁï-]
ⲧⲉ ⲑⲉ ⲛ̅ⲟⲩⲟⲛ [ⲛⲓⲙ']
ⲉⲛⲧⲁⲩⲱⲡ' [ⲉⲡⲉ-]
ϫⲡⲟ' ⲛ̅ⲕⲉⲥⲟ[ⲡ ϩ̅ⲙ̅-]
ⲡⲉⲩⲁⲅⲅⲉⲗ[ⲓⲟⲛ]
ⲕⲁⲛ ⲉⲛⲥⲉⲥ̣[ⲟⲟⲩⲛ]
ⲁⲛ, ⲛ̅ⲛⲉⲩⲉ[ⲣⲏⲩ ⲙ̅-]
ⲡϩⲟ· ⲁⲗⲗⲁ ⲛ̣[ⲉⲧ-]
ϩ̅ⲙ̅ⲙⲁ' ⲛⲓⲙ [ⲥⲉⲥⲟ-]
ⲟⲩⲛ, ⲛ̅ⲛⲉⲩⲉⲣ[ⲏⲩ]
ϩⲓⲟⲩⲥⲟⲡ· ⲁⲩ[ⲱ ⲥⲉ-]
ϣⲟⲟⲡ' ϩⲓⲟⲩ[

margin

Fol. 28. *Recto* (*v.* Am. 444). . . . the] sun, rising upon the earth.[1] And (δέ) [its] appearance (*lit.* likeness) was bright[2] exceedingly. It befell that when the fear had reached him, he fell down and continued twitching (*lit.* leaping) upon the ground, [even] as a live fish twitcheth upon the ground,[3] after it (*sc.* the fear) had entered into[4] his limbs (μέλος) and his joints (ἁρμός) and his marrow[5] [and] all his body (σῶμα) and his soul (ψυ.). But (δέ) when he had been very sorrowful, even unto (ὥστε) giving himself over unto death, [the angels] looked toward him with a part (μέρος) of their face(s) . . . . .

. . . not bear all [the fear] of the Lord ?'[6] After he had been troubled (θλίβειν)[7] . . ., he cried [out] many times, 'Lord, have mercy upon me.' Forthwith the ray[8] (ἀκτίν) of fear went, little by little, and returned to its [place]. And (δέ) thereafter too the [image] of mercy moved, little by little, until[9] it reached [him]. And its appearance [was] like unto oil exceeding thick.[10] And (δέ) when it had come to him, forth[with ? . . . . .

Verso (*v.* Am. 444). . . . thus . . . . . this figure that the Lord had shown [him[11]], how that every fruit (καρ.) of the Spirit (πν.) that is in any (*lit.* every) man doth come forth upon them[12] from Him, according to (κατά) the word that James spake,[13] saying, 'Every good gift (δῶρον) and every perfect gift (δ.) is from heaven, coming down from the father of lights.' And he knew also . . . . .

. . . with you. But (ἀλλά) I am with you in the Spirit (πν.), in the type (τύπος) of the [sun], which riseth upon all the [earth], and men that are in all countries (χώρα) do walk in his light. This is the manner of all such as are reckoned [of the] second birth [in ?] the Gospel (εὐ.), albeit (κἄν) they know not one another by sight (*lit.* face), yet (ἀλλά) do they that (?) are in every place know one another at once, and are in (?) . . . . .

[1] Am. should be, 'like the sun, when he riseth upon the earth. And their appearance was green exceedingly.'

[2] *Cf.* Br. Mus. Or. 7029 ζ, ⲡⲟⲩⲟⲧⲟⲩⲉⲧ ⲙⲡⲛⲟⲩⲃ. Am., misunderstanding, اخضر.

[3] Am. *sic*.

[4] Am., 'were broken, injured,' *sc.* his limbs.

[5] Am., 'the place without bones,' translating Bo. ⲁⲧ-ⲕⲁⲥ.

[6] Am. *om.* 'of the Lord'.

[7] Am. should be, 'And when the anxiety had reached him.'

[8] Am. *sic*, sing. [9] G *sic*, Am. 'and'.

[10] Am. should be, 'a very heavy perfume.'

[11] Am. should be, 'And thus passed this similitude that the Lord showed him;' G ⲣⲛ̄ⲃ b reading 'And thus it passed. And this similitude the Lord showed him, so that'.

[12] Am. should be, 'upon men.'

[13] Jas. i. 17.

Fol. 29. → *Recto* (?).

]. .

[. . . . . . ⲉϣ]ϫⲉ
[ⲛϯϩⲁⲧⲉⲧ]ⲏⲩⲧ̅
[ⲁⲛ] ϩ̅ⲛ̅ⲧⲥⲁⲣⲝ̅· ⲁ[ⲗ-]
ⲗⲁ ϯⲛ̅ⲙ̅ⲙⲏⲧⲛ̅
ϩ̅ⲙ̅ⲡⲉⲡⲛ̅ⲁ̅· ⲉⲡⲉⲓ-
ⲇⲏ̣' ⲇⲉ ⲟⲩⲛ̅ϩⲟⲉⲓⲛⲉ
ϩ̅ⲛ̅ⲙ̅ⲡⲓⲥⲧⲟⲥ' ⲉⲁⲩ-
ϫⲡⲟ' ⲛⲁⲩ ⲛ̅ⲟⲩⲙⲉ-
ⲣⲟⲥ ⲛ̅ⲛ̅ⲕⲁⲣⲡⲟⲥ ⲙ̅-
ⲡⲉⲡⲛ̅ⲁ̅ ⲙ̅ⲡϫⲟⲉⲓⲥ.
ⲛ̅ⲕⲉⲙⲉⲣⲟⲥ ⲇⲉ ⲛ̅ⲧⲟϥ
[ⲙ̅ⲡⲁ]ⲧⲟⲩⲉϣϭⲙ̅-
ϭⲟⲙ' ⲛ̅ϫⲡⲟⲟⲩ ⲛⲁⲩ·
[ⲉⲧ]ⲃⲉⲡⲁï ϥⲡⲣⲟ-
[ⲧⲣⲉ]ⲡⲉ' ⲛ̅ⲛⲁï ⲛ̅ⲧⲉï-
ⲙⲓⲛⲉ ⲛ̅ϭⲓ ⲡ̅ϩ̅ⲙ̅ϩⲁⲗ' (*sic*)
ⲙ̅ⲡⲛⲟⲩⲧⲉ ïⲁⲕⲱ-
ⲃⲟⲥ ⲉϥϫⲱ ⲙ̅ⲙⲟⲥ
ϫⲉⲡⲉⲧϣⲁⲁⲧ' ⲛ̅-
ⲟⲩⲥⲟⲫⲓⲁ ⲛ̅ϩⲏⲧ-
ⲧⲏⲩⲧⲛ̅ ⲉⲧⲉϩⲟⲉⲓ-

ϩⲁⲡⲗ[ⲱⲥ ⲉⲛϥⲛⲟϭ-]
ⲛⲉϭ ⲁⲛ, ⲁ[ⲩⲱ ϥ̅ⲛⲁ-]
ϯ ⲛⲁϥ· ⲡⲉⲓ̣ϣ[ⲁϫⲉ]
ⲇⲉ ϫⲉϩⲁⲡⲗⲱ[ⲥ ⲉⲛϥ-]
ⲛⲟϭⲛⲉϭ ⲁⲛ ⲁⲩ[ⲱ]
ϥ̅ⲛⲁϯ ⲛⲁϥ. ⲉⲧⲉ̣-
ⲡⲁïⲡⲉ ⲉϥϯ ⲛ̅ⲟⲩ-
ⲟⲛ ⲛⲓⲙ' ϩ[ⲛ̅]ⲟⲩⲙ̅[ⲛ̅ⲧ-]
ϩⲁⲡⲗⲟⲩⲥ ⲛ̅ϭⲓ ⲡϫ[ⲟ-]
ⲉⲓⲥ, ⲉⲛϥ̅ⲛⲟϭⲛⲉϭ [ⲛ̅-]
ⲗⲁⲁⲩ ⲛ̅ⲛⲉⲧⲁⲓⲧ[ⲉⲓ']
ⲙ̅ⲙⲟϥ ϫⲉⲁⲕⲣ̅ⲛⲟ-
ⲃⲉ ⲉⲣⲟï ⲏ (+ above) ⲁⲕⲣ̅ϣⲁϥ-
ⲧⲉ ⲛ̅ϯⲛⲁϯ ⲛⲁⲕ
ⲙ̅ⲡⲉⲕⲁⲓⲧⲏⲙ[ⲁ·]
ⲛ̅ⲧⲟϥ' ϩⲱⲱϥ' ⲡ[ⲉⲧ-]
ⲁⲓⲧⲉⲓ' ϥ̅ϫⲱ' ⲙ̅ⲙⲟ[ⲥ]
ⲉⲧⲃⲏⲏⲧϥ̅ ϫⲉⲙⲁ-
ⲣⲉϥⲁⲓⲧⲉⲓ ϩ̅ⲛ̅ⲟⲩⲡⲓ-
ⲥⲧⲓⲥ, ⲉⲛϥ̅ⲇⲓⲁⲕⲣⲓ-
ⲛⲉ ⲛ̅ⲗⲁⲁⲩ ⲁⲛ· ⲉⲧ[ⲉ-]

margin

↑ *Verso* (?).

[. . . . . . .]ⲡ̣ⲙⲁ
[ⲉⲧⲉⲣⲉⲡⲣⲱ]ⲙⲉ ϣⲱ-
[ⲡⲉ ⲛ̅]ϩⲏⲧϥ̅ ⲉⲃⲟⲗ
[ϩⲓ]ⲧⲙ̅ⲡⲛⲟⲩⲧⲉ·

ⲛ̅ⲥ̣[
ⲑⲓⲉ̅ ϩⲏ̣[ⲧ ? ⲛ̅-]
ⲧⲟϥ ⲙ̅ⲡⲛ̅ⲥ[ⲁⲧⲣⲉⲥ-]
ⲙⲓⲥⲉ ⲛ̅ⲧⲉⲡⲕ̣[ⲟⲩï]

[ⲛ̄]ⲑⲉ ⲛ̄ⲟⲩⲥϩⲓⲙⲉ
ⲉϣⲁⲥⲱ̄ⲱ̄ ⲕⲟⲩⲓ̈
ⲕⲟⲩ[ⲓ̈ ⲙ̄]ⲛ̄ⲛ̄ⲥⲱⲥ
ⲛ̄ⲥⲙ[ⲓ]ⲥⲉ· ⲛ̄ⲧⲉ-
ⲡⲕⲟⲩⲓ̈ ϫⲁⲧⲉ ϣⲏⲙ’
ϣⲏⲙ’ ϣⲁⲛⲧϥ̄-
ⲣ̄ⲧⲉⲗⲉⲓⲟⲥ ϩⲛ̄ⲑⲏ-
ⲗⲓⲕⲓⲁ· ⲧⲁⲓ̈ⲧⲉ ⲑⲉ’
ⲛ̄ⲛ̄ⲕⲁⲣⲡⲟⲥ ⲙ̄ⲡⲉ-
ⲡ̄ⲛ̄ⲁ̄ ⲉϣⲁⲣⲉⲡⲣⲱ-
ⲙⲉ ϫⲡⲟⲟⲩ ⲛ̄ϩⲏ-
ⲧϥ̄ ⲕⲟⲩⲓ̈ ⲕⲟⲩⲓ̈ ϩⲙ̄-
ⲡⲧⲱϣ’ ⲙ̄ⲡⲉϥ-
ϩⲏⲧ’ ϣⲁⲛⲧϥ̄ⲣ̄-
ⲧⲉⲗⲉⲓⲟⲥ· ⲛ̄ϩⲏⲧⲟⲩ
ⲛ̄ⲑⲉ ⲉⲧⲥⲏϩ’· ϫⲉ-

ⲙⲟⲩ ⲛ̄ⲧⲉⲩⲛⲟⲩ·
ⲧⲁⲓ̈ⲧⲉ ⲑⲉ ⲛ̄ⲟⲩⲣⲱ-
ⲙⲉ ⲙ̄ⲛ̄ⲛ̄ⲥⲁⲧⲣⲉϥ-
ⲥⲙ̄ⲛ̄ ⲇⲓⲁⲑⲏ[ⲕ]ⲏ
ⲙ̄ⲛ̄ⲡⲛⲟⲩⲧⲉ ⲉⲣ̄-
ⲡⲉϥⲟⲩⲱϣ’ ⲁⲩⲱ
ⲉϥⲁⲣⲉϩ’ ⲉⲛⲉϥⲉⲛ-
ⲧⲟⲗⲏ· ⲁⲩⲱ ϥⲡⲣⲟ-
ⲕⲟⲡⲧⲉ ⲕⲁⲧⲁ ⲧⲇⲓ-
ⲁⲑⲏⲕⲏ ⲉⲛⲧⲁϥ-
ⲥⲙ̄ⲛ̄ⲧⲥ̄ ⲁⲩⲱ ⲙ̄ⲛ̄-
ⲛ̄ⲥⲱⲥ ⲛ̄ϥⲕⲁ ⲧⲟ-
ⲟⲧϥ̄ ⲉⲃⲟⲗ’ ϩⲛ̄ⲛ̄ -
ⲕⲁⲣⲡⲟⲥ ⲙ̄ⲡⲉⲡ̄ⲛ̄ⲁ̄
ⲉⲛⲧⲁϥⲁⲣⲭⲉⲓ’ ⲛ̄-
7 ϩⲏⲧⲟⲩ: ⲛ̄ⲧⲟϥ

margin

Fol. 29. (The right position of this fol. is uncertain.)

Recto. . . . 'If I am not among you in the flesh (*σάρξ*), yet (*ἀλλά*) am I with you in the spirit (*πν.*).'[1] And since then (*ἐπειδή δέ*) there are some of the faithful (*πιστός*) have brought forth for themselves a portion (*μέρος*) of the fruits (*καρ.*) of the Spirit (*πν.*) of the Lord, while (*δέ*) as for the other portion (*μέ.*), they have not been able to bring them forth; for this cause doth the servant of God, James, exhort (*προτρέπειν*) such as these, saying,[2] 'He that lacketh wisdom (*σοφία*) among you—that is,[3] some . . . . .

. . . liberally (*ἁπλῶς*), upbraiding not, and he shall give unto him.' And (*δέ*) this saying: 'liberally (*ἁπ.*), upbraiding not, and he shall give unto him,' it(s meaning) is this: the Lord giveth unto every one with liberality (-*ἁπλοῦς*), upbraiding not any one of them that ask (*αἰτεῖν*) Him, (saying,) 'Thou hast sinned against Me, or (*ἤ*) Thou hast done iniquity; I will not

[1] Col. ii. 5.

[2] Jas. i. 5.

[3] An explanatory insertion; so too at end of this page.

grant thee thy request (*αἴτημα*).' Rather, of him that asketh (*αἰ.*) he saith,[1] 'Let him ask (*αἰ.*) in faith (*πίστις*), nothing doubting (*διακρίνειν*)—that [is . . . . .

Verso. . . . the place [where]in a man is, through God['s will]. Even as a woman conceiving, little by little, and afterwards bringing forth, and the little (one) growing by small degrees, until he reach completion (-*τέλειος*) in age (*ἡλικία*); such is the fashion of the fruits (*κα.*) of the Spirit (*πν.*), a man bringing them forth within himself, little by little, in the measure of his heart, until he be complete (*τέλειος*) therein, as it is written, ...

. . . cause abortion[2]; [but] then, after that she hath brought forth, straightway the little (one) dieth. This is the fashion of a man who, after that he hath established a covenant (*διαθήκη*) with God, to do His will and to keep His commandments (*ἐντολή*), and hath progressed (*προκόπτειν*) according to the covenant (*κατά, διαθ.*) that he hath established, doth afterward renounce the fruits (*κα.*) of the Spirit (*πν.*), wherein he had made beginning (*ἄρχειν*). He . . . . .

Fol. 30. ↑ *Recto.*

?
]ⲧⲉ
ⲙⲏ] ⲛ̄ⲧⲁⲧⲉ-
[ⲧ̄ⲛ̄ . . .] . ϥ' ⲛⲁï
[ⲉⲧⲣⲁϯ ⲡⲉϥ]ϩⲁⲡ'
[ⲟⲩⲡⲉ[a]] ⲡⲉⲧⲛ-
[ϩⲱⲃ ⲁⲛⲁⲭ]ⲱⲣⲉⲓ ⲛⲏ-
[ⲧ̄ⲛ̄ ⲙ̄ⲡϥ]ⲟⲩⲱϣ ⲇ̣ⲉ̣
[ⲉϫⲟⲟⲥ] ϫⲉⲛ̄ⲧⲟϥ
[ⲁⲛⲡⲉ ϫⲉ]ⲕⲁⲥ, ⲉ . ⲛ̄-[b]

ϩ̣ⲟⲟⲩ ⲛ̄ⲧⲉϥⲙⲛ̄ⲧ̄-
ⲕⲟⲩï ⲉϥⲥⲟⲃⲧⲉ ⲛ̄-
ⲛⲉⲥⲛⲏⲩ · ⲁϥϯ
ϩⲧⲏϥ' ⲉⲟⲩⲁ' ϩ̄ⲛ̄ⲛ[ⲉ-]
ⲧⲟⲩⲱⲙ' ⲉϥⲟⲩⲉ[ⲙ']
ϩⲁϩ' ⲛ̄ⲏϭⲉ ϩⲓⲧⲉ-
ⲧⲣⲁⲡⲉⲍⲁ · ⲡⲉⲧ̄ⲙ̄-
ⲙ̣ⲁⲩ ⲇⲉ ⲛⲉⲙ̄ⲡⲁⲧ[ϥ-]
ⲱⲥ̄ⲕ̄ ϫⲓⲛⲧⲁϥⲉⲓ' [ⲉ-]
ⲛⲉⲥⲛⲏⲩ · ⲁϥⲙⲉⲕ-
ⲙⲟⲩⲕ̄ϥ̄ ⲇⲉ ϩⲣⲁï ⲛ̄-

[a] This does not sufficiently fill the space. [b] Reading surely mistaken. The Greek word perhaps ⲇⲓⲥⲧⲁⲍⲉ; ⲛⲟⲙⲓⲍⲉ is too rare to be probable.

[1] Jas. i. 6.

[2] *Cf.* Lagarde, *Aeg.* 240 ⲛⲛⲉⲕⲑⲓⲉ ϩⲏⲧⲥ ⲛⲟⲩⲥϩⲓⲙⲉ ⲉⲡⲉⲥⲏⲧ; Curzon MS. 108, ⲡ̄ⲁ̄, ⲑⲉ ⲟⲛ ⲛⲧⲁⲕⲑⲓⲉ ϩⲏⲧϥ (*sic*) ⲛⲛⲉϩⲓⲟⲙⲉ ⲉⲧⲉⲉⲧ ⲛⲁⲕ.

[ ]ⲍⲉ ⲉⲕⲉⲟⲩⲁ·
[ⲁⲗⲗⲁ ⲁϥ]ⲕⲁⲣⲱϥ' ⲉ-
[ⲛϥϫⲉ ⲗ]ⲁⲁⲩ ⲛⲁⲩ,
[ⲁⲛ ⲉ]ⲙⲛⲧⲓ' ⲉ-
[ⲡⲁⲓ ⲙ̅ⲙⲁ]ⲧ̣ⲉ ϫⲉⲁϊ-
[ⲧⲱϣ ⲙ̅ⲡϩⲱ]ⲃ̣ ⲉⲧⲉ̣-

ϩⲏⲧϥ̅ ⲛ̅ϭⲓ̈ ⲑⲉⲟⲇ[ⲱ-]
ⲣⲟⲥ ⲉϥϫⲱ ⲙ̅ⲙⲟⲥ
ϫⲉⲉⲛⲟⲩⲛⲟϥⲣⲉ̣ [ⲁⲛ-]
ⲧⲉ ⲙ̅ⲡⲉϊⲥⲟⲛ, ⲉⲧ-
ⲣⲉϥⲟⲩⲉⲙ' ϩⲁϩ' ⲛ̅ⲛ-
ϭⲉ ϫⲉⲟ[ⲩ]ϩⲣ̅ϣⲓⲣⲉⲡⲉ

margin

→ *Verso.*

ⲙⲙⲟⲛⲁⲭⲟⲥ ⲛϣ-
ϣⲉ ⲁⲛ ⲉⲣⲟϥ ⲉⲟⲩⲉⲙ
ⲛϭⲉ ϣⲁⲛⲧϥ̅ⲥⲉⲓ.
ⲉⲃⲟⲗ' ϫⲉⲟⲩⲟⲩⲟⲟⲧⲉ-
ⲡⲉ ⲉϥⲧⲣⲉⲡⲣⲱ-
ⲙⲉ ϭ̅ⲙ̅ϭⲟⲙ· ⲙ̅ⲛ̅ⲛ̅-
ⲥⲁⲧⲣⲉϥϫⲱ ⲇⲉ ⲙ̅-
ⲡⲉϊϣⲁϫⲉ ⲁϥⲗⲩ-
ⲡⲉⲓ' ⲉⲙⲁⲧⲉ ϩ̅ⲙ̅ⲡⲉϥ-
ϩⲏⲧ' ⲛ̅ϭⲓ ⲑⲉⲟⲇⲱ-
ⲣⲟⲥ ⲉϥϫⲱ ⲙ̅ⲙⲟⲥ ϫⲉ-
ⲙⲉϣⲁⲕ' ⲙ̅ⲡⲟⲩⲱϣ
ⲙ̅ⲡϫⲟⲉⲓⲥ ⲁⲛⲡⲉ
ⲡϣⲁϫⲉ ⲉⲛⲧⲁϊϫⲟ-
ⲟϥ' ϫⲉⲙ̅ⲡⲓⲣ̅ϩⲁⲣϣ̅
ϩⲏⲧ' ϣⲁⲛⲧϥ̅ⲧⲱ-
ⲃ̅ⲥ ϩ̅ⲛⲧⲉϥⲡⲣⲟϩⲁⲓ-
ⲣⲉⲥⲓⲥ ⲙⲁⲩⲁⲁϥ· ⲛ̅ϥ-

ⲣ̣[
ⲑⲉⲟ̣[ⲇⲱⲣⲟⲥ ⲇⲉ ⲛ̅-]
ⲧⲉ̣ⲣⲉ[ϥⲉⲓⲙⲉ ϫⲉ-]
ⲡⲉⲓ̣ⲥ̣[ⲟⲛ ⲟⲩ-]
ⲱϩ' ⲉⲧ[ⲟⲟⲧϥ̅ ⲉⲟⲩ-]
ⲉⲙ' ⲛ[ϭⲉ
ⲛϭⲉ ⲙ̅[ⲙⲁⲧⲉ ⲛ̅-]
ⲧⲁϥϫ[ⲟⲟⲥ ⲁϥϩⲁ-]
ⲣⲉϩ' ⲉⲣⲟ̣[ϥ ⲉⲧ̅ⲙ̅ⲟⲩ-]
ⲱⲙ' ⲉⲡ[ⲧⲏⲣϥ̅ ϣⲁ-]
ⲡⲉϩⲟⲟ[ⲩ ⲉⲣⲉⲡϫⲟ-]
ⲉⲓⲥ ϭ̅ⲙ̣̅ [ⲡⲉϥϣⲓⲛⲉ]
ⲛ̅ϩⲏ[ⲧϥ

margin

Fol. 30. *Recto* (*v.* Am. 458). ... Have ye [(μή) brought] him unto me [that I should give] judgement [upon him? What then (?) is] your [affair?[1] De]part (ἀναχωρεῖν).' And (δέ) he wished [not to say,] It [was not] he, lest they should (?)[2] suspect (?) another; [but[3] (ἀλλά) he] kept silence, [saying] naught unto them, except (εἰμήτι) [this a]lone: 'I have [ordered the] matter that .....

... in the] days of his youth, while making ready for the brethren, he observed one of them that did eat, eating many leeks at table (τράπ.). But (δέ) it was not long since he had come to the brethren. And (δέ) Theodore thought within himself, saying, 'It is not a good (thing) for this brother that he eat many leeks, for he is a youth .....

Verso (*v.* Am. 458, 459). ... monk[4] (μον.) it befitteth him not to eat leeks until he be sated; for it is a herb that causeth a man to be strong.' But (δέ) when Theodore had said this word, he was much grieved (λυπεῖν) at heart, saying, 'If so be it is not the Lord's will, the word that I have spoken, seeing I had not patience until he should be stirred up by his own purpose (προαίρεσις) and he .....

... [But (δέ) Theo]dore when [he] had [known that this] [brother ... not] contin[ued to] eat leeks[5] .... that he had spo[ken, he ke]pt himself [from ea]ting (them) at all, [until] the day where[on] the Lord visited him .....

Fol. 31. → *Recto.*

margin

ⲟⲩ ⲧⲱϥ’ ⲁⲩⲱ
ⲙ̅ⲛ̅ⲛ̅ⲥⲁⲧⲣⲉϥϩⲟⲃ-
ⲥ̅ϥ̅ ⲛ̅ⲧⲉⲧⲙⲏ ⲛ̅-
ϭⲓ ⲑⲉⲟⲇⲱⲣⲟⲥ · ⲁϥ-
ⲛⲉϫ’ ⲧⲟⲟⲧ̅ϥ̅ ⲉϩⲣⲁï
[ⲉ]ⲩⲛ̅ⲕⲁ̀ ⲉϥⲙⲉϩ ⲛ̅-
[ⲃ]ⲛ̅ⲛⲉ ⲁϥⲙⲉϩ’ ⲧⲉϥ-
ϭⲓϫ’ ⲁϥⲥⲟⲟⲩⲧ̅ⲛ̅
[ⲙ̅]ⲙⲟⲟⲩ ⲉⲣⲟϥ’ ϫⲉⲉ-
[ϥ]ⲉϫⲓⲧⲟⲩ ⲛ̅ϥ̅ⲟⲩⲟ-

ⲙ̣[ⲟⲛⲟⲛ ϫⲉⲙⲡⲉⲕⲟⲩ-]
ⲱϣ̣ ⲉϩ[ⲟⲃ̅ⲥ̅ⲕ̅ ⲙ̅ⲡⲉⲓ-]
ⲡⲣⲏϣ̣ [ⲛ̅ⲥⲟⲣ̅ⲧ̅ ⲁⲗⲗⲁ]
ⲧⲕⲉϭⲓ[ϫ’ ⲛ̅ⲃ̅ⲛ̅ⲛ̅ⲉ ⲟⲛ]
ⲛ̅ϥ̣̅ⲟⲩⲱ[ϣ ⲁⲛ ⲉϫⲓⲧ̅ⲥ̅]
ⲛ̅ⲧⲟⲟⲧ̣[· ⲁϥⲟⲩⲱ-]
ϣ̅ⲃ̅ ⲇⲉ ⲡⲉ̣[ϫⲁϥ ⲛⲁϥ]
ϫⲉⲉⲕⲙ̣ⲉ̣[ⲉⲩⲉ ϫⲉⲛ̅-]
ϯⲟⲩⲁϣ[ⲟ]ⲩ ⲁ[ⲛ ⲧⲁ-]
ⲟⲩⲟⲙⲟⲩ̣ ⲁ[ⲗⲗⲁ ϯⲣ̅-]

[1] Am. 'Have ye brought him &c.? What is it to you?' *Cf.* AS. § 58 end, Bo. 112.

[2] Copy inadequate. Am. has 'think'.

[3] Am. *sic.*

[4] Preceded by an adjective, or by ⲣⲱⲙⲉ or the like.

[5] The 2nd ⲛϭⲉ 'leeks' must be wrongly read.

[ⲙ]ⲟⲩ. ⲛ̄ⲧⲟϥ ⲇⲉ ⲉⲙ-
[ⲡ]ϥϫⲓⲧⲟⲩ· ⲟⲩⲧⲉ
[ⲙ̄]ⲡϥϫⲟⲟⲥ ⲟⲛ ⲛⲁϥ
[ϫ]ⲉⲥⲉⲕ' ⲧⲟⲟⲧⲕ̄ ⲉⲣⲟⲕ·
[ⲁⲗ]ⲗⲁ ⲁϥϭⲱϣ̄ⲧ ⲛ̄-
[ⲥⲱ]ϥ ⲉⲣⲉⲛⲉϥⲣ̄ⲙ̄ⲉⲓⲟ̣-
[ⲟ]ⲩⲉ ϣ̣ⲟⲩⲟ' ⲉⲡⲉⲥⲏⲧ'
[ⲛ̄]ⲧⲉ̣[ⲣ]ⲉϥⲛⲁⲩ ⲇⲉ ⲉ-
[ⲣⲟϥ' ⲛ̄]ϭⲓ ⲑⲉⲟⲇⲱⲣⲟⲥ
[ⲉⲣⲉⲛ]ⲉϥⲃⲁⲗ ϯ ⲣ̄ⲙ̄-
[ⲉⲓⲏ] ⲁϥⲣⲓⲙⲉ ϩⲱⲱϥ
[ⲡⲉϫ]ⲁϥ ⲛⲁϥ ϫⲉⲁ-
[ϩⲣⲟⲕ ⲉⲕ]ⲣⲓⲙⲉ· ⲛ̄ⲧⲟϥ
[ⲇⲉ ⲡⲉϫⲁ]ϥ ⲛⲁϥ ϫⲉ-
[ⲉⲧⲃⲉ]ϫⲉϯⲛⲁⲩ ⲉ-
[ⲣⲟⲕ ⲉⲕϣ]ⲱⲛⲉ· ⲟⲩ'

ϩⲟⲧⲉ ⲉⲧⲃⲉ̣ⲡ̣[ϩⲁⲡ]
ⲙ̄ⲡⲉⲭ̄ⲥ̄ ϫ̣ⲉⲛ̣[ⲛⲉⲩ-][a]
ⲕⲣⲓⲛⲉ ⲙ̄ⲙⲟ[ⲓ· ⲡⲉ-]
ϫⲁϥ ⲛⲁϥ ϫⲉ[ⲉⲧⲃⲉ-]
ⲟⲩ' ⲉⲩⲛⲁⲕⲣⲓ[ⲛⲉ ⲙ̄-]
ⲙⲟⲕ· ⲙⲏ ⲛⲉⲧ̣-
ϣⲱⲛⲉ ⲧⲏⲣⲟⲩ ϩ̄[ⲛ̄-]
ⲛⲉⲥⲛⲏⲩ ⲙⲉⲛⲁ̣[b]
ⲛⲁⲩ· ⲛ̄ ⲉⲩϣⲁⲛ[ⲣ̄-]
ⲭⲣⲓⲁ ⲛ̄ⲟⲩⲡⲣⲏϣ [ⲛ̄-]
ⲥⲟⲣ̄ⲧ̄ ⲛ̄ ⲟⲛ ⲕⲉⲧ̣
ⲙⲉⲛⲧⲁⲁϥ ⲛⲁ[ⲩ·]
ⲛ̄ⲧⲟϥ ⲇⲉ ⲡⲉϫ[ⲁϥ]
ⲛⲁϥ· ϫⲉⲁⲕⲙ[ⲉϣ̄ⲧ]
ⲛ̄ⲕⲁⲗⲩⲃⲏ ⲛ̄[ⲛⲉⲥ-]
ⲛⲏⲩ ⲙ̄ⲡⲉⲓ̈[ⲛⲁⲩ]
ⲁⲕⲉⲓⲙⲉ ϫⲉⲙ̄[ⲙⲛ̄-]

margin

[a] Or ⲛⲉϥ-.

[b] ⲁ is faint; read ⲙⲉⲛⲛⲁ.

↑ *Verso.*

margin

]ⲩ̣ⲛ̣ⲡⲉⲧ-
[ϣⲱⲛⲉ ⲉϩ]ⲟⲩⲉⲣⲟⲓ̈ ⲙ̄-
[ⲡⲱⲣ ⲛ̄ⲛⲉⲥ]ϣ̣ⲱⲡⲉ
[ⲛ̄ⲧⲉⲓϩⲉ ⲉ]ⲣ[ⲉ]ⲛ̣̄ⲥⲕⲉ̣ⲩ-
[ⲏ ⲛ̄ⲛⲉⲥ]ⲛⲏⲩ ⲛⲧⲟ̣ⲟ̣-
[ⲧⲛ̄]ⲛ̣[a] ⲉⲣ̣̄ⲡⲉⲙ̄ⲙ̄-
[ⲧⲟⲛ ⲛ̄ϩ]ⲏⲧⲟⲩ ⲉϩⲟⲩⲉ-

ⲟⲟⲙ' ⲛ̄ⲧⲁⲓ̈ⲡⲁⲥⲧ̄ⲉ̄
ⲛ̄ϥ̄ⲛⲁⲣⲱϣⲉ ⲁⲛ
ⲉⲣⲟⲟⲩ· ⲁϥϭⲱϣ̄ⲧ
ⲇⲉ ⲛ̄ⲥⲱϥ' ⲛ̄ϭⲓ ⲡⲉⲛ-
ⲉⲓⲱⲧ' ⲡⲁϩⲱⲙ[ⲉ]
ⲁϥⲉⲓⲙⲉ ⲉⲡⲙⲟⲛ-
ⲙⲉⲕ' ⲉⲛⲧⲁϥⲁⲗ[ⲉ]
ⲉϩⲣⲁⲓ̈ ⲉϫⲙ̄ⲡⲉϥϩ[ⲏⲧ'·]

[a] Perhaps ⲁ]ⲛ.

[ⲣⲟⲟⲩ·] ⲁ[ⲥ]ϣⲱⲡⲉ
[ϩⲙ̄ⲡ]ⲉ̣ϩⲟⲟⲩ ⲉⲧⲙ̄ⲙⲁⲩ
[ⲛⲉⲣⲉ]ϩ̣ⲉⲛⲥⲛⲏⲩ ⲉⲓ'
[ⲉⲡⲃ̄]ⲟ̣ⲟⲩ[a] ϩⲓⲟⲩϫⲟⲉⲓ
[ⲙ̄ⲡ]ⲛⲁⲩ ⲛ̄ⲣⲟⲩϩⲉ
[ϫⲉⲕ]ⲁ̣ⲥ ⲉⲩⲉⲧⲁⲗⲉ ⲟⲩ-
[. . .]ⲙ'[b] ⲛ̄ⲕⲁⲙ ⲉⲣⲟϥ·
[ⲛ̄]ⲧⲟϥ ⲇⲉ ⲑⲉⲟⲇⲱⲣⲟⲥ
[ⲛ]ⲉ̣ⲁϥⲡⲓⲥⲉ' ⲛ̄ⲟⲩϭⲓⲛ-
[ⲟⲩ]ⲟ̣ⲟ̣ⲙ' ⲛ̄ⲛⲉⲥⲛⲏⲩ
[ϩⲙ̄]ⲡ̣ⲉ̣ϩⲟⲟⲩ ⲉⲧⲙ̄ⲙⲁⲩ·
[ⲁⲩ]ⲱ̣ ⲛ̄ⲧⲉⲣⲉϥϭⲱ-
[ϣ]ⲧ̣ ⲁϥⲛⲁⲩ ⲉⲛⲉ-
[ⲥ]ⲛⲏⲩ ϩⲓⲡϫⲟⲓ̈ ⲙ̄-
[ⲡⲁ]ⲧ̄ϥ̄ⲙⲟⲟⲛⲉ ⲁϥ-
[ⲙⲉ]ⲕⲙⲟⲩⲕ̄ϥ̄ ϩⲣⲁⲓ̈
[ⲛ̄ϩ]ⲏⲧ̄ϥ̄ ⲛ̄ⲧⲉⲩⲛⲟⲩ
[ⲉϥⲙⲟ]ⲕ̄ϩ̄ ⲛ̄ϩⲏⲧ ϫⲉ-
[ⲙⲉϣ]ⲁⲕ' ⲧϭⲓⲛⲟⲩ-

ⲡⲉϫⲁϥ' ⲉϩⲟⲩⲛ ⲉ-
ϩⲣⲁϥ' ϫⲉⲟⲩ'ⲡⲉ ⲡ[ⲉⲓ̈-]
ⲙⲟⲕ'ⲙⲉⲕ' ⲉⲛⲧⲁ̣[ⲕ-]
ⲙⲟⲕⲙⲉⲕ' (*sic*) ⲉⲣⲟϥ' ⲑ[ⲉⲟ-]
ⲇⲱⲣⲉ·[c] ⲟⲩⲡⲉⲧϣ̣[ⲟⲩ-]
ⲉⲓⲧ' ⲧⲁⲣⲡⲉ' ⲉⲡ[ⲉⲓ]
ⲛ̄ⲧⲟϥ ⲛ̄ϩⲟⲩⲟ' ⲛ[ⲧⲁⲕ-]
ⲛⲁⲩ ⲉⲛⲉⲥⲛⲏⲩ [ⲉⲩ-]
ⲉⲓ' ϣⲁⲣⲟⲕ ⲉ̣.ⲛ̄.[d
ϩⲙ̄ⲡⲉⲕϩⲏ[ⲧ ϩⲛ̄-]
ⲟⲩϣ̄ⲡ̄ϩ̄ⲙ̄[ⲟⲧ ϫⲉⲱ]
ⲡϫⲟⲉⲓⲥ ⲛ̄ⲑ̣[ⲉ ⲛ̄ⲧⲁⲕ-]
ⲉⲓⲛⲉ ⲛ̄ⲛⲉ[ⲥⲛⲏⲩ]
ϣⲁⲣⲟⲛ ⲉⲧ̣[ⲣⲉⲛ-]
ⲛⲁⲩ ⲟⲛ ⲉ[ⲛⲉⲛⲉⲣⲏⲩ]
ϩⲙ̄ⲡⲉⲓ̈ⲙ[ⲁ'· ⲁⲗⲗ]
ⲟⲛ ⲛ̄ⲙ̄ⲡ[ϣⲁ]
ⲉⲧⲣⲉⲛ[ⲛⲁⲩ ⲉⲛⲉⲛ-]
ⲉⲣⲏⲩ ϩⲙ̄[ⲡⲕⲉⲙⲁ]

margin

[a] Or ϣⲁⲣ]ⲟⲟⲩ. [b] ? ⲉⲧⲡⲱ. [c] Note the vocative form. [d] ⲉ̣. may be ϣ (? ϣⲁϫⲉ).

Fol. 31. *Recto* (*v.* Am. 552). . . . his (*sc.* mat).'[1] And after that Theodore had covered him with the mat, he put forth his hand to a vessel full of dates and filled his hand and reached them forth unto him (*sc.* Pachômius), that he might take and eat them. But (*δέ*) as for him, he took them not, neither (*οὐδέ*) said, Draw back thy hand. But (*ἀλλά*) he looked at him, while his tears flowed down. And (*δέ*) when Theodore beheld him, his eyes shedding tears, he also wept. He (Pach.) said unto him, 'What (lackest) thou, (that) thou weepest?' But (*δέ*) he said unto him, 'Because that I see thee sick. Not [only (*οὐ*

[1] ⲟⲩⲧⲱϥ as prep. + suff. seems improbable.

μόνον) that thou] wouldest not [cover thee with this woollen] coverlet, but (*ἀλλά*)] even the hand[ful of dates also], thou wouldest [not receive it] at my hand.'[1] But (*δέ*) [he answer]ed and [said unto him,] 'Thinkest thou I desired them not, to eat them? Ra[ther (*ἀλλά*) do I] fear because of the judgement of Christ (*Χρ.*), lest I be condemned[2] (*κρίνειν*).' He said unto him, 'Where[fore] shouldest thou be condemned (*κρ.*)? All they that are sick among the brethren, do we not (*μή*) charity unto them? Or (*ἤ*) if they have need (*χρεία*) of a woollen coverlet or (*ἤ*) aught besides, do we not give it unto them? But (*δέ*) he said unto him, 'Hast thou vis[ited] the cells (*καλύβη*) of [the] brethren at this [time] and hast found (*lit.* known) that that there is [not

Verso (*v.* Am. 553). any among them] that is more sick than I? Nay, [let it not] be [thus, while] the things (*σκεύη*) [of the] brethren are in our hands[3] (?), . . . have our com[fort there]from more than [they.'] It befell on that day that brethren came [to] Pbow (?)[4] in a boat, at eventime, that they might load a . . . of reeds thereon.[5] But (*δέ*) as for Theodore, he had cooked food for the brethren that day. And when he had looked, he beheld the brethren in the boat,[6] ere it had come to land; and he thought within himself forthwith, being sad at heart, (saying,) 'Perchance the food that I have cooked shall not suffice for them.' But (*δέ*) our father Pachômius looked toward him and knew the thought that had risen into his heart; and he said unto him, 'What is this thought that thou hast thought, Theodore? Vanity is it indeed (*γάρ*). For (*ἐπεί*) rather the more when thou sawest the brethren coming unto thee, [thou shouldest have said?[7]] in thy heart, in thankfulness, [' O] Lord, even as [Thou hast] brought the [brethren] unto us, that we may see [one another] in this world (*lit.* place[8]), [make us] also wor[thy] that we may [see one] another in [the other world (*lit.* place)].'

[1] Am. *om.* 'at my hand'.

[2] Or 'He condemns me'.

[3] *I.e.* 'in our keeping'. But if ⲛⲧⲟⲟⲧⲛ ⲁⲛ, '. . . are not in our hands, that we should have . . .' Am. differs somewhat. For *couverture*, read *nourriture et vêtement*. [4] Or 'unto them'.

[5] ? 'a load'. Am. should be 'that they might load it with *halfâ*'.

[6] Am. should be, 'And when he looked, he beheld the brethren that had come, and he thought within himself, Perchance the cooked food that he had cooked should not suffice for all.'

[7] Or imperat., 'say', if tense of preceding clause would permit.

[8] Am. 'here'.

Fol. 32. → *Recto* (?).

margin

margin

ϫⲉ ⲙ̅ⲡ̣[ⲓϩⲉⲡ ⲗⲁⲁⲩ]
ⲉⲣⲱⲧ[ⲛ̅ ⲛⲛⲉⲧⲣ-]
ⲛⲟϥⲣⲉ [ⲉⲓⲣⲙⲛⲧ-]
ⲣⲉ ⲛ̅ⲛⲓ̈[ⲟⲩⲇⲁⲓ ⲙ̅ⲛ̅-]
ⲛ̅ϩⲉⲑⲛⲟ[ⲥ ⲛ̅ⲧⲙⲉ-]
ⲧⲁⲛⲟⲓⲁ [ⲉϩⲟⲩⲛ ⲉ-]
ⲡⲛⲟⲩⲧ[ⲉ ⲁⲩⲱ]
ⲧⲡⲓⲥⲧ[ⲓⲥ ⲉϩⲟⲩⲛ]
ⲉⲡⲉⲛϫ̣[ⲟⲉⲓⲥ ⲓ̅ⲥ̅ ⲡⲉ-]
ⲭ̅ⲥ̅ · ⲉ[
ⲛ̅ⲧⲉ[
ⲙⲉ · [
ϫⲉⲁ̣[
ⲛ̅[

↑ *Verso* (?).

margin

margin

ⲟⲩⲟ]ⲉ̣ⲓϣ’ ⲛ̅ⲛ̅-
]ⲧⲉ ⲛ̅ⲣⲉϥ-
]ⲉ · ⲛ̅ⲧⲉⲣⲉϥ-
ϫⲉ]ⲧⲁⲓ̈ⲧⲉ ⲧϭ̅ⲓ̅
[ⲱⲛ̅ϩ̅ ⲛ̅]ⲛⲉⲧⲟⲩⲁⲁⲃ ·
]ⲩ̣ⲉ ⲁⲡϫⲟⲉⲓⲥ
ⲟ]ⲩⲟⲉⲓⲛ ⲛ̅-
]ⲁϥϫⲓ̈
ⲟⲩ]ⲟⲉⲓϣ ⲛ̅-
]ⲧ̣ⲉⲛⲉ
]ⲛⲁⲓ̈
[ⲛ̅ⲧⲁϥϫⲟⲟⲥ] ⲉⲧⲃ̣ⲏ-
[ⲏⲧⲟ̣ⲩ̣ ⲛ̅ϭ̣ⲓ ⲇⲁ]ⲩⲉⲓⲇ’

Fol. 32. (The position of this fol. is quite uncertain.)

Recto (?). . . . 'I [1] have not [hidden aught] from you [of the things that are] profitable, [testify]ing to the Jews and Gentiles (ἔθ.) repentance (μετάν.) [toward] God [and] faith (πίσ.) toward our Lord [Jesus the] Christ (Χρ.) . . . . .

Verso (?). . . . time of the . . . . . When he had [seen? how] this was the manner-of[-life of] the saints . . . . . the Lord had . . . . . light . . . . . he took (?) . . . . time of . . . . [where]of David [spake] . . . . .

[1] Acts xx. 20, 21, but differing considerably from Budge and Woide.

No. 26.

This story of Apollo, ⲫⲓⲗⲟⲥ [ⲡ]ⲡⲁⲅⲅⲉⲗⲟⲥ,[1] and Ammonius of Thône figures in the account of the latter in the *Synaxarium*.[2] A woman had attempted to beguile Ammonius, but had been converted by him. The devil, jealous at this triumph, spreads scandalous reports of the saint among the monasteries, and induces Apollo to visit him and be convinced. Apollo finds there the penitent woman, who, after eighteen years passed in Ammonius' cell, expires in their presence.

→ *Recto.*

[. . .]ⲛ̣ϩ·
[ⲡⲉϫ]ⲁ̣ϥ ⲙ̄ⲡⲁ-
[ⲧⲡ]ⲩ̣ⲗⲏ ϫⲉ-
[ⲃ]ⲱⲕ ⲧⲁⲙⲉ
ⲡⲉⲛⲉ̈ⲓⲱⲧ ⲁ-

[ⲉⲓ ⲉϩⲟ]ⲩⲛ ϣⲁ-
ⲣⲟϥ [ⲁ]ϥⲁⲣⲭⲉⲓ
ⲛ̄ⲣⲓⲙⲉ ⲛϭⲓ
ⲡⲁⲓ̈ⲁⲃⲟⲗⲟⲥ
Ⲡⲉϫⲉ· (sic) ⲁⲡⲁ ⲁ-

[1] His Life by بوهى ⲡⲁⲛⲟϩⲉ in Paris *arabe*, 4888, f. 139 b, whence in *Synax.* 25 Bâbeh. That this is the Apollo of Bawit has already been pointed out (*PSBA.* xxix. 291. The *Antiphonarium*, at the latter date, calls him ⲡⲓϩⲩⲥⲟⲥ [ⲡ]ⲡⲁⲅⲅⲉⲗⲟⲥ). He appears in the Diptychs, usually confounded with the martyr, son of Justus (*e.g.* Renaudot, *Lit.*, *ed.* 1847, i. 18), rarely distinct (*e.g.* Cairo *Euchology.* 358). Clédat's *Baouit* ii. 91 gives Hamoi as his father's name; *cf. Synax.* امانى, Life اموية. To what has been elsewhere collected regarding Apollo and his namesakes (Br. Mus. no. 322 n., *Aeg. Z.* xl. 60), I may add: *Miss.* iv. 818 (= Paris 129[13], f. 63) relates probably to this saint. A Life of A. was in the White Monastery Library (*J. Th. St.* v. 566). He is repeatedly invoked at the Jeremias Monastery, alone or with Phib and (or) Anoup; indeed, two Apollos are there commemorated (Quibell-Thompson, *Saqqâra* nos. 27, 76, 226). The calendaric mention of him with ⲡⲁ ⲡⲉϩⲓⲉⲓⲃ (= ⲁⲡⲁ ⲫⲓⲃ), Leyd. *MSS.* p. 216, remains obscure. The pilgrimage of Herminos and Hôr, related in the Life of the former (Paris *arabe* 148), took them to the church of Apa Apollo. There they beheld the saint's corpse 'adorned and mitred' مزينا متوجا (f. 322 b). Their preceding visits had been on the W. bank to Apa Jeremias ارميا (? of Saqqâra), then alive; thence to the church of Elias the Syrian; while from Apollo's relics they proceeded to those of Apa Mina in Gebel al-Khaṭṭaf (? Lybian Desert) (f. 323 a). This itinerary is too erratic to make it more than probable that its Apollo is he of Bawit. From the Arabic Life (f. 159 b &c.) it seems that the site of 'The Monastery' (ⲡⲁⲟⲩⲏⲧ Bawit) was جبل ازكوهى *i.e.*? ازكبوهى = [ⲡ]ϣϭⲉⲛⲟϩⲉ, where a legend placed the cell of Phib (Zoega 367). (Paris 4787, another copy, reads ادكوهى.) A further corruption of this may be ابلوج, *Synax.*, *l.c.* Several other names in this text await elucidation from its Coptic original, announced as in the P. Morgan collection (*Journ. d. Sav.* 1912, 181). J. Maspero points out that the monastery of A. at (?) Aphrodito is named after its historical founder, otherwise identifiable (Pap. Cairo no. 67096). Can this be the same with that near Kom Esfaht (Petrie, *Gizeh and Rifeh* 39), where the patron A. is often called ἅγιος?

[2] 20 Bashans (Forget ii. 130). Tûnah el-Gebel, W. of Ashmunain, is some 25 miles N. of Bawit. But Apollo was perhaps not, at this time, resident at Bawit; *v. Aeg. Z.*, *l.c.* Thône often occurs in Ashmunain MSS., *e.g.* Br. Mus. 1042, Rylands 119, Krall *Rechtsurk.* cxxxiv. This Ammonius is invoked, *Deir el-Gebrawi* ii, pl. xxix, Clédat *Baouit* ii. 91.

ⲡⲁ ⲁⲡⲟⲗⲗⲱ
ϫⲉⲉⲓ̈ⲥ ⲟⲩⲙⲟ-
ⲛⲁⲭⲟⲥ ⲉⲁⲡⲁ (*sic*)
ⲁⲡⲁ[a] ⲁⲙⲙⲱ-
ⲛⲉⲡⲉ · ⲙⲡⲧⲟ-
ⲟⲩ ⲛⲑⲱⲛⲉ
ⲉϥⲟⲩⲱϣ ⲉ-
ⲁⲡⲁⲛⲧⲁ ⲉ-
ⲧⲉⲕⲙⲛⲧⲉⲓ-
ⲱⲧ ·
Ⲛⲧⲉⲣⲟⲩϫⲓ̈
ⲡⲟⲩⲱ ϫⲉ
(*sic*) ⲛⲁⲁⲡⲁ ⲁⲡ[ⲟ-]
[ⲗⲗⲱ

ⲡⲟⲗⲗⲱ ⲛⲁϥ
ϫⲉⲡⲉϣⲃⲏⲣ
ⲁϩⲣⲟⲕ ⲉⲕⲣⲓ-
ⲙⲉ · ⲁⲣⲁ ⲛⲧⲁ-
ⲡⲁⲥⲟⲛ ⲁⲙⲙⲱ-
ⲛⲉ ⲙⲟⲩ ·
Ⲡⲉϫⲉ ⲡⲉⲧⲙ-
ⲙⲁⲩ ⲉⲧⲉⲡ̣[ⲇⲓ-]
ⲁⲃⲟⲗⲟ[ⲥⲡⲉ
?

[a] Reading ? ⲉⲡⲁⲁⲡⲁ.

↑ *Verso.*

ⲥ̣ⲛ[. . . . . .]ϥ
Ⲁⲡⲇⲓ̈ⲁ[ⲃⲟⲗⲟⲥ ⲑ]ⲃ-
ⲃⲓ̈ⲟϥ ⲁϥϩⲉ ⲉⲃⲟⲗ
ⲙ̄ⲡⲟⲩⲥϩⲓ̈ⲙⲉ
ⲁⲩⲱ ⲛⲧⲉⲣⲉϥϩⲉ
ⲉⲃⲟⲗ ⲛ̄ⲙ̄ⲙⲁⲥ
ⲁⲛϩⲓ̈ⲥⲉ ⲉⲛⲕⲱ-
ⲣ̄ϣ · ⲉⲣⲟϥ ϫⲉⲛⲟ-
ϫ̄ⲥ ⲉⲃⲟⲗ ⲙ̄ⲙⲟⲛ
ϫⲉⲛⲛⲉϩⲉⲛⲕⲟ-
ⲟⲩⲉ ⲧⲁⲕⲟ ⲛⲧⲉⲕ-
ⲗⲟⲉⲓ̈ϭⲉ · ⲙⲡⲉϥ-
ⲗⲟ ϩ̄ⲙ̄ⲡⲉϥⲛⲟ-

[
ⲛⲁϥ [ϫⲉⲛⲛⲉ-]
ϩⲉⲛⲕⲟ[ⲟⲩⲉ ⲧⲁ-]
ⲕⲟ ⲛⲧⲉϥ[ⲁⲫⲟⲣ-]
ⲙⲏ · ⲏ ⲙ̣ⲙ̣[ⲟⲛ]
Ⲧⲛⲛⲟⲟⲩ ⲙⲙ[ⲛⲧ]
ⲛ̄ⲥⲟⲛ ⲛⲙⲙ[ⲁⲛ]
ⲛ̄ⲧⲛϭⲟⲡϥ ⲛ̄-
ⲧ̄ⲡⲁⲣⲁⲇⲓ̈-
ⲇⲟⲩ ⲙ̄ⲙⲟϥ ⲛ-
ⲧⲉⲝⲟⲩⲥⲓ̈ⲁ ⲧⲁ-
ⲣⲟⲩⲥⲱⲧⲙ̄ ⲛ̄-
ⲥⲉϣⲗⲁϩ · ϫⲉⲛ-

ⲃⲉ ⲁⲗⲗⲁ ⲁϥ-
[. . .]ⲉ̣ ⲙ̅ⲙⲁⲧⲉ
[. . . .]ⲟ̣ⲥ ⲛⲙ-

ⲛⲉⲙⲙⲟⲛⲁ-
ⲭⲟⲥ ⲧⲏⲣⲟⲩ ⲧⲁ-
ⲕⲟ ⲛ̄ⲧⲉϥⲁⲫⲟ[ⲣ-]
ⲙⲏ· ⲥⲙⲟⲧⲛ [ⲅⲁⲣ]
Ⲧⲁⲣⲡ̄ⲛⲉϫ ⲟⲩ̣[ⲁ]
ⲉⲃⲟⲗ ⲉⲛ̣ϩⲟⲥ̣[ⲟⲛ]

Recto. ... He said unto the door-keeper (-πύλη), 'Go, tell our father Apa Apollo that, lo, (here is) a monk (*μον.*), namely one from Apa Ammône, of the hill of Thône, who desireth to meet with (*ἀπαντᾶν*) thy paternity.' But (*δέ*) when they had brought the news to Apa Apollo .....

... come] in unto him, the devil began (*ἄρχειν*) to weep. Apa Apollo said unto him, 'Friend, what (aileth) thee, that thou dost weep? Is then (*ἄρα*) my brother Ammône dead?' That one, who was the devil, said, ...

Verso. ... 'The devil (*διάβ.*) humbled him and he fell with a woman. And after that he had fallen with her, we were at pains, beseeching him, (saying,) 'Cast her forth from thee, lest others perish by thine example.' He ceased not from his iniquity, rather (*ἀλλά*) he ... much' .....

'... lest] others perish on his account (*ἀφορμή*). Or (*ἤ*) if not, send ten brethren with [us] and we will take him and give him over (*παραδιδόναι*) unto the authority (*ἐξουσία*), that they may hear and be afraid; lest all the monks (*μον.*) perish on his account (*ἀφ.*). [For? (*γάρ*)] it is easi(er?) that we should cast forth one whilst yet (? -*ὅσον*)' .....

No. 27.

This narrative relates (here at least) to a saint named Hôr. Seven of this name can, I believe, be distinguished,[1] and it is impossible so far to decide which of them is here in question. He appears to have visited Alexandria and presumably in peaceful times; he should therefore not be sought among the martyrs.

[1] **A**, Anchorites (1) *Hist. Laus.* ix (in Nitria) = Sozomen vi. 28 (in Thebaid); (2) companion of Hatre, *Vitae Patr.* v, lib. xv, § 43 = Zoega 299; (3) companion of Ambrosius (*cf.* ? the name 'Apa Rasios', Crum, *Ostr.* no. 116, and ? بدا سيوس = ابراسيوس *Synax.* 23 Tûbah) *PSBA.* xxix. 290, Quibell-Thompson, *Saqqâra* nos. 26, 295; (4) hermit of 2 Kihak, in Ludolf's Calendar 'the younger', and identical with biographer of Herminos, for in that story his and that saint's deaths are foretold for same date (Paris *arabe* 148, f. 328 b). *Cf.* too his epithets 'Dyer' القصار

	↑ *Recto* (?).	→ *Verso* (?).	
	margin	margin	
	ϩⲱⲣ ⲉϥϯ ⲉ[ⲟⲟⲩ]	ⲉϩⲟⲩⲛ ⲉⲡⲧⲟ-	
	ⲙⲡⲛⲟⲩⲧⲉ [ⲙⲛ-]	ⲡⲟⲥ ⲙⲙⲁⲣⲕⲟⲥ	
]ⲱⲥ	ⲛⲉϥⲁⲅⲅⲉⲗⲟ̣[ⲥ]	ⲡⲉⲩⲁⲅⲅⲉⲗⲓⲥ-	Ⲏ[
]ⲉ	Ⲁⲡⲥⲱⲧⲏⲣ ϯ̣ ⲛⲁ̣[ϥ]	ⲧⲏⲥ ⲁϥⲣⲥⲁ-	
	ⲛϯⲣⲏⲛⲏ ⲁϥⲃⲱ[ⲕ]	ϣϥ ⲛϩⲟⲟⲩ ⲉϥ-	
	ⲉϩⲣⲁⲓ ⲉ[ⲙ]ⲡⲏ̣ⲩ[ⲉ·]	ⲛⲏⲥⲧⲉⲩⲉ ϩⲛ-	
	Ⲡⲁ̣[ⲓⲕⲁⲓⲟⲥ	[. . . .]ⲡⲉⲕⲟ.	

Recto (?). . . . Apa] Hôr,[1] giving glory unto God and His angels (ἄγγ.). The Saviour (σωτ.) gave (?) him peace (εἰρήνη) and went up to heaven. The ri[ghteous ? . . . . .

Verso (?). . . . in unto the church (τόπος) of Mark the evangelist[2] and passed seven days fasting (νηστεύειν) in . . . . .

No. 28.

From the history of Apa Cyrus, the hermit, narrated by Pambô.[3] Cyrus, reputed a brother of Theodosius I, dwelt in a κατάγαιον,[4] 'at the edge of the world, nigh unto hell.' On Pambô's arrival he falls ill, and, before his death, is aware of that of Shenoute, which, in the Calendar, occurs on the day preceding his own.

(*Synax. ad loc.*) and الابرجتى (Paris 148, ff. 294 a, 321 b, 330 b), for which I propose ابرختى, *i.e.* ⲡⲣⲁϩⲧ, so explaining the obscure name of his home ابرجت (*alias* اتريب). Yet Amél. *Géogr.* 12 suggests that the latter is a real place-name: B, Martyrs (5) Zoega p. 23 = *CSCO.* vol. 43, 127; (6) *Synax.* 12 Abîb = Amélineau, *Actes* 104: C, Bishop (7) اور (but Abû Sâlih 71 b اورا) Amélineau, *Contes* i. 109. Of these, no. 4 visited Alexandria, as did the subject of our text.

[1] May be subject of a foregoing verb.

[2] *V.* Amélineau, *Géogr.* 37, A. J. Butler, *Arab Conq.* 372.

[3] Br. Mus. Or. 6783 has a complete Life, differing slightly from the other versions (*v.* Rustafjael, *Light of Egypt* 137). Fragments in Sa'idic: Paris 129[18], f. 26, 131[8], f. 37. *V. Synax.* 8 Tûbeh (Hamlê). The Ethiopic text, *ed.* Turaieff, *Zapiski*, Orient. Sect. Imp. Russ. Archaeol. Soc., xv. (1903), is but a slightly longer form of the *Synax.*; but Br. Mus. Or. 701 (Eth. Cat., p. 184) appears to be different.

[4] Paris, *l.c.* So used *Miss.* iv. 763, Rossi I. ii. 11,

→ *Recto.*

ⲧⲁⲟ̣ⲩ[a] ϣ[ⲱⲡⲉ ⲱ]
ⲡⲁⲉ̈ⲓⲱⲧ [ⲡⲉ-]
ϫⲁϥ ϫⲉⲁⲩⲛ[ⲟϭ]
ⲛⲥⲧⲩⲗⲗⲟ[ⲥ]
ϩⲉ ϩⲙⲡ[ⲧⲟ-]
ⲟⲩ ⲛⲁⲧⲣⲓ̈ⲡ[ⲉ]
ⲙⲡⲟⲟⲩ ⲁⲡⲙⲁ-
ⲕⲁⲣⲓ̈ⲟⲥ ⲁⲡ[ⲁ]
[ϣⲉⲛⲟ]ⲩⲧⲉ ⲙ-
[ⲧⲟⲛ ⲙ̅ⲙ]ⲟϥ ⲙ-
[ⲡⲟⲟ]ⲩ ⲁⲗⲏⲑⲱ̣ⲥ̣
[. . .]ⲟⲥ . . ϣϯ
[. .]ⲛ . . [ⲛⲣ]ϥϯ
ⲥ[ⲃ]ⲱ ⲁⲩⲱ ⲛⲣϥ-
ⲥⲙⲛ ⲛ̄ⲛⲟⲙⲟⲥ ⲛ̄ⲛ̄-
ⲙⲟⲛⲟⲭⲟⲥ ⲙⲛ-
sic ⲛⲕⲁⲥⲙⲓ̈ⲕⲟⲛ[.]

ⲉⲩ[
ϣⲓ[
ⲧⲟⲟ[
ⲥ̣[
ϫ̣[
ⲡⲉϫ[ⲁⲓ ⲛⲁϥ
ϫⲉϩⲛⲟⲩ[ⲙⲉ ⲡⲁ-]
ⲉ̈ⲓⲱⲧ̣ [
ⲧ̣ⲁⲩ[ⲉⲧ-]
ⲃⲏⲏ[ⲧϥ

margin

↑ *Verso.*

ⲡ]ⲕ̣[ⲟ]ⲥⲙⲟⲥ
]ⲡ̣ⲁϥ-
]ⲧ̣ⲉⲗⲓ̈ⲟⲥ̣
?
]ⲛϥ
]ⲁⲟ̣ϩ.
]ϩⲁ
]————
[ⲙ]ⲛⲛⲥⲁⲛⲁⲓ̈ ⲇⲉ
[ⲡ]ⲉϫⲁϥ ⲛⲁⲓ̈
[ϫⲉ]ⲙ[. .]ⲧⲡ
]ⲱ̣

]ⲟ
. . . ⲛ̣ⲟ̣ⲩ ϫⲓ̣ ⲙ-
ⲡⲉⲓ̈ⲕⲟⲩ[ⲓ] ⲉⲛⲱ-
ⲡⲉ ⲛ̄ⲧⲁⲁϥ ϩⲁ-
ⲧⲁⲁⲡⲉ ⲙⲙⲟⲛ
[ⲁ]ⲓ̈ⲗⲟ ⲉⲓⲉϣϭⲙ-
ϭⲟⲙ ⲉϩⲙⲟⲟⲥ ⲉ-
[ϩⲣ]ⲁⲓ ϫ̣ⲉⲁⲡⲁⲥⲱ-
[ⲙ]ⲁ ⲣⲁ̣[ⲧϭⲟ]ⲙ̣ ⲁ-
ⲛ̣ⲟ̣[ⲕ ⲇⲉ ⲁ]ⲓϥⲓ̣[b] ⲡⲱ-
ⲛ̣ⲉ [ⲁⲓⲧⲁⲁϥ ϩ]ⲁ-
ϫ̣ⲱϥ [. . . .]ⲩ
. . ⲛⲣⲟ̣[. . .]ⲡ̣ⲉ̣
[. .]ⲧ[. . . ⲉ]ⲧ-
ⲣⲉϥϣⲟⲡ[ϥ] ⲉ-[c]
ⲣⲟϥ ⲛⲟⲩⲉⲓⲣⲏ-
ⲛⲏ· ⲁⲩⲱ ⲟⲛ ⲛⲉ̣-
ⲣⲉⲡϥⲥⲧⲟⲙⲁ-
ⲭⲟⲥ ϣⲟⲩⲱ ϩ[d][
. ϥⲡ̄ⲛⲟ . [

[a] ⲛ]ⲧⲁ-. [b] I have noted that ϫⲓ cannot be read. [c] Or ϩⲙⲡ]ⲧⲣⲉϥ-. [d] Or ϣⲟⲩⲱϩ[or as = ϣⲟⲩⲟ.

Recto. . . . What hath happened, O] my father?' He said, 'A great pillar (στῦλος) hath fallen in the mount of Atripe this day; the blessed (μακ.) Apa [Sheno]ute is gone to rest this day. Verily (ἀληθῶς) . . . . teacher and law-maker (-νόμος) for monks (μον.) and worldlings (κοσμικός) . . . . [I?] said [unto him?,] 'In [truth (?), my] father . . . . . concerning [him . . . . .

Verso. . . . the] world (κόσ.) . . . . perfect (τέλειος) . . . . (*dividing line*). And (δέ) thereafter he said unto me, ' . . . . .

. . . take this small stone and place it beneath my head; verily I am no longer able to sit down, for my body (σῶ.) is become powerless.' [But (δέ)] I took (?) the stone [and I placed ? it] beneath him . . . ., that He would[1] receive him unto Him in peace (εἰρ.). And also his stomach (στόμ.) was[2] . . . . .

No. 29.

This should be part of one of those tales of wandering visits through the desert, paid by a devout inquirer to the cells of various ascetic celebrities, and met with in the collections of *Apophthegmata*, in the Life of Onnophrius,[3] that of Cyrus,[4] of Paul of Tammah,[5] and the like.[6] Here the scene is presumably in the far south, as certain of the characters are connected with Nubia.

Of fol. 3 no translation can be attempted.

Fol. 1. ↑

margin p. ⲥ̅ⲅ̅

ϣⲱⲛⲉ ⲙ̄ⲛ̄ⲛ̄ⲇⲁⲓⲙⲟⲛⲓⲟⲛ ⲉϥ-
ⲛⲟⲩϫⲉ ⲙ̄ⲙⲟⲟⲩ ⲉⲃⲟⲗ· ⲕⲁⲧⲁ ⲑⲉ ⲉⲧⲉ-
ⲣⲉⲡⲉⲛϫⲟⲉⲓⲥ ϫⲱ ⲙ̄ⲙⲟⲥ ϫⲉⲙ̄ⲛ̄-
ϣⲏⲛ ⲉⲛⲁⲛⲟⲩϥ ⲛⲁⲧⲁⲩⲉ ⲕⲁⲣ-
ⲡⲟⲥ ⲉⲃⲟⲗ ⲉϥϩⲟⲟⲩ· ⲁϥϫⲓ ϩⲁϩ ⲙ̄-
ⲙⲉⲣⲟⲥ ⲛ̄ⲁⲡⲟⲥⲧⲏⲑⲟⲩⲥ ⲉⲃⲟⲗ ϩ̄ⲛ̄-
ⲛⲉⲅ̅ⲣ̅[ⲁⲫⲏ] ⲉⲧⲟⲩⲁⲁⲃ· ⲁⲩ̣ⲱ ⲛⲉ-
[ϣⲁϥ. . . .]ⲡ̣ϥ ⲉⲃⲟⲗ ⲉϥⲙ̣ⲉ̣ⲗⲉⲧⲁ
ⲡ]ⲉϩⲟⲟⲩ ⲙ̄ⲛ̄ⲧⲉⲩϣⲏ·
].ϫ̣ⲉ̣ ⲛ̄ⲧⲉⲩϣⲏ ⲧⲏ-
[ⲣ̅ⲥ̅]ⲧ̣ⲥ̄[a] ϫⲉⲛⲁ ⲛⲁⲓ̈
]..ⲧ̣ⲱ̣ⲛ[b] ⲉⲣⲟⲟⲩ
]...ⲱⲧ

[a] Not ⲙⲙ]ⲟⲥ.

[b] ? ⲧⲛⲧⲱⲛ.

[1] Or 'when He should'.

[2] This might be read variously: 'was not able to . . .', 'was pouring forth . . .'

[3] *Acta SS.*, June 12, Amélineau in *Rec.* vi. 166.

[4] *Synax.*, 8 Abîb (Forget ii. 215. The Ethiop., 8 Hamlê, differs much).

[5] *Miss.* iv. 759. The true title of this narrative is not known.

[6] *E.g.* the Life of Herminos, alluded to in No. 26.

→ p. ⲥ̅ⲇ̅ margin

ⲧⲙ̅ⲙ̅[a] ⲛ̅ⲥⲱⲃⲉ ⲛ̅ⲟⲩⲟⲉⲓϣ ⲛⲓⲙ ⲡⲉ-
ϫⲁï ⲛⲁϥ ϫⲉⲉⲡⲉⲓⲇⲏ ⲟⲩⲛ̅ⲧⲁïⲉⲓ̣[b]
ⲉϣⲁϫⲉ ⲙ̅ⲡⲉⲕⲙ̅ⲧⲟ ⲉⲃⲟⲗ· ϯⲟⲩ-
ⲱϣ ⲉⲧⲣⲉⲕϫⲱ ⲉⲣⲟï ⲙ̅ⲡⲃⲓⲟⲥ ⲛ̅-
ⲛⲉⲥⲛⲏⲩ ⲧⲏⲣⲟⲩ ⲉⲧⲙ̅ⲡⲉⲕⲕⲱ-
ⲧⲉ ϫⲉⲛⲉⲟⲩⲛ̅ⲕⲉⲟⲩⲟⲛ ⲙ̅ⲡⲥⲁⲣⲏⲥ
ⲙ̅ⲙⲟⲛ· ⲡⲉϫⲁϥ ⲛⲁï ϫⲉⲁïⲧⲁϩⲉ
ⲥⲟⲛ ̓ⲥⲛⲁⲩ ⲙ̅ⲡⲓ̣ⲙⲁ̣ⲛ̣[. . . .]ⲛ
ϩⲛ̅ⲛ̅ⲁⲛⲟⲩⲃⲁ· ⲉ[ⲣⲉⲡⲣⲁⲛ[c] ⲙ̅ⲡⲟⲩⲁ]
ⲙ̣ⲙⲟⲟⲩⲡⲉ ⲑ̣ⲁⲣⲁ[ⲡⲣⲁⲛ ⲙ̅-]
ⲡⲕⲉⲟⲩⲁⲡⲉ ïⲁⲕ̣[ⲱⲃ ⲡⲛⲟⲩ-]
ⲧⲉ ⲧ̅ⲛ̅ⲛⲟⲟⲩⲥⲟⲩ ⲙ̅[ⲡⲉⲡⲓⲥⲕⲟⲡⲟⲥ]
ⲁⲡⲁ ϩⲉⲣⲙⲓⲁⲥ ⲉⲧ̣[ⲣⲉϥⲧⲥⲁⲃⲱⲟⲩ]
ⲉⲥϩⲁï ⲛ̅ⲧⲉⲧ̣[[d]

[a] ⲥⲱⲧⲙ̅ seems the only possibility. [b] For ⲛⲧⲁⲓⲉⲓ. [c] Instead of stop, possibly a letter, ⲛⲉⲣⲉⲡⲣⲁⲛ. [d] ? ⲛⲧⲉⲣ[ⲉ.

Fol. 1. P. 203. . . . maladies and the devils (*δαιμόνιον*) that he cast out; according (*κατά*) as our Lord saith, 'A good tree doth not bring forth evil fruit (*καρ.*).'[1] He got many portions (*μέρος*) by heart (*ἀπὸ στηθοῦς*) from the holy scriptures (*γρ.*). And [he used to . . . . .], repeating (*μελετᾶν*) . . . . ., day and night . . . . . all the night . . . . . Have mercy upon me . . . . . resemble (?) them . . . . .

P. 204. . . . laughter[2] at all times.' I said unto him, 'Seeing, then (*ἐπειδὴ οὖν*), that I have come to speak before thee, I desire that thou wouldest tell me of the life (*βίος*) of all the brethren that are in thy neighbourhood, as to whether there be any other to the south of us.'[3] He said unto me, 'I came upon two brethren . . . . . among the Nubians,[4]

[1] Luke vi. 43.

[2] Or as an adjective.

[3] *Cf.* a phrase in Br. Mus. no. 336.

[4] This form, ⲡⲁⲛⲟⲩⲃⲁ (sing. ⲟⲩⲁⲛⲟⲩⲃⲁ, pl. ϩⲉⲛⲁⲛⲟⲩⲃⲁ) is used throughout Br. Mus. Or. 7029, where the barbarians about Philae are so called; also in *Miss.* iv. 642. (Wessely's Ἀννουβάδων, *Ein biling. Majestätsgesuch* 44, is confirmed by Wilcken, *Chrest.* i. II, p. 13.) In Paris 131[1], f. 62 (homily of Philip, bishop of

[the name of the one] of them being Thara . . .[1], [the name of] the other Jacob (?) . . . . . God sent them to [the bishop (ἐπ.) ?] Apa Hermias,[2] that [he should teach them] to write. After that (?) . . . . .

Fol. 2. → *Recto.*

margin (*page no. here*)

ⲡⲉⲩⲁⲓ̈ⲧⲏⲙⲁ ⲙ̄ⲡⲛ̄ⲥⲱⲥ ⲁⲡⲛ[ⲟⲩ-]
ⲧⲉ ⲥⲱⲧⲙ̄ ⲉⲡⲉⲩⲥⲟⲡⲥ̄· ⲙ̄ⲛ̄ⲛ̄ⲥⲁϩ[ⲉⲛ-]
ϩⲟⲟⲩ ⲇⲉ ⲁⲛⲉⲩⲉⲓⲟⲧⲉ ⲃⲱⲕ ⲉⲡⲡ[ⲟ-]
ⲗⲉⲙⲟⲥ ⲁⲩⲙⲟⲟⲩⲧⲟⲩ· ⲛ̄ⲧⲉⲣⲉϥⲥ[ⲱ-]
ⲧⲙ̄ ⲇⲉ ⲛ̄ϭⲓ ⲡⲉⲡⲓⲥⲕⲟⲡⲟⲥ ⲉⲡⲟⲩⲱ̣
ⲁϥϫⲱⲕ ⲉⲃⲟⲗ ⲙ̄ⲡⲉⲩⲁⲓⲧⲏⲙ[ⲁ·]
ⲁϥϯ ⲛⲁⲩ ⲙ̄ⲡⲃⲁⲡⲧⲓⲥⲙⲁ· ⲛ̄ⲧ[ⲉ-]
ⲣⲉϥⲛⲁⲩ ⲇ[ⲉ] ⲉⲑⲟⲧⲉ ⲙ̣̄ⲡ̣ⲛⲟⲩⲧⲉ .
][a] ⲛ̄ϩⲏⲧⲟⲩ ⲁϥϯ ϩⲓⲱⲟⲩ ⲙ̣̄-
[ⲡⲉⲥⲭⲏⲙⲁ] ⲛ̣ⲧⲙⲛ̄ⲧⲙⲟⲛⲁ̣ⲭⲟⲥ ⲁⲩ̣-
[ⲱ]ⲓ̣ⲟⲩ[b] ⲉⲥϩⲁⲓ̈· ⲁⲩⲱ̄ ⲛ̄ⲧⲉ-
[ⲣⲉϥ]ⲟⲩ ⲛ̄ⲡⲥⲟⲟⲩⲛ ⲧⲏⲣϥ̄
[ⲁϥϯ ⲛⲁⲩ ⲛⲧⲉ]ⲭⲉⲓⲣⲟⲇⲟⲛⲉⲓⲁ· ⲡⲉ̣
]ⲁ̣ⲛ̣ⲁ̣ⲁϥ ⲙ̄[

↑ *Verso.*

margin

[ⲙ̄]ⲙⲟϥ ⲙ̣ⲡϥ̄ⲗⲩⲡⲉⲓ ⲙ̄ⲙⲟⲟⲩ· ⲉ̄-
[ϫ]ⲱⲕ ⲉⲃⲟⲗ ⲙ̄ⲡⲉⲩⲁⲓ'ⲧⲏⲙⲁ ⲕⲁⲧⲁ
[ⲑⲉ] ⲛ̄ⲧⲁⲩϫⲟⲟⲥ· ⲁⲩⲱ ⲁⲩⲃⲱⲕ ⲉⲣⲏ[ⲥ]
[ⲉ]ⲡ̣ⲉⲩⲙⲁ ⲉϥⲟⲩⲏⲩ ⲙ̄ⲙⲟⲛ ⲛ̄ⲁϩⲟⲟⲩ
[ⲥ]ⲛⲁⲩ ⲙ̄ⲙⲟⲟϣⲉ ⲉⲁⲩⲧⲁⲙⲓⲟ ⲛⲁⲩ
ⲛ̣ⲟⲩⲙⲁ ⲛ̄ϣⲱⲡⲉ ⲁⲩⲱ ⲟⲩⲕⲟⲩⲓ̈
[ⲛ]ⲉⲕⲕⲗⲏⲥⲓⲁ ⲁⲩⲟⲩⲱϩ ⲛ̄ϩⲏⲧⲥ̄·
[ⲁ]ⲩⲱ ⲛⲉⲩϯ ⲛ̄ϩⲧⲏⲩ ⲉⲣⲟⲟⲩ ϩ̄ⲛ̄ϩⲱⲃ
[ⲛ]ⲓⲙ· ⲁⲩⲱ ⲁⲩϣⲱⲡⲉ ⲛ̄ϩⲏⲩ ⲛ̄-
[ⲟ]ⲩⲟⲛ ⲛⲓⲙ ⲉⲧⲛⲁⲩ ⲉⲣⲟ[ⲟⲩ ⲁⲩ]ⲱ ⲁⲛ-
[ⲥ]ⲱⲧⲙ [ⲉ]ϩⲁϩ ⲛ̄ⲁⲣⲉⲧⲏ [ⲉⲧⲉⲟⲩⲛ-]
ⲧ̣ⲁⲩ ⲛ̄[ⲑ]ⲉ ⲛ̄ⲛⲁⲛⲉⲛ[ⲉⲓⲟⲧⲉ ⲛⲁⲣⲭⲁⲓ-]
[ⲟ]ⲛ· ⲁⲛⲟⲕ ⲇⲉ ⲛ̣̄[ⲧⲉⲣⲉⲓⲥⲱⲧⲙ]
[ⲉ]ⲛⲁⲓ̈ ⲁⲓ̈ⲡⲁⲣⲁⲕⲁⲗ[ⲉⲓ
[. . . . .]ⲁ̣ⲓ̈ ϫⲉ . . . [

[a] ⲉⲧ[ⲟⲩⲟⲛϩ ⲉⲃⲟⲗ] or ⲉⲧ[ⲟⲩⲏϩ ϩⲣⲁⲓ].

[b] ⲁϥⲧⲥⲁⲃ]ⲟⲟⲩ?

Fol. 2. *Recto.* . . . ' their request (αἴτημα). Afterwards God heard their prayer and (δέ) after some days their parents went to the war (πόλ.) and were slain. But (δέ) when the bishop (ἐπ.) heard the news, he fulfilled their request (αἴτ.) and gave them baptism (βάπ.). But (δέ) when he heard of the fear of God [that dwelt[3]?] within them, he put upon them [the habit (σχῆμα)] of monkhood (-μοναχός) and [taught] them to write. And when . . . . . them all knowledge, [he gave them] ordination (χειροτονία) ' . . . . .

ⲧⲁⲛⲁⲧⲟⲗⲏ, *cf.* Zoega pp. 266, 267) it is ⲛⲟⲩⲃⲁ. *Cf.* Arab. *Nûba*, Ethiop. *Nôba* (Ludolf, *Comment.* p. 68).

[1] My copy would not justify Serapion.

[2] I find no such bishop or saint elsewhere.

[3] Or ' that was manifested '.

Verso. '. . . him and he grieved (λυπεῖν) them not as to fulfilling their request (αἴτ.), according (κατά) as they had said. And they departed southward to their place, distant from us about two days' walk, when they had made for themselves a dwelling place and a little church (ἐκ.), and therein they dwelt. And they gave heed unto themselves in everything and became profitable unto every one that beheld them; and we heard of many "virtues" (ἀρετή) [which were] theirs, like those of our [ancient (? ἀρχαῖος) fathers']. But (δέ) I [, when I had heard?] these things, I besought (παρακαλεῖν) . . . . (saying), '. . . . .

Fol. 3. ↑ *Recto* (?).

margin

ⲁⲗ]ⲗⲁ ⲉϩⲛⲏⲧ̅ⲛ̅
]ϫⲱ ⲙ̅ⲙⲟⲥ
]ⲉ̣ϥⲛ̣̅ⲁϯ
].ϩⲃ̅ⲏ̣ⲩ̣ⲉ
]ϫ̣. . . ⲧⲉ̣ ⲉ
]ⲙ̣. . . . ⲟⲩⲛ
]ⲏ̣. . . ⲛ̣̅ⲑ̣ⲉ
].ⲛ̅ⲛ̅. . . ⲧⲟ̣ⲛ̣
].ⲱⲕ ⲉⲃⲟⲗ
ⲧ]ⲁϣⲉⲟⲉⲓϣ
ϫ]ⲱ ⲙ̅ⲙⲟⲥ
]ⲡ̣· ⲛ̅ⲑⲉ

→ *Verso* (?).

margin

ⲇⲟⲭⲓⲟ̣ⲛ[a] ⲇ[. . . . . ⲉⲕ-]
ⲕⲗⲏⲥⲓⲁ· ⲧ[
ⲧⲏⲣ̅ⲛ̅ ⲡⲉ[
ⲡⲣⲱⲙ[ⲉ
ϩⲓⲧ̅ⲙ̅[ⲡ . . . . ϫⲓ-]
ⲧ̅ϥ̅ ⲉⲧⲉⲕⲕⲗ[ⲏⲥⲓⲁ
ⲛ̅ⲧⲉϥⲯⲩⲭ[ⲏ
ϩⲓⲟⲩ̣[ⲥⲟ]ⲛ ⲁ[
ⲛⲟⲙⲟⲥ ⲙ[. . . . . ⲛⲧⲉ-]
ⲣⲉϥⲉⲓ ⲇⲉ ⲉ[
ⲡⲉϥⲉⲓⲱ̣[ⲧ
ⲙⲉⲛ ⲁ[

[a] ? ⲡⲁⲛⲇⲟⲭⲓⲟⲛ, ⲝⲉⲛⲟⲇⲟⲭⲓⲟⲛ.

APPENDIX

ABBREVIATIONS EMPLOYED.

GREEK TEXTS:

AS.	*Vita* in *Acta Sanctorum*, Maii iii.
§	refers to paragraphs of the above.
Par.	*Paralipomena*, *ibid.*
Nau A	*Patrol. Or.* iv. 425–503.
Nau D	*ibid.*, 504–511.
Sur.	Surius, *De Prob. SS. Vit.*, iii and Nau's copy of the Greek original.

COPTIC TEXTS:

Sa (1 to 6)	Sa'idic recensions, *v. below*, pp. 183ff.
SaX	The new text, No. 25 *above.*
Bo.	Bohairic recension, *ed.* Amélineau.

ARABIC TEXTS:

Ap.	Paris, MS. arabe 261.
Ac.	Cairo, printed edition.
Am.	Amélineau's printed text.
Av.	Vatican, Cod. Arab. 172.

THE main object of this Appendix is to draw attention to two hitherto unnoticed Arabic versions of the Life of Pachomius. Three texts are indeed here described, but two of them (Ap. and Ac.) are, in great part, so closely related that they may be regarded as representing a single version.

M. Amélineau, in publishing his Arabic text, was aware of the existence of the MSS. in Rome and Paris, besides those which he employed[1]; but one must suppose that he did not examine either, since he says nothing of their wide divergence from his own text; and it has thence been hitherto assumed[2] that but one form of the Arabic Life exists.

To the descriptions of these I have added what can provisionally be said as to the six Sa'idic recensions,[3] awaiting for their final valuation the investigations which, it is to be hoped, Professor Lefort will before long publish.

I have no pretext for attempting here a rediscussion of the question of origins; neither our new Sa'idic text nor the new Arabic versions contribute anything

[1] *Mus. Guim.* liv.

[2] Ladeuze 52.

[3] Each of the extant MSS. represents a somewhat different recension. When it is remembered that the White Monastery alone (whence all these six came) once possessed twenty (*sic?*) copies of the Life of P., besides that of P., Horsiese and Theodore together, such an amount of variation is not surprising (*J. Th. Stud.* v. 566).

available as arguments against Ladeuze's contention in favour of a Greek text as the original basis whence the other versions sprang.[1] Yet a reader of AS. and Par., having the requisite familiarity with the popular literary idiom of Egypt in the earlier Byzantine period, and if conversant too with Coptic, would probably be struck by the uncouthness of much of their phraseology, and would incline to admit at least the possibility of certain parts of these texts having been directly translated from Coptic—whether written or oral—and so incorporated in the Greek biography.[2] Not a few examples occur of those ambiguous locutions which, being of identical usage in both languages, it is difficult to assign as original property to either. Such are *χεῖρα δοῦναι* *help* (Nau D. 511, 15), *τόπον εὑρεῖν* (AS. § 76 *sup.*, but *cf.* N. Test. *τόπον δοῦναι*), *ὀνόματα λαβεῖν* (AS. § 80 *sup.*). Are these to be reckoned evidence for a translation from the Coptic or merely for a Greek composition, written in a Coptic 'atmosphere'; or are they in fact passable Greek and their identical Coptic counterparts simple translations, naturalized and current, like many another Greek phrase and idiom, in the native language?[3]

PARIS, MS. ARABE No. 261 (= Ap.).

De Slane's catalogue assigns this MS. to the end of the 14th century. A reader's note on the last fol. is dated A. M. 1066 = A. D. 1350. The title runs: 'In the Name of the Father .... the History of our father, the great Pachomius, the saintly, and his favourite disciple, Theodore, the beloved.' *Cf.* the title of Am., where the latter is not mentioned. The limits of this recension are practically conterminous with those of AS. + Par. (*s.* the Table, p. 189). It is indeed a direct translation from the Greek, as we learn from the subscriptions to the MSS. in Cairo[4]; and confirmation of their statements may be had from many of the personal and place-names, where the transcription often reproduces even the Greek case-endings (*e.g.* in § 3 بحوميا voc.,

[1] The main argument against this now generally accepted view (*e.g.* Butler, *Laus. Hist.* ii. 206) is of course its inherent improbability. Despite Prof. Ladeuze's ingenious marshalling of reasons why the Life should have been first composed in Greek, one cannot but feel that such a literary product, in such a time and place, is scarcely credible. (*Cf.* C. H. Turner, in *J. Th. St.* vi. 324.)

[2] Hence there might be instances of mistranslations which have resulted in obscure or improbable readings in the Greek. One case of probable misunderstanding of the Coptic appears to me to be the simile of the devil, bound and placed under foot *ὡς στρουθίον* (Par. § 4 = Nau A § 15). I suggest that the Coptic here read ϫⲁϫⲉ *enemy*, which the translator mistook for ϫⲁϫ *sparrow*. The corresponding AS. § 67 has *θηρίον*, but Am. 531, 9, in paraphrasing that (and translating probably the missing parallel from SaX), has *enemy*. As to *στρουθίον*, *cf.* Jerome's comment on Eccles. xii. 4, *nunquam passerem in malam partem legisse me novi*, *PL.* 23, 1109. But *v.* Par. § 26, where the word is scarcely open to the explanation here offered.

[3] Ladeuze 43, 44, quotes Tillemont to like effect, but criticizes his remarks. The late E. A. Sophocles (*Lexicon*, List of Authors) appears to have taken the Greek for a 'barbarous translation'. If the much needed revision of the edition of AS. be ever undertaken, we shall learn how far the Bollandists adhered to one MS., how far they compiled their text (*v.* Nau, 409 n.).

[4] *V.* description of Ac.

§ 7 طبانسين acc., § 20 تنتيرون gen. pl., *ib.* سيينس gen., § 38 بلامنس gen., § 68 صورن acc., § 72 فيلونس gen., *ib.* مغضولو gen.), while discarding those forms usual in the parallel texts of Coptic origin (نطريات for برنوج, بانوس for اخميم, شينوفسكيا for شاناسات, زكشاوس; Ζακχαῖος sometimes for زكا, زكى). Of features positively significant of a non-Coptic origin, the most noteworthy is the transmutation of the date of Pachomius' death, 14th Pachôns, into its Syrian (or ? Melkite) equivalent, 15th Iyâr, and similarly that of Theodore from 2nd Pachôns to 16th Iyâr; further, the fantastical 'Coptic' etymology of the name Panopolis,[1] and perhaps such omissions as that of the local names in § 52 (fol. 188 b).

The precise relationship between this and the various Greek recensions could only be ascertained by a series of comparisons far more systematic than I have undertaken. This much however may be said: that Ap. is a patchwork of (1) a version following closely AS. + Par.,[2] (2) another, once substantially identical with Am., but since provided with stylistic embellishments—here a further epithet or synonym, there a longer phrase[3]—and (3) independent alterations or additions, sometimes of considerable length. Of these elements (1) is represented, for example, in §§ 1–19, with the exception of §§ 7, 15 (partly), again in §§ 22–25; (2) in §§ 35, 71–96 and in the sections taken from Par. As examples of (3) we may cite (*a*) many additional biblical quotations, throughout the whole text; (*b*) several homiletic developments, *e.g.* in §§ 11, 12, 24, 31, 46, 49, Par. 6, 22, this last of over 7 pages; (*c*) additions or changes in detail, presumably due to the translator, *e.g.* § 2 Abyssinia the scene of P.'s military service; §§ 4, 25 P. and Theodore both tonsured; § 22 P.'s sister writes to him, asking to see him (the whole section is peculiar); § 36 after Υἱοῦ τοῦ Θεοῦ, reference to the Ode of Habakkuk, which, if the wise man meditate, he may dispense with the rest of the Prophets; § 39[2] P. asks water to wash his hands, lest he defile the book he reads; Par. 5 'Permit us to bury him, lest the jackals devour him'; Par. 6 begins with P.'s question, 'Have ye yet more words and blame? They answered, No'[4]; Par. 26 P. exorcises the phantom with a charm[5]; Par. 12 P. in his reply quotes 'a sage'[6]; § 62 (?) referring to P.'s innumerable virtues, 'Who may number the flowers of the desert or the waves of the sea?'; § 65 subsequently P. gave to some the interpretation of his vision, 'and what I long after heard from them I tell to you'; § 72 P. says his monasteries have 7,000 monks.[7] Further, certain additions

[1] Fol. 186, 13 (§ 51[2]) الذى هو اسم الزيتون باللغة القبطية.

[2] An instructive specimen of their combination is §§ 66, 67 (ff. 121–129 b). Practically all of AS. and of Par. 2, 3, 4 is included, but the narrative is made up of regularly alternating sections from these two sources.

[3] Often with the object of effecting a rhyme (*cf.* description of Ac.).

[4] So too in Par. 16. *Cf.* Nau A (*Patr. Or.* iv. 443).

[5] Fol. 167, 7. Begins يا لشركم الذى لا ينام وقتالكم الذى ما يكل ويسام.

[6] Fol. 179, 11 بعض الحكماء, 'Whoso setteth fire and water in a vessel without understanding hath done so in madness.'

[7] *Cf.* Am. 380, Ladeuze 204.

would seem to aim at exalting the monastic dignity: § 25 Pekusius first asks P.'s leave to introduce Theodore; § 49 Theodore, before preaching, begs P.'s blessing; Par. 5 the funeral procession reverently salutes P. and takes his blessing; § 50[2] Petronius, on arrival, performs the humblest menial service during three years (*quot.* Mat. vii. 14); § 51[1] the bishop's deference to P., as if he had been his disciple. Of sheer misunderstandings we may note the name 'Archelaus', given to the anonymous brother in § 42[2] and originating presumably in the words ἀρχαίῳ ἀδελφῷ.

As is natural in a recension of non-Coptic origin, Ap. shows none of those additional passages which make up so much of Am. (*i. e.* those in Butler's table without Greek, though often with Coptic, equivalents), excepting where taken from the *Laus. Hist.* (*viz.* Am. 366–9, 377, 382–4) and the two anecdotes on Am. 641,[1] which figure in Nau D (*v. Patr. Or.* iv. 509, 43) and are, here as there, followed by the passage *l. c.* 510, 6, ending with Gal. ii. 2.[2] Indeed a number of the minor peculiarities which differentiate the texts printed or analysed by Nau from those of AS. and Par. reappear in Ap., which likewise has not a few features in common with the pseudo-metaphrastic text of Surius. The following references will suffice to confirm the former statement: Par. 6 ends in Ap. as in Nau D (*l. c.* 440); § 50[2] Ap. more like Nau D than AS., but much longer; § 52 Ap. = Nau D in certain details, but is longer; § 53 Ap. = Nau D in ref. to πορνεία (*l. c.* 507, 27); § 55[2] Ap. has συγχωροῦνται κτλ., as in Nau D; § 57 Ap. has τὰ τοῦ πνεύματος; § 58 Ap. = Nau D in omitting 2nd section (AS. καὶ πολλάκις), reading ὑπακούετε—Θεοῦ and in 3rd section οὐ μόνον—ἁμαρτία; § 71 last two lines *om.* Ap. and Nau D. Thenceforth Nau D as well as Ap. generally = Am.

As regards sequence of the paragraphs in Ap., it will be seen from the table, p. 191, that there is an undeniable similarity between their grouping here and in Ac., while in several of the other texts groups appear, identically composed with those in Ap., though at relatively different intervals.

The Cairo Edition (= Ac.).

This print, edited in 1891 by the hegumenus of the monastery of El-Baramûs for the Coptic Orthodox Educational Society in Cairo,[3] professes (*s.* Preface) to be reproduced unaltered [from the MS.], so far as the sense remained intelligible. Nothing is said as to sources; but from the colophon in a modern copy in the

[1] A Boh. version of the 2nd in Br. Mus. no. 915.

[2] Instead of being direct translations from AS., the additions in Am. 'from another copy' (Am. 599) must now appear more likely to have come from Ap. (fol. 76 a), which text contains moreover the other passages regarded as directly from AS. (*v.* Ladeuze p. 60).

[3] Title . . . كتاب القديس انبا باخوميوس
نقحه . . . القمص عبد المسيح المسعودى . طبع
على نفقة جمعية التعليم المسيحى الارثوذكسية
بالقاهرة ١٨٩١

Patriarchal Library, very kindly communicated by Marcus Bey Simaika, we learn that the print was made from it. My informant tells me that the original of this copy (as well as of another in the same library, which expressly states as much) was a MS. in Deir Abû Maḳâr, dated A.M. 975 = A.D. 1251 (*sic*). A third copy of this is, I am further informed, at Deir el-Moḥarraḳ and was made in A.D. 1842. Now this last copy bears the important statement (copied for me by Simaika Bey) that the old MS. at Abû Maḳâr was 'translated from the Greek into the Arabic in the handwriting of one of the Greek Melkites, named John, son of Metri, son of Ḥamzah, in Cairo.[1] Apparently therefore the date of the MS. is that of the translation itself, which was made only in the 13th century; and if so, we further obtain a *terminus ante quem* for the writing of Ap. The scribe of the Patriarch's copy whence the print was made further observes that from the latter many clauses in rhymed prose (الكلم المسجّع) have been omitted, while, at the same time, such of the more important dates have been inserted as the editor was able to ascertain.[2]

The text as printed is, like Ap., a mixture of the two recensions: the majority of its sections show the same version of AS. + Par. as Ap., and in all but identical wording, while a lesser number agree with Am., though often with modifications in phraseology. But, beyond this, the compiler of Ac. has made a large selection from those independent additions of Am. which Ap. discards (*e.gg.* Ac. p. 8 has Am. 348 *inf.*, p. 29 Am. 390, p. 33 Am. 406, p. 37 Am. do., p. 61 *inf.* Am. 432, p. 65 Am. 562, p. 80 Am. 502, pp. 89–91 Am. 509–18, p. 112 Am. 435, p. 126 Am. 448, p. 136 Am. 591), while in a few cases omitting passages to be found in Ap. (conspicuously that from *Laus. Hist.* = Am. 366 ff., § 27[1] and Par. 32 + § 40[1]). There remain, as elements peculiar to Ac., besides a homiletic development of § 71 (p. 131) and a short apophthegm (p. 163),[3] a long section consisting of excerpts from P.'s sermons (pp. 115, 2–121, 7). Their Sa. original is to be found in Br. Mus. Or. 7024, ff. 18–49 b, while short extracts, partly identical with these, are in Arabic in Or. 4523 (*v.* below), f. 182b ff.[4] For the sequence of paragraphs, *v.* the table, p. 191. How far this is the arrangement of the modern editor it is impossible at present to ascertain.

[1] بخط احد الأروام الملكية اسمه جونة بن مترى بن حمزة بمحروسة مصر.

[2] These occur on pp. 4, 8, 12, 141, 168 of the edition. The Coptic month-names are of course here employed; *cf.* Ap.

[3] 'By what road can a man expel Satan from within him?' Theodore replies that, as a guest cannot be expelled except his belongings be first put without, so only by first casting forth the vices, can Satan be himself expelled.

[4] Sa. is about to be published by Dr. Budge. It is entitled: '*An Exhortation* (κατήχησις) *pronounced by . . . Apa Pahomô, concerning a brother that had been wroth, being one of the time of Apa Ebônh, who had brought him to Tabennêse.*' Ebônh is presumably the abbot of Shenesêt (§ 35). *Cf.* perhaps Br. Mus. no. 268. It may be noted here that, among these extracts added after the text in Or. 4523, there is one (f. 185) from the Life of Herminus (= Paris 148 f. 320 *inf.* *Cf.* No. 27 above).

Amélineau's Text, *Musée Guimet* xvii. 337 (= Am.).

It is not necessary to describe afresh this recension. Of the four MSS. available to me only that at Göttingen (Universitätsbibliothek, Nr. 116, here G) is of any antiquity; it is assigned to the 16th century.[1] The others are all modern copies, the age of whose originals I do not know. M. Amélineau says (*Introd.* liv, lvi) that he had at his disposal copies of three practically identical MSS., in Luxor, El-Moḥarraḳ, and the Patriarchate, but that his text and translation were made from the last of these. Confronting this statement with Simaika Bey's information (*v.* above), it would appear that the Patriarchate (if not El-Moḥarraḳ also) possesses copies both of the Ap. and Am. recensions. The MS. which M. Amélineau printed is now Or. 4523 of the British Museum (A.D. 1816), his other two being Nos. 4783 and 4784 (A.D. 1886 and 1839 respectively) of the Bibliothèque Nationale. And yet it is difficult to believe that the translation was indeed made, as one would gather from the author's words (*Introd.* liv), strictly upon his printed text.[2] Wide divergence in detail between them is incessant, and often enough it is possible, by reference to the Am. sections in Ap. and Ac., to account for the discrepancy (*e.gg.* Am. 595 '. . . dont Dieu l'avait sauvé,' *cf.* Ac. 137, 20; Am. 699 'Une certaine nuit . . .', *cf.* Ac. 166, 18; Am. 413 'Quand on eut préparé . . .', *cf.* Ac. 51, 8; Am. 418 '. . . près de moi', *cf.* Ac. 53, 20; Am. *ib.* '. . . Satan qui se montre', *cf.* Ac. *ib.*, 23). The translation in such cases clearly follows the readings of a second MS., more closely related to that whence Ac. (and doubtless Ap.) derived its Am. sections.

As regards the older MS. G, its text is not seldom preferable to that of the printed Am. and agrees occasionally with Ac. Its chief interest however lies in its length as compared with that of Am. For, while containing nothing not found in Am., it omits the incident of Hieracapollo (Am. 365),[3] the passage from the *Laus. Hist.* (Am. 366–9), two other passages (Am. 373, *ult.*–380, 6 and 382, 6–384, 6) and, finally, the long section consisting mainly of Par. (Am. 599, 7–644, 5).[4] The text ends with the death of P., thus, so far as I know, alone of the MSS. of this recension, justifying its title, which in all copies is practically the same as that printed Am. 337 (*cf.* above, title of Ap.).

It may be doubted whether comparative study of the Coptic materials can ever attain to distinguishing among the sources whence Am. was compiled. Help towards such an object might at any rate be had from a tabulation of the Arabic forms under which the commoner personal and place-names appear. It would, I think, then be

[1] Flemming in *Vers. d. Hss. im Preuss. Staate* i. (3), 373.

[2] In order to be sure that no other of the three MSS. would account for the peculiarities of the translation, I have collated a number of passages of the latter with each of them. They agree in differing constantly from it.

[3] Otherwise omitted only by Bo. Av.

[4] The connecting link reads as follows (G. ϲ̄κ̄ℏ̄ b), after 'Ainsi faisait notre père [P., *sic*], '*And when he had said this to the brethren, and he lying sick*', 'il resta trois jours &c.'

found that *Tabennése* and *Pbow*[1] occur as طبناسين and بافوا in both the earliest and latest portions of the text, while in the intermediate sections[2] they are written دوناسة and ادفوا. So too *Cornelius* is قرناليا in its earlier and later occurrences, قرناليوس between these. The name *Pachomius* offers more confusing evidence; for the form باخوميوس (or بخوميوس), far less common here than the native باخوم—it occurs only 19 times—is found generally in close proximity to the other, sometimes in the selfsame section.[3] The Greek form does not occur between pp. 380 and 600; 14 of the instances are between p. 600 and the end.

It may be noted here that, while Amélineau supposes the 13th–14th century as a probable date for the execution of this translation, Casanova considers that its linguistic character points rather to the tenth.[4]

From some form of Am. is clearly derived the compressed biography of the *Synaxarium* (14 Bashans): *cf.* the forms of place-names, reference to P.'s objection to ordained monks (*cf.* Am. 372), his vision of heaven and hell (Am. 547 ff.), and to his forty years (*sic*) as head of the congregation (Am. 650). Only Athanasius' use of Lu. vi. 48, in praising P.'s institution, does not appear to come from known texts.

VATICAN, Cod. arab. 172, foll. 1–98 b (= Av.).

This MS. is dated A.M. 1061 = A.D. 1345. We have here a text of an entirely different type from those already described and one, to all interested in the reconstruction of the Coptic Lives, of far greater importance. Indeed for that purpose Ap. + Ac. are practically negligible, except in so far as their recension affords further testimony to the text of Am. The first 9 leaves of the MS. were unfortunately long ago lost and replaced by a hand probably not much younger than the original scribe's,[5] but from a quite incongruous source, namely the recension Ap.[6] The last words written by this second scribe (fol. 9 b *ult.*) are the first of § 5 and correspond to Ap. f. 15, 5. They are 'And on a certain day', and they are followed in Ap. (and Ac.) immediately by 'there came to them a certain one of the monkish brethren, visiting them; and this brother had been conquered by pride and self-conceit'. But in Av. the two recensions are clumsily pieced together as follows: (f. 9 b) 'And once on a time, (f. 10) in the morning, and they working at their handiwork and repeating by heart (the Scriptures), a brother knocked at the door who dwelt near them.' The preceding context, identical in Ap. and Av., makes it practically certain that the sequel too should have been identical; whereas, with our return to the original scribe, the narrative, forsaking Ap., proceeds as in Bo. (18) and Am. (353).

[1] Sa. 1 (*v.* p. 183 *below*) uses the form *Pbau*. *Cf.* the two Greek forms Πβόου and Παβαῦ (Παβῶ).

[2] Respectively pp. 380–595 and 384–639.

[3] On pp. 380, 632–3, 668, 699. It may be noted that the sections of Ac. coinciding with Am. constantly prefer the Greek to the native form.

[4] *Bull. Instit. Franç.* i. 19, 20.

[5] So Prof. Guidi, who kindly examined these folios for me.

[6] The opening passage in Ac., on the contrary, belongs to the Am. recension.

With the exception, then, of the extraneous title and opening sections (§§ 1–4), we have in Av. a complete, uninterrupted text, closing with P.'s death—a limit which further demonstrates the incongruity of the title transferred here from Ap. Yet the abruptness of the ending (f. 98 b), '. . . lest he should fall into bodily weakness (which would have been) contrary to His will' (*cf.* Am. 650, 3), may point to Av. being but the translation of a first volume, the sequel to which would, like certain of the Coptic Lives, have carried on the story beyond the death of Theodore. Now this abrupt ending happens to coincide exactly with that of an excerpt from the Life in a Sa. anthology of various popular writers,[1] the MS. of which is already known by its extracts from P.'s sermons (= *Miss.* 612–616). The passage here in question is in Paris 129[13], 43 (paged ϥⲉ̅, ϥⲋ̅) and corresponds to Am. 649 *infra*–650, 3. Hence we may assume that one Sa. version did in fact end just as does Av. Moreover the subscription[2] to the excerpt is of some interest; for after *A portion* (μέρος) *from the Life* (βίος) *of our father Pahôm*, we read *Apa Theodorus, the archimandrite of Tabennêse*, which is proof that in the 11th century at any rate (for that is doubtless the date of the MS.), one Sa. version of the Life was attributed to Theodore himself.[3] Indeed the colophon of Av. (fol. 98 b) refers to the work as a Discourse or Encomium,[4] and P. is, in the course of the narrative, often called *my father, Apa P.*, instead of the elsewhere usual *our father*. However, in face of the unvarying reference to Theodore in the 3rd person, these arguments cannot have much weight.

To judge from the identity in sequence between Av. and Bo. up to the point where the latter breaks off (Bo. 214), it may be assumed that what is thereafter lost of P.'s Life followed a course parallel with the remainder of Av. (*i.e.* from f. 88, 5 ظهر له ملاك). Turning now for parallel texts to Am., we find the following correspondence: Av. ff. 88, 5–98 b, 2 = Am. 562, 7–564, 8, 542, 1–548, 5, 643 *infra* (only approximate), 596, 5–599, 7, 596, 9–597, 2, 644, 7–650, 3. But though parallel here in matter, details of narrative and phraseology differ widely; and this is true of Av. and Am. as a whole. I have collated many parallel passages and found nowhere more than a transient identity: a relationship about as close—and this was indeed to be expected—as that between Bo. and Am.

For, at first sight, Av. might be taken for a translation of Bo.: the sequence of paragraphs is identical, and identical too is much of the phraseology, down often to

[1] Besides Pachomius and Athanasius, other foll. (Paris 131[1], 66, 87) have extracts from John of Hermopolis, Severus and Epiphanius; possibly too from *Acta* (Claudius, Paris 129[16], 43).

[2] *V.* Br. Mus. no. 184, note. That this is the subscription and not the title is clear from the succeeding piece, headed *Likewise* (ὁμοίως) *upon the great Antonius, the anchorite*, the text of which is by *me Athanasius*, and is closed by the words *Apa Athanasius, the archbishop of Rakote*; then follows an account of Anthony's death, headed *Likewise upon the death of &c.*

[3] Prof. Lefort had arrived at the same conclusions from these facts (Letter of 12. ii. 1911).

[4] ميمر القديس انبا بخوم. But ميمر is not an uncommon title where the work is merely narrative and biographical: *e.g.* Bodl. Hunt. 470 (Mart. Pshai and Peter), Paris 148 (Life of Herminos).

the closest details of wording. Yet a comparison with Sa. shows indisputably that it, and not Bo., was the source translated. I have collated them through all passages where the three texts are extant, and have found that, in an overwhelming majority of places—some 140 against 30—Av. agrees with Sa. rather than with Bo. The following examples will illustrate their interrelationship[1]:—

I.

	Bohairic (*Mus. Guim.* 91)		Sa'idic (*Mus. Guim.* 318)		Av. fol. 41
	avec joie		*om.*		= Sa.
92	= Sa.		et toi vieillard		+ that art above the well
	dans les saints		*om.*		= Sa.
	en présence de tous les frères		*om.*		= Sa.
	les saintes Écritures		*om.*		= Sa.
	terrible		glorieuse		= Bo.
	pleuraient &c.		couverts &c.		= Bo.
	communauté	319	faisceau	41 b	= Sa.
93	sortir		= Bo.		be delivered
	fosse		falaise		= Bo.
	je pense		*om.*		= Bo.
	om.		de sorte . . . la mort		= Sa.
	om.		continuèrent		= Bo.
	arrivés		où il arriva (*sic leg.*)		= Sa.
	à la barque (2°)		= Bo.		*om.*
	près de		*om.*		= Bo.
	tous		*om.*		= Sa.
	envoya (ογωρπ)		envoya (ϫεγ)		said to (? Sa. misunderstood)
94	dans ta cellule		*om.*		= Sa.
	de l'esprit	320	des esprits	42	= Sa.
	om. (*sic leg.*)		(fit manger) le frère		= Sa.
	ordonnait (*sic leg.*)		t'eût dit		= Sa. (*om.* dative)
	om.		ô mon père		= Sa.
	lui dit aussi (*sic leg.*)		aussi dit		= Sa.
	Je sais que		= Bo.		*om.*
	sagesse, longanimité		patience, sagesse		= Sa.
	à tous &c.		Et nous . . . arrivé		= Sa.
95	démon, démon	321	un, un autre		= Sa.
	en tout ce qu'il fait		en tout ce qui est à lui (*sic leg.*)		= Sa.
	vers le Seigneur		*om.*		= Sa.
	om.		aussitôt		= Sa.
	dit		répondit	42 b	= Sa.
	promptement, beaucoup		*om.*		= Sa.

[1] In these illustrative passages *all* variant places are, of course, recorded.

Bohairic (*Mus. Guim.* 91)	Sa'idic (*Mus. Guim.* 318)	Av. fol. 41
si quelqu'un	si un homme (*sic leg.*)	= Sa.
l'ennemi	= Bo.	the lord (? of the house)
96 *om.*	322 comme assis sur un trône	= Sa.
inspirant . . . âmes	*om.*	concerning their salvation (*cf.* Bo.)
en dessus de la barque	l'endroit . . . abordé	beside the boat
Le lendemain &c.	et ensuite &c.	= Sa.

II.

Bohairic (*Mus. Guim.* 119)	Sa'idic (*Miss. fr.* 547)	Av. fol. 51 b
aussitôt	= Bo.	*om.*
il n'y avait . . . deux	à cette heure . . . seulement	alone (*pl.*)
om.	Levons-nous	= Sa.
120 sa main (*sic leg.*)	ses mains	= Bo.
om.	disant	= Sa.
Aussitôt	Sur-le-champ	*om.*
à Dieu	au Seigneur	= Sa.
disant	ils . . . firent prières	= Sa.
et avec larmes	*om.*	= Sa.
Seigneur [notre] Dieu	*om.*	= Sa.
ta . . . sur nous	sa . . . sur eux	= Sa.
fût rendu à lui	548 l'eût [vu]	= Sa.
avant sa mort	*om.*	= Sa.
A l'heure du soir	Mais après l'heure du soir (*sic leg.*)	= Sa. (literally)
à Tmouschons	au couvent	= Sa. + Bo.
le frère	*om.*	= Sa.
121 *om.*	et lorsque . . ., aussitôt	= Bo.
om.	*om.*	52 the holy (40 days)
Nous . . . baptiser	Nous . . . prêtre	= Sa.
lui révéla	549 leur révéla	= Sa.
de la part du Seigneur	*om.*	= Sa.
conduite (ἀναστροφή)	= Bo.	dignity (قدر)
pour le conduire à Dieu	*om.*	= Sa.
s'il . . . vertus	si c'est . . . conduite (2°)	And if his deeds be small
122 Dieu	le Seigneur	= Sa.
envoyait	aillent	= Sa.
om.	avec légèreté	= Sa.
om.	magistrature évidente	= Sa.
puissances	= Bo.	52 b angels
ordre	volonté	= Sa.
om.	sans acception de personnes	= Sa.

III.

Bohairic (*Mus. Guim.* 175)	Sa'idic (Zoega cccix)	Av. fol. 72 *ult.*
et qu'ils reçussent la vie éternelle	even as he that asked the Saviour, saying, What shall I do &c.	= Sa.
176 vains	*om.*	73 = Sa.
le besoin du corps	the cares of their maintenance	= Sa.
volonté de Dieu	will of Him that created them	of God that created them
qu'ils fussent . . . éternel	and be saved	*om.*
om. (*sic leg.*)	Likewise too (he prayed)	= Sa.
se trouvaient dans	remain complacently in	= Sa.
parce que . . . égarés	*om.*	= Sa.
qu'ils se connaissent (*sic leg.*) . . . temps	that they should know . . . worthy of life	= Sa.
ainsi, il fait que	and all the other created-things that He hath created for their satisfaction	= Sa.
pendant le jour	daily	= Sa.
afin . . . besoin	*om.*	= Sa.
nous	*om.*	= Sa.
om.	which He hath fixed for them	= Sa.
177 que l'on sème dans les champs	which He hath made on their behalf	73 b *om.*

As a further illustration we may take the passage §§ 26–34, where Sa. chances to be available in two decidedly, if slightly, differing forms.[1] A comparison in their variant places of these two and Bo. with Av. shows, as before, a large preponderance of agreements between Av. and Sa.:—

Av. and both Sa.	agree	58	times
Av. and Sa. 1	„	8	„
Av. and Sa. 1 + Bo.	„	13	„
Av. and Sa. 5	„	6	„
Av. and Sa. 5 + Bo.	„	16	„
Av. and Bo.	„	5	„
Av. against all[2]	„	34	„

If it has been sufficiently demonstrated that Av. is translated from Sa., it yet remains to decide which version of that recension was used. The solution of this question involves a comparative examination of all the Sa. material with Av. such as I have not undertaken. In the case of the passage last analysed the claims of the two Sa. versions represented are practically equal; for another, still more fragmentary and

[1] *Miss.* 800–810, here called Sa. 1 (= Mingarelli *Cod.* ix), and *Miss.* 521–534, here Sa. 5.

[2] Including of course mere omissions.

only partially parallel Sa. version (Brit. Mus. no. 342) the terms of comparison must be different, for here Bo. is wanting. Pp. ⲛ̄–ⲛ̄ⲏ̄ of this Sa. correspond to Am. 542–544 and Av. ff. 89–91; there are some 30 variant places, whereof 20 show agreement between Av. and Sa., 7 between Av. and Am., 3 between Sa. and Am., Av. being independent.[1] As regards the relation of Av. to the other Copto-Arabic text, Am., their paragraph-sequence will, of course, differ, since that of the former coincides with Bo. (*v.* Table, p. 191); while the collation of a number of passages—among them those where no Bo. is extant—has shown that they diverge widely, in detail of phrasing, even where not in the construction of the narrative.

Testimony to the Sa'idic origin of Av. could however be had without recourse to comparative methods such as the above. The proper and place-names, to begin with, are, in cases where the Arabic transcript might be ambiguous, generally added (interlined) in Coptic. Of 21 such names, it is true that the majority are not such as to show forms distinctively Sa'idic. ⲡⲉϭⲟϣ (*sic*) Av. 17 b, for instance, persists in Bo. 44, 48, beside the true ⲡⲓⲉⲑⲱϣ, *ib.* 32. But ϣⲉⲛⲧⲁⲥⲉ Av. 16 b (Bo. ⲡϣⲉⲛⲧⲁⲏⲥⲓ), ⲧⲃⲁⲕⲱⲧ Av. 17 b (Bo. ⲑⲃⲁⲕⲁⲧ), ⲡⲛⲟⲩⲙ Av. 35 b (Bo. ⲫⲛⲟⲩⲙ), ⲡϣⲛⲁⲛⲁϩⲧⲉ *ib.* (Bo. ⲡϣⲉⲛⲁⲛⲁϩⲓ[2]) and ϯⲁⲟⲩⲉ Av. 65 b (Bo. ϯⲧⲟⲩⲏ) speak clearly enough.[3] Then there is a word of frequent occurrence throughout the text which alone goes far to support the claim we make. 'Monastery' is, in Bo. with rare exceptions, represented by ⲙⲟⲛⲏ (*μονή*). This corresponds normally to Sa. ϩⲉⲛⲉⲉⲧⲉ[4] and in Am. to دير. So too in Av., this last is the usual Arabic equivalent. However, in 11 cases[5] ϩⲉⲛⲉⲉⲧⲉ is simply transcribed as هناة (هنادات, هنادتين). But ϩⲉⲛⲉⲉⲧⲉ is a word unknown so far in Bohairic literature. In this Arabic form, it is to be met only as a place-name[6]: the dictionaries do not record it.

It is probable moreover that careful examination of the text would reveal unintelligible or questionable readings explicable only when retranslated into Sa'idic. I am only able to point to one undoubted case: Sa. (*Miss.* 526, 2) ⲁϥϩⲱⲛ ⲉⲣⲟϥ 'he approached him' = Bo. 62, 1 ⲉⲧⲁϥϧⲟⲛⲧϥ ⲉϧⲟⲩⲛ 'when he approached' = Av.

[1] One other independent reading of Av. (90 b) الاودية, where Am. 544, 7 المواضع, Sa. ⲛ̄ⲛⲉ̄ ⲛⲧⲟⲟⲩⲉⲓⲏ, might be due to resemblance in sound between the Arabic words, though neither represents the Coptic accurately.

[2] Prof. Mallon confirms this reading, but doubtless Sa. is correct; *v.* Griffith, *ÄZ.* xxxviii. 88.

[3] Conversely in Bo. ⲉⲃⲱⲛϩ, ⲡⲉϭⲱϣ, ⲫⲃⲟⲟⲩ (*cf.* ⲫⲃⲱⲟⲩ), ⲧⲥⲙⲓⲛⲉ confirm the Sa. origin of that version. The remaining Coptic glosses of interest in Av. are: ϣⲉⲛⲉⲥⲏⲧ, ⲉϥⲱⲛϩ 31 b, ⲡⲓⲥⲱ 32 b, ϣⲉⲛⲧⲉϩϥⲱ 35 b, ⲧⲁⲙⲁⲩⲟ (=[ⲁ]ⲡⲁ ⲙⲁⲩⲟ) 43 b, also ⲙⲁⲱ, ⲙⲁⲩⲱ *ib.*, ⲡⲁⲧⲗⲟⲗⲉ 57 (*v.* Bo. 133), ⲫⲙⲟⲩⲛ 95 b (*cf.* ⲡⲛⲟⲩⲙ), ϩⲟⲣⲥⲉⲥⲓⲟⲥ 96, ⲥⲙⲓⲛⲉ 96 b (*cf.* ⲧⲥⲙⲓⲛⲉ).

[4] *E.gg.* Bo. 30, 57, 61, 71, 101, corresponding to Sa. *Miss.* 543, 522, 525, 533, *M. Guim.* 326.

[5] Av. foll. 22 b, 35 b, 36, 37 a, b, 51 b, 52, 54, 66 b, always = Bo. ⲙⲟⲛⲏ. Once, 32 b = Sa. (*Miss.* 535) ⲥⲟⲟⲩϩⲥ.

[6] Abû Ṣâliḥ 89 a gives a monastery so named at Rîfah, S. of Siût, while in *Synax.*, 21 Hatûr (Basset ii. 322, Forget i. 305), it is the name of one at any rate close by Siût, presumably the same. The same too probably is 'the ϩⲉⲛⲏⲧⲉ of Siût' in the colophons Zoega 453 and Paris 132^1, 67, though this is hardly a true place-name.

f. 28, 10 اوصاه 'he bade him', the translator mistaking Sa. ϩⲱⲛ 'approach' for ϩⲱⲛ 'bid', a mistake impossible if his original had been Bo., since there the two words are different. That the right meaning here is 'approach' is proved by AS. § 29, *πλησιάσας*. Perhaps the following also is an error of like origin: Sa. 528, 2 ⲁϥϫⲟⲟⲩ 'he sent' = Bo. 64, 8 ⲁϥⲟⲩⲱⲣⲡ = Av. f. 29, 6 فقال 'he said', reading apparently ⲁϥϫⲟⲟⲥ, though elsewhere ϫⲟⲟⲩ is rightly recognized. Had we a more complete Sa., further conclusions might doubtless be drawn from the numerous corrections in Av., made, with scarcely an exception, by the original scribe, in the actual course of writing. That these are not subsequent alterations is clear; for, in some instances, a word but half written is cancelled and immediately followed by the correction or preferable alternative, *e.g.* f. 95b, 4 بعنون was begun, but altered to ابمون. This would seem to point to Av. being, not a copy from another Arabic MS., but the original holograph of the translator, written directly from the Coptic before him.[1] The nature of many of the alterations—different readings generally,[2] seldom mere errors corrected—may point to the text being the result of an eclectic process, the translator having perhaps drawn upon more than one of the Coptic versions.

The Sa'idic Recensions.

The prospect of an exhaustive edition of all the Coptic recensions by Professor Théodore Lefort relieves me of the necessity of more than a short description of the MSS. Professor Lefort has expended much labour upon the disentanglement of their mutual relationships; we may therefore leave to him the statement and solution of the various problems involved.

Besides our two new papyri (Nos. 24 and 25 above), fragments are known of six parchment MSS. preserving parts of the Lives.

1 (Lefort No. 4). The Life of P. alone. The script of this MS.[3] is of about the 12th century: facsimile, Mingarelli p. 223, no. 9. Its fragments are:—

Paris 129^{12} ff. 45, 46	= *Mus. Guim.* 314 pp. ⲍ–ⲓ̄	= § 2.
„ „ f. 60	= *Miss.* 537	§ 4.
Venice (Ming. no. 9)	= *Miss.* 800	ⲡ̄ⲁ̄–ϥ̄ⲥ̄ = §§ 27^2–33^2, *cf. Miss.* 522.
Paris 129^{12} f. 47		ϥ̄ⲍ̄, ϥ̄ⲏ̄ (communicated by Prof. Lefort).

[1] The frequent Coptic transcripts of names (*v.* above) may testify to this.

[2] *E.gg.* Av. 14, 9 تعرق altered to تصير = Sa. (Paris 129^{12}, 11) ⲱⲙⲥ 'were drenched (with blood)'; Bo. wanting; *cf.* Am. 361, 2. Av. 18b, 8 ليهى altered to ليهتموا, Bo. 35, 4 has both. Av. 21b, 15 لذات الأطعمة, first word cancelled, as *τροφή* had been mistaken for *τρυφή*, *v.* Bo. 46, 11. Av. 62, 13 تمتحنه altered to تتميزه = Bo. 148, 10 ⲉⲣⲁⲓⲁⲕⲣⲓⲛⲓⲛ. Av. 69b, 5 و عند ما ارادوا ان يرسوا الى البر ليطلعوا الى الاسكندرية altered to و فى كل ترة يريدوا يصعدوا الى البر فى حال مضيهم الى الا, which better agrees with Bo. 168, 1, Sa. being here lost.

[3] The same as that of Zoega cxcii, ccxiii** (Shenoute).

Vienna, Hofbibl. = Wessely, *Stud.* xi, no. 112 a, b pp. ⲣⲓⲁ, ⲣⲓⲃ = §§ 52, 35[2].
" " " " 112 c, d ⲣⲕⲍ, ⲣⲕⲏ } = §§ 43–50, 55[1].
Paris 129[12] ff. 48–54 = *Mus. Guim.* 317 ⲣⲕⲑ–ⲣⲙⲇ }
" 78 ff. 27–30 = *Miss.* 547 ⲣⲝⲉ–ⲣⲟⲃ (*v.* Bo. 119), *cf.* Br. Mus. no. 355 (1).
Vienna, *ut supra* = Wessely, *l. c.*, 112 e–h ⲣϥϛ–ⲣϥϛ = § 60, *cf. Miss.* 553 *inf.*

The text corresponds with another Sa. version in three passages, as here indicated; but, so far as extant, it offers no material not to be already found elsewhere.

2 (Lefort No. 2). This would also appear to consist of the Life of P. alone, although, as in the last case, we have only the argument *e silentio* to support the assumption. The MS. may be of the 6th or 7th century: the script much resembles Br. Mus. *Cat.*, pl. 2, no. 971 (datable about 650). Described with extracts, *l.c.*, no. 342. Its text seems to be generally parallel with Am. (*cf.* sequence of sections), though in detail they differ considerably. One of the passages (p. ⲡϛ) omitted by Am. (543) reappears in Av. (f. 90, 3–8), and in the same context as here.

3 (Lefort No. 1). Neither is there any evidence here that the MS. included more than the Life of P. The script should be of about the 6th century: facsimile, Hyvernat, *Album*, pl. 2, 2. The two extant fragments are published *Miss.* 538–543 and correspond apparently to §§ 13, 11, 16, though both text and sequence are very different from those of any other recension.

4 (Lefort No. 6). This MS. related solely to Theodore, for on p. ϛ we see that P. is already dead. The script is of an easily datable type: it must belong to A.D. 1000 or thereabouts: facsimile, Wessely, *Studien* xi, p. 152 (9440). Its fragments are[1]:—

Paris 129[12] ff. 67 + 65 = *Miss.* 560 pp. ϛ, ⲇ = § 75.
Naples (Zoega clxxv) = *Mus. Guim.* 297 = § 77, *cf. Miss.* 567.
Paris 129[13] f. 54 = *Miss.* 823
Berlin, *Kopt. Urk.*, Nr. 191 ⲕⲍ, ⲕⲏ, *cf. Miss.* 594.
Paris 129[12] f. 63 = *Miss.* 586 ⲗⲉ, ⲗϛ = § 81.
Paris 129[12] f. 62 = *Miss.* 584 and *Muséon* xi. 215 (*v.* Bo. 238).
Berlin, Kgl. Bibl., Or. 1607, f. 3 pp. ⲙⲁ, ⲙⲃ = § 84 (?).
Vienna, Hofbibl. = Wessely, *l. c.*, no. 111 a, b ⲙϛ, ⲙⲇ = §§ 82, 83, *cf. Miss.* 588.
Paris 129[13] f. 60 + 129[12] f. 58 ⲙⲉ, ⲙϛ = § 93 (?).
" 129[12] ff. 55–57 = *Mus. Guim.* 328 *ult.* ⲡϛ–ⲡⲏ (*v.* Bo. in Leipzig, Univ. Bibl., vol. xxv, f. 3).

[1] On this list *cf.* Lefort in *Muséon* xi. 206, to whom the identification of two of the Paris fragments is due.

The three passages here which have parallels in another MS. (Sa. 5) make it probable that the present is but the second volume of the combined Life, since in the parallel MS. they occur midway in the work, which afterwards proceeds with the history of Theodore.

5 (Lefort No. 5). This is the only MS. which unquestionably combined the history of Theodore with that of P. It was written most probably in the 9th century. Facsimiles: Mingarelli p. 30, nos. 7, 8, Cairo, *Catal. Gén.* no. 8016. Its fragments are:—

Paris 129[12] f. 11		pp. ⲕⲑ, ⲗ	= § 9.
Naples (Zoega clxxiii)	= *Mus. Guim.* 295	ⲙⲉ, ⲙⲋ	= § 40[2].
Paris 129[12] ff. 18–25	= *Miss.* 521	ⲝ-ⲟⲉ	= §§ 26–35, 51, *cf. Miss.* 800, Br. Mus. no. 342, p. ϥⲉ.
" f. 26	= *Miss.* 545	ⲡⲏ, ⲡⲑ	= §§ 41, 42.
Brit. Mus. no. 355, f. 1		ⲣⲕⲋ, ⲣⲕⲍ	(*v.* Bo. 122), *cf. Miss.* 549.
Paris 78 f. 40	= *Miss.* 552		= §§ 61[2], 56[1], *cf. Mus. Guim.* 328.
" 129[12] f. 27	= *Miss.* 553	ⲣⲗⲑ, ⲣⲙ	= § 60, *cf.* Wessely, *l.c.* 112e, f, g.
" " f. 39	= *Miss.* 555	[ⲣⲙⲑ, ⲣⲡ]	(*v.* Am. 477).
Brit. Mus. no. 355, f. 2		ⲣⲡⲁ, ⲣⲡⲃ	(*v. ib.* 478).
Paris 129[12] f. 28	= *Miss.* 557	ⲣⲡⲍ, ⲣⲡⲏ	= § 66.
Naples (Zoega cccix)		ⲣϥⲋ, ⲣϥⲍ	(*v.* Bo. 175).
Leyden no. 88		ⲥⲍ, ⲥⲏ	(*v.* Am. 507).
Venice (Ming. no. 7)	= *Miss.* 562	ⲥⲡⲍ–ⲥⲟ	= § 77, *cf. Mus. Guim.* 297.
" (Ming. no. 8)	= *Miss.* 577	ⲥⲟⲋ, ⲥⲡ	= § 77.
Paris 129[12] f. 37	= *Miss.* 588		= § 83, *cf.* Wessely, *l.c.* 111b.
" " ff. 29–35	= *Miss.* 592	ⲧⲁ–ⲧⲓⲍ	*cf.* Berlin, *Kopt. Urk.* Nr. 191.
Brit. Mus. no. 355, f. 3		ⲧⲓⲍ, ⲧⲓⲏ	
Paris 129[12] f. 36	= *Miss.* 604	ⲧⲗⲁ, ⲧⲗⲃ	= § 88.
" " f. 38	= *Miss.* 559		= §§ 94, 95, *cf.* Wessely, *l.c.* 111 c, d.

To the following fragments I do not venture to assign a sequence:—

Cairo Museum no. 8016 (*v.* Am. 515).

Cairo, a fragment in Patriarch's collection (*v.* Bo. 243–5), *cf. Mus. Guim.* 306–8 and p. ⲣⲝⲍ of next MS.

6 (Lefort No. 3). This is the MS. of which the largest number of fragments are extant; but so bad is the state of preservation of many, and so obscure or unfamiliar the contents of others, that the character of the recension is hard to define. Its most obvious feature is the homiletic element, more or less prominent in the majority of fragments, and consisting of discourses (or prayers), attributed usually to Theodore, but having little or no visible relation to the narrative or indeed to the incidental discourses of the other recensions or versions. It relates the history of both P. and Theodore. The following list gives the paged fragments, in their order of pagination and irrespective of their contents :—

Naples (Zoega ccxcvi, f. 1)		pp. ⲅ, ⲇ = § 1.
Br. Mus. Or. 6954, 40		ⲙⲁ, ⲙⲃ = § 10 (?).
Berlin, Kgl. Bibl., Or. 1350, f. 1		ⲙⲍ, ⲙⲏ = § 12.
Br. Mus. no. 356		ⲛⲑ, ⲝ.
Paris 129[12] f. 59	= *Miss.* 543	ⲝⲉ, ⲝⲋ = §§ 16, 17.
Naples (Zoega ccxcvi, f. 2)		ⲝⲑ, ⲟ.
Br. Mus. no. 343, f. 1		ⲟⲉ, ⲟⲋ.
Naples (Zoega ccxcvii, 1 fol.)		ⲣ, ⲣⲁ.
Br. Mus. Or. 6954, 36		ⲣⲏ, ⲣⲑ.
Paris 131[8] ff. 29–33		ⲣⲓⲇ–ⲣⲕⲅ.
Leyden no. 70		ⲣⲕⲇ, ⲣⲕⲉ.
Br. Mus. no. 343, f. 2 (last of qu. ⲓⲅ)		[ⲣⲕⲏ, ⲣⲕⲑ ?].
Naples (Zoega ccxcvi, f. 3)		ⲣⲙⲍ, ⲣⲙⲏ.
Paris 131[7] f. 50		ⲣⲝ, ⲣⲝⲁ
Naples (Zoega clxxvii, ff. 1–4)	= *Mus. Guim.* 299	ⲣⲝⲇ, ⲣⲟⲁ.
Oxford, Clar. Pr., no. 35 (*v.* below)		ⲥⲏ, ⲥⲑ.
Vienna, Hofbibl.	= Wessely, *Stud.* xi, no, 111 c, d	ⲥⲛⲇ, ⲥⲛⲉ = §§ 94, 95, *cf. Miss.* 559.
Naples (Zoega clxxvii, ff. 5–7)	= *Mus. Guim.* 308–314	ⲥⲝⲇ–ⲥⲝⲑ = §§ 80, 96.
Berlin, Kgl. Bibl., Or. 1350, f. 2		ⲥⲟⲍ, ⲥⲟⲏ.
Paris 129[12] f. 42	= *Miss.* 605	ⲧϥ, ⲧϥⲁ.

Here follow those fragments which lack pagination, in a sequence, as far as possible, parallel to Bo. or Am. :—

(*a*) Narrative passages:

Br. Mus. Or. 6954, 35.	
Cairo, a fragment in the Patriarch's collection	*cf.* Bo. 184, Am. 500.
Naples (Zoega ccxcvi, f. 4)	*cf.* Bo. 186, Am. 503.
Br. Mus. no. 343, f. 2	*cf.* Am. 525.
Paris 129[12] f. 61	*cf.* Bo. 260, 276.

(*b*) Homiletic passages:

Br. Mus. no. 343, f. 3.

Naples (Zoega ccxcvii, 2 foll.).

Br. Mus. Or. 6954, 2 fragments (the subject is closely related to that of pp. ⲥⲏ, ⲥⲑ above).

Besides these 6 MSS., mention may be made of others relating to the founders of the Pachomian institutions, although they do not contain biographies of them:

α. Paris 129^{13} ff. 43, 44 (*v*. above, p. 178). This is an extract from the Life of P., narrating his death and burial. The MS. was written about A.D. 1000.

β. Paris 129^{12} ff. 70–72 = *Miss.* 609–611. From an Encomium (?) on P., attributed, no doubt falsely, to Athanasius. The MS. may be of the 11th century.

γ. Paris 129^{12} f. 68 = *Miss.* 590 *ult.*, 591. Hand of about the 11th century: facsimile, Cairo, *Catal. Gén.* no. 8017. This leaf is from an anecdote of Horsiesius. The paging in the edition,[1] ⲣⲟⲍ, ⲣⲟⲏ, shows that, if indeed it is from the same volume as the other extant leaves by this hand,[2] we may (as M. Amélineau has suggested, *Miss.* 488) have to do with an independent Life of Horsiesius; for the preceding leaves, paged ⲟⲑ, ⲡ, ⲣⲗⲁ, ⲣⲗⲃ, ⲣⲙⲅ–ⲣⲙⲋ, all relate to the patriarchs Peter I and Achillas of Alexandria and the suppression of paganism: they have, that is to say, no apparent relation to the Pachomian communities.

δ. Paris 129^{12} f. 74 = *Miss.* 812. The hand may be of the 9th century. This small fragment refers indeed to certain of P.'s companions, but it cannot—if we have regard to the other leaves by this hand and their pagination—belong to any of the Lives. The other extant work of the same hand is: Zoega no. ccxxx, Paris 130^{3} ff. 59–74, 130^{4} ff. 131–162. There is nothing in the pagination of these long fragments to forbid their being, together with our leaf, all parts of a single volume. On the leaves from 130^{3} see Leipoldt's observations (*Schenute*, p. 11 n.). The fact that those from 130^{4} are certainly Shenoute's supports his opinion that Zoega's text has at least been edited by that writer.[3]

ε. This fragment is obviously concerned with P. and his disciples, but its relationship to the Lives is obscure, no such incident being discoverable in any other text. I print it from a copy kindly given me (1899) by Professor Guidi, who says the hand is that of the late E. Teza. The copy offers not the slightest information either as to the MS. copied or the number and pagination of its leaves.

[1] I have not noted any pagination. Possibly it has (as too often) disappeared in binding.

[2] Cairo no. 8017, Paris 129^{16} f. 74, 129^{14} ff. 105–108.

[3] The title ⲁⲡⲁ, without following name, rightly claimed by Leipoldt for Pachomius, is however applied to other venerable persons besides, *e.g.* Jeremias of Saqqara (Quibell-Thompson, no. 226, l. 14 n.), Peter of Alexandria (*Texte u. Unt.*, NF. v. 4b, p. 10), Zoega p. 303, 19, Br. Mus. nos. 691, 597 (?). See also the text here following.

ⲙⲛⲛⲥⲱⲥ ⲟⲛ ⲁϥϯ ⲕⲉⲕⲟⲧ ⲁϥⲡⲱϩ ⲉⲣⲟϥ ⲟⲛ ⲡⲉϫⲁϥ ⲛⲁϥ ⲙⲡⲙⲉϩⲥⲉⲡⲥⲛⲁⲩ ϫⲉⲡⲏⲓ ⲉⲛⲧⲁⲡⲣⲱⲙⲉ ⲕⲟⲧϥ ϥⲉⲓⲣⲉ ⲛⲟⲩⲏⲣ ⲛⲟⲩⲁϩⲙⲉ· ⲙⲡϥⲉϣϯ ⲁⲡⲟⲗⲟⲅⲓⲁ ⲛⲁϥ ⲡⲁⲗⲓⲛ ⲟⲛ ⲁϥⲕⲟⲧϥ ⲙⲡⲙⲉϩϣⲟⲙⲧ ⲛⲥⲟⲡ· ⲁϥⲡⲱϩ ⲉⲣⲟϥ ⲟⲛ ⲡⲉϫⲁϥ ⲛⲁϥ ϫⲉⲡⲏⲓ ⲉⲛⲧⲁⲡⲣⲱⲙⲉ ⲕⲟⲧϥ ϥⲉⲓⲣⲉ ⲛⲟⲩⲏⲣ ⲛⲟⲩⲁϩⲙⲉ· ⲡⲉϫⲁϥ ⲛⲁϥ ⲙⲡⲙⲉϩϣⲟⲙⲧ ⲛⲥⲟⲡ ϫⲉϥⲉⲓⲣⲉ ⲙⲙⲏⲧⲉ ⲛⲟⲩⲁϩⲙⲉ· ⲛⲧⲉⲣⲉϥϫⲟⲟⲥ ⲛⲁϥ ϫⲉϥⲉⲓⲣⲉ ⲙⲙⲏⲧⲉ ⲛⲟⲩⲁϩⲙⲉ ⲁⲡⲁⲅⲅⲉⲗⲟⲥ ⲛⲱⲧϥ ⲣⲱϥ ⲛⲥⲱⲃⲉ ⲁϥⲙⲟⲟϣⲉ· ⲛⲧⲉⲣⲉⲁⲡⲁ ⲧⲁⲩⲟϥ ⲉⲣⲟⲛ ⲁⲛϫⲛⲟⲩϥ ϫⲉⲧⲁⲙⲟⲛ ⲉⲡⲉϥⲃⲱⲗ· ⲡⲉϫⲁϥ ⲛⲁⲛ ϫⲉⲡⲣⲱⲙⲉⲡⲉ ⲡⲛⲟⲩⲧⲉ· ⲧⲙⲏⲧⲉ ⲛⲟⲩⲁϩⲙⲉ ⲙⲡⲏⲓⲡⲉ ⲧⲥⲁϣϥⲉ ⲙⲡⲉ· ⲙⲡⲉⲥⲧⲉⲣⲏⲱⲙⲁ ⲙⲡⲕⲁϩ ⲙⲛⲁⲙⲛⲧⲉ ⲡⲉϫⲁϥ ⲛⲁⲛ ϫⲉⲛⲑⲉ ⲉⲛⲉ(ⲛ)ⲧⲁⲓⲣⲁⲧⲥⲟⲟⲩⲛ[1] ⲙⲡⲙⲉϩϣⲟⲙⲧ ⲛⲥⲟⲡ ⲉⲙⲛⲓϭⲛⲧϥ ⲉⲧⲁⲩⲟϥ ⲛⲁϥ ⲛⲉⲣⲉⲧⲙⲛⲧⲁⲧⲥⲟⲟⲩⲛ ⲛⲁⲕⲓⲙ ⲁⲛ ϩⲛⲛⲉⲥⲛⲏⲩ ϣⲁⲉⲛⲉϩ· ⲡⲉϫⲁⲛ ⲛⲁϥ ϫⲉⲁⲕⲛⲁϩⲙⲛ ⲙⲛⲡⲉⲛⲥⲡⲉⲣⲙⲁ ϣⲁⲉⲛⲉϩ· ⲛⲁⲓⲛⲉ ⲛϣⲁϫⲉ ⲉⲛⲧⲁⲁⲡⲁ ⲧⲁⲩⲟⲟⲩ ⲉⲣⲟⲓ ⲉⲓⲧⲁⲗⲏⲩ ⲉⲡϫⲟⲉⲓ ⲛⲙⲙⲁϥ ⲁⲛⲟⲕ ⲙⲛⲡⲁⲉⲓⲱⲧ ⲕⲟⲣⲛⲏⲗⲓⲟⲥ· ⲡⲉϫⲉ ⲁⲡⲁ ⲕⲟⲣⲛⲏⲗⲓⲟⲥ ⲛⲁϥ ϫⲉⲧⲁⲩⲉⲛϣⲁϫⲉ ⲉⲣⲟⲛ ⲙⲡⲉϩⲟⲟⲩ ⲉⲛⲧⲁⲩϥⲓⲧⲕ ⲉϩⲣⲁⲓ ⲉⲧⲡⲉ· ⲡⲉϫⲁϥ ⲛⲁⲛ ϫⲉⲙⲡⲓⲧⲁⲩⲉⲛⲣⲉⲙⲏⲧ ⲙⲡⲁⲥⲁⲗⲁⲡⲓⲛ ⲉⲣⲱⲧⲛ· ⲡⲉϫⲉ ⲁⲡⲁ ⲕⲟⲣⲛⲏⲗⲓⲟⲥ ⲛⲁϥ ϫⲉⲡⲉⲧⲡⲏϩ ϣⲁⲣⲟⲛ ϩⲱⲱⲛ ⲧⲁⲩⲟϥ ϣⲁⲣⲟⲛ· ⲡⲉϫⲁϥ ⲛⲁⲛ ϫⲉⲡϣⲟⲣⲡ ⲙⲙⲁ ⲉⲛⲧⲁⲩⲛⲧ ⲉϫⲱϥ (*sic expl.*).

'And thereafter he turned about[2] again and came up again to him and said unto him the second time, "The house that the man did build, how many stories hath it?" He was not able to give him account (ἀπολογία). Again he turned about the third time and came up to him again and said unto him, "The house that the man did build, how many stories hath it?" He said unto him the third time, "It hath ten stories." When he had said unto him, It hath ten stories, the angel smiled and departed.' When Apa had told it us, we asked him, saying, 'Tell us its meaning.' He said unto us, 'The man is God. The ten stories of the house are the seven heavens, with the firmament (στερέωμα) and the earth and hell (*amente*).' He said unto us, 'Supposing I had been ignorant the third time, not finding what to say unto him, so would ignorance not have ceased from[3] the brethren evermore.' We said unto him, 'Thou hast saved us and our seed (σπέρμα) for ever.' These be the words that Apa spake unto me, I being on board the boat with him, I and my father Cornelius. Apa Cornelius said unto him, 'Tell us the words (spoken) on the day when thou wast taken up to heaven.'[4] He said unto us, 'I have not told you the tenth part of my heart (?)'[5]. Apa Cornelius said unto him, 'That which reacheth (? = concerneth) us, tell it us.' He said unto them, 'The first place whereunto I was brought (*sic expl.*).

[1] The copy has ⲉⲛⲉ̄ ⲧⲁⲓ &c.

[2] ϯ ⲛⲕⲟ́ⲧ seems equivalent to ⲕⲱⲧⲉ a little below. Recurs perhaps in Rylands Cat., no. 368. Whether = ϯ ⲟⲩⲕⲟⲧⲥ (Exod. xxxii. 27 &c.) is doubtful.

[3] *Cf.* this rare use of ⲕⲓⲙ in Acts v. 42 = παύεσθαι.

[4] *Cf.* ? Am. 543.

[5] ⲥⲉⲗⲉⲡⲓⲛ = ὑποχόνδρια (or καρδία) in 1 Sam. xxxi. 3. *Cf.* ? σπλήν. Seems not impossible here.

TABLE I, SHOWING WHERE THE PARAGRAPHS OF AS. AND PAR. OCCUR IN THE UNPUBLISHED ARABIC TEXTS.

AS., §§	Ap., foll.	Ac., pp.	Av., foll.	AS., §§	Ap., foll.	Ac., pp.	Av., foll.
2	7 b		3 b	38^{1}	98 b	79 (?)	
3	10 a	5	5	38^{2}	99 b		36 b
4	11 a	6	6	39^{1}	100 a	88	37 a
5	15 a	10	9 b	39^{2}	102 a		
6	17 b	11	11 b	40^{1}	174 a	41	37 b
7	20 a		12 b	40^{2}	66 b, 103 a	33	
8	21 a	12	12 a	41	67 a	34	38
9	22 b	13	13 b	42^{1}	70 b	36	38 b
10	24 a		14 b	42^{2}			
11	25 b	14	15 a	43	104 a	56	39 b
12	28 b	16	15 b	44	106 b	50	40 b
13	30 b	”	16	45	107 b	”	41
14	32 b	17		46^{1}	108 b	53	41 b
15	34 a		16 b	46^{2}	109 b		
16	37 b	18	”	47^{1}	111 a	54	
17	39 a	”	”	47^{2}	112 a		42 b
18	39 b	19	17 b	48	113 a	58, 113	42 b *ult.*
19	42 b	20	18 b	49	115 a	58	44
20^{1}	73 b	43		50^{1}	119 a	60	44 b
20^{2}	75 a			50^{2}	183 a	122	35
21	76 a	44		51^{1}	184 b	123	33 a, 35 b
22	49 a	24	18 b	51^{2}	185 b		33 b
23	54 a	26	21 b	52	188 b	125	35 b
24	56 a	27	20	53	189 b	112	
25	59 b	30	20 b *ult.*,	54			
			22 b	55^{1}	190 b	74	45
26	61 b	31	24 b	55^{2}			
27^{1}	77 a			56^{1}	192 a	”	45 b
27^{2}		87	26	56^{2}			
28	78 b	63	26 b	57	194 a	76	47 b, 49
29	80 b	68	28	58^{1}	195 b	126	24 b
30	83 b	64	29	58^{2}			48
31		66	30	59^{1}	198 a	128	55
32	88 b	”		59^{2}			
33^{1}	65 a	52		60	199 a	129	59 b
33^{2}	90 b		30	61^{1}	202 b	71	
34^{1}	92 a	77	30 b	61^{2}			45 b
34^{2}				62	202 a (?)	130 (?)	
35^{1}	47 a	23	31 b	63			
35^{2}	93 a	78		64^{1}	206 a	69	63, 74 b
36	94 b	79		64^{2}			71 b
37	96 b	79 (?)		65^{1}	207 a	106	75 b

AS., §§	Ap., foll.	Ac., pp.	Av., foll.	AS., §§	Ap., foll.	Ac., pp.	Av., foll.
65[2]			63 b	81	238 a	149	
66	121 a	91		82	239 a	150	
67	125 a	93		83	240 b	151	
68	208 b	132	63 b	84	242 a	152	
69	211 a	133	65	85	244 b	153	
70	213 a	134	68 b	86	246 b	155	
71	215 a	130		87	247 a	„	
72	217 b	136		88	249 a	157	
73	221 a	137	70	89[1]	251 b		
74	222 b	138	95	90	256 a	160	
75	224 a	140	95 b	91	256 b	161	
76	226 a	142		92	260 b	164	
77	230 a	144		93[1]	263 b	165	
78	232 a	146		94	266 b		
79	234 a	147		95	268 a	168	
80	236 a	148		96	270 a	169	

Paralipomena.

Par., §§	Ap., foll.	Ac., pp.	Par., §§	Ap., foll.	Ac., pp.
2	121 a	91	*20*	147 a	
3	125 b	94 (?)	*21*	148 b	83
4	127 a	„	*22*	150 b (?)	84 (?)
5	129 b	96	*23*	155 b	82
6	131 a		*24*	161 b	103
7	140 a	45	*25*	164 a	104
8	157 a	101	*26*	167 b	105
9	158 a	„	*27*	„	108
10	159 b	102	*28*	169 a	81
11	160 b	103	*29*	170 a	109
12	177 a	121	*30*	171 b	110
13	135 a	98	*31*	169 b	82
14	136 a	„	*32*	172 b	
15	136 b	99	*33*	175 a	107
16	138 a	„	*34*	180 a	70
17	142 a	46	*35*	181 a	110
18	144 a	47	*36*	182 b	111
19	147 a	48			

TABLE II, SHOWING SEQUENCE OF PARAGRAPHS OF AS. AND PAR. IN CERTAIN OF THE RECENSIONS.

Italics here = Paralipomena.

Am.	Bo.	Av.	Ap.	Ac.	Sur.	Nau A.
1	1	As Bohairic.	1	1	1	*1*
2	2		2	2	2	*2*
3	3		3	3	3	*3*
4	4		4	4	4	*4*
5	5		5	5	5	*5*
6	6		6	6	7	*6*
8	8		7	7	8	*13*
7	7		8	8	9	*14*
9	9		9	9	10	*15*
10	10		10	11	11	*16*
11	11		11	12	13	7
12	12		12	13	14	*17–23*
13	13		13	14	15	*8*
15	15		14	16	16	*9*
16+17	16+17		15	17	17	*10*
18	18		16	18	18	*11*
19	19		17	19	19	*24–33*
17	22		18	35^{1}	20	*12*
35^{1}	20^{2}	(*om.*)	19	22	21	40^{2}
22	24		35^{1}	23	22	38^{2}
20^{2}	25		22	24	23	39^{1}
23	23		*Hist. Laus.* xxxiii.	25	24	40^{1}
24	25	As Bohairic.	23	26	25	41
25	58^{1}		24	40^{2}	26	43
40^{2}	26		25	41	27	47
26	27^{2}		26	42	28	45
42^{2}	28		33^{1}	40^{1}	29	50^{1}
41	29		40^{2}	20	30	44 (*cf.* 62)
42^{1}	30		41	21	33	51
44	31		42	7	34	57
45	33^{2}		20	*17*	35	55^{1}
46	34		21	*18*	*28*	*34*
43	35^{1}		27	*19*	*29*	*35*
47^{2}	51^{2}		28	44	*32*	*36*
48	50^{2}		29	45	*12*	74
49	51^{1}		30	33^{1}	*33*	75
50	52		32	46	38	31
53	35^{2}		33^{2}	47	39	
54	38^{2}		34	43	40	
56^{1}	39^{1}		35^{2}	48	41	
55^{1}	40^{1}		36	49	*1*	
56^{2}	41		37	50^{1}	43	

Am.	Bo.	Av.	Ap.	Ac.	Sur.
57	42	As Bohairic.	38	28 (?)	47
58	43		39	30	45
59^{1}	44		40^{2}	31	50
61^{2}	45		43	32	*2*
60	46		44	29	*3*
64^{2}	47^{2}		45	64	*4*
68	48		46	*34*	51^{1}
64^{1}	49		47	61	*5*
65^{1}	50^{1}		48	55	*6*
66	55^{1}		49	56	59 }
67	61^{2}		51^{1}	57	*13* }
55^{2}	56^{1}		66	33^{2}	51^{1}
33^{2}	57		67	34	51^{2}
27^{2}	58^{2}		*3*	35^{2}	*15*
29	57		*4*	36	*16*
28	59		*5*	37 (?)	7
30	60		*6*	38	*17*
31	64^{1}		*13*	*28*	*18*
34	65^{2}		*14*	*31*	*19*
35	68		*15*	*23*	*21*
51	69		*16*	*21*	*22*
50^{2}	70		7	*22* (?)	*23*
52	73		*17–23*	27^{2}	*8*
38^{2}	64^{2}		*8*	39	*9*
39^{1}	64^{1}		*9*	66	*10*
68	65^{1}		*10*	67	57
69	lacuna	addition	*11*	*2*	55^{2}
70	89^{1}	74	*24–28*	*3*	*24*
73	88	75	*31*	*4*	*25*
72	89^{3}	addition	*29*	*5*	*26* (?)
21	90		*30*	*6*	64^{2}
32^{1}	91		*32*	*13*	58
38^{1}	89^{2}		40^{1}	*14*	27
39^{2}	93^{2}		*33*	*15*	*34*
40^{2} (?)	92		*12*	*16*	*35*
47^{1}	93^{1}		*34*	*8*	74
48	94		*35*	*9*	75
50^{1}	95		*36*	*10*	31
5	96		50^{2}	*11*	
6			51	*24*	
13			52	*25*	
15			53	*26*	
16			55	65	
7			56	*33*	

Am.	Bo.	Av.	Ap.	Ac.
17			57	*27*
18			58	*29*
19			59	*30*
21–27			60	*35*
29			62 (?)	*36*
30			61	53
32			64	48
33			65	addition
12			68	*12*
34			69	50[2]
35			70	51
36			71	52
52			*v.* Nau	58
71			72–96	59
v. Nau*				60
72–96				62 (?)
				71
				v. Nau
				68
				69
				70
				72–87
				90–93
				95
				96

* The two additional sections in Nau D (pp. 509–10); *cf.* Am. 640 *infra*.

ADDITIONS AND CORRECTIONS

Page 1, note a, *read* Should be **ⲉⲛⲧ̅[ⲉⲛⲟⲥ.**

,, 9, note 2, *read* vol. 43.

,, 31, note 1. **ϣⲁⲙⲓⲥⲉ** occurs in 1 Sam. vi. 7.

,, 57, No. 11, *verso*, l. 8, *read* **ⲉⲓϣⲁⲛⲕⲧⲟⲓ.**

,, 71, note 1. **ⲇⲓⲟⲕⲗⲏ** in Rossi, *Papiri* I. iii. 24, 26, 31 &c.

,, 73, note 6, *for* 42 *read* 43.

,, 75, note 1. [Ap]a Moui might possibly be a variant of Hamoi. *Cf.* their Arabic forms, here and p. 162, note 1.

,, 77, note 1, *read* vol. 43.

,, 83, note 2, ditto.

,, 98, note 1. With **ⲉϩⲟⲩⲛ ⲉϩⲣⲁ-** *cf.* **ⲉϩⲟⲩⲛ ⲉϩⲛ-** Num. xiv. 11, Rossi I. i. 19, and **ⲉϩⲟⲩⲛ ϩⲛ-** 2 Sam. iii. 31; *v.* also Stern § 572.

INDEX

PERSONS

(*In sequence of Coptic alphabet*)

PLACES

COPTIC

(*A selection only*)

GREEK

ARABIC

SUBJECTS

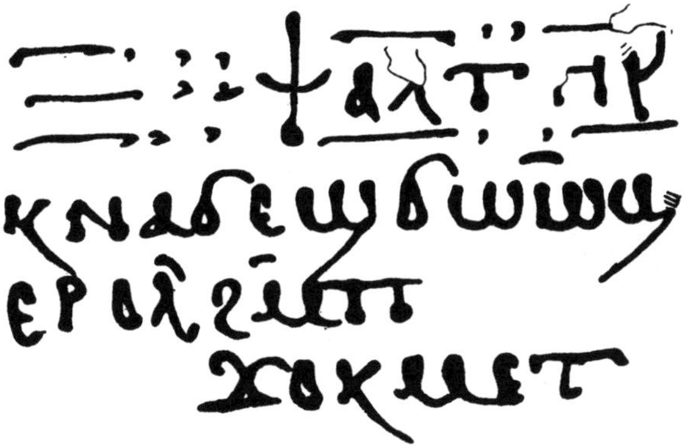

No. 2

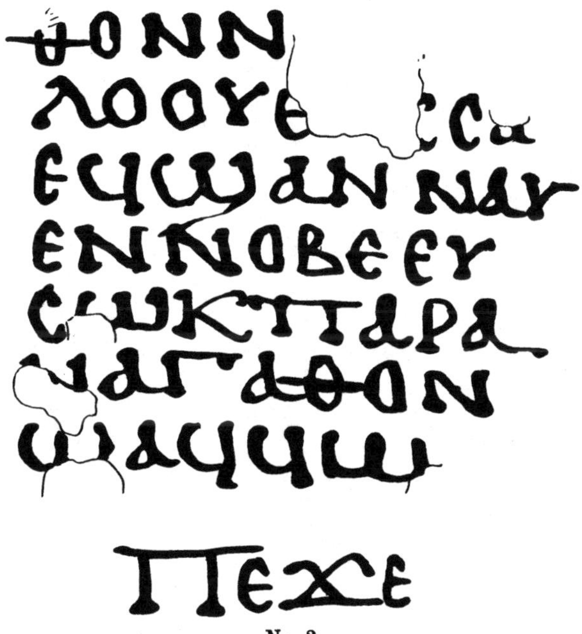

No. 3

No. 4

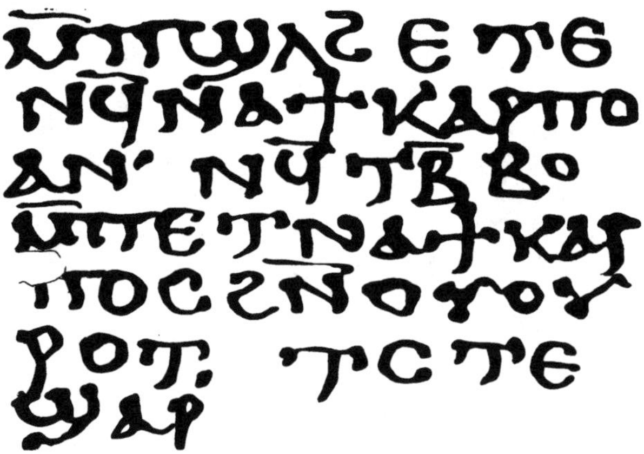

No. 6

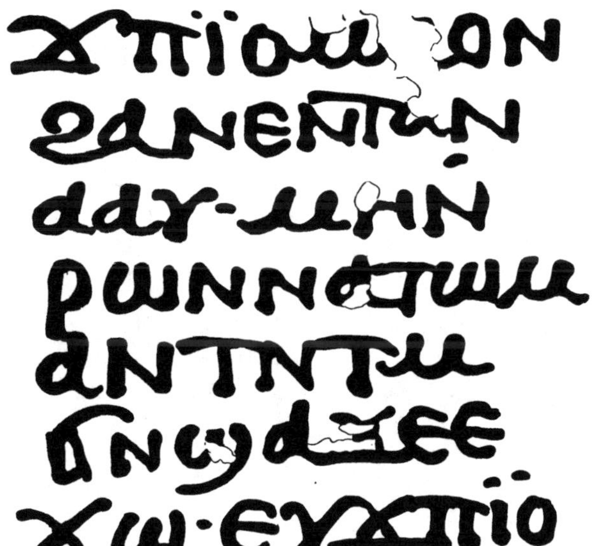

No. 8

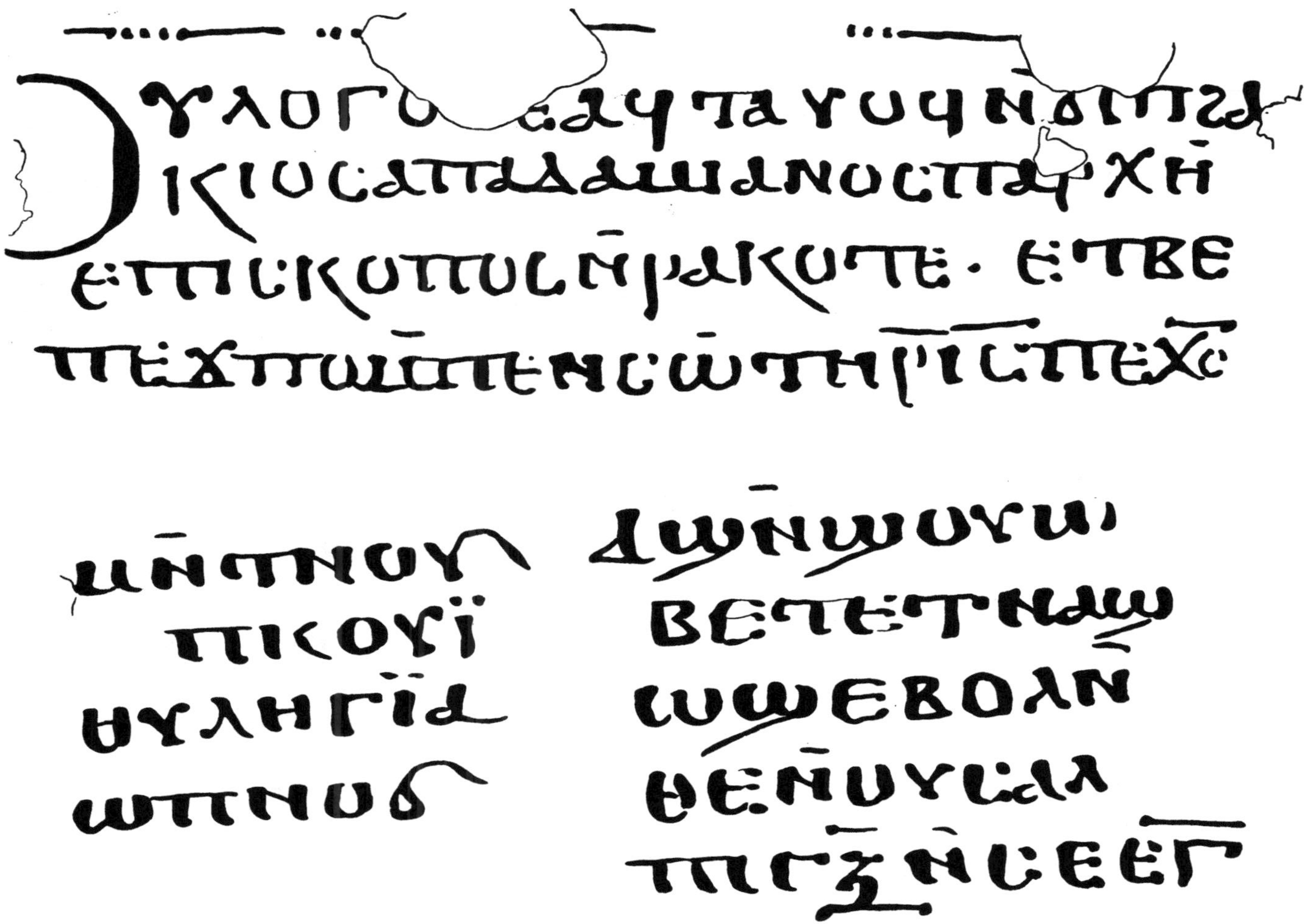
ⲕⲓⲟⲥ ⲁⲡⲁ ⲇⲁⲙⲓⲁⲛⲟⲥ ⲡⲁⲣⲭⲏ
ⲉⲡⲓⲥⲕⲟⲡⲟⲥ ⲛ̀ⲣⲁⲕⲟⲧⲉ · ⲉⲧⲃⲉ
ⲡⲉϫⲡⲟ ⲙ̀ⲡⲉⲛⲥⲱⲧⲏⲣ ⲓ̅ⲥ̅ ⲡⲉⲭ̅ⲥ̅

No. 7

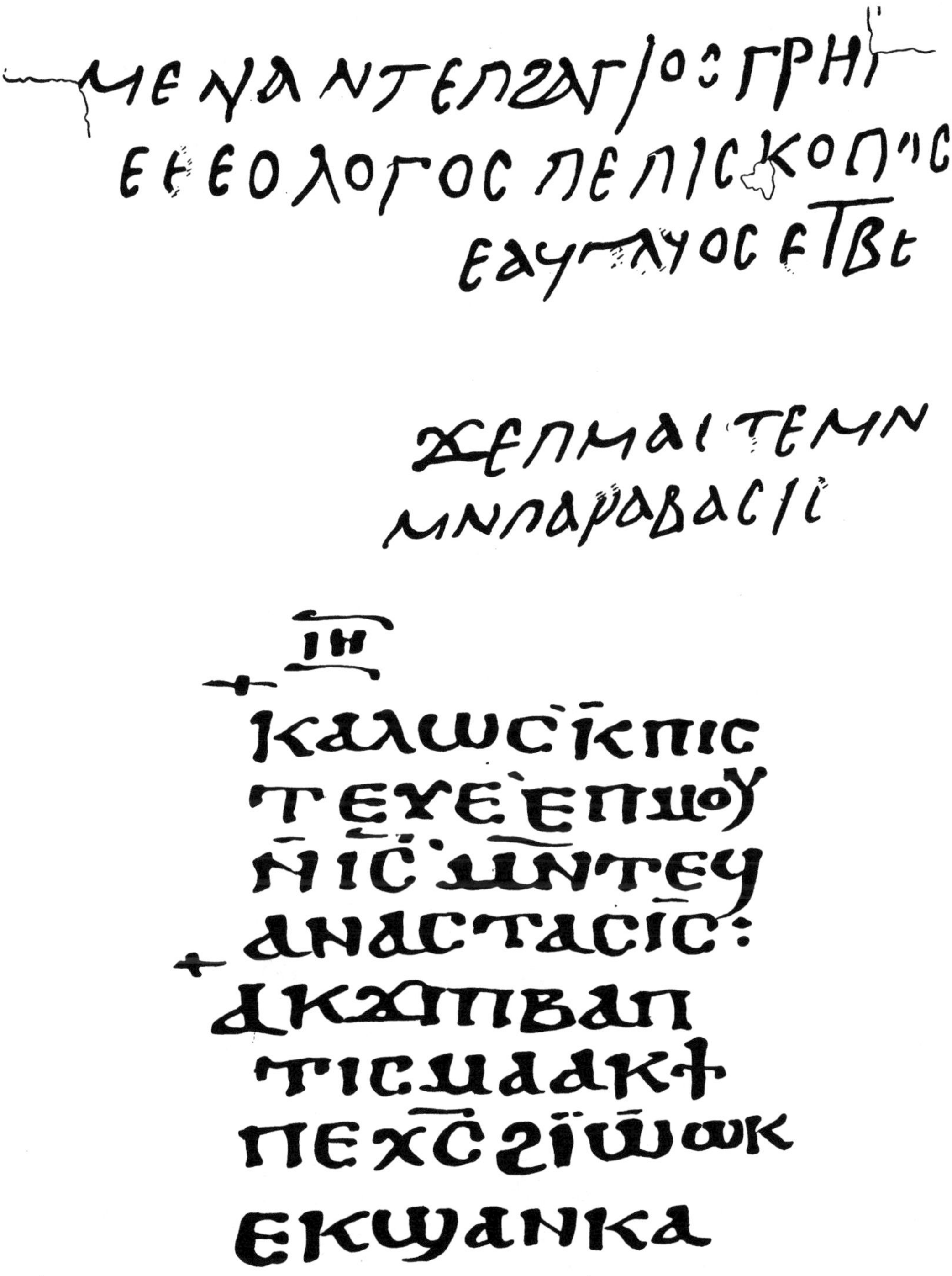

No. 9

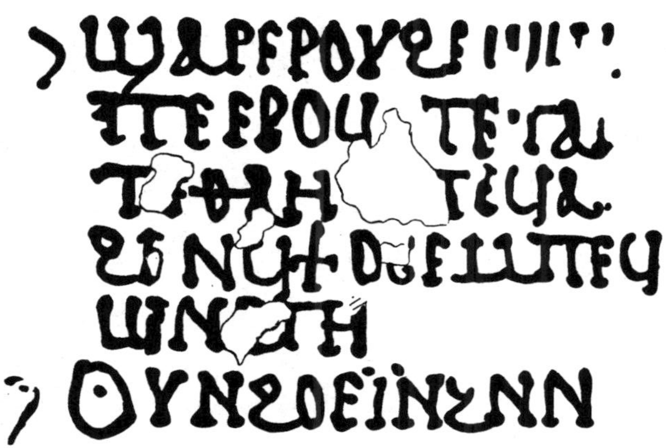

No. 10

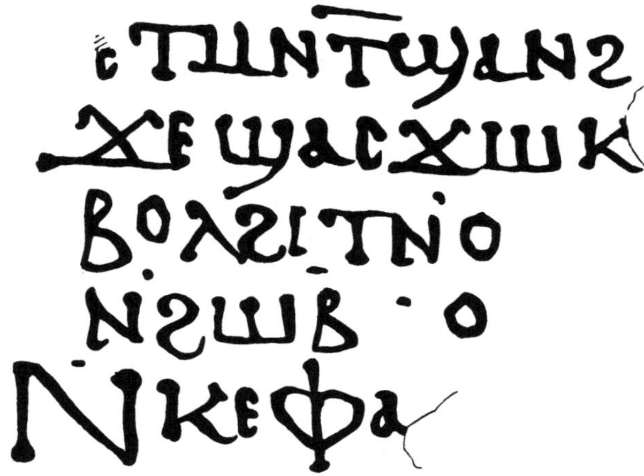

No. 11

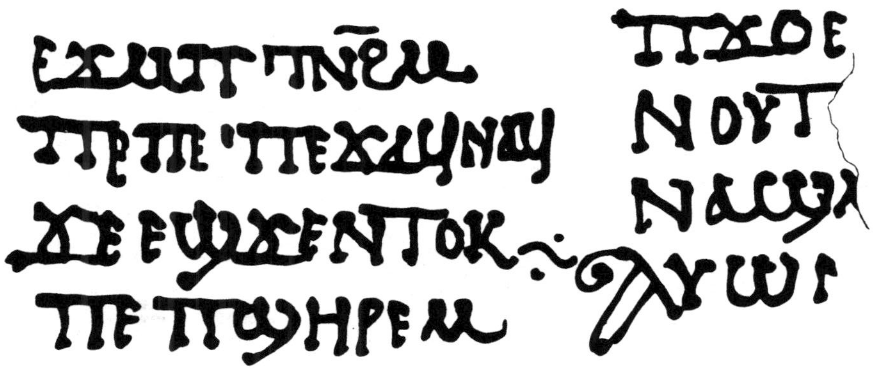

No. 12

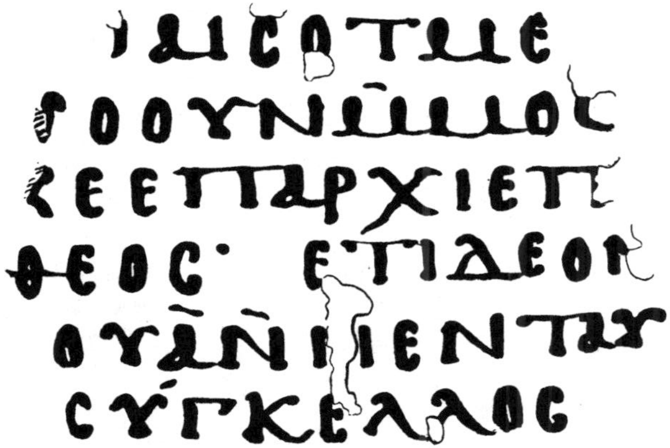

No. 13

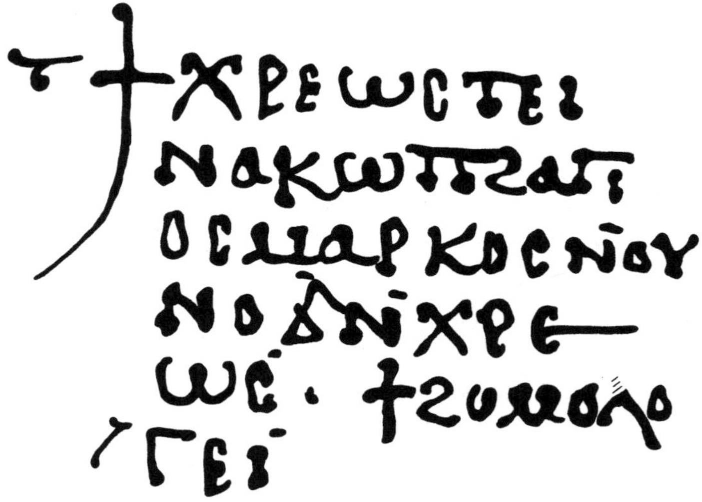

No. 15

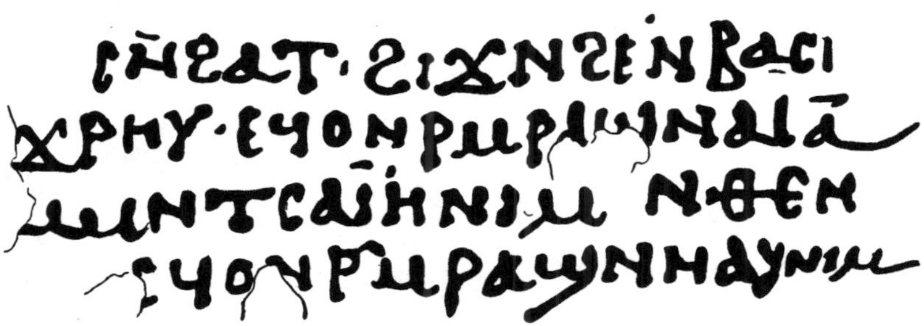

No. 16

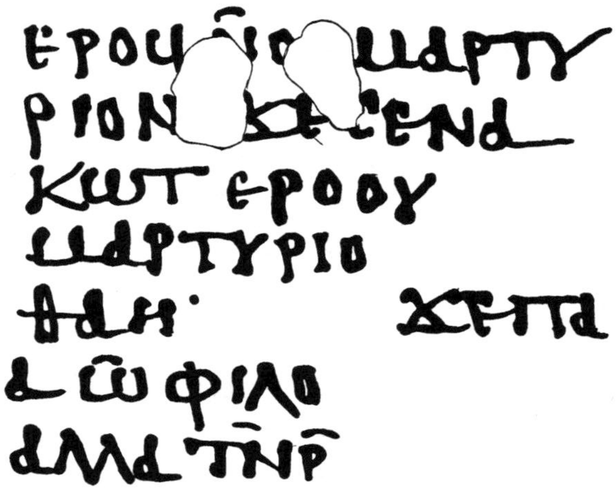

No. 17

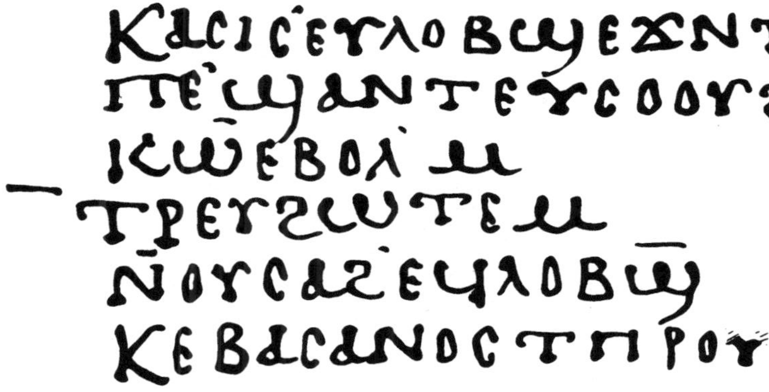

No. 19

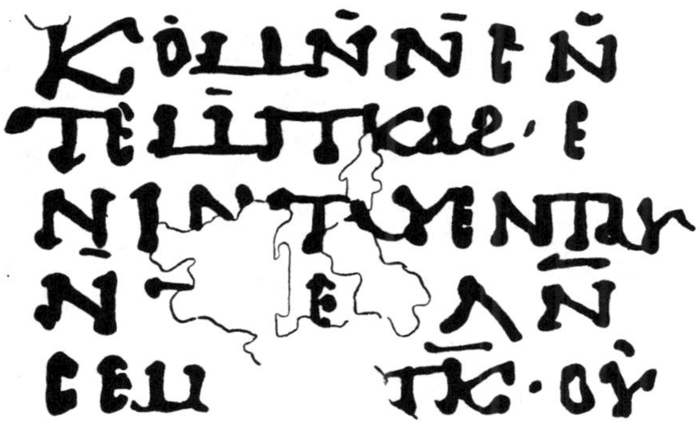

No. 21

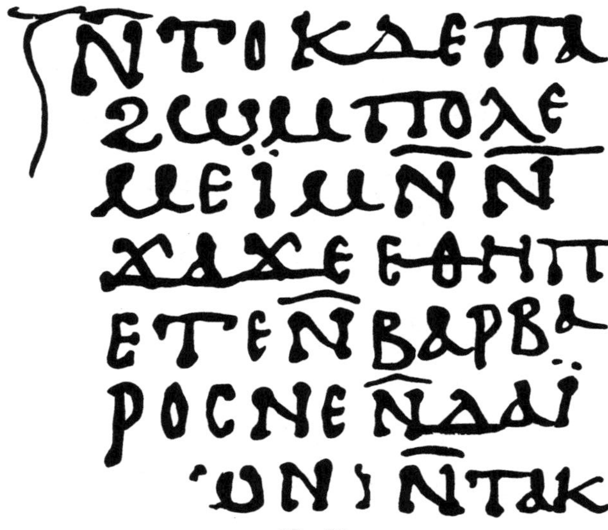

No. 24

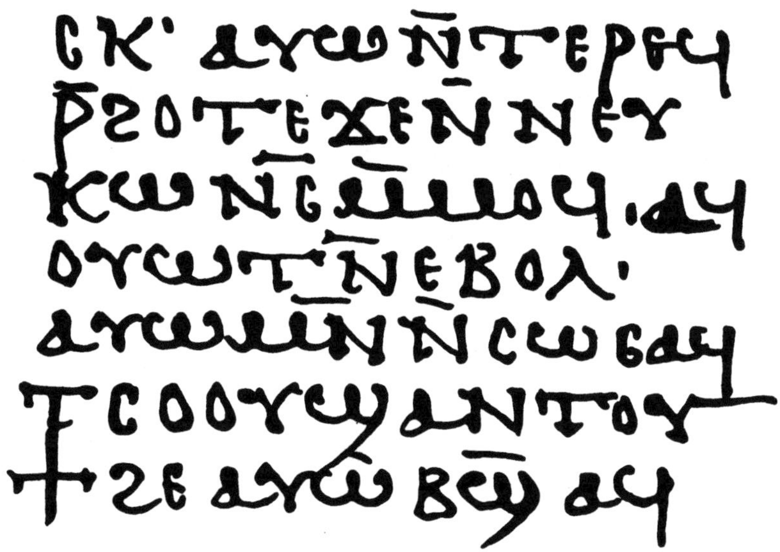

No. 25

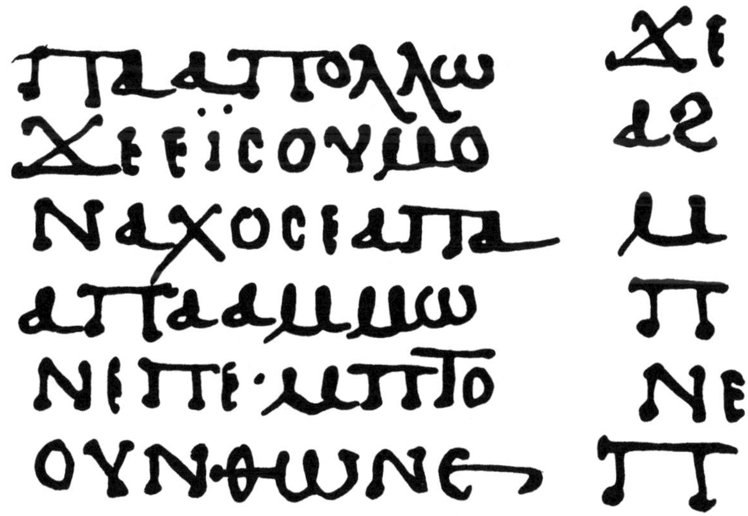

No. 26

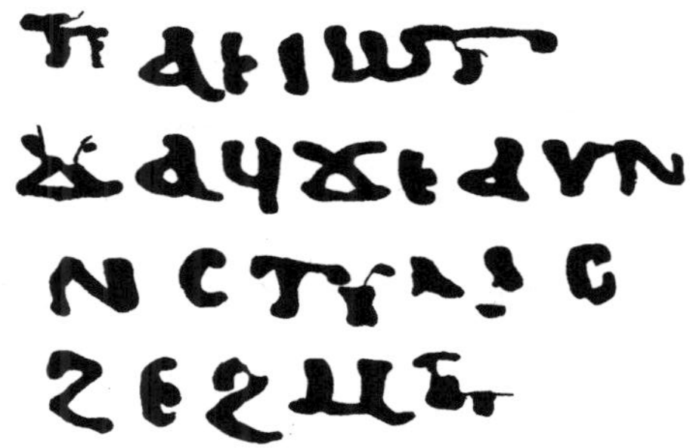

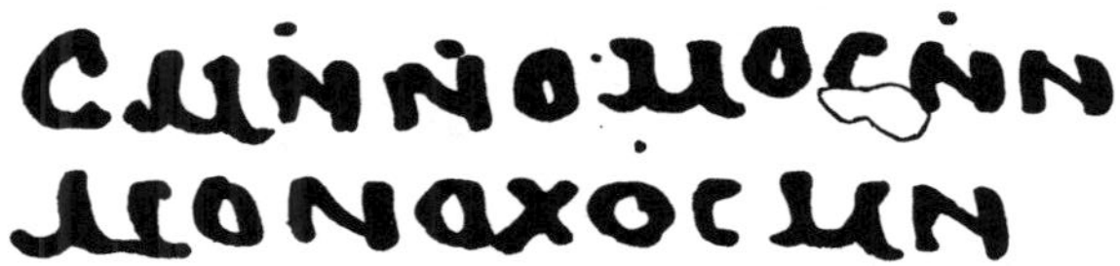

No. 28

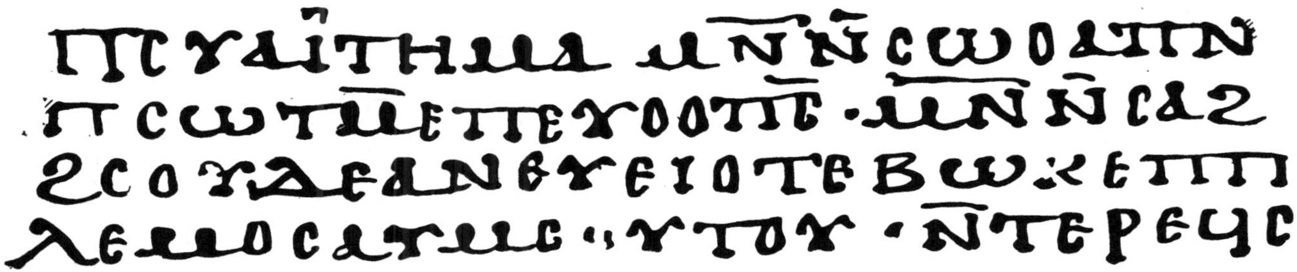

No. 29